15^{oc}

Producible Interpretation

EIGHT ENGLISH PLAYS 1675–1707

JUDITH MILHOUS and ROBERT D. HUME

Southern Illinois University Press

Carbondale and Edwardsville

88 87 86 85   4 3 2 1

Library of Congress Cataloging in Publication Data

Milhous, Judith.
    Producible interpretation.

    Includes bibliographical references and index.
    Contents: The concept of producible interpretation—
The production process—The country-wife (1675)—
[etc.]
    1. English drama—Restoration, 1660–1700—History
and criticism.   2. Theater—Production and direction.
I. Hume, Robert D.   II. Title.
PR691.M55   1984   822'.4'09   84-5634
ISBN 0-8093-1167-4

For Sybil Rosenfeld

CONTENTS

ILLUSTRATIONS

TABLES

FIGURES

Illustrations

PREFACE

THIS book has been written in the belief that useful interpretation of late seventeenth-century plays is best accomplished by methods that go beyond a close reading of texts. The new criticism of the last twenty-five years has made a substantial contribution to our understanding of these plays, but the limitations of such an approach have become increasingly evident. Is interpretation reaching a dead end? We think not, but new methods must be sought. Given the paucity of evidence about the reception of the plays by their original audiences, a "historical" approach must inevitably remain highly speculative. What can a critic do to get away from the ruts in which recent interpreters have got bogged down? What should the critic be trying to accomplish?

Most critical accounts of these plays seem excessively dogmatic to us. Our starting point is the assumption that a playscript (especially one of some complexity) is seldom limited to just one "valid" interpretation. Given the variables legitimately introduced in production, a play can vary considerably in meaning and impact without violence being done to the sense of the text. A playscript should be interpreted as what it is—a vehicle to be completed in performance—not as an aesthetic object complete in itself. Where a poem or a novel stands on its own, a play does not—an obvious fact, but one all too often ignored by recent critics.

We have tried to offer a critical approach to late seventeenth-century plays which uses a variety of methods and kinds of evidence to yield readings which show some diversity of possible meanings and impacts in performance. For each play we have tried to use deductions drawn from several kinds of investigation:

1. close reading (undertaken on the assumption that a director could validly present the text in one of a number of ways);
2. analysis of the original cast and the reception of the original production;
3. study of the scenery and machines required for performance in a changeable-scenery theatre;
4. historical reading in terms of seventeenth-century values and views of subject matter;
5. survey of eighteenth- , nineteenth- , and twentieth-century production history;
6. analysis of modern critical opinion.

We wish to argue neither that a play was interpreted in thus-and-such a way in the seventeenth century nor that it should be interpreted in thus-and-such a way now. Rather, we have tried to work out a variety of stageable interpretations for each text. Literary critics are too apt to imagine that there must be a "right" reading and to forget that vast differences can be wrought by perfectly reasonable directorial choices. We might cast Horner as a dashing young scamp, as a goatish lout, or as an increasingly middle-aged roué. Lady Fidget can be made young and sexy or blowsily middle-aged. The text will work for any of these choices.

Our selection of plays has been affected by a number of considerations. We make no pretense at historical coverage, but we wanted to include both Carolean works and some from the transitional 1688–1710 period. We have tried to avoid undue concentration on a single company, theatre building, or set of actors. Generic diversity was a desideratum: we have included five quite distinct sorts of comedy, a split-plot tragicomedy, and a pair of tragedies. With the exception of *The Wives Excuse*, all of these plays were extremely successful on stage, and all of them could, in our opinion, be made to work on the stage today.

Our object in this book is both to illuminate the particular plays we have studied and to illustrate a critical method for approaching drama. Just as a Beethoven sonata can be played in a variety of ways, so a play changes its character in different directors' hands. We have tried, as far as possible, to deduce the probable impact of the original production, but beyond that we have sought to work out alternative possibilities, using information about a number of productions as an aid to imagination. We are particularly concerned to identify those choices in production which would make an interpretation work on stage. This seems to us the decisive touchstone in assessing any interpretation. If it can be staged effectively it must possess some kind of validity, even if it is demonstrably remote from the apparent intention of the author and the original production.

A word of explanation is in order about texts, dates, and citation of scholarship. For the eight plays analyzed in detail here we have used the standard edition if one exists (e.g., the Oxford *Country-Wife*). Lacking a standard edition we have given page or line references to the most adequate modern edition that is widely available (e.g., the Regents Restoration Drama Series [RRDS] *Beaux' Stratagem*), even though this means that we sometimes cite old-spelling texts and at others modernized ones. References to plays not otherwise identified are to the first London edition, with the original spelling and punctuation preserved, though we have silently reversed italics as appropriate. Titles are given as found in our copytexts.

All dates are Old Style, and following the practice of *The London Stage*, the new year is considered to begin 1 January rather than 25 March. Where dates differ from those given in *The London Stage* the grounds for the change will be explained in the new edition of parts 1 and 2 on which we are now at work.

Except in the case of *The Country-Wife*, we have tried to concentrate on the plays themselves rather than on modern critical disagreements about them. In preparation for writing each chapter we attempted to read essentially all published criticism, but we have felt no obligation to cite books and articles unless they seemed directly relevant to our discussion. We apologize to any critic who may feel slighted, but even with this attempt to limit scholarly clutter our footnotes have become all too numerous.

We want to thank the editors of *Theatre Journal* for permission to reprint in altered form "*The Beaux' Stratagem*: A Production Analysis," which appeared in *Theatre Journal*, 34 (1982), 77–95.

We are grateful to Philip H. Highfill, Jr., Kalman A. Burnim, and Edward A. Langhans for allowing us access to yet-unpublished accounts of performers whose names fall beyond "Keyse" and the end of volume 8 of the *Biographical Dictionary*.

We would like to express our special gratitude to Professors John T. Harwood and Arthur H. Scouten for reading the entire manuscript and offering us many valuable suggestions and criticisms. For assistance with musical matters we are indebted to Curtis A. Price. For help with the index we are grateful to William J. Burling. Kit Hume has as always been our kindest and firmest critic.

WORKS FREQUENTLY CITED

Birdsall, *Wild Civility*
Virginia Ogden Birdsall, *Wild Civility: The English Comic Spirit on the Restoration Stage* (Bloomington: Indiana Univ. Press, 1970).

Biographical Dictionary
Philip H. Highfill, Jr., Kalman A. Burnim, and Edward A. Langhans, *A Biographical Dictionary of Actors, Actresses, Musicians, Dancers, Managers, and Other Stage Personnel in London, 1660–1800*, 10 vols. to date (Carbondale: Southern Illinois Univ. Press, 1973–).

Cibber, *Apology*
Colley Cibber, *An Apology for the Life of Mr. Colley Cibber*, ed. Robert W. Lowe, 2 vols. (1889; rpt. New York: AMS, 1966).

Downes, *Roscius Anglicanus*
John Downes, *Roscius Anglicanus* (London: H. Playford, 1708).

Genest	John Genest, *Some Account of the English Stage from the Restoration in 1660 to 1830*, 10 vols. (1832; rpt. New York: Burt Franklin, n.d.).
Holland, *The First Modern Comedies*	Norman N. Holland, *The First Modern Comedies: The Significance of Etherege, Wycherley and Congreve* (Cambridge, Mass.: Harvard Univ. Press, 1959).
Holland, *The Ornament of Action*	Peter Holland, *The Ornament of Action: Text and Performance in Restoration Comedy* (Cambridge: Cambridge Univ. Press, 1979).
Hume, *Development*	Robert D. Hume, *The Development of English Drama in the Late Seventeenth Century* (Oxford: Clarendon Press, 1976).
The London Theatre World	Robert D. Hume, ed., *The London Theatre World, 1660–1800* (Carbondale: Southern Illinois Univ. Press, 1980).
The London Stage	*The London Stage, 1660–1800.* Part 1: 1660–1700, ed. William Van Lennep, Emmett L. Avery, and Arthur H. Scouten (Carbondale: Southern Illinois Univ. Press, 1965). Part 2: 1700–1729, ed. Emmett L. Avery, 2 vols. (1960). Part 3: 1729–1747, ed. Arthur H. Scouten, 2 vols. (1961).

Rothstein   Eric Rothstein, *Restoration Tragedy*
                                       (Madison: Univ. of Wisconsin
                                       Press, 1967).

Part One

BACKGROUND

1

The Concept of Producible Interpretation

B Y "producible interpretation" we mean a critical reading that
a director could communicate to an audience in performance. Not all "valid" literary readings can be made to work in
the theatre. Conversely, some readings whose critical or historical
validity may be questioned have proved highly effective in performance. Ernest Jones' Oedipal interpretation of *Hamlet*, for instance, is certainly producible, as Olivier has demonstrated.

We have written this book as a response to our own dissatisfac-
tion with much of the dramatic criticism published in recent
years. Criticism has been chaotic in its aims and methods, and
contradictory in its conclusions. The resulting interpretations
often seem remote from theatrical reality, past or present. Our
particular concern is with late seventeenth-century English
drama, but the problems we are responding to are unrelated to
country or period. The bulk of this book is devoted to eight detailed analyses of particular plays, but those analyses have been
written to illustrate the application of a critical method. This
book—like the critical method that it embodies—has grown out
of our attempt to answer a disturbingly basic question: What
should an interpreter of drama undertake to accomplish?

WAYS OF WRITING ABOUT DRAMA AND THEATRE

As a means of defining the particular nature of this book, we would like to contrast its method and object with those of several other sorts of critical and scholarly writing about drama and theatre. At least nine sorts of work can usefully be distinguished.

Prescriptive directions to authors. In its original guise, this mode is so thoroughly out of vogue that one tends to forget it, but since such prominent examples as Aristotle's *Poetics* and Dryden's *Essay of Dramatic Poesy* are so often cited in other sorts of criticism, some acknowledgment of this one seems in order. Neither Aristotle nor Dryden would have been comfortable with the suggestion that he was "prescribing": Aristotle's procedure is inductive; Dryden's, speculative. But de facto, both are telling playwrights how good plays are to be made. In the postromantic world prescriptive criticism remains in permanent ill repute, though one can find a few dramatic cookbooks addressed to student playwrights. A glance at such tomes will tell you the obvious: the novice can be cautioned against fundamental error, but cannot really be told how to write a good play.

The most interesting writing directed at authors is broadly theoretical, addressed to larger questions of the nature and point of theatre, and the kinds of theatrical effect to be sought. Artaud's *The Theatre and Its Double* (1938), Brecht's *Short Organum* (1948), and Grotowski's *Towards a Poor Theatre* (1968) are manifestoes asking—with radically different programs—for a basic reorientation of our theatrical enterprise. In all three cases, the ultimate concern is with altering the nature of the interchange between performers and audience, reducing spectator passivity, demanding involvement and response from the audience. Handke's *Offending the Audience* (1965) is an extreme instance of such theory carried into practice. We raise these examples as evidence that prescriptive criticism is far from dead, but with the arguable exception of Brecht, most such theoreticians have little relevance to what they dismiss as "classic" theatre.

Literary analysis treats the printed playscript as an isolated artifact. Only the extreme frequency with which such criticism is practiced makes it seem anything but bizarre. Well over 90 percent of the criticism of plays published today is of this sort—written as though plays were poems. At this date we hardly need to claim that plays should be treated as plays: the argument has been a commonplace for thirty years.[1] Widespread lip service to this principle has, however, produced little change in practical criticism. No kind of article on drama is to be found in current journals more frequently than that which purports to explain a play by identification of a hitherto undiscovered "central theme." We would not for an instant deny the excellence or usefulness of many strictly literary studies. A great deal is to be learned from Norman Holland's *The First Modern Comedies* (1959) or Rose Zimbardo's *Wycherley's Drama* (1965) or from a host of articles about particular plays. But if the critic does not inquire whether the reading proposed could be communicated in performance, he is ignoring a crucial point in the validation of an interpretation of a play. A critic who is treating a play strictly as a text ought to say so. Lacking such a disclaimer, any interpretation seems to us implicitly to claim producibility, and ought therefore to be judged by that criterion. We should, however, point out certain definite advantages enjoyed by textually-oriented criticism. First, writer and reader can both examine the evidence: a printed text is available to both parties in a way that live performances are not. (Movies or television versions of plays are less vulnerable to this objection.) And second, a playscript is a bundle of potentialities, and a production is not only a completion of one of those potentialities but also a suppression of the others. In one way the words are more alive on stage, but in another, deader, because more determined.[2]

Drama history generally traces trends in plays through a partic-

---

1. Some of the most widely-cited examples are Raymond Williams, *Drama in Performance* (1954; rev. ed. New York: Basic, 1968), and J. L. Styan, *The Elements of Drama* (Cambridge: Cambridge Univ. Press, 1960).
2. We are indebted to Eric Rothstein for suggesting that we acknowledge this important point.

ular chronological period. The basis of comparison may be generic features (as in Hume's *The Development of English Drama in the Late Seventeenth Century*, 1976), treatment of subject matter (Loftis' *Comedy and Society from Congreve to Fielding*, 1959), or ideological analysis (Staves' *Players' Sceptres: Fictions of Authority in the Restoration*, 1979). A more limited sort of study may claim merely to characterize a given kind of play in a limited period (Fujimura's *The Restoration Comedy of Wit*, 1952, or Rothstein's *Restoration Tragedy*, 1967). Drama history can be written with attention to the theatrical circumstances that shaped and affected the plays—or not. A book like Volume V (1660–1750) of *The Revels History of Drama in English* (1976) illustrates the problems of combining texts and background. The four authors—Loftis, Southern, Jones, and Scouten—provide erudite but entirely disjunct accounts of intellectual background, theatre buildings, acting companies, and plays. For the drama historian, no problem is so pressing as the discovery of how to integrate study of practical theatre background with analysis of play texts.

Theatre history usually signifies study of theatre buildings, company management and finances, and acting style. At its best, theatre history is a sophisticated historical discipline, recreating performance circumstances from scrappy and scattered records. At its worst, it amounts to no more than sodden description of particular productions from readily available sources. Critics all too often dismiss the theatre historian as a maker of lists and a scavenger for unnoticed facts. The question, obviously, is what the facts are to be used for. To reconstruct the finances of the United Company in the 1680s is hardly an end in itself. But if such a reconstruction ultimately leads us toward an understanding of why the company adopted the repertory policies it did, then this bit of esoterica may be a key to helping us understand some quite puzzling developments in drama history. Likewise physical reconstruction of the stages used in the 1670s may seem uninteresting to the critic bent on understanding Wycherley's outlook; but his plays were written with very specific staging possibilities in mind, and to ignore the effect of his stage on what Wycherley chose to do can make the critic look very foolish indeed.[3] Except in textbook form (Brockett's *History of the Theatre* and its ilk), theatre history has rarely presumed to encompass drama. Logically, this need not be so. The best account of Wycherley would probably be one starting with a thorough study of the King's Company, its theatres, repertory, actors, and audience. But whether theatre history co-opts criticism or criticism learns to use theatre history hardly matters: either will serve to advance our understanding of the plays.

Instructions for performers can be either notes provided by the author to explain how a play is to be staged and to what ends (Shaw's for *Arms and the Man* or records of Brecht's Berliner Ensemble rehearsals) or similar guidance provided by a director for his or her actors. In the latter case communication is usually oral rather than written; but in principle it could be written, however much that goes against the norm of directorial practice. Directors are often more skilled in eliciting an effect from their actors than in explaining—even ex post facto—what that effect is. Critics tend to be deeply suspicious of all such information. ("New Critics" long worried about falling foul of the "intentional fallacy"; even today there is a widespread feeling that the text is sacrosanct and that it must be considered autonomous.) Directorial pronouncement is suspect to literary critics because directors inevitably and necessarily make myriad decisions for which there is no textual warrant. To cast Tartuffe as a scrawny little fellow against a big, bluff Orgon can work beautifully in the theatre,[4] but without textual authority most critics are at best uncomfortable about treating such points of casting as a significant part of interpretation. Such timidity is deplorable. Plays come to life only in performance, and to insist upon analyzing them in terms of text alone is methodological cowardice. Our particular interest in "instructions for performance" lies in the usefulness of such material

3. As witness the embarrassingly ill-informed criticisms of so redoubtable a theatre person as Harley Granville-Barker, *On Dramatic Method* (1931; rpt. New York: Hill and Wang, 1956), Chapter 4 ("Wycherley and Dryden").

4. Indeed, this actually runs counter to Molière's text ("Gros et gras," I.v.234). But had Molière been writing for a different actor he would presumably have described Tartuffe differently. Few directors would care to be bound by physical description, nor should they be.

in judging designed potentialities. The heart of actual production is choice: the more conscious the critic is of possible choices and the effects of those choices, the better.

Reviews. Reviewing is a critical mode rarely held in high estimation. Most newspaper reviews are little more than the subjective responses of an allegedly trained viewer, writing to inform potential customers what they would see and whether they would enjoy it. The brevity of most reviews militates against much explanation of the reviewer's judgment and ideological position. The inevitably and unfairly hostile review is a commonplace of the form. Reviewers are prone to talk about what they think should have been done, often without regard to whether (or how) it could have been done, and with little concern for what the production actually tried to do. A more interesting sort of "review" is that to be found in *Theatre Journal*, published long after the production has closed and devoted to a broader kind of evaluation. The audience for such a review is not potential patrons but directors, performers, and scholars interested in the theatrical potentialities of playtexts. Properly executed, such a review should ask what the production tried to do; whether the aim was reasonable; how it tried to achieve those aims; and how well the aim was fulfilled.[5]

Records of performance, by which we mean several things. A promptbook, a detailed descriptive review, a phonograph recording, a videotape recording—all are records of a sort. We would suggest that some of the most interesting drama criticism could be written by directors, explaining what they found in a text, why they made the choices they did, and how they tried to achieve the effects they wanted. Beyond such relatively conventional "records," we need to consider the feasibility of semiological nota-

5. Consider, for example, the Opera Factory production of *The Beggar's Opera* (London, February 1982), notorious for its nudity and punk rock interpolations. Most newspaper reviewers contented themselves with denouncing the production for ahistoricity and bad taste, without asking why David Freeman chose to do what he did, or considering whether the production succeeded on its own terms. Both of us disliked the production (hardly a surprising reaction from theatre historians), but found it highly effective.

8

tion.[6] How are we to "preserve" a performance in such a way that it remains accessible to analysis? An elaborate promptbook/score has its uses, though we lack the system of notation to render such relative intangibles as style and tempo universally accessible. A videotape solves a lot of notational problems, but imposes the limitations of the medium, and it freezes for us only a single representation, thereby losing the spontaneous variation of live performance. Records of performance are a particular concern for anyone who agrees (as we do) with the semiologists' argument that ultimately the best dramatic criticism will encompass the totality of text, theatre history, and actual performance. We do not at present possess adequate records of performance even of present-day productions.

Performance analysis. We included reviews in this survey of possibilities, trivial though most of them are, because they represent the principal form of attention to performance. But whereas a review is almost always appreciative or judgmental, concerned principally with a particular production, performance analysis should seek to identify and explain meaning and impact and is in no way debarred from extensive investigation of the text being communicated in performance. Few "literary" analyses of playtexts refer even in passing to production history, or treat the actuality of performance as a way of getting at a higher truth than the dead words of the script on the page. What we need is analysis attentive equally to the script and its realization. Almost all worthwhile performance analysis to date has concerned avantgarde plays or experimental and controversial productions of a few older ones. Such theatre journals as *The Drama Review* and *Performing Arts Journal* regularly publish extended analyses of recent performances. At present a camel will pass through the eye of a needle more easily than an analysis of the Guthrie *Beggar's Opera* or the National Theatre *London Cuckolds* will find its way

6. Some of the possibilities and problems are well discussed by Patrice Pavis in "Reflections on the Notation of the Theatrical Performance," *Languages of the Stage: Essays in the Semiology of the Theatre* (New York: Performing Arts Journal Publications, 1982), pp. 109–30.

into the pages of *Philological Quarterly*. Dare we hope that "scholarly" journals in "literature" will start to understand that an article analyzing *The School for Scandal* or *Man and Superman* on the basis of an interesting recent production may have more validity than one analyzing the language or meaning of the script in antiseptic isolation? Such prejudices aside, the principal obstacle to performance analysis remains our lack of more than the barest rudiments of a method and vocabulary for analyzing theatrical performance. Even more daunting is the formidable practical problem of collecting the evidence necessary to a serious analysis of performance. Videotape is preferable to scattered comments in eighteenth-century newspapers, but even when available it is not a panacea. For the present, performance-oriented criticism remains a utopian ideal. Consequently, we are principally concerned here with a more limited and accessible kind of criticism, namely—

Production analysis. By this term we mean interpretation of the text specifically aimed at understanding it as a performance vehicle—"reading with a directorial eye," if you like. While heavily grounded in textual analysis, such criticism will be undertaken on the principle that what should emerge is a sense of multiple possibilities in actual performance. Production analysis should draw freely on theatre history and drama history. Particular productions will be studied for what they can tell us about the potentialities of the script, but the critic is in no way limited to what has been staged. The results will sometimes resemble instructions for performance, but practically speaking they will be no more than a preliminary hint to the director, necessarily lacking the detail required for actual execution of a performance. *A production analysis is a series of architect's sketches, not the blueprints that would be necessary to bring any one of them to actuality.* The object is to clarify possible meanings and effects, primarily for readers, critics, and theatregoers, secondarily for the interested director. The result should be improved understanding of the performance potentialities of the play at issue.

Table 1.1
Kinds of Criticism

Kind	Subject	Method	Audience
directions to authors	principles of playwriting	speculation; empirical survey; a priori deduction	playwrights; secondarily critics
literary analysis	playtexts	analysis of structure, characters, content, etc.	readers of plays
drama history	playtexts	usually generic	readers of plays
theatre history	buildings, finances, performers	documentary history	historically-minded theatregoers; scholars
instructions for performance	playtexts visualized for performance	various	directors, actors, secondarily theatregoers
reviews	particular performances	description/judgment	potential theatregoers
records of performance	particular performances	various	directors, performers, critics
performance analysis	text and particular performances	analysis of actual performances	directors, actors, critics, readers, theatregoers
production analysis	text and particular productions	visualization of performance possibilities	directors, actors, critics, readers, theatregoers

SOME METHODOLOGICAL CONSIDERATIONS

Only very recently have critics started to consider producibility a touchstone for the evaluation of interpretations of plays. We agree with John Styan's dictum: "Criticism which ignores theatrical experience is peripheral, even irresponsible."[7] Michael Booth has gone so far as to argue that "no interpretation of

7. *Drama, Stage and Audience* (Cambridge: Cambridge Univ. Press, 1975), p. 241.

Shakespeare or any other dramatist is valid unless it is proved workable in performance; that is, unless it can be clearly communicated to the audience by the actors and the staging."[8] We are in considerable sympathy with this position, though ultimately it seems too extreme. Plays are printed and read, and in that form they can legitimately be interpreted as printed literature. But certainly the first question to be asked of any interpretation is *Does it claim to be communicable in performance?* Underlying this fundamental question are several problems of definition and method of which the critic trying to write production analysis should be aware.

Is theatre communication?

John Styan takes the position that "a play must communicate or it is not a play," and considers "*Does it work?*" the "ultimate question" for the critic.[9] We entirely agree that theatre is communication: to say otherwise is to abandon any claim for its meaning and significance. But *what* is communicated in performance? Reading literary criticism, one might suppose that plays exist as vehicles for some sort of central meaning, often defined by such critics as a comment on a "theme." This simplistic assumption has been widely if belatedly challenged in recent years.[10] Styan protests against the idea that a play "conceals a message which an audience has a duty to perceive." Thomas Whitaker cautions against any attempt to "try to extract from a play its apparent statement, its 'imitated' action, or its presented world, and call *that* the 'meaning.'"[11] That plays can be didactic is clearly true— from Lillo's *The London Merchant* to Hochhuth's *The Deputy*. But in very few good plays does "statement" outweigh the world presented. A writer desirous of making abstract statements should

8. "Theatre History and the Literary Critic," *Yearbook of English Studies*, 9 (1979), 15–27; quotation from p. 20.

9. *Drama, Stage and Audience*, pp. 1–2.

10. See particularly Richard Levin, "Some Second Thoughts on Central Themes," *Modern Language Review*, 67 (1972), 1–10, and *New Readings vs. Old Plays* (Chicago: Univ. of Chicago Press, 1979).

11. Styan, *Drama, Stage and Audience*, p. 241; Whitaker, *Fields of Play in Modern Drama* (Princeton: Princeton Univ. Press, 1977), p. 24.

be able to find forms better suited to the purpose than drama. Or as George Kaufman says, if you have a message to deliver, send a telegram.

A play can communicate ideas, attitudes, moods. More broadly, one might say that a "way of seeing" is preferred to the audience —ideology, if you will. Every play has an ideology, but a great many plays (especially those written for the commercial theatre) do not venture beyond the commonplace, and ideology has little to do with their effectiveness in the theatre. Ideology becomes important when it challenges or significantly reinforces that of the audience. When a play relies largely on formulas, asking what it communicates is usually a sterile exercise; the critic can more profitably inquire what sorts of response it tries to elicit from the audience. To expand on this point: not all communication involves significant content. A play demands both intellectual comprehension and emotional response. Shaw is heavily tilted toward the former; O'Neill, toward the latter. Feydeau demands no comprehension; his plays aim simply to amuse. To agree that theatre is communication does not commit us to a procrustean demand for message/meaning; nor should it inhibit us from studying subjective and variable response in the audience.

We must not refuse to recognize, however, that a significant part of the meaning is added in performance.[12] The point remains surprisingly controversial. Gareth Lloyd Evans has recently attacked Ralph Berry for views "disturbingly similar to Tyrone Guthrie's assertion that the text is nothing but a blueprint until the director completes, with major and vital creativity, the final edifice."[13] Guthrie's "nothing but a blueprint" shortchanges the verbal potency of plays as literary texts. But as Peter Brook has justly said, nowadays the director is inevitably "responsible" for what comes across in the theatre. "He cannot avoid this. An actor reads the lines out loud. How? At once a thousand choices

12. For a useful discussion, see Keir Elam, *The Semiotics of Theatre and Drama* (London: Methuen, 1980), Chapter 3.
13. Gareth Lloyd Evans, review of Ralph Berry, *Changing Styles in Shakespeare* (London: Allen and Unwin, 1981), in *Theatre Notebook*, 37 (1983), 38–39.

are before him. Does he read tonelessly? Does he give the sense with no 'expressive' colour? Does he use the intonations of realistic speech? Does he use a special voice? Does he move towards song? . . . An actor who speaks must also be seen. How will he appear? How will he be dressed? . . . None of these questions can be ducked."[14] As Berry comments: "In itself, this passage disposes of the 'straight' Shakespeare argument." Berry elaborates with the useful example of *Measure for Measure*, a play whose point and import turn almost entirely on Isabella's response (not specified by Shakespeare) to the Duke's proposal: "In determining this action the director determines the provisional meaning of the play." But even when what the director does is outrageous and wrongheaded, no real damage is done. Peter Hall says: "If I do *Macbeth*—as I did—in red rugs, I make a fool of no one but myself. *Macbeth* is still there at the end—staring at me. I have done nothing to *Macbeth*." Or as Berry interprets: "The text remains."

Almost every theoretician reminds us that the communication process (and the meaning involved) is rendered more complex by its transmission through performer to audience. One of the major deficiencies of almost all theories of drama is failure to deal with audience diversity and the inevitable disparateness of audience response. This failure extends, curiously, even to recent semiotic criticism, which devotes vastly more attention to defining and recording signs than to the process by which an actual audience decodes them.[15] Even Patrice Pavis, for us the most useful and stimulating of recent semiologists, tends to treat text and performance as the object of analysis, their reception as a given.

14. Peter Brook, "Production: total responsibility of a director," *Birmingham Post*, 17 April 1964; cited by Berry, p. 10.

15. For a number of stimulating contributions to semiotic study of drama and theatre see "Drama, Theater, Performance: A Semiotic Perspective," special issue of *Poetics Today*, 2, no. 3 (Spring 1981). Even semioticians are having trouble dealing with both text and performance. Thus Cesare Segre treats dramatic texts as a particular kind of narrative while Frank Coppieters—in a welcome departure from text-centered criticism—adopts a radically audience-oriented point of view and deals with audience perception basically as an empirical phenomenon. We cannot feel comfortable with either extreme.

We are not about to advocate wholesale importation of reader-response criticism (duly adapted for drama) as a panacea, but in response to Styan's query *"Does it work?"* we are inclined to ask *How can we tell?* Dryden's *Marriage A-la-Mode* (1671) was popular in the theatre—but according to contemporary testimony the audience went to salivate over what Dryden thought he was satirizing. Did the play "work"? In one sense, yes; in another, not at all.

What is unproducible?

An interpretation which cannot be put on stage in such a way that it is understood by a reasonable number of audience members is unproducible. Of course there are variables both in performers' skill and in audience receptivity. What fails with one actor or for one audience may work on another occasion. Most unproducible interpretations are the result of ingenious explication undertaken without regard for the practical realities of theatrical performance. Abstract propositions are extraordinarily hard to put across in performance—unless the text makes them flagrantly explicit, or the director resorts to banners with caption explanations. When a critic asserts that *King Lear* is an answer to the question "What is Man?" or that *The Country-Wife* expounds "the distinction between illusion and reality," the director generally despairs of any help from that quarter. How is the cast to send the audience out of the theatre thinking about illusion and reality? Plays tend to be about people, and audiences react on that basis. Until a play is as overtly abstract as *Waiting for Godot*, the audience is unlikely to start thinking about extrapolative abstractions. The critic may dream them up, but experienced performers will tell you that abstractions are nearly impossible to communicate without explicit statement—and not always easy even then. And stating them is one thing; making them meaningful and interesting to an audience, quite another.

We should not forget that even authorial interpretation may not prove communicable in performance. Brecht's *Mother Courage* is a notorious example of a play in which audiences have persistently identified with a character the author meant to pillory—

and kept right on doing so, even after Brecht rewrote the piece to blacken his unwanted heroine.[16] In this extreme case the interpretation declared "correct" by the author proved impossible to communicate successfully in performance.

Reading versus seeing

The difference between reading and seeing a play can hardly be overemphasized.[17] The reader controls the pace at which he proceeds. He can stop to think; go back and reread a passage; turn back to Act I to check a detail or hunt down a possible discrepancy. He can pause to daydream; can impose the set, cast, and performance style of his choosing; or can resolutely ignore everything but the words. The theatregoer has none of these options, and his experience is thereby both richer and more limited. He sees what is put before him, and he cannot lift his eyes from the page (or push a button) to stop the play while he thinks. The many choices of characterization and sympathy left to the reader are made by the director, like them or not. Theatregoing is an experience—one usually designed to engender an immediate response that is largely beyond the control of the spectator, though his personal predilections may play a large part in governing that response. Reading is an altogether more self-controlled enterprise, and one which invites both fantasy and ratiocination. The responses of the reader are naturally less governed and controllable than those of the theatregoer, and the range of reasonable interpretive responses concomitantly wider.

As an example of criticism better suited to the reader than the theatregoer we would offer Aubrey Williams' *An Approach to*

16. Such failure to control audience response is by no means limited to the theatre. Richardson's revisions of *Clarissa* show him struggling to make the rapist Lovelace hateful to a multitude of readers who persisted in finding him attractive.

17. We should add that readers seldom "see" even what the author specifies by way of stage movement and theatrical effects. For a vivid reconstruction of "Shakespeare's direction of his plays" from the speeches and stage directions of his plays, see Ann Pasternak Slater, *Shakespeare the Director* (Brighton, England: Harvester, 1982). Slater makes especially good use of stage directions from "bad" quartos, but what she can pull out of familiar folio texts is also extremely revealing.

Congreve (1979). Williams presumes an "audience" both explicitly Christian and decidedly inclined to extract moral edification from its entertainment. We can hardly deny that anyone so minded can moralize practically any text—from *The Miller's Tale* to *The Country-Wife* or Molière's *Dom Juan*. But how many theatregoers of 1693 saw *The Old Batchelour* in anything like the terms of Professor Williams' discussion? Outcry at the time about "The Bawdy Batchelour," not to mention the howls of the Reverend Jeremy Collier, suggest that some part of the audience reacted to the play's obvious bawdry. Of course this by no means invalidates Williams' reading: Congreve's detractors may have been misreading him. But in our view the play could not have been staged to elicit Williams' reading—unless the audience was as exegetically-minded as Professor Williams would have us believe. Lack of Christianized response to comedy from Congreve's audience (except in denunciations) seems to us to argue strongly against such a hypothesis.

Both readers and playgoers tend to see what they are predisposed to see. If, for example, you want to find a moral center for *The Country-Wife*, an obvious solution is to hail the marriage of Harcourt and Alithea as the "right way" for this society, and Alithea as a high moral norm for the play—as Norman Holland has done.[18] For the reader in the reflective solitude of his study, brooding over the play and pondering its implications, this is by no means an unreasonable idea. The theatrical experience of the play, however, is quite different. Harcourt and Alithea are thin and peripheral characters compared to Horner and the Pinchwifes. To stage the play to make them memorable, let alone normative, would be extremely difficult.

Producibility versus validity

By "valid" we mean that an interpretation is (a) compatible with the plain verbal sense of the text, and (b) in accord with known facts about the author and the original performance conditions. D. W. Jefferson's "comic" interpretation of Dryden's he-

18. Holland, *The First Modern Comedies*, Chapter 8.

roic plays, for example, seems to us at odds both with the plays (from which he concentrates on a few selected passages) and with Dryden's critical commentary on them.[19] Without very strong evidence indeed we would not be prepared to believe that Otway wrote satires on the Tory party, or that Etherege saw his comedies as moral treatises. Common sense does have a place in criticism.

Not all producible interpretations are valid. The eighteenth-century productions of *Venice Preserv'd* in which Pierre became a heroic opponent of government tyranny were evidently highly effective in the theatre, but their republican ideology was radically at odds with the original Tory purport of the play in 1682. (In this case substantial cutting was necessary to make the script suitable to the changed ideological purpose.) For the literary critic, validity in the sense of conformity to the author's basic concept of the play (if apparent) is a significant criterion in assessing an interpretation. For the director, it is much less an issue.

Consider Shadwell's *The Squire of Alsatia* (1688), an adaptation of Terence's *The Brothers*. The play traces the fortunes of two brothers, one given a liberal "city" education, the other raised in the country. The country brother quickly proves to be a booby and a gull. We soon learn that the town brother, though advertised as a model of moral rectitude, has a bastard by a mistress he has cast off, and has just seduced a lawyer's previously innocent daughter. He sweet-talks his new mistress for three acts, until he finds a wealthy heiress to marry, at which point he both swears that the lawyer's daughter is sexually innocent and pays her father £1,500 (easily $50,000 in current buying power) to drop the matter—i.e., to shut up. Our hero then marries the heiress, solemnly assuring her that he is a reformed character. What are we to make of this? Is Shadwell satirizing the corruption and hypocrisy of the "town" mores? Or is he—as the text says—holding the town brother up as a model of gentlemanly reform and good

19. D. W. Jefferson, "The Significance of Dryden's Heroic Plays," *Proceedings of the Leeds Philosophical and Literary Society*, 5 (1940), 125–39.

behavior? Given what we know of Shadwell, the original production circumstances, and other plays of the time, we would be rash to imagine that he did not take this offensive bilge quite seriously. For the audience of 1688 the philandering was normal (at least in plays), the generosity and reform at least technically admirable. But suppose Brecht were to have hit on this play (instead of *The Recruiting Officer*) as a vehicle for displaying exploitation by the ruling classes. Without changing a word Brecht could stage the play to make it a searing indictment of the gentry's callous disregard for the humanity of the lower classes, a revealing illustration of the amorality of the money ethic, and so forth. And it would work. Indeed, almost any other production concept would be very hard to sell to an audience today.

Let us try to summarize our position on some thorny issues. A producible interpretation may not be historically valid, though any stageable interpretation possesses a certain de facto legitimacy for the theatre. Hamlet could certainly be played as a homosexual, remote though this appears from Shakespeare's view of his play, or anything implied by the text. We are dealing with three distinct concepts here. A *producible interpretation* is not necessarily *historically valid*; a *valid interpretation*, however, should be producible, unless the critic has specifically disavowed the applicability of his reading to actual performance. For the theatrical critic, a valid interpretation is a producible one.

Audience diversity

If we are to analyze "meaning" in terms of audience understanding, or a play's "impact" on an audience, then one of our crucial problems is to define and comprehend that audience. Uniformitarian assumptions are convenient but unsound.[20] To assert

20. We may have our pick in this period. According to K. M. P. Burton, the Restoration audience was a coterie consisting principally of "courtiers, hangers-on, and prostitutes" (*Restoration Literature* [London: Hutchinson, 1958], p. 63); Aubrey Williams suggests that what Restoration "playwrights and audiences had most in common" was "a shared upbringing and schooling in the basic doctrines and precepts of the Christian religion" (*An Approach to Congreve*, p. 1). Of course, upon reflection one may conclude that there is less contradiction in these positions than one might at first suppose.

uniformity in politics, morals, humor, and world view in members of the London audience of the 1980s would bring immediate derision upon the dimwitted proposer of such an idea. We see no reason to suppose that the audience was any less heterogeneous in the late seventeenth and eighteenth centuries.[21] A basic principle for the serious critic must be recognition of audience diversity.

Not all writers of comedy in the Carolean period—nor, we may suppose, all members of the audience—despised the country, approved of fornication, sneered at cast mistresses, and believed fervently in the Tory view of the Exclusion Crisis. As soon as we start to say that libertines were admired and fallen women despised in the late seventeenth century, we are adopting a set of blinders that will prevent us from reading a play like Aphra Behn's *The Revenge* (1680) at all accurately.

To admit the pluralism of audience values at all times debars us from easy appeals to "what the seventeenth-century audience would have thought." How then are we to analyze "meaning" as a contemporary audience understood it, especially given the relative dearth of audience testimony from the period at issue? This is not a problem to be lightly dismissed. To cling to simplistic generalizations (the court wit coterie, etc.) is irresponsible. To abandon the case as hopeless is equally so—an abdication of responsibility that exaggerates the difficult into the impossible. Serious study of audience composition and response is still in its infancy, and belongs more to performance analysis than to production analysis, but the critic should at least refrain from imposing false generalizations in defense of tidy interpretations. The audience member with violent moral objections to adultery will respond to *The Country-Wife* quite differently from the earl of Rochester, or from someone able to treat stage adultery as a lark or a joke. For the objector, production choices are irrelevant and will not work: the subject automatically irritates or offends, re-

---

21. For a discussion, see Robert D. Hume, *The Rakish Stage* (Carbondale: Southern Illinois Univ. Press, 1983), Chapters 1 and 2.

gardless of how it is presented. We can analyze the affective response apparently sought by play or production; we can study whatever actual audience responses are available to us; we cannot claim to dictate a "correct" response to the audience.

Producible then versus producible now

The popularity of historical criticism (claiming to recover meaning as perceived by an author's contemporary audience) has encouraged a widespread belief that the "original" meaning of plays is now unrecapturable in the theatre. Topicalities often do lose their significance. *Venice Preserv'd* could not be staged today to "mean" what it did as a comment on Whigs and the Popish Plot for the audience of 1682. Those plays—including *The Wives Excuse* and *The Beaux' Stratagem*—that protest the lack of a divorce law can try to appeal to modern views of women's rights, but the impact of their protest against a specific injustice is inevitably diminished. *Uncle Tom's Cabin* suffers from the same difficulty. But perhaps because plays are art, not life, good ones often retain a surprising theatrical viability long after they have lost the topical interest that was a prominent part of their original appeal. Buckingham's *The Rehearsal* (1671) held the stage decades after its butts had vanished into oblivion. Sir Robert Howard's *The Committee* (1662) was a repertory staple for a century, though the puritan sequestration committee it retrospectively satirizes must have been a dim memory by the 1690s.

Critics with uniformitarian assumptions have often cited the beliefs and values of that ubiquitous "seventeenth-century reader" (or playgoer) as justification for all sorts of assertions about what seventeenth-century plays allegedly meant and how they would have been taken. We may certainly agree that the attitude of the New York or San Francisco audience of the 1980s toward Catholics is very different from the attitude predominant in the London audience in 1680 during the Popish Plot hysteria. This difference will clearly affect reactions to *The Spanish Fryar*. We believe, however, that Dryden's play makes its attitude toward Catholics quite sufficiently explicit for audience comprehension, then or now. Dealing with the "problem of anachronism," Richard Levin challenges interpretations which "ask us to reject our felt experience of the play and to substitute for it an interpretation which we have not experienced" on the basis that the original audience would have responded this way.[22] We agree with Levin's conclusion: "The ideas and attitudes necessary to guide our response are established in the plays themselves"—so much so that there is hardly "any major English Renaissance drama where we would go seriously wrong in our interpretation without a special knowledge of some idea of the time."

Obviously, there is a difference between the audience's "understanding" what a play says or implies and a production's "working" effectively for a modern audience. Let us illustrate. Calderón's *The Mayor of Zalamea* relies heavily on a code of honor that was certainly accepted as a convention (if not personally shared) by the seventeenth-century Spanish audience, but is not particularly familiar today and is certainly not accepted by the twentieth-century London audience. Nonetheless, the play makes the code entirely comprehensible (as in the 1981 National Theatre production), even though many audience members now find it peculiar and repulsive. We must not lose track of the distinction between comprehension and response. The basic values of a good play should be readily deducible from the text, but how interesting and acceptable the play and its values may be to a later audience is a different problem altogether, one that concerns the director more than the critic.

The essentials of production analysis

An actual production almost always tries to control audience response. For a critic analyzing that production, two questions are central: What is the production concept? What response does the production try to elicit? Whether it succeeds—and for what proportion of the audience—is a third problem. Properly speak-

---

22. Richard Levin, *New Readings vs. Old Plays*, p. 159. Following quotation from p. 166.

ing, a serious performance analysis ought to deal with all three.

Precise determination of audience comprehension and response goes beyond the bounds of this book, belonging as it does to the realm of performance analysis. For the historical critic, evidence of audience response can be useful, but it is usually so scanty that most of what we know about the probable impact of a play has to be deduced from the text and known productions. The business of production analysis as we are trying to practice it for the late seventeenth-century period is to analyze the text and known productions to determine performance possibilities. Where the literary critic attempts to present the "correct" reading, or the "best" reading, the author of a production analysis claims merely to identify performable production concepts and to indicate the sort of response to be sought from the audience in each case. Unlike literary criticism, production analysis is essentially undogmatic, making no exclusive claim to truth for any one production concept. "Validation" is much less an issue than it is for a literary critic: it rests very simply on the claim to performability.

THE EXAMPLE OF *THE PLAIN-DEALER*

We are turning to *The Plain-Dealer* at this point in order to illustrate some of the practical problems of judging producibility. What follows is by no means a full-dress production analysis, but rather merely an indication of some of the kinds of issues that may arise. We have selected this play because of its particularly tangled critical history. We would like to suggest that what appears to be chaotic contradiction in literary criticism can sometimes be resolved very easily when considered in the light of the multiple performance possibilities that are the basis of production analysis.

Is Manly hero or satiric butt?

Wycherley's play (1676) was praised in its own time as a hard-hitting satire—presumably on a corrupt society. For nearly three hundred years critics assumed that Manly was the "hero" and that he served as a spokesman for the author. The nickname "Manly

23

Wycherley" naturally encouraged such an identification. Critics varied considerably in their response to Manly, some finding him unpleasant and unbalanced, but no one expressed doubts that Wycherley meant us to take Manly seriously. In 1950 Alexander H. Chorney published a brief but radical reassessment, arguing that "the real character of Manly is . . . neither serious, philosophical, nor misanthropic: Wycherley's contemporaries would have recognized him as a 'humours' character and an object of satire." Chorney sees Manly as "a recognizable comic type, a 'humourist' whose plain dealing is a folly to be castigated," even though his "social criticism may often be valid."[23] Chorney implies that instead of playing Manly's ranting dead seriously, we should present him as a comic butt who winds up as thoroughly discredited as the corrupt world in which he lives. The reading has been attacked by some historicists, but it is eminently producible.

In the following decade critics divided between the traditional and the humours interpretations. In 1961 K. M. Rogers set out to resolve the dispute by asking some fundamental questions. "Is *The Plain-Dealer* a mockery of social infirmities or a slashing attack on Restoration society? Few works of comparable importance are susceptible to such contrasting interpretations. The problem centers, of course, on the attitude one is intended to take toward Manly. Is he a satiric butt—a traditional humours character; a self-deluded, self-righteous fool; a fatuous rebel against society . . . ? Or is he a fundamentally noble character, embittered by the corruption around him and voicing Wycherley's own disgust with his society?"[24] What she finds (rather to her dismay) is that Wycherley's script offers ample warrant for either interpretation. Professor Rogers concludes that "the play is written from two incompatible moral viewpoints," and that consequently

23. "Wycherley's Manly Reinterpreted," *Essays Critical and Historical Dedicated to Lily B. Campbell* (Berkeley: Univ. of California Press, 1950), pp. 161–69.

24. "Fatal Inconsistency: Wycherley and *The Plain-Dealer*," *ELH*, 28 (1961), 148–62.

much of the play's "force is dissipated amid its inconsistencies." "Drama," she tells us, "cannot be fully effective when one's attitude toward the characters is made to fluctuate."

This excellent article illustrates very nicely the difference between literary criticism and production analysis. To the literary critic a play with multiple potentialities is at best suspect, at worst irretrievably flawed. The fallacy is easily seen: the script offers incompatible possibilities, but a competent director will make a choice and present *one* of them. Had Wycherley been writing a novel, we might well criticize him for such inconsistency, but unless the director fails to make a necessary choice about the character of Manly, it presents no problem in a playscript. This is a distressing assertion to the critic who believes as an article of faith that there is one valid interpretation, and only one—but to anyone prepared to consider the practical realities of performance, this idea has to seem preposterous. Manly is a problem only to the literary critic unprepared to reckon with the performance potentialities of the play.

Is the ending straight or ironic?

Should we be pleased at the end of the play when Wycherley rewards Manly with the wealthy, faithful, and virtuous Fidelia? This depends entirely on the production concept. Rewarding Manly the hero is fine. Letting the humours character be reformed and rewarded is no problem. But if Manly is seriously satirized as part of a hypocritical world, then rewarding him is flagrantly cynical and discordant. Consider, for example, Rose Zimbardo's widely admired reading of 1965, which treats *The Plain-Dealer* as a formal satire against hypocrisy in which Manly starts out as satiric spokesman and gradually becomes an object of attack himself.[25] In essence Zimbardo tries to cope with inconsistency by treating it as degeneration. In performance this would be possible, though tricky. Stripping sympathy from an initially

---

25. *Wycherley's Drama: A Link in the Development of English Satire* (New Haven: Yale Univ. Press, 1965), Chapter 3.

25

attractive protagonist and not directing it elsewhere rarely commends itself to performers. What to do with the end is certainly a problem. If this is not a case of Degeneration Rewarded, then what is it? Professor Zimbardo seems quite uncomfortable with the end and gives it minimal attention, a solution more readily open to the critic than to the director.

The issue of reward is even more sharply posed by Percy G. Adams in one of the best articles ever published on the play.[26] Adams points out that Manly either "rapes" Olivia (copulates with her while pretending to be Fidelia) or lies in claiming that he has slept with her. Critics have tended to skim over the point, but in the theatre a director would have to make a decision. The text is ambiguous, but "'the plain dealer' is one kind of person if he rapes Olivia and an entirely different kind if he does not." Neither reading is flattering, but a director must adopt one of them. A Manly-as-hero production would presumably minimize the damage by having him merely lie. A production bent on showing him up can display him, as Adams suggests, "adjusting his rumpled clothes." Rewarding the "plain dealer" with Fidelia (who has sat outside and wept during the crucial moments) can hardly be anything but brutal irony.[27] The ending is generally treated as "conventional," but given what it follows critics seem surprisingly complaisant about it.

Virginia Ogden Birdsall, also writing in 1970, swung back to

26. "What Happened in Olivia's Bedroom? or Ambiguity in *The Plain Dealer*," *Essays in Honor of Esmond Linworth Marilla*, ed. Thomas Austin Kirby and William John Olive (Baton Rouge: Louisiana State Univ. Press, 1970), pp. 174–87.

27. Eric Rothstein offers us an alternative response in a personal letter. "I think Manly 'rapes' Olivia, if you want to call that 'rape,' and that the audience is delighted (as with other bed tricks in comedies) by the revenge, and that Manly is all the more the hero as the result of action rather than railing. . . . Why would *anyone* think it wrong to screw Olivia? or cuckold Vernish? or humiliate both of them by making this known?" There is a good probability that the gallants in the audience of 1676 did respond this way, though we would argue that *The Plain-Dealer* invites a more complicated kind of judgment than most "bed trick" comedies.

the old Manly-as-hero view, but with a difference.[28] Declaring that "Manly is himself at no time being satirized by Wycherley," she argues that we are not to laugh at him as an unrealistic idealist, but to pity him for his inability to cope with a corrupt society. The reading is plausible, though ineffectuality is hard to make attractive, and little in the text makes Manly easy to play for pity—he is too abusive, both verbally and physically. This reading at least makes sense of the ending, but we would have to regard its producibility as questionable.

Is Wycherley alluding to Dryden or Molière?

At least two recent critics have suggested that "outside" allusion is a key to understanding Wycherley's satiric aims in *The Plain-Dealer*. Perhaps the most ingenious account of Manly is Cynthia Matlack's.[29] In essence, she argues that Manly is a deliberate parody of Dryden's Almanzor in *The Conquest of Granada* (1670–71). Some of the parallels were first pointed out by John Harold Wilson: both are intensely masculine, fierce fighters, rugged individualists, rough and blunt, devoted to honor, intolerant of sycophants and courtiers, very much in love, and deceived by villains.[30] All very true. But did Wycherley write with Almanzor consciously in mind? Did he hope or assume that the audience, unprompted, would see and respond to the parallel? (We have no evidence that any member of the seventeenth-century audience did in fact see the resemblance and interpret the play in light of it.) Did Wycherley assume that the play could "work" even for an audience that failed to see this alleged connection? We doubt that Wycherley would have attempted specific parody without making it explicit. Matlack's reading is in fact simply a variant on the Chorney school. The audience of 1676 might well have

28. Birdsall, *Wild Civility*, Chapter 7. Following quotation from p. 161.
29. "Parody and Burlesque of Heroic Ideals in Wycherley's Comedies: A Critical Reinterpretation of Contemporary Evidence," *Papers on Language and Literature*, 8 (1972), 273–86.
30. *A Preface to Restoration Drama* (1965; rpt. Cambridge, Mass.: Harvard Univ. Press, 1968), p. 161.

recognized the "heroic" nature of Manly's ethos, whether played straight or as a comic target. But to see *The Plain-Dealer* as aimed specifically at Dryden, or as necessarily a burlesque, is unconvincing.

Equally questionable, in our view, is the idea that the play should be interpreted with one eye on a quasi source in Molière. Peter Holland states unequivocally that the first scene "establishes from the beginning the parodic distance of *The Plain-Dealer* from *Le Misanthrope*. Molière's play is recalled so that Wycherley can mark his distance from it."[31] We have all sorts of problems with this breezy assertion. Exactly how is *Le Misanthrope* "recalled" to the audience's attention? Critics since Langbaine have generally concluded that Molière's play served as "the initial impulse" for *The Plain-Dealer*, an assumption we would not dispute.[32] But the play does not announce itself as a translation or adaptation, either in the prologue or later in published form on the title page or in the dedication. The character names are entirely different. Molière's play (1666) had not previously been translated or adapted on the English stage, and no English translation had been published. Many members of a modern academic audience would have read or seen it, but in 1676 what proportion of Wycherley's audience would have been familiar with the play, let alone drawn the connection unaided? No doubt a literary critic can learn something from the comparison, but we would argue that in performance *The Plain-Dealer* must be considered entirely on its own terms.

Does the 1676 cast imply satire of Manly?

In a very helpful discussion of the impact of the cast on the original production, Holland brings up Thomas Davies' 1784 comment associating Manly with Pinchwife in *The Country-Wife* (p. 185). The attraction of such cross-association is obvious, but so are the dangers. In this case Davies wonders why Michael

31. *The Ornament of Action*, Chapter 6. Quotation from p. 187.
32. John Wilcox, *The Relation of Molière to Restoration Comedy* (New York: Columbia Univ. Press, 1938), p. 94.

Mohun was not cast for both parts. But suppose Charles Hart (the original Manly) had also taken Pinchwife? This would prove nothing at all, unless we had overwhelming evidence that he stuck rigidly to a single "line." Repertory companies cast parts as best they can, not always to ideal advantage. Critics have pointed to Almanzor and Pinchwife as hints for Manly—but one can just as well look to Alexander (in *The Rival Queens*), Aureng-Zebe, Brutus, Mosca, Nero, and a flock of Hart's other roles. The more skilled and varied the actor, the less use the critic will find a study of roles in determining what any one of them was like.

A somewhat different sort of problem is raised by Holland's comment that "the juxtaposition of heroic Hart and comic Haines [Lord Plausible] hints at ridicule. No audience could have forgotten the famous story of Haines' mocking Hart during a performance of Jonson's *Catiline*" (p. 187). As far as we are aware, this "famous story" was first published in an obscure pamphlet in 1701. It concerned an incident that occurred in a single performance, probably in 1668, and no later than 1672. How many members of the audience in 1676 would conclude that Haynes—in a role in which he was typecast—was presented as a hint that Manly is "a bubble ripe for bursting," as Holland would have it? Haynes was perennially in trouble, and his employment with the King's Company was intermittent. To assume that any significant part of the audience would recall an incident at least four and probably eight years earlier seems more than a little farfetched, and to say that Haynes' presence as Plausible was "inevitably . . . a hint" of ridicule seems hard to justify. Moreover, as soon as either cast member dropped out, the hidden message would be lost.

What does the audience "learn"?

One of the most interesting and sophisticated readings of *The Plain-Dealer* to date, and as literary criticism perhaps the most convincing, is Peter Holland's, which concentrates on miscommunication and misinterpretation within the play. Using the ambiguities and contradictions that have confused or annoyed other critics, Holland assumes that the ambiguity is functional, designed to frustrate the audience. The point, in Holland's view, is that by the end "*The Plain-Dealer* has taught the audience that judgement is a fraud, that there are few means by which we can guarantee knowledge and none at all by which we can talk about it" (p. 202). In our opinion, this is an excellent illustration of a plausible and ingenious literary reading that is virtually unproducible. *The Plain-Dealer* shows us Manly, Freeman, Olivia, Vernish, Fidelia, the Widow Blackacre, et al., and an audience is going to respond to the fortunes of these characters. Holland's reading focuses on the judgmental processes of the viewer (or really the reader)—but how is a production to force the audience to make the leap to abstraction and conclude that "judgement is a fraud"? Indeed, such a conclusion is appropriate principally to a production that tries—against theatrical logic—to play the "inconsistencies" decried by literary critics. Holland's reading is a gallant attempt to make "literary" sense of the play, but neither the "humours character" nor the "satiric scourge" interpretation suggests that judgment is particularly difficult, let alone fraudulent. Dryden's praise for *The Plain-Dealer* as "one of the most bold, most general, and most useful Satyres which has ever been presented on the English Theater" does not suggest any doubts about the judgments it calls for.[33] Holland's reading is, in fact, peculiarly modern, born of 1970s doubts about the very possibility of meaningful communication.

Our skepticism about the producibility of Holland's interpretation is reinforced by what seem to us inconsistencies of method. Holland is naturally concerned with "authority" as the audience perceives it in the play. Fair enough, but just what counts as "the play"? Holland opens his analysis with a consideration of "confusion over the identity of the speaker of the dedication and prologue. Author, actor, and character are intertwined; the audience is dubious about the relative authority of

33. "The Authors Apology for Heroique Poetry; and Poetique Licence," prefixed to *The State of Innocence* (1677).

the various voices" (p. 171). True for the reader, no doubt, but in a book that claims attention to performance, this is a shocking lapse in method. Dedications were not spoken in the theatre, and indeed Wycherley is unlikely to have written the dedication by the time of the premiere. The dedication is illegitimate evidence; the prologue, questionable. Holland here muddles the very reading/performance distinction he so rightly insists upon.

Reflecting on this little survey of *Plain-Dealer* criticism, we would like to stress four points on which production analysis and literary criticism differ in practice. First, the "inconsistencies" or multiple interpretive possibilities that bedevil the literary critic are meat and drink for the production analyst. Second, the literary critic is at least de facto much freer to deal selectively with his text. Ignoring "what happens in Olivia's bedroom" may do the critic scant credit, but many have done so. Such selectivity merely renders a production analysis ridiculous: the contriver has to take a position on choices necessary to any production. Third, the supposed allusions and comparisons (Almanzor, Alceste) that critics freely introduce are much harder to justify in production analysis, where one must ask how, in a performance, the audience might be induced to make such a jump. Fourth, the abstract lessons devised by literary critics are the very devil to get across to an audience in a theatre.

CODA: THE OBJECTS OF DRAMATIC CRITICISM

The glaring inadequacy of most literary criticism applied to drama results from the longstanding assumption that there is *an* interpretation to be found. Many critics who would deny that they believe any such thing have in fact written as though they accepted such a premise. A playscript is by definition a vehicle designed for completion in performance, and the chances that only a single, "ideal" interpretation is appropriate are remote indeed. Recent trends in literary criticism suggest that future critics may be much less dogmatic. Deconstructionists and reader-response critics are now prepared to allow for multiplicity of meaning even in poems. This is a healthy trend, though the justifications offered by these cognitive nihilists take us dangerously far in the direction of complete anarchy.[34] Even more than poems and novels, plays invite critical pluralism, and we must agree with Gerald Rabkin that the application of deconstructionist criticism to drama is overdue: "Questions of textuality, intertextuality, demystification, hermeneutics . . . have profound implications for the study of theatre."[35] The first step would seem to be willingness to deal with the special problems posed by works written for performance.

Who would claim that music is best left on the page? To anyone who argues that the performer inevitably puts his own imprint on the work, changes it, twists it in directions not specified on the page, there is a simple answer: Exactly. That's what it's there for. If we could imagine a player piano that could take the text of *As You Like It* or *King Lear* and render a letter-perfect "performance," the results would be as lifeless and boring as a machine-punched player piano performance of the "Moonlight" Sonata.

Drama criticism should not be tied entirely to performance. Many plays never get revived, and any one production is inevitably limited by the very choices that give it performance validity, even if the performance itself is magnificent. "How was it done?" is an interesting question. "How could it be done?" is usually more fruitful. As the late Daniel Seltzer pointed out, the "real problem" in relying on actual performance "is that performance, while by nature unlike an act of literary criticism, always has one of the same results: *it cannot avoid implying a point of view*."[36] A

34. For a sensible attempt to mediate between the claims of "radical pluralists" (Derrida & Co.) and the objections of "critical monists" (Hirsch, Wellek et al.) see Paul B. Armstrong, "The Conflict of Interpretations and the Limits of Pluralism," *PMLA*, 98 (1983), 341–52.

35. Gerald Rabkin, "The Play of Misreading: Text/Theatre/Deconstruction," *Performing Arts Journal*, 7 (1983), 44–60. Quotation from p. 46.

36. "Shakespeare's Texts and Modern Productions," *Reinterpretations of Elizabethan Drama*, ed. Norman Rabkin (New York: Columbia Univ. Press, 1969), pp. 89–115.

director must do one thing and thereby conceal other possibilities. The great virtue of production analysis is that it leaves us free to explore multiple possibilities.

Dramatic criticism comprises two basic activities: analysis of the script (production analysis) and analysis of actual performance of the script (performance analysis). The connection between production analysis and performance analysis is real, and so is the difference. Performance analysis enjoys the distinct advantage of dealing with actuality, with a production complete in all its details, with the experience of the real thing. Of course, the advantage is also a disadvantage: the critic is stuck with what the performance gives him. The production analyst is far freer to pursue hypothesis and speculation, to envision interpretive possibilities. Both approaches deal with such matters as "concept," dominant mood, effect of casting choices, style, tempo, intensity, energy/violence level, impact of scenery and costumes. Both must grapple with the slippery problem of "dominant idea." Is there one? If so, what? How is it communicated?

Legitimate performance analysis requires answers to at least four basic questions. (1) What does the text say? (2) What is the production concept—i.e., the view of characters and events presented? (3) What reaction does the production try to elicit from the audience? (4) Does the production succeed in its apparent aims? Production analysis is much less tied to the specifics of any single performance or concept. The writer of production analysis has a choice: whether (a) to concentrate on the multiplicity of possible choices, treating the text as an empowering agency, or (b) to present discrete, coherent interpretations in which all the choices are made. Our procedure in this book comes much closer to the latter. For each play we have sketched out two or three sharply different productions, striving to give a sense of the range of performance possibilities. Consequently our production concepts (e.g., "pathetic vehicle" versus "pessimistic satire" for *Venice Preserv'd*) should be regarded as paradigmatic rather than prescriptive, and readers must remember that in practice a director might legitimately opt for a middle way. Obviously, future critics will find other production concepts for the plays we analyze in this book: we regard this as a healthy and desirable state of affairs. Good plays should be susceptible of a variety of different production concepts—this is the premise of our book—and to analyze or produce a play in one way does not in any sense invalidate another interpretation or production concept.

Production analysis and performance analysis must both deal with an experience (whether potential or actual), not just with a message to be decoded. John Styan speaks of the "emergent meaning" in drama, as opposed to the "immanent meaning" found in poems.[37] The literary critic who sticks firmly to text falsifies that text by treating it without regard for what it is—a performance vehicle. Our hope in writing this book has been to encourage a production-oriented dramatic criticism, a criticism that is neither limited to the text nor dependent upon the availability of actual performance.

37. Styan, *Drama, Stage and Audience*, p. 27.

2

The Production Process

Second Player. So it gets us money, 'tis no great matter.
                                   The Rehearsal (Q1672), p. 5.

T HIS CHAPTER is a bridge between critical theory and the specific analyses presented in the remainder of the book. Our
aim is to sketch the original production circumstances for the late
seventeenth-century plays we are about to discuss. For some
readers this chapter will function as a reminder of the theatrical
practicalities that impinge on the drama; for others, it will have
to serve as a capsule introduction to the performance conditions
in which these plays came to the stage. For most of the substance
we can claim no originality, but we have tried to let this discussion serve as a way of bringing recent research to the attention of
both sorts of readers. The Introduction to Part 1 of *The London
Stage* remains the best general account of the background for the
late seventeenth century, but a gratifying amount of new research
has been done in the twenty years since its publication.[1]

Despite this new scholarship, the evidence from which we
have to work remains scrappy and unsatisfactory. How were
plays chosen? How were they cast? What went on during the re-

1. For a recent overview, see Robert D. Hume, "English Drama and Theatre
1660–1800: New Directions in Research," *Theatre Survey*, 23 (1982), 71–100.

hearsal process? How much "directing" was done, and by whom? What was the acting like? What did the scenery look like? The costumes? How much "production concept" was there? To such questions we can return no more than halting and often speculative answers. Anecdotes must be used with caution, and extrapolation backwards from known eighteenth-century practices is historically questionable. Plays like *The Rehearsal* (1671) and *The Female Wits* (1696) are rich in allusion to playhouse practices, but how much does one allow for comic exaggeration? Such practical problems notwithstanding, a brief survey of what can be inferred about late seventeenth-century production circumstances should shed light on both the way they influenced playwrights and the kinds of meaning plays could be given in performance.

THE NATURE OF THE LATE SEVENTEENTH-CENTURY THEATRE

To understand attitudes toward new plays, and the ways in which the theatres produced them, we must first consider some basic features of the professional theatre as it was established in late seventeenth-century London. The facts are familiar, but their implications are often ignored.

The patent monopoly granted to Sir William Davenant and Thomas Killigrew settled the basic outlines of London theatre.[2] By no means, however, were the two companies established on an equal basis. Killigrew got almost every experienced actor in London, and he was also given a near-monopoly on classic English drama.[3] Davenant had perforce to stage new plays, and he compensated for his inexperienced actors by moving immediately to equip and open a theatre with changeable scenery—the "first"

2. For discussion of the nature of the competition established by the patent grants see Judith Milhous, *Thomas Betterton and the Management of Lincoln's Inn Fields, 1695–1708* (Carbondale: Southern Illinois Univ. Press, 1979), Chapter 1.

3. See Robert D. Hume, "Securing a Repertory: Plays on the London Stage 1660–5," in *Poetry and Drama 1570–1700: Essays in Honour of Harold F. Brooks*, ed. Antony Coleman and Antony Hammond (London: Methuen, 1981), pp. 156–72.

Lincoln's Inn Fields, opened in June 1661. So successful was the changeable scenery that Killigrew's troupe found itself forced to build the Bridges Street theatre in order to remain competitive. The pattern of competition as it developed in the 1660s soon taught the managers that they had to stage new plays, and that effective scenery, costume, song, and dance were likewise vital to success at the box office.

In the period covered by this book (broadly conceived as 1660–1710) there are six distinct managements in charge of various companies. Their diversity is striking. Thomas Killigrew and his son Charles delegated authority to actors and then meddled with them, interested chiefly in profits (1660–82). Davenant served as both proprietor and manager (1660–68). The Thomas Betterton–Henry Harris and the Betterton–William Smith managements (1668–87) were actor oligarchies. Christopher Rich was an owner-tyrant who delegated theatrical detail but kept an iron hand on the budget (1693–1709). The company formed at Lincoln's Inn Fields in 1695 was an actor cooperative (1695–1704). John Vanbrugh was an intelligent amateur who relied heavily on his senior actors (1704–8). Management made a tremendous difference to the contentment of the actors (for whom alternative employment was practically nonexistent), but the demands of competition were such that management made less difference to a company's offerings than one might expect. Four factors seem pretty well to govern repertory decisions.

1. These were commercial theatres. Owners of the early companies included both "adventurers" (outsiders who bought stock as an investment) and "sharers" (senior actors whose pay was a percentage of the profits).[4] Because the senior actors' incomes depended on having profits to distribute, the company had to make money if the sharers were not to starve.[5] A venal proprietor like Christopher Rich cared only for money, but however genuinely

4. For such specific figures as we possess on theatre profits and sharers' income, see Judith Milhous, "The Duke's Company's Profits, 1675–1677," *Theatre Notebook*, 32 (1978), 76–88, and "United Company Finances, 1682–1692," *Theatre Research International*, 7 (1981–82), 37–53.

5. Benefits became a regular part of the actors' income in the late 1690s dur-

concerned the actors may have been about artistic excellence, they too were committed to the proposition that the theatre should be profitable. New plays were staged in the hope that they would make money—or at least that they would provide variety without losing any money.

2. Mounting new plays was an important competitive tactic. The pattern established in the 1660s carried right through to the Union of 1682 and picked up again with the reestablishment of competition in 1695. At the height of competition in the 1670s, the two companies put on anywhere from twelve to twenty-five new plays each season—at considerable nuisance and some expense. After the union, in contrast, the United Company grudgingly mounted only three or four—generally surefire scripts from established playwrights (Dryden, Aphra Behn, and John Crowne) or company insiders (actors like Thomas Jevon and William Mountfort). The importance of new plays is obvious in the early 1660s, when the King's Company found itself forced to offer new plays, despite its virtual monopoly in the principal Elizabethan, Jacobean, and Caroline plays. And it is apparent again after 1695, when the Lincoln's Inn Fields stars obviously believed that they could not afford to compete without a lot of new plays, even against the shabby group of castoffs and beginners left to Rich. Yet the resistance of these companies to mounting new plays is manifest in times of noncompetition. In the days of the United Company and again after the Union of 1708 (and yet again after the Licensing Act of 1737), the managers adopted an ultraconservative policy of taking few chances and sticking with revivals. The contrast between the 1670s and the 1680s makes clear how troublesome and risky these companies found new plays.

3. Runs were extremely short, even for successful new plays. Because only a few hundred people regularly came to the the-

ing hard times when neither company was able to pay salaries in full and neither had profits to distribute to sharers. See Robert D. Hume, "The Origins of the Actor Benefit in London," *Theatre Research International*, 9 (1984), 99–111.

atre,[6] rapid turnover in the offerings was unavoidable. Eight or ten consecutive performances was exceptional success for a new play, and many lasted only three nights—i.e., long enough to give the author a benefit. Competition put great pressure on a company to mount new plays, but no one play was going to keep the house going more than one or two weeks at best. Not many plays appear to have been revived after their first three-to-six day run. An even smaller number were ever revived after their initial season. Performance records are far too incomplete to let us guess at a figure, but the survival rate of new plays was clearly discouraging.

4. The repertory made brutal demands on the actors. Theatres involved in competition felt obliged to stage a lot of new plays, but they depended on a repertory of proven favorites for day-to-day survival. All of the major companies active in London during this period appear to have operated on essentially the same schedule—a season of 180–200 acting days running from September or October into June. During the summer (and sometimes in Lent) the hirelings (nonsharing actors) were allowed to perform for their own profit. During most of the nine-month season, however, the company performed six days a week. Limited evidence suggests that even newly revived plays were rarely performed more than two or three days in succession, and that a company often mounted six different plays in the course of a week. We do not know how many different plays any company performed in a season before 1700. But the theatre is a conservative institution, and if we judge by eighteenth-century norms we may guess that a late seventeenth-century company performed between forty and sixty different plays each season. The carryover from season to season was probably very high, or so both logic and eighteenth-century practice would suggest.

The implications of these figures for the actors are rather staggering. In the height of competition in the 1670s a company

6. Our knowledge of the late seventeenth-century audience remains sketchy. See Emmett L. Avery, "The Restoration Audience," *Philological Quarterly*, 45

might have expected to mount ten new plays during a season. With average luck they would probably occupy no more than sixty performance dates, leaving at least 120–140 days to be filled by about forty "old" plays. A handful of those plays might be run six or seven times, but most of them just two or three, unless the seventeenth-century pattern of offerings was very different from the eighteenth. This meant that a principal actor or actress might need to be able to perform some thirty or more different parts in the course of a single season—perhaps twenty old plays carried over from the previous season, five revivals, and five new plays.[7] As we have noted, the number of new plays varied greatly; but in the 1680s, for example, the United Company was busy reviving old King's Company plays, and so the demands on actors cannot have lessened significantly. Actors and actresses certainly tended to have particular "lines" (often quite different in comedy and tragedy), which probably let them use a standard bag of tricks in many parts, but the number of roles involved remains astonishing.

The variety afforded by new plays was important to these companies, but work on new plays and revivals had to be squeezed into the midst of schedules which were already quite demanding. There was no possibility of stopping to work intensively on a single production. New plays were a necessary evil, a drain on energy and attention added to the burdens already imposed by a high-turnover repertory system. Given these conditions, we need to inquire how the theatres went about acquiring and producing these not altogether welcome new scripts.

(1966), 54–61; Harold Love, "Who were the Restoration Audience?" *Yearbook of English Studies*, 10 (1980), 21–44; Arthur H. Scouten and Robert D. Hume, "'Restoration Comedy' and its Audiences, 1660–1776," *Yearbook of English Studies*, 10 (1980), 45–69; Harry William Pedicord, "The Changing Audience," Chapter 8 of *The London Theatre World*.

7. For example, in 1681–82 William Smith, in addition to his duties as co-manager of the Duke's Company and parts in a great many of the repertory plays, took on at least five substantial roles in new plays—Don Carlos in *The False Count*, Ramble in *The London Cuckolds*, Kinglove in *The Royalist*, Pierre in *Venice Preserv'd*, and King Harry in *Vertue Betray'd*. He may also have taken parts in three new plays for which we lack casts. And with the King's Company in the process of collapse, this was not a particularly strenuous season for the Duke's Company.

Scripts

The theatres got new plays from three distinct sources—amateurs, professionals, and attached professionals.[8] The amateurs ranged from a stage-struck teenager like Elizabeth Polwhele[9] to the likes of Sir George Etherege and the duke of Buckingham. By "professional" is meant anyone who earned his or her living as a free-lance writer. People like Edward Ravenscroft and Thomas Durfey[10] seem usually to have written their plays on speculation, hoping to peddle them somewhere. Free-lance writers did not, however, necessarily compose without specific actors in mind. On the contrary, they probably tailored roles to particular actors to help get the piece accepted by that company. "Attached professionals" had signed an exclusive agreement with one company. The famous example is Dryden, who contracted with the King's Company circa May 1668 to provide three new plays each year in return for a share and a quarter of the company's profits.[11] How much money this deal produced we do not know. To judge from the facts we possess about the rival Duke's Company's finances and the checkered history of the King's Company, we might guess at just about nothing in some years, but as much as £200 in others. When Dryden defected to the Duke's Company in 1678, the aggrieved King's Company claimed that he had received as much as "3 or 4 hundred pounds, Comunibus annis"—probably a considerable exaggeration.[12] This share was in lieu of author's

8. We borrow these terms from Gerald Eades Bentley, *The Profession of Dramatist in Shakespeare's Time* (Princeton: Princeton Univ. Press, 1971).

9. Polwhele's *The Frolicks* (1671) is dedicated to Prince Rupert with the explicit request that he help her get it staged.

10. According to PRO LC 3/24, Thomas Durfey was sworn in as a member of the King's Company on 8 May 1676. See John Harold Wilson, "Players' Lists in the Lord Chamberlain's *Registers*," *Theatre Notebook*, 18 (1963), 25–30. The exclusive arrangement was evidently short-lived: Durfey's *Madam Fickle* was staged by the Duke's Company in November.

11. See James M. Osborn, *John Dryden: Some Biographical Facts and Problems* (1940; rev. ed. Gainesville: Univ. of Florida Press, 1965), pp. 200–207. In the prologue to *The Virtuoso* (1676) Shadwell implies that the usual contract called for two plays a year, but he does not specify the retainer.

12. Leslie Hotson reaches the same conclusion from a completely different

benefits, though the company (perhaps fearing his defection in hard times) gave him a benefit for *All for Love* in 1677. Dryden never achieved his promised output, but the company paid him his share and a quarter anyway, probably recognizing that it was getting value for money. Nathaniel Lee evidently had an exclusive contract with the King's Company in the 1670s, and the King's Company was heavily fined by the Lord Chamberlain when it persuaded John Crowne to breach his contract with the Duke's Company.[13] The usual arrangement was probably a cash retainer for right of first refusal, with the author to get a benefit for any play the company chose to perform. Or so we would deduce from evidence that in 1673 Elkanah Settle was allowed £50 per annum by the Duke's Company "upon Condition they might have the Acting of all the Plays he made. But he expecting a greater third day, if acted by the King's Servants, notwithstanding his Pension, put his play into their hands."[14]

Celebrated amateurs and attached professionals had an obvious advantage in getting their plays staged and in getting some trouble taken over the production. Managers probably figured that producing some weak scripts was preferable to offending prominent people or company insiders. One of the few documentable cases of a company manager's refusing a play from an attached professional is Colley Cibber's *Xerxes*, which appeared at Lincoln's Inn Fields in late 1698. In this case Christopher Rich's judgment was sound: *Xerxes* died in a single night.[15]

angle. See *The Commonwealth and Restoration Stage* (1928; rpt. New York: Russell and Russell, 1962), p. 245.

13. Osborn, *Dryden*, pp. 204–5. Why the Duke's Company was not fined for stealing Dryden we do not know.

14. *Reflexions Upon a late Pamphlet, intituled, A Narrative Written by E. Settle* (London: J. H. for the Author, 1683), p. 2. The Duke's Company protested, and either Charles or James (contemporary testimony is contradictory) ruled that the play belonged to the Duke's Company, which duly performed it with great success.

15. Cibber signed an exclusive contract with Drury Lane on 29 October 1696 (PRO LC 7/3, fols. 76–77). He got that rather lucrative contract after the success of *Love's Last Shift* and a temporary defection to Lincoln's Inn Fields. The fine print, however, reveals that Cibber was obliged to sell all his plays on the terms specified, but that Rich was not obliged to buy them.

How did scripts get chosen? Some, of course, were commissioned. When the King's Company wanted a Molière adaptation in a hurry from an experienced hand in the winter of 1671–72, it turned to Thomas Shadwell, who provided *The Miser* "in less than a moneth," according to his prefatory note. The play appeared anonymously—because his "great hast" made him doubtful of its success, according to the author, but perhaps also because his agreeing to work for the King's Company was politically touchy. When the Duke's Company decided to get up a major opera, *Psyche* was chosen as the subject and Shadwell (by 1673 a company regular, and probably "attached") was given the job of producing the libretto. Ravenscroft tells us that he wrote *The Careless Lovers* (1673) in less than a week because the Duke's Company's hirelings needed a nonrepertory play to act for their own benefit in Lent (preface). In the fall of 1698, when Lincoln's Inn Fields produced a successful if small-scale opera, Rich responded by commissioning Peter Motteux (who had hitherto done all his work for Lincoln's Inn Fields) to make an operatic alteration out of *The Island Princess*, which he proceeded to do with great dispatch. A dispute subsequently arose over whether Motteux was entitled to a benefit or only a flat fee—apparently settled to Motteux's advantage by the authorities.[16]

The vast majority of new plays, however, were simply submitted to the company manager for his decision. Because getting managers to read plays—let alone read them sympathetically—was never easy, authors often sought the endorsement of prominent litterateurs, successful playwrights, and members of the company.[17] Famous cases include Southerne's interceding with Rich on behalf of Cibber's *Love's Last Shift*, and Lord Halifax's interesting himself in Vanbrugh's *The Provok'd Wife* on behalf of the Lincoln's Inn Fields Company.[18] Little is known about the

16. See Milhous, *Thomas Betterton*, pp. 130–31.
17. An aspiring playwright in *The Female Wits* (Drury Lane, 1696) accosts two of the company's senior actresses, Mrs. Knight and Mrs. Cross: "Well, Ladies, after this Play's over, I hope you'll think of mine; I have two excellent Parts for ye" (p. 19).
18. See *The London Stage*, Part 1, p. cl.

details of reviewing scripts before 1700. Davenant and Betterton appear to have made decisions for the Duke's and United companies, with what advice we can only guess. Both Thomas Killigrew and Christopher Rich seem often to have delegated repertory decisions to the senior actors. Cibber, for example, was certainly reading scripts for the Patent Company by 1704.[19] The Lincoln's Inn Fields company presumably required a vote of the sharers before accepting new plays.

How much "fixing" was done, and who carried out such play doctoring? The evidence is scanty but suggestive. The host of authors who thank Betterton for such assistance in prefaces indicates that he regularly helped clean up scripts during the process of production. The best known instance is probably Dryden's *Don Sebastian* (1689), which Betterton shortened by twelve hundred lines after the first performance—with the author's approbation and gratitude. According to a memorandum written by Thomas Southerne, Congreve's *The Old Batchelour* (1693) was shown to Dryden in rough draft, and Dryden "putt it in the order it was playd" after consulting with Southerne and Arthur Maynwaring.[20] Despite the scarcity of such evidence, everything we know about the theatre (amply borne out in eighteenth-century sources) suggests that scripts were subject to managerial blue penciling, and that a considerable amount of revising and fixing must have gone on during rehearsals and occasionally afterwards. Thus Thomas Durfey's *The Richmond Heiress* had a rough reception in April 1693, but was revived the following October "with Alterations and Amendments." And sometime during the first month of Farquhar's extremely popular *The Constant Couple* (1699), the author saw fit to rewrite a key scene, entirely

19. In October 1704 Cibber signed a contract with Rich giving him £3 10s. a week for acting, plus 10s. a week for reading and casting plays and another 20s. for other managerial work. See Richard Hindry Barker, *Mr Cibber of Drury Lane* (1939; rpt. New York: AMS, 1966), p. 61 (citing PRO C10/537/22).

20. See British Library Add. MS 4221, cited in *The London Stage*, Part 1, p. 419. For performance cuts made by Thomas Killigrew in his own plays, see Albert Wertheim, "Production Notes for Three Plays by Thomas Killigrew," *Theatre Survey*, 10 (1969), 105–13.

altering its tone and impact.[21] We have strong evidence that the character of Count Bellair disappeared from *The Beaux' Stratagem* almost immediately, perhaps after the first night. It was ever thus in the theatre, and one can hardly imagine that late seventeenth-century playwrights were exempt from production changes and the agonies of rewriting.

In theory, all new plays had to be licensed by the Master of the Revels. Sir Henry Herbert fought bitterly to continue this practice in the early 1660s, and succeeded.[22] Since the fee was £2 per play (£1 for revived plays), it was worth collecting. Herbert diligently went through each script, striking out words and phrases to which he objected, a practice he continued until his death on 27 April 1673.[23] All available evidence suggests that after that date licensing was a pro forma process, except during a couple of short-lived flaps about it. A number of plays got banned (sometimes just temporarily) during the height of the political crisis of 1680–1682, and pressure from the Lord Chamberlain late in the 1690s produced a spate of rather arbitrary excisions. The removal of Act I of Cibber's *Richard III* (1699) in its entirety, for example, suggests pique on the part of Charles Killigrew (then Master of the Revels) more than any attempt to review the play in the fashion of Herbert. Only during the Exclusion Crisis was censorship a major issue during this period.[24] Direct intervention

21. Both versions are printed in *The Complete Works of George Farquhar*, ed. Charles Stonehill, 2 vols. (1930; rpt. New York: Gordian, 1967), I, 141–44, 361–63.

22. Some of the relevant documents in the dispute are preserved in *The Dramatic Records of Sir Henry Herbert*, ed. Joseph Quincy Adams (New Haven: Yale Univ. Press, 1917).

23. The famous example of his censorship is *The Cheats* (1663). See *John Wilson's The Cheats*, ed. Milton C. Nahm (Oxford: Blackwell, 1935). For more typical examples, see Elizabeth Polwhele's *The Faithful Virgins* (ca. 1670), Bodl. Rawl. Poet MS 195, fols. 49–78, and prompt copies of Cartwright's *The Ordinary* and *The Lady Errant*, licensed by Herbert in 1672. These copies, now in the University of Illinois Library, are discussed in *The Poems and Plays of William Cartwright*, ed. G. Blakemore Evans (Madison: Univ. of Wisconsin Press, 1951), pp. 85, 260.

24. See Arthur F. White, "The Office of Revels and Dramatic Censorship in the Restoration Period," *Western Reserve Univ. Bulletin*, n.s. 34 (1931), 5–45;

by the King was a different matter. When Charles II took personal offense at Edward Howard's *The Change of Crownes* (1667) or James II decided "that ye play called ye Spanish Friar should bee noe more Acted,"[25] the play simply disappeared, with or without a formal order.

The playwright's remuneration was normally the profits of the third performance—i.e., the gross minus "house charges." These daily expenses ran about £25 early in the period and about £35 by the turn of the century. A passably full house at Drury Lane or Dorset Garden brought in something over £100 at ordinary prices.[26] A playwright might therefore hope to make something between £75 and £100, plus whatever extra he could get by peddling tickets to friends and patrons at more than list price. There was no guarantee of such good fortune. Cibber's rueful admission that the author's benefit for *Richard III* "did not raise me Five Pounds" (preface to *Ximena*) is notorious, but it can hardly have been a unique occurrence. At what point playwrights began trying to bargain for the sixth night (if the play lasted that long) we do not know, but Southerne refers to his receiving two benefits for *Sir Anthony Love* in 1690, and in due course custom granted the author every third night for the duration of the initial unbroken run. This was all the writer got for his play, save what he might get from a publisher.[27] After the first production an author had no control whatever over performance rights to his play, derived no income from revivals, and had no control over changes

---

Calhoun Winton, "Dramatic Censorship," Chapter 10 of *The London Theatre World*.

25. PRO LC 5/147, p. 239 (8 December 1686).

26. John Downes states that £130—received by Shadwell for *The Squire of Alsatia* at Drury Lane in 1688—"was the greatest Receipt they ever had at that House at single Prizes." See *Roscius Anglicanus*, p. 41. Whether this was gross or net Downes does not say.

27. Each play was subject to negotiation, but £30 or £35 was a good price for outright sale of copyright in this period—after which all profits accrued to the publisher. Farquhar sold *The Beaux' Stratagem* to Lintot for £30 in 1707; a year earlier he received only £16 2s. 6d. for *The Recruiting Officer*. See Shirley Strum Kenny, "The Publication of Plays," Chapter 11 of *The London Theatre World*.

introduced by any company that chose to revive the piece.[28] The importance of new plays in the late seventeenth century is evident both in the number that got produced and in the arrangements for "attached" playwrights. Plays were not, however, thought of as particularly individual creations. In a letter of 4 March 1699 Dryden comments: "This Day was playd a reviv'd Comedy of Mr Congreve's calld the Double Dealer, which was never very take-ing; in the play bill was printed,—Written by Mr Congreve . . . the printing an Authours name, in a Play bill, is a new manner of proceeding, at least in England."[29] The theatre is a conservative institution, but this is an absolutely astonishing statement. Dry-den presumably knew whereof he spoke, and he tells us in so many words that before 1699 no theatre had ever advertised a play with its author's name attached. The difference between late seventeenth-century and twentieth-century views of a play could hardly be made clearer. In Dryden's theatre plays were thought of not as art but as a necessary commodity—and the skillful con-triver of useable scripts was regarded as an artificer worthy of his far from extravagant hire.

CASTING

After a play was accepted by the manager the author read it aloud to the actors, though whether this public reading preceded or followed the casting process we cannot be certain. Cibber's well-known description of the process is worth quoting.

28. A rare instance of protest is George Granville's request in December 1706 that a revival of his semiopera *The British Enchanters* be suppressed by the Lord Chamberlain because it was to be done without "singing & dancing"—which Granville considered "no other than a design to murder the Child of my Brain." Granville got the performance stopped, probably because his plea was addressed to his brother-in-law, who was the Lord Chamberlain's secretary. By March 1707 the actors were allowed to proceed with the exhibition of this op-era sans music, the unhappy author's feelings notwithstanding. See *Vice Cham-berlain Coke's Theatrical Papers, 1706–1715*, ed. Judith Milhous and Robert D. Hume (Carbondale: Southern Illinois Univ. Press, 1982), No. 7.

29. *The Letters of John Dryden*, ed. Charles E. Ward (Durham: Duke Univ. Press, 1942), pp. 112–13.

As we have sometimes great Composers of Musick who cannot sing, we have as frequently great Writers that cannot read. . . . Of this Truth *Dryden*, our first great Master of Verse and Harmony, was a strong Instance: When he brought his Play of *Amphytrion* to the Stage, I heard him give it his first Reading to the Actors, in which, though it is true he deliver'd the plain Sense of every Period, yet the whole was in so cold, so flat, and unaffecting a manner, that I am afraid of not being believ'd when I affirm it.

On the contrary, *Lee*, far his inferior in Poetry, was so pathetick a Reader of his own Scenes, that I have been inform'd by an Actor who was present, that while *Lee* was reading to Major *Mohun* at a Rehearsal, *Mohun*, in the Warmth of his Admiration, threw down his Part and said, Unless I were able to *play* it as well as you *read* it, to what purpose should I undertake it? (*Apology*, I, 113–14)

How the casting process was conducted we do not know. No evidence of actor tryouts has come down to us, and the best guess seems to be that since the company had a particular set of actors and actresses available, the most plausible candidates were simply assigned where they seemed to fit best. Most actors had a particular "line" (fop, villain, coquette, etc.), which constituted a significant part of what the company gave them to do—though as Peter Holland points out, many performers had entirely distinct lines for comedy and tragedy.[30]

The probability seems to be that roles were assigned by the manager with the advice of the author. David Garrick is reported to have said (three generations later) that "every author, since my management, distributed his parts as he thinks will be of most service to his interest, nor have I ever interfered, unless I perceive that they would propose something contrary to common sense."[31] At times company politics were an issue. Jane Rogers claims that Ambrose Philips walked her home from his reading of *The Dis-*

30. Holland, *The Ornament of Action*, pp. 78–80.

31. Garrick, *Private Correspondence*, II, 30, cited by Kalman A. Burnim, *David Garrick, Director* (1961; rpt. Carbondale: Southern Illinois Univ. Press, 1973), p. 27. Burnim notes that this is "an overstatement." For an anecdotal overview of casting and rehearsal practices, see W. J. Lawrence, *Old Theatre Days and Ways* (London: George G. Harrap, 1935), Chapter 4 ("Old-Time Rehearsing").

trest Mother (1712) and promised her the part of Andromache, but that Mrs. Oldfield demanded it and got it from the Drury Lane managers.[32] Authors were sometimes consulted even about emergency substitutions. Cibber reports that Congreve recommended him as a replacement for the ailing Edward Kynaston at a command performance of *The Double-Dealer* (13 January 1694).[33]

For veteran actors, a new role was a mixed blessing. It meant a great deal of work, probably for nothing. Except for those hirelings paid extra for each performance,[34] no additional pay was involved. For hirelings, new parts could mean status and perhaps a step toward eventual advancement into sharer status. Glory aside, the real appeal of new parts was that by custom anyone cast in a part kept that part permanently. If, therefore, the new play survived and went into the repertory, the original performers would be called for all future revivals as long as they remained with the company—sometimes for decades. To memorize a fat part in a flop was a nuisance, but if the piece "proved a living play" (as Downes liked to say), then the part would definitely provide status and continued exposure. Cibber craved good parts in the early 1690s, and Robert Wilks found the United Company situation so discouraging that he went back to Dublin for several years. But only for beginners and ambitious hirelings did new plays represent an opportunity eagerly sought. The actors' lack of enthusiasm for new parts is evident in a set of King's Company rules, adopted in 1675. Number 2 reads: "That neither Man or Weoman shall refuse any part the Company shall thinke them fitt for Subpoena a weekes wages."[35] If actors had to be threatened with so stiff a fine to keep them from refusing parts, we may de-

---

32. See *The Memorial of Jane Rogers* (1712), reprinted and discussed in Judith Milhous and Robert D. Hume, "Theatrical Politics at Drury Lane: New Light on Jane Rogers, Anne Oldfield, and Letitia Cross," *Bulletin of Research in the Humanities*, in press.

33. *Apology*, I, 185–86.

34. An arrangement specified in the hypothetical "Company Plan" of 1703 (PRO LC 7/3, fols. 160–63), but not definitely in use before the later 1690s.

35. PRO LC 5/141, p. 307. (Printed by Allardyce Nicoll, *A History of English Drama, 1660–1900*, rev. ed., 6 vols. [Cambridge: Cambridge Univ. Press, 1952–59], I, 324–25.)

duce that senior members would probably have been glad to duck out of roles in all but the most promising new plays.

Even a desultory survey of late seventeenth-century casts shows the high proportion of plays in which essentially all parts were typecast.[36] Cibber illustrates the degree of audience expectation amusingly in an anecdote that probably refers to Aphra Behn's *The Widdow Ranter* (1689):

> So unusual had it been to see *Sandford* an innocent Man in a Play, that whenever he was so, the Spectators would hardly give him credit in so gross an Improbability. Let me give you an odd Instance of it, which I heard *Monfort* say was a real Fact. A new Play (the Name of it I have forgot) was brought upon the Stage, wherein *Sandford* happen'd to perform the Part of an honest Statesman: The Pit, after they had sate three or four Acts in a quiet Expectation that the well-dissembled Honesty of *Sandford* (for such of course they concluded it) would soon be discover'd, . . . when, at last, finding no such matter, but that the Catastrophe had taken quite another Turn, and that *Sandford* was really an honest Man to the end of the Play, they fairly damn'd it, as if the Author had impos'd upon them the most frontless or incredible Absurdity. (*Apology*, I, 132–33)

In comic plays Sandford was acceptable in other sorts of roles, but in serious plays he did not ordinarily take heroic parts.[37]

The rigidity of typecasting can be overstressed. Betterton, for example, took a tremendous variety of roles in both comedy and tragedy, including both villains and heroes in both genres.[38] Peter Holland's valuable analysis makes plain that the better writers sometimes cast parts counter to type and audience expectation— as for example in Farquhar's *The Twin-Rivals* (1702).[39] Whether audience confusion caused by the casting contributed to that

36. The best general discussion of casting in this period is by Peter Holland, *The Ornament of Action*, Chapter 3.

37. See Robert H. Ross, Jr., "Samuel Sandford: Villain from Necessity," *PMLA*, 76 (1961), 367–72.

38. For documentation of his versatility throughout his long career, see Judith Milhous, "An Annotated Census of Thomas Betterton's Roles, 1659–1710," *Theatre Notebook*, 29 (1975), 33–43, 85–94.

39. Holland, *The Ornament of Action*, pp. 86–98.

play's initial failure we can only speculate. But Holland is correct in saying that surprising cast choices in 1690s plays by Dryden, Southerne, and Congreve must have contributed significantly to their complexity and impact for the original audience.

Professional and attached professional writers were extremely conscious of the performers available to them in any particular company. To write a part for which there was no suitable performer would at best hurt the play and at worst get it refused. To write a play without parts for the company's best actors made no sense at all. Thus Cibber tells us in the preface to *Woman's Wit* that when he went (very temporarily) to Lincoln's Inn Fields in 1696 he naturally wrote parts for the stars available there, but that when he took the piece back to Drury Lane he had to rewrite in order to provide a character suitable for Doggett, the company's best comic performer. Even amateurs must quickly have become conscious of special talents to be exploited. The flock of gay couple comedies done by the King's Company in the late 1660s obviously reflects the availability of Charles Hart and Nell Gwyn, just as the Elizabeth Barry-Anne Bracegirdle tandem inspired a whole series of tragedies in the 1690s designed to capitalize upon their complementary talents. Farquhar plainly tailored his romantic leads to the talents of his friend and compatriot Robert Wilks.[40]

As we will see in discussing particular plays, one can often deduce a surprising amount about a production from the cast, even when almost all other sources of information are lacking. We should remember, however, that although the wise author tried to write parts calculated for the talent available, authors did not always get the actors they wanted. Actresses got pregnant with distressing frequency, and even male actors sometimes got sick or left a company.[41] We can usefully debate the implications of par-

40. See Shirley Strum Kenny, "Farquhar, Wilks, and Wildair; or, the Metamorphosis of the 'Fine Gentleman'," *Philological Quarterly*, 57 (1978), 46–65.
41. For example, Nahum Tate's dedication to *Cuckolds-Haven* (1685) says that its poor success "was for this Reason: The principal Part (on which the Diversion depended) was, by Accident, disappointed of Mr. *Nokes*'s Performance, for whom it was design'd, and only proper." A notorious (if confusing)

ticular choices (why Mrs. Barry rather than Mrs. Mountfort as Mrs. Friendall in *The Wives Excuse?*), but we must not forget that casts from these repertory companies reflect the personnel available, not necessarily the author's preferences.[42]

SCENERY AND STAGING

At some point between the acceptance of the script and the beginning of rehearsals a promptbook had to be made up and "sides" written out. Because of the recent appearance of Edward A. Langhans' monumental *Restoration Promptbooks*, we now know a great deal more than we did about promptbooks in this period.[43] Promptbooks generally indicate scene shifts, warnings for actor entrances, and special effects, but they are silent on stage movement and blocking, line delivery, and broader questions of effect and interpretation. The prompter ran the performance from his own marked master copy; other annotated copies were evidently used by the machinist and the musicians. Since new plays were almost invariably staged before publication, each actor was given his own part written out in longhand by the prompter or one of his assistants, with just enough words from each preceding speech to let the actor recognize his or her cue.[44]

---

instance of cast changes is Congreve's *Love for Love*, discussed in Chapter 9, below.

42. Two of Flecknoe's plays, published before performance, give complete King's Company casts as the author envisioned them. In *Erminia* (1661) he specifies either Theophilus Bird or William Cartwright for the "Duke of Missina"; whether the company ever performed the play we do not know. *The Damoiselles a la Mode*, printed for the author in 1667, has a special explanatory note: "Together with the Persons Represented . . . I have set down the Comedians, whom I Intended shou'd Represent them, that the Reader might have half the pleasure of seeing it Acted, and a lively imagination might have the pleasure of it all intire." The King's Company mounted the play a year later, but whether it used the intended cast we do not know.

43. Carbondale: Southern Illinois Univ. Press, 1981. Langhans prints eleven major promptbooks complete in facsimile (elaborately annotated), as well as transcriptions of all known prompt markings (and traces of prompt copies in printed books) from the late seventeenth century.

44. On the one set of such "sides" discovered in modern times, see Edward

Before the promptbook could be completed, someone (the prompter? the machinist?) had to draw up a scene plan and decide exactly which scenes would be used and when they would be changed. This is hardly the place for a full-dress description of the physical workings of changeable scenery in the late seventeenth-century theatre, a topic discussed in a number of useful works.[45] For our purposes here, two points about the scenery are crucial. First, the scenery for most new plays (like the costumes) was simply pulled from stock, not specially designed and painted for each play. Downes remembered which productions had been "new-dressed" decades afterwards. The amount of fuss made over new scenery and new costumes in turn-of-the-century ads is clear evidence of their rarity. Every company had a "Wood," a "Tavern," a "Lodgings," a "City Street," a "Throne Room," and so forth. Regardless of what the author specified in his script, he got what the company had or chose to provide. The promptbook for the earl of Orrery's *Guzman* (1669), for example, shows that the King's Company used a scene they designated "The Forest" when Orrery called for "a Field with Trees" and then for "A Grove of Trees." We are probably safe in assuming that almost any standard setting could be approximated from the company's stock, if the manager thought it worth the bother. A demand for an arcane setting was likely to be met by the substitution of something already extant. No doubt companies that had lost

A. Langhans, "A Restoration Actor's Part," *Harvard Library Bulletin*, 23 (1975), 180–85.

45. The classic account is Richard Southern's *Changeable Scenery* (London: Faber and Faber, 1952), now badly in need of revision and updating but still useful. The fullest description of the use of scenery and scenic effects in this period remains Chapter 4 of Montague Summers' *The Restoration Theatre* (1934; rpt. New York: Humanities Press, 1964). For a lucid and helpful account of "Scenery and Technical Design" between 1660 and 1800, with some useful diagrams of stage machinery, we refer the reader to Colin Visser's fine study of the subject in Chapter 3 of *The London Theatre World*. For discussion of scene design per se, Southern's book and Sybil Rosenfeld's *A Short History of Scene Design in Great Britain* (Oxford: Blackwell, 1973) remain standard. The early portions of Rosenfeld's excellent *Georgian Scene Painters and Scene Painting* (Cambridge: Cambridge Univ. Press, 1981) are also helpful.

their stock of scenes (the King's Company by fire in 1672, for example) simplified ruthlessly. Late seventeenth-century companies did at times indulge in extremely fancy scenic and machine effects, but they tended to do so in expensive and elaborately mounted semioperas rather than in ordinary legitimate drama.[46] The £335 for which Isaac Fuller sued the King's Company over scenes painted for *Tyrannick-Love* or the "very glorious scenes & perspectives" done for *The Conquest of Granada* by Robert Streeter are exceptional in the extreme, special efforts made on behalf of plays for which management decided to go all out.

The second point we need to emphasize about scenery is that the practices and conventions of the mid-eighteenth-century cannot safely be read back into the earlier period, as Richard Southern often does. The elaborate scene-changing Southern postulates for Tuke's *The Adventures of Five Hours* (1663) seems to us implausible before 1700. Further, we must distinguish between what a company could do and what it did do in staging a given play. Discussing *All for Love* in Chapter 4 we postulate four distinct settings, but feel constrained to point out that the play could be staged with two or even with just one. Changeable scenery permits the presentation of very precise locations, but its availability is no proof of full changes for all implied shifts of venue. The conventions of the sceneryless Elizabethan public theatre were a living memory in 1660, and a great many old plays originally without scene designations were in the repertory. Colin Visser convincingly argues for a rather simple concept of scene changes in this period and for acceptance of a convention in which "The Street" can be represented by the proscenium front, regardless of which set is displayed on wings and shutters.[47]

An obvious question we must face is the differences among the four theatres at which the plays analyzed in this book were origi-

46. On the production scale of such shows, see Judith Milhous, "The Multi-Media Spectacular on the Restoration Stage," *British Theatre and the Other Arts, 1660–1800*, ed. Shirley Strum Kenny (Washington, D.C.: Folger Lib.), pp. 41–66.

47. See Colin Visser, "The Anatomy of the Early Restoration Stage: *The Adventures of Five Hours* and John Dryden's 'Spanish' Comedies," *Theatre Notebook*, 29 (1975), 56–69, 114–19.

nally staged—Drury Lane, Dorset Garden, the "second" Lincoln's Inn Fields, and Vanbrugh's Haymarket. What we know about these theatres varies considerably. We have passably full information about Drury Lane and the Haymarket; Dorset Garden is vague and hotly debated; about the 1695 Lincoln's Inn Fields we know almost nothing. Despite the galling inadequacies of our information, great progress has been made in this part of theatre history during the last twenty-five years.[48]

How different were the four theatres at issue here? Very. Dorset Garden was built to accommodate Betterton's English opera spectaculars, and seems to have been fitted for really elaborate scenic spectacle—mostly unused when the company mounted ordinary plays, to be sure. The 1695 Lincoln's Inn Fields was refitted on a shoestring budget and was cramped and minimal by

48. As the best introduction to the theatres of the period we would recommend Richard Leacroft's splendid *The Development of the English Playhouse* (London: Eyre Methuen, 1973), especially notable for its scale reconstructions. Leacroft was not, unfortunately, able to muster enough information to attempt reconstructions of Dorset Garden and the second Lincoln's Inn Fields. For meticulous analyses of the staging capacities at Drury Lane and Dorset Garden through 1682, see Edward A. Langhans, "Staging Practices in the Restoration Theatres, 1660–1682," Ph.D. diss., Yale University, 1955, available from University Microfilms. For detailed consideration of particular theatres and plans, the reader may wish to consult the following articles. On Drury Lane, see Edward A. Langhans, "Wren's Restoration Playhouse," *Theatre Notebook*, 18 (1964), 91–100, and "Pictorial Material on the Bridges Street and Drury Lane Theatres," *Theatre Survey*, 8 (1966), 80–100; Donald Mullin and Bruce Koenig, "Christopher Wren's Theatre Royal," *Theatre Notebook*, 21 (1967), 180–87. On Dorset Garden, see Langhans, "A Conjectural Reconstruction of the Dorset Garden Theatre," *Theatre Survey*, 13 (1972), 74–93; John R. Spring, "Platforms and Picture Frames: A Conjectural Reconstruction of the Duke of York's Theatre, Dorset Garden, 1669–1709," *Theatre Notebook*, 31 (1977), 6–19; Robert D. Hume, "The Dorset Garden Theatre: A Review of Facts and Problems," *Theatre Notebook*, 33 (1979), 4–17; Spring, "The Dorset Garden Theatre: Playhouse or Opera House," *Theatre Notebook*, 34 (1980), 60–69; Hume, "The Nature of the Dorset Garden Theatre," *Theatre Notebook*, 36 (1982), 99–109. No such reconstructions are currently available for the second Lincoln's Inn Fields or Vanbrugh's Haymarket, though Graham Barlow should be publishing some soon. For the best overview, see Edward A. Langhans, "The Theatres," *The London Theatre World*, Chapter 2. Langhans' chart of "Statistical Comparisons" (giving known and conjectural dimensions for all theatres in the period) is especially helpful.

all contemporary accounts. Jokes were made about Iliads in a nutshell when John Dennis's opera *Rinaldo and Armida* was produced there in 1698. Such difficulties notwithstanding, we are inclined to think that for regular plays the differences among these theatres would have imposed few changes in staging. None of the technical demands are out of the ordinary.

For the eight plays we analyze we have presented a scene plan put together on some simple principles. We have assumed no more scenic or technical capacity than we believe to have been available at all major London theatres after the opening of the first Lincoln's Inn Fields in 1661 and Bridges Street in 1663. We have assumed the availability of six different sets of shutters (with coordinating wings and borders), divided into two distinct groups so that the drawing apart of shutters in the first group can "discover" action in progress against a setting in the second group. We have presumed the use of the proscenium arch as "The Street" where convenient. We have tried to ensure that the progress of scenes in the script can be conveniently accommodated by the scene plan, especially for "discoveries" specified or implied in the script. We have felt free to combine different sets of "Lodgings" and the like where such combination was needed to reduce the total number of sets to six. (Differentiation by means other than wings and shutters would be easy enough if wanted.) We are aware that some productions were doubtless more scenically elaborate than we have allowed for, and that others were more minimal in actual practice. Our aim has been to suggest a staging plan that could have been carried out routinely at any of these theatres. We should point out that in late seventeenth-century theatres there were probably two grooves at each shutter and wing position. Any number of scenes could be displayed in a single groove by putting different shutters into the groove in the "off" position. Likewise there is no reason that four or five of the sets should not be shown in the second shutter position if the requirements of a particular play made that desirable. Our restriction to six sets divided into two groups of three is essentially an arbitrary approximation of what we would guess to have been common practice in the period. Readers must re-

2.3   The City
2.2   Palace Yard
2.1   Throne Room

1.3   Queen's Bed Chamber
1.2   Queen's Antechamber
1.1   A Chamber

Proscenium

Figure 2.1. Scene plan for *The Spanish Fryar*.

member, however, that specification of three sets at each group of shutters does not imply a separate groove for each one.

As a shorthand description of the scene plan we have employed the formula illustrated in Figure 2.1. Translated, this means that there are three shutters available in each of the two groups of shutters (1 and 2). Each shutter displays the setting specified ("Palace Yard" and the like) in conjunction with matching wings and borders. There is enough open stage space between the two shutter positions to permit a scene-in-progress in the Throne Room to be discovered as a scene in the Queen's Bed Chamber ends, and those shutters are drawn off to either side. Figure 2.2 shows the same scene plan in a more representational pictorial form. We have discussed a few special effects and staging problems as they have arisen, but in general anyone accustomed to the concept of wing-and-shutter changeable scenery and the uses of proscenium doors and balconies should have little difficulty following the implied staging of these plays.

Knowledge of lighting arrangements in the late seventeenth-century theatre is almost wholly inferential. By the standards of the nineteenth century (with gaslit theatres), illumination would have seemed dim indeed. Donald Mullin has recently calculated that some 1,200 square feet of stage space were lit by "less than 200 watts of modern illumination."[49] Dim as this seems, we should remember Pepys' complaints about the brightness of the

49. Donald Mullin, "Lighting on the Eighteenth-Century London Stage: A Reconsideration," *Theatre Notebook*, 34 (1980), 73–85. For a different view, see

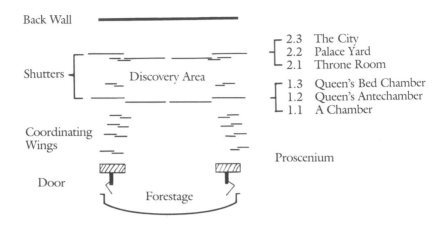

Figure 2.2. Scene plan for *The Spanish Fryar* in pictorial form.

candles hurting his eyes.[50] And beyond that nontechnical piece of evidence, we would offer two points for consideration. First, we do not know how many candles were in simultaneous use, or what reflector systems were employed. Mullin makes his calculation largely from chandeliers in contemporary drawings—but what sorts of added illumination may have been employed in the wings? And second, the human eye has remarkable compensatory powers, and once accustomed to a low level of light viewers find that they can see many things initially obscured. Since seventeenth-century audiences felt themselves able to distinguish nuances of facial expression, we see no reason not to suppose that

Allardyce Nicoll, *The Garrick Stage* (Manchester: Manchester Univ. Press, 1980), pp. 115–18.

50. E.g., Pepys' *Diary*, 22 February 1669: "I was in mighty pain to defend myself now from the light of the candles." To be sure Pepys was having serious problems with his eyes, but he continued going about his business out of doors in the daytime and the candles *seemed* painfully bright to him. Congreve too had trouble with his eyes, and is described in a contemporary pamphlet sitting in the theatre "with his Hat over his Eyes"—presumably to shade them from the light (cited in *The London Stage*, Part 1, p. 486).

a seventeenth-century performer could communicate pretty much what would be possible today, especially considering the relatively small size of the theatres involved.

Rehearsals and Acting

Documentary evidence about rehearsal practices before 1700 is practically nonexistent. Our best sources of information are *The Rehearsal* (1671) and *The Female Wits* (1696)—little used, presumably because scholars have hesitated to draw on works in which the degree of comic exaggeration is hard to estimate.[51] We believe, however, that these rehearsal plays are a valid indication of what authors did at rehearsals. Bayes and Marsilia do things badly, but this should not distract us from the fact that they do them. Allowing for some satiric malice, what can we deduce about rehearsals?

Most significantly, the author was in charge of rehearsals. The precise limits of authority are unknown, but both plays show us an author taking most of the responsibilities we would regard today as directorial, and neither suggests that the author is usurping a function belonging to someone else or doing anything novel. If the author were unavailable for some reason,[52] or did not care to appear in low company at the theatre, then presumably the manager or one of the senior actors took over the author's functions, as must also have been the case for revivals.[53] A play written by an unknown or an absentee author was some-

51. Quotations from these two plays in this section are identified by *R* and *FW* in parentheses with page numbers referring to the first quartos. Many of the directorial practices represented in these plays also appear in Molière's *L'Impromptu de Versailles* (1663). Molière's angle of vision is significantly different, but French production practices as represented in that play seem quite similar to English customs of the time.

52. For example, Otway was reportedly serving in the army in Flanders at the time *Friendship in Fashion* (1678) was first performed.

53. Regular daily rehearsals were normally supervised by the manager or a designated senior actor. We know, for example, that on 15 August 1706 Robert Wilks signed an agreement with Vanbrugh to act at the Haymarket for £150 per annum, plus £50 "For his care and Managemt of Rehearsalls," and a benefit play at £40 charges. (PRO LC 7/2, fol. 2.)

times "seen to the stage" by an actor, in which case the actor functioned as director of rehearsals and collected the proceeds of the third night.[54] An experienced professional (especially an "attached" one) was probably allowed a good deal more leeway and authority than an amateur.

Rehearsals were evidently called for 10:00 A.M. ("Must not I be at the Rehearsal by Ten?"—*FW*, p. 1). This would give time for a complete run through (including an early afternoon dinner break—*R*, p. 52) before the late afternoon curtain for the day's show. All but the final rehearsal were normally done in street clothes. ("This morning is its last Rehearsal, in their habits, and all that"—*R*, p. 3.) This point is reinforced in *The Female Wits*, where we see a very early rehearsal, and an actress asks, "What's the Whim, that we must be all dress'd at Rehearsal, as if we play'd?" (p. 13).

Both plays clearly imply that the author was expected to be able to explain meanings and motivations that actors found obscure.

> *First Player*: Have you your part perfect?
> *Second Player*: Yes, I have it without book; but I do not understand how it is to be spoken.
> *Third Player*: And mine is such a one, as I can't ghess, for my life what humour I'm to be in: whether angry, melancholy, merry, or in love. I don't know what to make on't.
> *First Player*: Phoo! the Author will be here presently, and he'l tell us all. (*The Rehearsal*, p. 5)

In *The Female Wits* Mrs. Knight laments that she "can't find the Ladies meaning out," though she is said to "read much" and is called "a Judge" (p. 18). Mrs. Cross complains that "this is the most incomprehensible Part I ever had in my Life; and when I complain, all the Answer I get is, 'tis New, and 'tis odd; and nothing but new things and odd things will do" (p. 13). In the midst of the rehearsal Mrs. Cross despairs of doing anything

---

54. Examples are "Mountfort's" *Edward the Third* and *Henry the Second*, "Underhill's" *Win Her and Take Her*, "Powell's" *The Cornish Comedy*, and "Pinkethman's" *Love without Interest*—all false attributions spawned by this practice.

with a part she cannot understand, and gets only abuse by way of explanation (p. 38). The point is comic, but the author's proper function is plain. Indeed, since the actors came to the first rehearsal knowing the play *only* from the author's reading and their own "sides" (having no complete text available), the author's explanation of overall point must have been doubly important if the actors were to make any sense of the play as a whole.

From the two rehearsal plays we deduce that the author conventionally did the following:

1. Suggested, corrected, and illustrated line delivery. Thus Bayes says "Mr. *Cartwright*, pr'ythee speak a little louder, and with a hoarser voice. I am the bold *Thunder?* Pshaw! speak it me in a voice that thunders it out indeed: I am the bold *Thunder*" (p. 10). Of "A forward exit to all future end" Bayes says: "Pish, there you are out; to all future end? No, no; to all future end; you must lay the accent upon end" (p. 25). Marsilia constantly exhorts the actors to the deliveries she fancies. "O Heav'ns! You shou'd have every thing that is terrible in that Line! You shou'd speak it like a Ghost, like a Giant, like a Mandrake, and you speak it like a Mouse" (p. 27). "Louder . . . strain your Voice: I tell you, Mr. *Pinkethman*, this speaking Loud gets the Clap" (p. 57). "This last Speech to the highest pitch of raving" (p. 62).

2. Approved the scenery provided. Marsilia calls for "one of your finest Scenes, and the very best that ye know must be, when the Emperour and Empress appear." The "Scene-Men" slide the shutters into view and she responds, "Aye, aye, that will do" (p. 63).

3. Handled the blocking and business. Bayes' play is in its dress rehearsal, and blocking would have been settled much earlier, but Marsilia tries to control stage movement—"Now quick, quick, get behind her, Mr. least she shou'd resist; the rest disarm Mr. *Powell*" (p. 59), and she complains when the storming of a castle is insufficiently spirited: "Drums beat; mount, ye Lumpish Dogs: what are you afraid of? you know the Stones [thrown by defenders] are only Wool: Faster, with more Spirit? Brutes" (p. 52).

4. Tried to direct and demonstrate individual movement. Thus

Marsilia: "Dear Mrs *Knight*, in this Speech, stamp as Queen *Statira* does,[55] that always gets a Clap; and when you have ended, run off, thus, as fast as you can drive. O Gad! Duce take your confounded Stumbling Stage. (*Stumbles*)" (p. 32). "Now make haste off, Mrs. *Betty*, as if you were so full of Thought, you did not know what you did" (p. 33). "Laugh heartily, Mrs. *Betty*, go off Laughing" (p. 37). "Well, Mr. *Pinkethman*, I think you are oblig'd to me for choosing you for a Heroe; Pray do it well, that the Town may see, I was not mistaken in my Judgment:[56] Fetch large Strides; walk thus; your Arms strutting; your Voice big, and your Eyes terrible" (p. 51). "Now, Mr. *Powel*, enter like a Lyon" (p. 52).

5. Tried to indicate emotion and explain how to convey it. "Good Mrs. *Knight* speak that as passionately as you can, because you are going to Swoon, you know; and I hate Women shou'd go into a Swoon, as some of our Authors make 'em, without so much as altering their Face, or Voice" (p. 30). "Your pardon, Mrs. give me leave to instruct you in a moving Cry. Oh! there's a great deal of Art in crying: Hold your Handkerchief thus; let it meet your Eyes, thus; your Head declin'd, thus; now, in a perfect whine, crying out these words, *By these Tears, which never cease to Flow*" (p. 50). "Look dreadfully, sweet Mr. *Powell*, look dreadfully" (p. 58).

6. Controlled the progress of the rehearsal. Bayes: "So, So; pray clear the Stage. . . . So, now let down the Curtain" (p. 41). Marsilia insists that George Powell (deputy manager to Rich) stay with her, but definitely keeps direction of the rehearsal in her own hands. "Now clear the Stage; Prompter give me the Book! Oh, Mr. *Powell*, you must stay, I shall want your Advice; I'll tell ye time enough for your Entrance" (p. 26). She even orders the scenemen to "Change the Scene to the Orange Grove" (p. 48).

7. Presumed to direct, criticize, and correct the dancing.[57]

55. I.e., like Elizabeth Barry in *The Rival Queens*.

56. Marsilia's choice of the low comic actor William Pinkethman is a comically incongruous piece of casting, and his attempts to strut as directed must have been extremely funny.

57. This may well have been a sore point. Few authors can have known

Bayes' famous mishap occurs while he is trying to show the dan-cers their business. "Out, out, out! Did ever men spoil a good thing so? no figure, no ear, no time, no thing? . . . if you observe, there are two several Designs in this Tune; . . . you shall see me do't. Look you now. Here I am dead. . . . (*As he rises up hastily, he tumbles and falls down again.*) Ah, gadsookers, I have broke my Nose" (p. 19).[58] Marsilia's rehearsal ends with a rebellion by her unhappy dancers:

> *Dance upon all Four. . . .*
> *Marsilia.* What's the whispering for?
> *One of the Men.* Why, Madam . . . we are not able to continue in
>   this Posture any longer, without we break our Backs; so we have
>   unanimously resolv'd to stand upright.
> *All the Men and Women Stand up. . . .*
> *Marsilia.* Oh! the Devil; you have spoilt my Plot! you have ruin'd
>   my play, ye Blockheads! ye Villains, I'll kill you all. (p. 64)

8. Explained special effects to the property man, whether he needed the explanation or not. "D'ye hear, Property-Man, be sure some red Ink is handsomely conveyed to Mrs. *Knight*" (p. 60). This may be a joke at Marsilia's expense: sheep's blood was usually used for gore.

All this must be taken with a grain of salt, but these plays would not have made sense if they did not present something re-cognizably like reality. Burlesque satire depends on satiric exag-geration, but also on likeness to the object satirized. A lot of de-tails ring true—the promise of a treat in the greenroom (*FW*, p. 18); actors late or missing when wanted (*R*, p. 11; *FW*, p. 13); grumbles about authors who are unable to remember the actors' names (*R*, p. 5; *FW*, p. 62—"Good Mr. What-d'call'um"). The attitudes and flavor of interchanges in the rehearsal plays are so true to modern experience in the theatre that we are inclined to conclude that some things have changed remarkably little from

---

enough to direct dancers properly, and both plays satirize authors meddling with dance routines.

58. The edition of 1675 adds another bit of dance business at the end of Act III. "Pray Dance well . . . you should be light and easie, tah, tah, tah. (*All the while they Dance*, Bayes *puts 'em out with teaching 'em*)."

century to century. A celebrated seventeenth-century rehearsal anecdote reveals the low comedian's perennial view of pompous, self-important authors.

> Then the Conquest of *China* by the *Tartars*, by Mr. *Settle*; in this Play Mr. *Jevon Acting* a *Chinese* Prince and Commander in it, and being in the Battle Vanquisht by the *Tartars*; he was by his Part to fall upon the point of his Sword and Kill himself, rather than be a Prisoner by the *Tartars*: Mr. *Jevon* instead of falling on the point of his Sword, laid it in the Scabbard at length upon the Ground and fell upon't, saying, now I am Dead; which put the Author into such a Fret, it made him speak Treble, instead of Double. *Jevons* answer was; did not you bid me fall upon my Sword. (*Roscius Anglicanus*, p. 35)

Such tomfoolery has always been the way of the theatre and should be remembered when solemn writers of textbooks start to pontificate about "the neoclassical acting style."

Almost all reports of acting are both impressionistic and personal. A great many of the surviving accounts of Betterton, Barry, and their contemporaries tell us how the audience responded but have precious little to say about technique or what the performer actually did. Tidy-school historians used to assume that each generation of actors became more "realistic" (presumably a great virtue), with Garrick improving upon Quin, who had in his turn improved upon Booth, and so forth. Recent scholars have been forced to admit that back in the seventeenth century Betterton had quite a "natural" style for his time (whatever that means). The problem of "what was the acting like?" is just not very soluble short of access to a time machine.[59]

We do want to make a few specific points about seventeenth-

---

59. For the best available sense of what eighteenth-century acting looked like in terms of gesture and movement, the reader should consult a valuable series of articles by Dene Barnett, "The Performance Practice of Acting: The Eighteenth Century. Part I: Ensemble Acting," *Theatre Research International*, 2 (1977), 157–86; Part II: "The Hands," ibid., 3 (1977), 1–19; Part III: "The Arms," ibid., 3 (1978), 79–93; Part IV: "The Eyes, the Face and the Head," ibid., 5 (1980), 1–36; Part V: "Posture and Attitudes," ibid., 6 (1981), 1–32. Mr. Barnett's book is eagerly awaited.

century acting. First, the concept of over-acting is at least as old in this period as *The Rehearsal*, where we are told: "*Volscius* sits down to pull on his Boots: *Bayes* Stands by and over acts the Part as he speaks it."[60] Second, scholars often assume radical differences in the staging of comedy and tragedy in this period. Peter Holland, for example, asserts that tragedy was staged largely in the scenic area, comedy largely on the forestage, and that "The theory of acting, the intentions of the dramatist, the relation of actor to audience were all profoundly different when the action was carried on within the scene."[61] Holland postulates profoundly different "characteristic methods of producing the two forms." This view derives from the school of criticism that finds "Restoration comedy" and "Heroic tragedy" "implacably opposed forms."[62] With respect, we disagree. We do not find so vast a gulf between the comedies and the tragedies of the 1670s, different though they indubitably are. Nor can we find any historical evidence for the scenic stage/forestage division between the genres. We would certainly expect a stylistic difference between a performance of *Aureng-Zebe* and *The Country-Wife* (both premiered by the King's Company in the spring of 1675), but then we would not want stylistically identical performances of *King Lear* and *As You Like It* from the same group of actors. The popularity of split-plot tragicomedy in the late seventeenth century seems to us a good argument against radical incommensurability in the performance styles of tragedy and comedy, unless we are to assume that the contrast was always to function in a flagrantly ironic way. As far as we are concerned, the radical discontinuity theory remains an unproven (and unattractive) hypothesis.

Our third point about acting takes us back to the vital and unanswerable question: what was the acting like? In our opinion,

---

60. This stage direction (in III.v. of the revision) was added in the 3d ed. (1675). We take this to imply exaggeration, not just duplication of the sort practiced by ballet teachers. The point has to be that Bayes cannot do it right. For this sense of "overact" as early as 1631, see *OED* definition 2.

61. Holland, *The Ornament of Action*, p. 36.

62. Anne Righter, "Heroic Tragedy," in *Restoration Theatre*, ed. John Russell Brown and Bernard Harris (London: Edward Arnold, 1965), p. 138.

the best way to get a sense of what late seventeenth-century actors thought they were doing is to read Charles Gildon's *The Life of Mr. Thomas Betterton* (1710), although there are some problems with this source. Gildon gives little "life," but a great deal of precept and admonition about acting in theory and practice. Much of the specific commentary Gildon plagiarized wholesale from French rhetoric handbooks, so we cannot attribute this material directly to Betterton. We would argue, however, that if these sentiments and dicta had not seemed appropriate to Betterton, Gildon (not the most popular of men) would have been laying himself open to severe ridicule. And if we discount the somewhat unfamiliar vocabulary, the advice we find "Betterton" giving seems astonishingly naturalistic—indeed, at times downright Stanislavskian. Aspiring actors should study their parts (p. 22); should "consult e'en the most indifferent Poet in any Part" (p. 16); should study art, literature, and psychology diligently (pp. 36, 63); should "enter into" a part, and be the person represented (pp. 40–41); should avoid mere copying of another actor's characterization of a part (p. 56); should think about the emotions felt by the character and enter into them, not merely project a mechanical simulation of them (p. 70)—and so forth. What Betterton's companies did in performance would no doubt look very odd and mannered to us, but the point is how they looked to an audience familiar with their conventions. A reading of the *Life of Betterton* suggests that the kinds of impact sought by seventeenth-century actors were very similar to what we might seek today, and that similar techniques were employed in performance.

Seventeenth-Century Production Concepts

Johnson. But wilt thou do me a favour, now?
Bayes. I, Sir: what is't?
Johnson. Why, to tell him the meaning of thy last play.
Bayes. How, Sir, the meaning? do you mean the Plot.

(*The Rehearsal*, p. 3)

A theoretical problem remains to be confronted. Can we assume that our notions of interpretation and meaning were shared by seventeenth-century writers, actors, and audiences? And if not, is this a major difficulty? Our answer to both questions is no.

Such criticism as was practiced in the seventeenth century did not produce the sort of broad, conceptual accounts of plays that we now take for granted. Does this mean that seventeenth-century writers and audiences would simply not have seen the things in their plays that we find there? If we could see the original productions of *The Conquest of Granada* and *The Plain-Dealer*, would we find them entirely innocent of production concept and meaning as we understand those notions?

Because there was no one called the director in the late seventeenth-century theatre and because authors' participation in rehearsals has remained largely undocumented, many scholars have assumed that interpretation was minimal in this theatre and that the actors simply played all parts in accordance with procrustean and antiindividualistic conventions. Brockett epitomizes a long tradition when he says that "Little time was spent on blocking or movement patterns. . . . Actors stood throughout and gave little thought to creating realistic stage pictures. . . . Roles were passed down from one generation to the next, and with them went the traditional interpretation. . . . Until about 1750, the dominant approach was oratorical."[63] This seems to us pernicious nonsense. The rehearsal plays imply nothing of the sort; nor do the

63. Oscar G. Brockett, *History of the Theatre*, 4th ed. (Boston: Allyn and Bacon, 1982), p. 346. Similar assumptions can be found in the work of so fine a scholar as John Harold Wilson—e.g., *A Preface to Restoration Drama* (1965; rpt. Cambridge, Mass.: Harvard Univ. Press 1968), Chapter 3. We can certainly agree with Langhans that the demands of the repertory system must have encouraged acceptance of "simple conventions . . . that governed many of the things [e.g., movement] about which the promptbooks are silent" (*Restoration Promptbooks*, p. xxiv). There is, however, a difference between the "stock characterizations" that must have been a commonplace in the seventeenth-century theatre (as indeed they are today), and the sort of rigid preservation of inherited tradition practiced in Kabuki drama—an example proffered by Langhans as a possible parallel. The truth is that we have almost no evidence about acting style in the late seventeenth century.

rich collection of anecdotes about theatre in this period. The picture of acting that emerges from the *Life of Betterton* is far from suggesting mechanical application of conventions and rote imitation of predecessors. Nor do the plays themselves make such a view in any way plausible. If they were written for the most rigid and mechanical kind of acting, their suitability to an altogether different sort of performance style is a very happy and surprising coincidence.

The myth that there was little or no directing done in the late seventeenth-century theatre has naturally led to simplistic and derogatory estimates of the original productions. Mr. Bayes may have been incapable of keeping track of either "plot" or "meaning," but then that is precisely why he is the object of Buckingham's ridicule. Lack of abstract critical vocabulary need not imply simplistic (or nonexistent) production concepts. We see no reason to believe that seventeenth-century writers and performers would not have seen and used the complexities we find in their plays. Most playwrights were probably as verbose and incoherent then as playwrights are now (or alternatively, as uncommunicative), but the evidence of the plays themselves suggests that the best of them knew their business.

A great many directors today work intuitively and shy away from the abstract concepts preferred by academic critics. If anything, this tendency was probably even more pronounced in the seventeenth century. From our reading of the original criticism and performance commentary, we suspect that seventeenth-century productions stressed the characters' emotions and the concomitant response they were designed to arouse in the audience. Both the rehearsal plays and the *Life of Betterton* suggest the importance of the actor's understanding "who he is" and trying to make the audience respond appropriately. Our best guess—and we offer it as no more than that—is that a seventeenth-century director (whether author or actor/manager) would have thought of contrasting production concepts largely in terms of sympathy with and alienation from the characters. One does not need the abstractions of modern Wycherley criticism to generate contrasting production concepts of *The Country-Wife*—one need merely ask "How sympathetic or unsympathetic shall we make Horner?" Problems of convention and critical vocabulary notwithstanding, we have found little barrier between seventeenth-century plays and twentieth-century assumptions about performance and meaning.

Part Two

PLAYS

3

The Country-Wife (1675)

W YCHERLEY'S THIRD PLAY is the best known, the most admired, and the most hotly disputed comedy of the period.
Scandalous but successful in its own day, it has been denounced
by moralists and defended by admirers as everything from a
value-free farce set in Cloud Cuckooland to a fervent manifesto
on the virtues of honesty and sexual liberation. Although the
events and speeches of the play seem quite straightforward, modern critics have been able to agree on almost nothing. Is Horner
the hero or a satiric butt? Do Harcourt and Alithea represent a
pro forma secondary love interest or the moral center of the play?
Does the play make a statement about something, and if so,
what? Sex? Marriage? Lust? Honor? Hypocrisy? Unfortunately,
critics have seldom attempted to rebut their predecessors, with
the predictable result that the efforts of some fifty critics add up
to total confusion.

Even if we ignore those critics who are morally outraged, division of opinion on *The Country-Wife* is astonishing. Nor is this a
recent development. In 1913 John Palmer (adapting Lamb's defense) called it "the most perfect farce in English dramatic literature—a whirlwind of inspired buffoonery. . . . All questions of
motive and moral value disappear." Writing a decade later, Bonamy Dobrée found the play an expression of "deep pessimism"
reminiscent of "the *saeva indignatio* of Swift." Dobrée described
Horner as a "grim, nightmare figure," and the play as "a savage

snarl," Wycherley's attempt to face down the utter vileness of his world with bitter laughter.[1] This fundamental contradiction in interpretation is echoed half a century later by Anne Righter (taking the gloomy view) and Robert D. Hume (reading the play as a farce).

The Country-Wife makes a good starting point for this book because more than any other play of the period it forces us to confront chaotically diverse and contradictory criticism—much of it intelligent, well-argued, and, by itself, seemingly persuasive. We are going to argue that the failure of modern critics to arrive at any consensus—or even at clearly demarcated disagreements— is a result of their assumption that the play contains a single intrinsic "meaning." Because Wycherley does not specify standards of judgment within the play, the critic—or the director—is free to make what he or she wishes of a text susceptible to radically contradictory interpretations. To ask "Should we identify with Horner or despise him?" or "Are Harcourt and Alithea a moral norm?" is fundamentally misguided. Rather, we need to enquire what is communicable in performance. The play could be staged with Horner portrayed as a dashing scamp, a glamorous libertine, or a debauched roué. The results would be about as different as the irreconcilable readings of Palmer, Fujimura, and Zimbardo. However distressing the idea may seem to a critic who believes that a text possesses a single, "correct" meaning, the play can be made to mean pretty much what the director wants it to mean.

Unlike the other plays analyzed in this book, *The Country-Wife* is sufficiently familiar and has been subjected to such extensive critical interpretation that it requires relatively little textual analysis. Our principal concerns here are (a) to show that contradictory interpretations usually reflect different implicit assumptions and production choices; (b) to identify some interpretations that seem unstageable; and (c) to suggest that if we abandon the notion that there is a unique "right" reading, we will find that most

1. John Palmer, *The Comedy of Manners* (London: Bell, 1913), p. 128; Bonamy Dobrée, *Restoration Comedy* (Oxford: Oxford Univ. Press, 1924), pp. 78, 94, 95, 102.

of the critics fall into coherent subgroups, each of which offers us a viable way to conceive and stage the play. Approaching the play undogmatically, we will find a surprising range of performance possibilities consonant with the text.

THE CRITICAL MUDDLE

To make any sense of the chaotic diversity of critical opinion, we must start by seeing that critics have disagreed about some largely unacknowledged fundamental questions. A brief survey should be helpful.

What is the play about? For Palmer, no subject is necessary: like the racier tales in the *Decameron*, Wycherley's play is merely a romp. Most critics, however, have started from the assumption that there is a "theme" or a "point," and that by identifying it the critic has somehow "solved" the play. Dobrée says that "the sex question" (not further defined) is central. H. T. E. Perry sees the play as a satire on the pettiness of jealousy; Charles Hallett considers it a satire on hypocrisy, while Kenneth Muir feels that the main thrust of the satire is specifically against "female hypocrisy"; David Vieth and William Freedman suggest from quite different points of view that the play is about "masculinity"; David Morris tells us that "*The Country Wife* is a play about honor," while Ronald Berman finds Wycherley's "idea of friendship" central. R. Edgley sensibly criticizes other critics' readiness to make themes the "main interest" of a play, and then announces that the subject of *The Country-Wife* is the exposure of "folly."[2]

2. Dobrée, p. 94; Henry Ten Eyck Perry, *The Comic Spirit in Restoration Drama* (New Haven: Yale Univ. Press, 1925), pp. 43, 45; Charles A. Hallett, "The Hobbesian Substructure of *The Country Wife*," *Papers on Language and Literature*, 9 (1973), 380–95; Kenneth Muir, *The Comedy of Manners* (London: Hutchinson, 1970), p. 76; David M. Vieth, "Wycherley's *The Country Wife*: An Anatomy of Masculinity," *Papers on Language and Literature*, 2 (1966), 335–50; William Freedman, "Impotence and Self-Destruction in *The Country Wife*," *English Studies*, 53 (1972), 421–31; David B. Morris, "Language and Honor in *The Country Wife*," *South Atlantic Bulletin*, 37, no. 4 (1972), 3–10; Ronald Berman, "The Ethic of *The Country Wife*," *Texas Studies in Literature and Language*, 9 (1967), 47–55; R. Edgley, "The Object of Literary Criticism," *Essays in Criticism*, 14 (1964), 221–36.

There is some truth in each of these views. *The Country-Wife* does indeed show us something about folly, jealousy, honor, hypocrisy, masculinity, and so forth. Obviously, a critic can use any of these themes as a focus for a discussion of the play. But whether any one of these themes constitutes the defining and organizing subject of the play is an altogether different matter. The variety of proposals put forward to date casts some doubt on the utility of the approach. If we assume that Wycherley built his play around such a theme, then we ought in honesty to admit that he made a mess of the job. To be effective, especially in the theatre, such a subject must be conspicuous, clear, and unmistakable. And since hardly any two critics can agree on what the theme is, we are probably wisest to regard the search for one as misguided. A theme that genuinely defined and organized the play would not have to be hunted for.

Are we to approve of the sex? Before the last twenty-five years, few critics other than the disapproving Macaulay cared to claim that Wycherley meant us to enjoy, let alone approve of, the action of the play, except with the proviso that its world is unrelated to our own. Recent critics have felt much less hesitation in admitting that we might enjoy sex for the sake of sex. C. D. Cecil reads the play as a comic celebration of a libertine ideal. Gorman Beauchamp finds it an expression of a "pagan ideal of sensual hedonism" in which "Horner is very much the hero" and "Wycherley's imaginative identification with Horner is almost total, and certainly adulatory."[3] Virginia Ogden Birdsall has gone even further in this direction, taking the play as an argument for the virtues of sexual liberation, with Horner as a representation of the "élan vital" and "the life force triumphant," "a wholly positive and creative comic hero . . . squarely on the side of health, of freedom, and . . . of honesty."[4]

By no means, however, has the trend in criticism been entirely

---

3. C. D. Cecil, "Libertine and *Précieux* Elements in Restoration Comedy," *Essays in Criticism*, 9 (1959), 239–53; Gorman Beauchamp, "The Amorous Machiavellism of *The Country Wife*," *Comparative Drama*, 11 (1977–78), 316–30.

4. Birdsall, *Wild Civility*, pp. 136, 156.

toward a positive reading of Horner and an enjoyment of sex in the play. Rose Zimbardo reads the play as a systematic satire on lust.[5] Anthony Kaufman considers Horner a psychologically sick character, a latent homosexual whose womanizing is a neurotic compulsion: "Horner . . . far from being the 'hero' of *The Country Wife*, the libertine free agent that some readers have thought him, would seem to be Wycherley's deliberate portrait of a haunted man."[6] H. W. Matalene believes that "the lesson of *The Country-Wife* is that 'Nature,' in the sense of a generalized instinctual drive to experience orgasm or to reproduce the species, has little or nothing to do with bringing about particular acts of sexual intercourse"—and that consequently the audience should learn to disdain Horner and his assumptions about sex.[7]

Obviously, the response to sex in the play depends heavily on the outlook of the audience. But granting that a favorable view of the sex is the easy and obvious way to stage the play, we must agree that a negative view could readily be communicated in the theatre. The text will permit either interpretation, and therefore we are compelled to treat the view of sex as a production choice, not as a critical problem.

What was Wycherley's view of marriage? Several influential critics have taken the point of the play to be Wycherley's view of marriage, though unfortunately they have not altogether agreed on what that view is. P. F. Vernon and W. R. Chadwick deduce a very negative attitude, holding that the main "thesis" of the play is "the failure of contemporary marriage arrangements." Anne Righter and Katharine Rogers find a positive comment in the play, and suggest that, in Harcourt and Alithea, Wycherley tried to show "a more decent basis for relationships between the sexes."[8] If we accept Horner as the author's spokesman, then we

5. Rose A. Zimbardo, *Wycherley's Drama: A Link in the Development of English Satire* (New Haven: Yale Univ. Press, 1965), pp. 147–65.

6. Anthony Kaufman, "Wycherley's *The Country Wife* and the Don Juan Character," *Eighteenth-Century Studies*, 9 (1975–76), 216–31. Quotation from p. 227.

7. H. W. Matalene, "What Happens in *The Country-Wife*," *Studies in English Literature*, 22 (1982), 395–411. Quotation from p. 397.

8. P. F. Vernon, *William Wycherley*, Writers and their Work (London: Long-

could take the play as a libertine protest against marriage as it was practiced in Wycherley's society. If we view Harcourt as spokesman, then we have to try to take a rather vapid stock lover as the ideological center of the play. A grave difficulty in making "marriage" the subject is the lack of attention paid to marriage per se. Wycherley portrays two bad marriages (the Pinchwifes and the Fidgets), but the positive alternative (Harcourt and Alithea) is shown not as a marriage but as a very farcical courtship. Harcourt and Alithea never have a serious conversation about their future life. While we could agree that Congreve shows us a reasoned concept of marriage in the courtship of Mirabell and Millamant, Wycherley does nothing of the sort here. That our pro forma sympathies are supposed to be with Harcourt and Alithea seems clear, but there is nothing in the text to suggest that they represent a serious ideal.[9]

The position taken by Righter and Rogers is in fact a variant on Norman Holland's right way/wrong way reading, probably the single most influential account of the play.[10] Holland sees Harcourt and Alithea as a high moral norm; Horner, as clever but misguided. Of course, for Virginia Ogden Birdsall, Horner represents the right way. How are we to be sure what constitutes the right way? Harcourt wins Alithea, but Horner too gets what he wants in the course of the play, enjoying his multiple seduc-

---

man for the British Council, 1965), pp. 20–29; W. R. Chadwick, *The Four Plays of William Wycherley* (The Hague: Mouton, 1975), Chapter 3; Anne Righter, "William Wycherley," *Restoration Theatre*, ed. John Russell Brown and Bernard Harris (London: Arnold, 1965), pp. 70–91; Katharine M. Rogers, *William Wycherley* (New York: Twayne, 1972), Chapter 3, quotation from p. 60.

9. The most extreme such reading is offered by J. Peter Verdurmen, who somehow succeeds in convincing himself that the play presents an "'emerging' society . . . composed of characters who fight for varieties of freedom at the expense of . . . blocking forces." In his view "Harcourt, Horner, Margery, and in their wake Horner's women . . . have . . . helped set up a 'new' society that gives greater scope than had the old to natural sensuality and human affection." See "Grasping for Permanence: Ideal Couples in *The Country Wife* and *Aureng-Zebe*," *Huntington Library Quarterly*, 42 (1979), 329–47. Harcourt wins his girl and Horner escapes exposure, but how this constitutes the emergence of a new society we do not see.

10. Holland, *The First Modern Comedies*, Chapter 8.

tions and escaping scot free. Neither the text nor the outcome of the plot tells us whom Wycherley approves or disapproves of. "Right way" readings rest firmly on the moral presuppositions of the critics who sponsor them.

What assumptions does the audience bring to the play? The degree to which critics have read their own values and preconceptions into the text brings us to an obvious but singularly neglected point: audience assumptions have a great deal to do with the way the play would work in performance. Lack of appeal by critics to the suppositions of Wycherley's original audience is surprising— not that it would settle much. Had the earl of Rochester and John Evelyn both attended a performance, their reactions would presumably have been quite different, regardless of the production concept. We might hypothesize, on the court wit coterie theory, that with the exception of some hypocritical "Ladies" and a few prudes, the audience enthusiastically approved of what it was shown. Alternatively, adopting Williamsite assumptions, we might suppose that everyone short of the earl of Rochester and his friends dutifully worked out a "lesson" in the fashion of Norman Holland, preferably with Christian trimmings. Seeking a more reasonable middle ground, we might suppose that some wits lapped up the sex, some ladies were offended, and a lot of ordinary playgoers were entertained and amused by actions and sentiments they would not have accepted comfortably in real life. Except for some Mrs. Grundys, most members of a present-day audience are usually willing to suspend both belief and moral judgment when the action does not seem "real." A hardened libertine is not going to disapprove of Horner or take Harcourt very seriously (Gorman Beauchamp's reading). A determined moralist will either condemn Wycherley for displaying such filth (William Archer found it "the most bestial play in all literature"[11]) or find a way to moralize it (as Norman Holland does). Wycherley himself was both a libertine and a moralist—psychologically a perfectly plausible combination.[12] A sound interpreta-

11. William Archer, *The Old Drama and the New* (Boston: Small, Maynard, 1923), p. 193.

12. For much the best biography, see B. Eugene McCarthy, *William Wycher-*

tion must both acknowledge its assumptions about audience views of what is presented and acknowledge the fact that the critic needs to ask not what the play "is" (or "is about") but rather what it can be made in performance.

Three basic production concepts. Bewildering as the critical contradictions are, we would be quite wrong to conclude in despair that meaning resides entirely in the eye of the beholder.[13] Certain interpretations do not seem communicable in performance—the psychological readings of Kaufman and Matalene, for example. A more extreme instance is offered by Douglas Duncan, who believes that the "depth" and significance of *The Country-Wife* lie in its "allusion" to such works as *Leviathan*, the 1674 *Tempest*, *Paradise Lost*, and religious myth.[14] But amidst the welter of possibilities suggested by critics, three basic production concepts seem implicit. A fair amount of diversity is possible within each of them, but almost all producible interpretations of the play make one of these assumptions about what the play is and does. (1) The play is a farce without significant point or moral value—Palmer, Hume. (2) The play is a libertine comedy that allows the audience to empathize with the rake—Cecil, Beauchamp, Birdsall. (3) The play is a satire that excoriates Horner, his society, or both of them—Zimbardo, Norman Holland, Righter. Unlike the thematic readings, the variants on these approaches are producible (some more readily and plausibly than others) and are worth our attention.

---

ley: A Biography (Athens: Ohio Univ. Press, 1979). For a good discussion of Wycherley's use of maxims and proverbs, and "l'influence des moralistes, de Sénèque à La Rochefoucauld, sur l'œuvre de Wycherley," see J. Auffret, "Wycherley et ses maitres les moralistes," *Études Anglaises*, 15 (1962), 375–88.

13. For a fuller account of Wycherley criticism in general, see Robert D. Hume, "William Wycherley: Text, Life, Interpretation," *Modern Philology*, 78 (1981), 399–415. For a helpful discussion of the fundamental and irreducible moral ambiguities of the text of *The Country-Wife*, see John T. Harwood, *Critics, Values, and Restoration Comedy* (Carbondale: Southern Illinois Univ. Press, 1982), Chapter 5, esp. pp. 98–114.

14. Douglas Duncan, "Mythic Parody in *The Country Wife*," *Essays in Criticism*, 31 (1981), 299–312.

VIEWS OF HORNER

Most of the arguments that have raged over *The Country-Wife* stem directly from contradictory readings of Horner, and the view taken of Horner is crucial to the way we interpret or produce the play. The assumptions necessary to the libertine, satiric, and farcical readings are extremely different.

Identification with libertine success. This is the basic presumption of the "libertine comedy" production: men will identify with the successful rake.[15] Fujimura describes Horner as Wycherley's "most striking Truewit . . . neither corrupt nor wholly cynical. . . . [He] believes in honesty and plain dealing, in common sense, in wit (judgment), and in fidelity to nature."[16] Fujimura finds Horner neither a "nightmare figure" (Dobrée) nor a "joyeux libertin" (Perromat) but rather an attractive young gentleman of "naturalistic views," spokesman for a play that is "a witty and often mordant statement of the Truewit's attitude toward life. Frankness, truth to nature, sound judgment, and wit are praised, while pretense to honor, unnatural jealousy, and stupidity are ridiculed." A less glamorized view is offered by W. R. Chadwick, who suggests that "the most productive way of looking at Horner and his function in the play is to see him as a picaresque hero. Like the *pícaro* he is untroubled by conventional morality, and he spends his time exploiting the fools with whom he comes in contact."[17] Like C. D. Cecil, Chadwick feels that we can enjoy Horner's success and approve his serving as scourge of false values in his society without taking his doings seriously in moral terms. But where Chadwick sees Horner primarily as a "satirical instru-

---

15. Critics have devoted singularly little thought to how the women in the audience are supposed to respond. A Horner contemptuous of his conquests would hardly appeal to the female part of the audience; if he seems genuinely to please and satisfy his women, then perhaps the identification would be with their interests.

16. Thomas H. Fujimura, *The Restoration Comedy of Wit* (Princeton: Princeton Univ. Press, 1952), p. 145. Following quotations from pp. 139, 140, 145–46.

17. Chadwick, p. 119.

ment," Cecil, in a reading closer to normal twentieth-century production practice, finds him the protagonist of an "uncomplicated sensual fantasy." "For a moment sex is the unalloyed fun that the youthful libertine hoped and pretended it might be. This is the raucous, English statement of an ideal which seems to have been under continual discussion in the salon of Ninon de Lenclos. In *The Country Wife*, as in the legend of that salon, the ideal is achieved."[18] Yet more uncritical views of Horner are offered by Beauchamp and Birdsall (already quoted), Birdsall going so far as to offer Horner as a model whose "naturalness and honesty" we should emulate. Without necessarily going to that extreme, we agree with all of these critics that the most obvious ways to produce the play make Horner an attractive rogue hero with whom the audience will tend to identify. A moralist is likelier to be offended by the play than to assume that it satirizes its successful libertine.

Rejection of the libertine. Bonamy Dobrée was the first critic to construct a positive moral reading of *The Country-Wife*. For Dobrée, Horner is essentially a villain (though he does not use the term)—like Tartuffe, someone we wholly reject.[19] Dobrée admits that Horner is successful within the play, but concludes that we reject him because he is "unselectively lecherous" and "seems to derive such a sorry enjoyment from his success," though he does not explain how this is to be shown. Norman Holland calls Horner "undeniably a bad man" (having failed to allow for the outlook of Rochester, let alone Birdsall). In a similar reading Anne Righter finds Horner an "agent of destruction," "nihilistic," and "wholly negative." In various ways Zimbardo, Kaufman, and Matalene fall in this camp. Zimbardo's reading is the most stageable. For her, the point is the ugliness of lust, especially lust cloaked by hypocrisy. The problem with this reading is

18. Cecil, pp. 249–50.
19. Dobrée, p. 94. The comparison is an odd one, for as Norman Holland observes, Horner "is not a villain in the sense that, say, Iago is, for he does not prey on innocents. The people Horner victimizes, his cuckolds and mistresses, are either far worse than he, or, like Margery, do not feel that they have been harmed." See *The First Modern Comedies*, p. 75.

that the text and action of the play do not make Horner repulsive or unsuccessful. "If the *plot* were to be 'instructive,' Horner ought to catch the pox from Lady Fidget and find himself impotent."[20] Horner can be made repulsive in performance, but the fact is that almost all productions take the opposite tack, and the audience does not automatically reject him, as Zimbardo suggests it should, when "he sacrifices Alithea's true honor to the preservation of his false disguise."[21] That episode comes too late in the play to affect the audience's view of Horner significantly, and in performance it tends to get lost in the rush of events in the finale, especially as Alithea comes to no harm.

All of these critics make the risky assumption that Wycherley condemned libertinism and believed in romantic marriage—i.e., in the kind of "permanent" and passionate relationship "that goes beyond the merely social and answers one's inner nature."[22] They also assume that Wycherley was capable of implicit condemnation, a point emphatically (and to us convincingly) denied by T. W. Craik. "Where Wycherley's satire is intentional it is unmistakable. . . . The strongest argument against interpreting [Horner] satirically is . . . that Wycherley allows him to comment disparagingly on most of the other characters, but provides no disparaging commentary on him. . . . Actions do not speak for themselves in Wycherley; if he disapproves, he tells us so."[23] Such reservations notwithstanding, we must certainly agree that Horner could be made repulsive in performance, a point to be taken up in due course.

Amused indifference towards the libertine. Critics inclined to see *The Country-Wife* as a lighthearted theatrical entertainment have generally taken Horner much less seriously. Palmer grants that Horner "is intimately modelled upon the fine gentlemen of Covent Garden," but holds that given the implausibility of the stratagem and the farcicality of the action, "it would be absurd in

20. Hume, *Development*, p. 99.
21. Zimbardo, p. 161.
22. Holland, *The First Modern Comedies*, p. 83.
23. T. W. Craik, "Some Aspects of Satire in Wycherley's Plays," *English Studies*, 41 (1960), 168–79. Quotation from pp. 176, 178–79.

a critical reader to feel towards Mr. Horner as he would feel towards an actual twentieth-century figure of Mr. Horner's character and habits."[24] Gerald Weales feels that Horner "is an extremely attractive character for several reasons. The hidden *Playboy* reader in all of us [well, in some of us] is bound to identify with his sexual triumphs; the audience's fondness for the con man . . . impels it to hope for the success of his scheme"; and we feel superior to his victims. Nonetheless, Weales believes that Horner's "seductions become merely mechanical. Horner is more like a chain smoker than a great lover."[25] Peter Malekin sensibly observes that "Horner is not a diabolical character; he seduces no unwilling virgins and commits no rapes. On the contrary it is the women who are only too happy to pursue him; and this goes for Mrs. Pinchwife as well as the others. His role is . . . passive."[26] Robert D. Hume sees little glamor in Horner's successes: "We are glad enough to see Horner succeed, but we cannot identify very seriously with his endeavours. . . . Even Margery . . . is made to appear more silly than lovable. In the world of fools and hypocrites in which he lives, Horner is welcome to his triumph."[27] None of these critics takes into account the degree to which our impression of Horner is susceptible to manipulation in performance.

The crucial step toward resolving the tangles in criticism of *The Country-Wife* is surely to admit that we could adopt any of these three positions and make it work in the theatre. A great deal depends on how Horner is cast and on what sort of women he is allowed to seduce. As a dashing young scamp—handsome, ingratiating, and aged no more than twenty-five—Horner threatens no one and need not be taken very seriously. He is playing a new and amusing game, and we can see him enjoying every minute of his escapade. Basically, he is an "extravagant rake" who has

24. Palmer, pp. 128–29.
25. *The Complete Plays of William Wycherley*, ed. Gerald Weales (Garden City, New York: Anchor, 1966), Introduction, pp. xii-xiii.
26. Peter Malekin, "Wycherley's Dramatic Skills and the Interpretation of *The Country-Wife*," *Durham University Journal*, n.s. 31 (1969), 32–40. Quotation from p. 39.
27. Hume, *Development*, p. 103.

not yet settled down.[28] We would guess that this was the production concept favored by Robert Wilks early in the eighteenth century. An older (mid-thirties) Horner, played as a powerful and
successful rake by someone like Charles Hart (who created the
role at the age of forty-five), would come across as a glamorous
libertine, more self-controlled and self-seeking than the scamp.
For this Horner the stratagem is not just a temporary diversion
but could become a way of life. There is, however, nothing in the
text to prevent our casting Horner as a fortyish debauchee, now
overweight, visibly dissipated, and inclined to leer. Few members
of the audience, *Playboy* readers or not, will be inclined to identify with him.

Beyond casting, the most important single factor in determining our response to Horner is the attractiveness of the women he
manages to seduce. And here again the director has a wide variety of choices. Lady Fidget can be cast and played as the pretty,
neglected young wife of a preoccupied older man, as a luscious
but inexperienced lady in her early thirties, or as an amorous
older woman in her forties whose looks are past their prime. She
is the chance object of Horner's attentions, not his predeter-
mined target. The older she is, or the more innocent, the better
test case she makes for his deception. In a farce production her
adultery can pass without emphasis. If she is inexperienced but
sex-starved, and we can enjoy her discovery of "safe" sex, she im-
plicates us in Horner's scheme (libertine comedy). Presenting her
as already promiscuous makes her far more hypocritical and
hence unpleasant (satire). The neglected young wife and the amorous older woman are clichés of Carolean sex comedy: how
much the men in the audience envy Horner's success depends on
which Lady Fidget he beds. Almost as much leeway is open to us
for Mrs. Dainty Fidget and Mrs. Squeamish. Dainty may be Sir
Jaspar's sister (aged forty-plus), or half-sister (aged almost anything), or wife of a brother (any age).[29] Squeamish is clearly

28. See Robert Jordan, "The Extravagant Rake in Restoration Comedy,"
Restoration Literature, ed. Harold Love (London: Methuen, 1972), pp. 69–90.
29. The Quack calls Lady Fidget and Dainty Sir Jaspar's "Wife and Sister"
(p. 250); "sister" often means "sister-in-law" in this period. Sir Jaspar addresses

young and unmarried (Old Lady Squeamish still looks after her); but whether she is a tempting flirt, a hypocritical slut, or an unappetizing cow, Wycherley does not specify. Mrs. Pinchwife is definitely young and very pretty. She could be played as a sweet girl who has the bad luck to be grotesquely innocent (as Elizabeth Bowtell probably portrayed her in 1675) or she could be an incipient slut who merely needs opportunity and a little instruction to become a Hoyden. A director might opt to make all Horner's women seem alike, or could choose to differentiate them sharply in age, looks, and character. If they are all young and attractive, a production will tend to tilt toward libertine comedy; if they are quite different, then the play tends to make a statement about female sexual voraciousness. We should note that while Lady Fidget and Margery definitely sleep with Horner in the course of the play, Dainty and Squeamish have not necessarily done so—yet another point on which the director has a considerable variety of options.

A really negative view of Horner must depend either on assumed audience hostility or on making him (and his conquests) repulsive. Within the world of the play, Horner does nothing particularly wicked or objectionable. Even less than in a case like *Volpone* does the structure of the play turn us against the principal character. Horner is a trickster who successfully avoids exposure and catastrophe, and consequently a negative view of him, though entirely possible, must be achieved in the face of audience inclination to identify with success.

We might reasonably ask why a nonmoralist member of the audience would take a negative view of Horner unless the production were tilted very heavily toward satire. Two arguments have been advanced, one concerning Horner's motivation, the other having to do with his social and financial standing.

Horner's motivation has only recently become a subject of debate. Most critics have been content to assume that the desire to

---

Dainty as "Sister, *Cuz*" (p. 281). All textual references are to *The Plays of William Wycherley*, ed. Arthur Friedman (Oxford: Clarendon Press, 1979).

bed as many women as possible is normal and have felt that as a comic donnée it needs no further explanation. Some have believed (with Norman Holland) that an intelligent viewer should learn better and decide to accept Harcourt as a better model; a majority have felt that in a comedy with a conspicuous farce component we need not find Horner's indiscriminate lust reprehensible. Anthony Kaufman, however, has chosen to treat Horner as though he were a real-life reprobate, subjecting him to psychological analysis. Unsurprisingly, Kaufman finds him neurotic, his compulsive womanizing an expression of sexual hostility and aggression toward women.[30] Kaufman has, in fact, committed almost exactly the error against which Palmer warned in 1913—forgetting that Horner is not a real person, and ignoring the literary context in which we find him. H. W. Matalene's reading is equally misguided. Matalene considers Horner a "homosocial" character whose principal aim in life is to achieve the reputation of being a great womanizer, not actually to take women to bed. As this reading flatly contradicts both Horner's testimony ("let vain Rogues be contented only to be thought abler Men than they are, generally 'tis all the pleasure they have, but mine lyes another way," p. 249) and the whole point of his pretended impotence, Matalene has to do some fancy footwork to explain away obvious objections. We see no reason to indulge in tortuous (and unproducible) subtleties here: for farce, libertine comedy, and satire alike, we can reasonably assume that Horner's motivation is an uncomplicated enjoyment of sex.

A more interesting question to emerge from Matalene's essay is Horner's financial and social standing. Matalene takes him as a parvenu social climber, laying great (and unwarrantable) stress on the scene description "Horners *Lodging*" (e.g., p. 335), which he assumes to mean that Horner lives in "a sort of 'bed-sitter,'"

---

30. Harold Weber seems more in accord with the facts of the play when he observes that "Horner emerges as the only male, other than Harcourt, who appreciates the needs of women." See "Horner and His 'Women of Honour': The Dinner Party in *The Country-Wife*," *Modern Language Quarterly*, 43 (1982), 107–20. Quotation from p. 117.

not in a "private space" of his own. This is a serious misinterpretation. The term *lodging* is used without prejudice in dozens of Carolean comedies (e.g., in *The Man of Mode*; "Lady Woodvil's *Lodgings*" and "Dorimants *Lodging*"). It only means the quarters are rented rather than owned. We are told specifically that Horner lives in Russell Street, Covent Garden (p. 257), a fashionable district. Pinchwife owns a "House" within walking distance. Matalene says that the servants sometimes announce Horner's visitors, sometimes not, and concludes that he "is probably not their employer." But "friends" need not be formally announced, and at page 346 the "Boy" enters to say, "O Sir, here's the Gentleman come, whom you bid me not suffer to come up, without giving you notice." None of Pinchwife's visitors are announced. Since we know that Horner's quarters contain fancy, possibly pornographic pictures (p. 321) and knick-knacks expensive enough to suggest the "china" dodge to Lady Fidget, we deduce that Horner lives not in a dingy boarding house but in the seventeenth-century equivalent of a posh bachelor flat, lavishly appointed. Squeamish says with admiration that it is "the prettyest lodging" (p. 321). On the matter of finances Sir Jaspar tells us that Horner "has money as much as I" (p. 279), and Pinchwife says that "his estate is equal to *Sparkish's*" (p. 333). We may not think much of these gentlemen, but Wycherley gives us clear hints that they are all genuinely part of high society. Sparkish is courtier enough that he is entitled to watch the king dine ("I must not fail the drawing Room," p. 291) and Sir Jaspar explains his lateness in III.ii. by saying "I was advancing a certain Project to his Majesty, about—" (p. 303).[31] In neither case do other characters indicate amusement or skepticism. Wycherley makes no great compliment to Charles II in these references, but we must conclude that whether we are to approve or disapprove of Mr. Horner, he is a wealthy gentleman who moves comfortably in high society, if not in the inner circles of the court.

31. Critics have sometimes assumed that Sir Jaspar is a nouveau riche cit (e.g., Chadwick, pp. 105–7). But as Friedman explains, "business" means government affairs for Sir Jaspar: "Business is never here 'Trade, commercial transactions' (illustrated in *OED* only from 1727)" (p. 252).

FOUR CRUXES

Beyond the presentation of Horner, four cruxes stand out among the host of problems and choices that confront the interpreter or director of *The Country-Wife*. What one does with them goes a long way toward determining the impact of the play in performance.

Realism

How "real" the world of *The Country-Wife* seems to the audience obviously affects the seriousness with which they take it. We need not rehash a longstanding critical debate here.[32] Critics who come to the play via its generic context tend to see it as highly formulaic (Hume), while those inclined to look for commentary on society stress its grounding in Carolean reality (Rogers).

Wycherley's scenic presentation of actual London settings (the "New Exchange" and "Covent Garden Piazza") weighs against any dismissal of the world of the play as Cloud Cuckooland. The massive amount of farce material, however, weighs against an audience's mistaking the play for a representation of real events in high society. Consider the following obstacles: the implausibility of Horner's stratagem; the floods of asides—a farce characteristic; the ancient clown routine in which the three friends push Pinchwife out of Horner's room only to have him pop back like a jack-in-the-box (p. 259); Margery's repeated incarcerations (pp. 269, 316, 331); the breaking up of the Sparkish-Harcourt duel (p. 273); Pinchwife's being routed by the honorable ladies (pp. 274–75); the rakes' teasing Pinchwife by kissing "Margery's brother"; "Ned Harcourt" deceiving Sparkish as a parson; the letter scenes and Pinchwife as letter carrier; Margery's disguise as Alithea (the third implausible disguise in a row); Margery's incredible ignorance of society ("you shall be my Husband now," p. 346). These are just some of the incidents in the play that will admit of a "realistic" presentation with difficulty, if at all. Enough violence will make Margery's getting locked up quite unfunny,

---

32. For a brief survey, see Hume, *Development*, pp. 49–54, 89–92.

but how on earth could one make Sparkish's obstinate refusal to believe that "Ned Harcourt" is Frank Harcourt in disguise anything but the stuff of farce? Or the kissing scene? Or Margery's claiming Horner? The presence of this material does not preclude the possibility of a satiric or libertine production concept, but it does generate a gusto, an exuberance and high spirits, that make solemn discussion of Wycherley's views of contemporary marital arrangements seem ill-attuned to the tone and spirit of the play.

Peter Malekin sensibly observes that

> neither the characters nor the action of *The Country-Wife* are realistic in the sense of copying the surface appearances of life in the ordinary world, although the play of course relates to that life in a less direct way. The world of *The Country-Wife* is a special world; the action is farcical and the characters are Hogarthian caricatures, that is, they isolate and exaggerate some moral (or immoral) characteristic of ordinary men. This remains true even if ordinary life occasionally throws up farcical situations like those in the play and odd individuals who markedly resemble Wycherley's characters. Each character of Wycherley's taken separately, lacks roundness, lacks the conflict and complexity of desires which beset real men.[33]

A director may legitimately choose to emphasize the farcical, the libertine, the pathetic, or the grotesque elements in the play, but nothing will make the farcical action and single-minded characters very real; and Gerald Weales has objected to critics' "using realistic criteria to judge non-realistic plays," arguing that Wycherley's plays "are artificial" in the sense that the characters are stereotypical and the exchanges between them are as set as vaudeville comic turns."[34] We are quite prepared to agree with Dobrée, Righter, and others that in some ways *The Country-Wife* was Wycherley's "comment" on his society—but even in 1675 it was a decidedly unrealistic presentation of that society, and today it functions primarily as a comic vehicle for the stage.

33. Malekin, p. 39.
34. Weales, p. xvii.

Our attitude toward Harcourt and Alithea

Most critics who take a negative view of Horner have wanted to see Harcourt and Alithea as representative of a countervailing virtue—a "right way." This approach is a relatively recent development: before the appearance of Norman Holland's book in 1959 almost all critics dismissed Harcourt and Alithea as standard plot-padding, the sort of secondary love interest added to dozens of comedies of the period for fullness and variety.[35] Young Bellair and Emilia in *The Man of Mode* come to mind: we wish them well, but we feel no profound concern or sympathy for them.

In search of a reading that would give *The Country-Wife* the sort of point and moral substance he approved of, Holland hit on the notion that it presents a right way/wrong way dichotomy. This allowed him to condemn Horner's philandering while exalting the courtship of Harcourt and Alithea into a serious message. As Holland reads the play, Alithea must learn to value "inner nature" rather than "mere appearance," while Harcourt's apparently "bumbling and ineffective" sincerity finally proves his "real faith." At the end Harcourt and Alithea have escaped the "social framework" and world of "pretense" because "they each realize the importance of an aim that goes beyond the merely social and answers one's inner nature."[36] This flowery language comes from Holland, not from Wycherley's text, and it could be applied with equal plausibility (or implausibility) to any of fifty Carolean courtship comedies. How the actors could convey such a message, or why the audience should depart with this realization Holland does not explain. Likewise, Rose Zimbardo simply asserts that Harcourt and Alithea constitute a "satiric antithesis" to Horner: "The opposing virtue in this play is embodied in Alithea and Harcourt . . . the twin virtues that oppose the double vice of the thesis. Alithea, as her name suggests, is the truth that opposes hypocrisy; Harcourt is the romantic love that stands against

---

35. Dobrée (p. 94) does refer in passing to "the charming figure of Alithea."
36. Holland, *The First Modern Comedies*, esp. pp. 77–78, 82–83.

lust."[37] Such a conclusion must be arrived at by audience ratioci-nation: Wycherley does not say this, and within the play neither Harcourt nor Alithea "opposes" Horner. Quite the contrary: Harcourt is his bosom friend, and Alithea can say to Horner, "I always took you for a man of Honour" (p. 347). We agree that any critic in need of a positive moral norm in *The Country-Wife* must seize on Harcourt and Alithea, but we do need to ask whether they can actually function this way.

Anne Righter wishes to read the play à la Holland but is more careful in qualifying her claims. She says flatly that the "two young lovers (Alithea and Harcourt) stand in the centre of the play" and that "it is by their standard that Wycherley intends the other characters, including Horner, to be judged." (How she de-duces Wycherley's intentions with such assurance she does not explain.) But she does admit the "surprising" fact that Harcourt and Alithea are "not the part of *The Country Wife* that one re-members. . . . The interest of the play no longer lies with them. In fact, there is something a little mechanical, a little weary, about the handling of this plot as it works towards its inevitable end. . . . Wycherley is not really interested in his young lovers."[38] She concludes that the play is flawed: "The trouble with *The Country Wife* is, that although the centre of the comedy clearly lies with Alithea and Harcourt, Wycherley cannot really bring himself to believe in them." Righter's sense of the vapidity of this plot seems exactly right; her insistence that the romance plot must properly be the center of the play seems to us misguided. (Are the young lovers whose names we hardly remember the cen-ter of *Tartuffe*?) Kenneth Muir, inclined toward a similar reading, more cautiously suggests that Harcourt and Alithea are merely a "hint" of Wycherley's standard of judgment.[39]

The objection to viewing Harcourt and Alithea as a moral norm is that they cannot carry that weight in performance: they have neither the time on stage nor the emphasis needed. As Peter Malekin says, Harcourt cannot "serve a normative function in

37. Zimbardo, p. 161.
38. Righter, esp. pp. 77–79.
39. Muir, p. 79.

this play" because "he is a peripheral character: the main emphasis in *The Country-Wife* falls heavily on the Horner plot [or plots], and Horner cannot be measured and found wanting by Harcourt."[40] W. R. Chadwick, like Malekin a theatrically-oriented reader of the play, observes that "the Harcourt-Alithea scenes" are "insipid."[41] Our experience is that in performance they are either insipid or farcical, and in neither case is the audience likely to take the characters very seriously, let alone as a moral standard.[42]

In performance, Alithea generally comes across as foolish in her allegiance to Sparkish, and not very witty. (Fujimura is caustic on the latter point.) She is the most passive woman in the play. Harcourt is comically ineffectual, as even Norman Holland admits. We cannot imagine how Peter Verdurmen can assert that "their elegance and substantiality, combined with the aura of calm that stability gives them, define the surrounding moiling characters who are agitated by varieties of unease."[43] Is Harcourt calm, stable, serene, and in control of everything as he tries to invalidate Alithea's marriage by pretending to be his imaginary twin brother the cleric?

Both the farcical nature of Harcourt's schemes and the relative weighting of parts in the play undercut the idea that Harcourt and Alithea can be the center of attention.[44] Given these facts, we need to ask whether the right way/wrong way reading is pro-

40. Malekin, p. 39.
41. Chadwick, p. 111.
42. Because the text does not specifically approve Harcourt and Alithea the audience is free to apply its own standards of judgment. Thus Cynthia Matlack finds their courtship a "parody of the love-honor conflict of heroic plays"—an idea probably impossible to communicate in performance, but not necessarily inappropriate for a reader to entertain. See "Parody and Burlesque of Heroic Ideals in Wycherley's Comedies: A Critical Reinterpretation of Contemporary Evidence," *Papers on Language and Literature*, 8 (1972), 273–86.
43. Verdurmen, p. 336.
44. As a rough indication of time on stage, consider the following page totals, calculated from the Friedman edition. Horner is on stage 67 pages; the Quack, 27; Sir Jaspar, 23; Lady Fidget, 30; Dainty, 24; Harcourt, 44; Dorilant, 36; Sparkish, 37; Pinchwife, 61; Margery, 42; Alithea, 44; Lucy, 30; Squeamish, 26; Old Lady Squeamish, 10.

ducible for an audience not predisposed to take plays that way. Our answer would be no: Harcourt and Alithea cannot be made explicitly normative. One could push a production in that direction. To make the pair memorable, one could costume them distinctively, put them at center stage whenever possible, and give them business to draw audience eyes to them from time to time even when they are not speaking. One would probably also want to make Sparkish prominent and memorable: he shares a lot of stage time with them, and Harcourt's stature is increased if Sparkish is a genuine obstacle, not just a pretentious fool. Most important, one could let Alithea show her love for Harcourt from their first meeting,[45] and thus emphasize their serious feeling in contrast to the rest of the characters.

The usual response to Harcourt and Alithea is the benevolent indifference appropriate to rather underdeveloped characters carrying out a plot formula. In performance that plot line can easily be farcicalized; less easily, it can be romanticized. Why one would want to do the latter we do not really see. Gorman Beauchamp says that "Critics in need of an ideal that will salvage *The Country Wife* for Mrs. Grundy and the college curriculum have lighted on the Alithea episodes as their touchstone, taking it for Wycherley's as well."[46] But whatever Wycherley thought he was doing, Harcourt and Alithea will not function in a normative way in performance, romanticize them though we will. To make *The Country-Wife* into a right way/wrong way play requires that we exaggerate a stock comic formula into a moral exemplum.

The presentation of the Pinchwifes

Critics have not been especially interested in the Pinchwifes, but they are in fact quite important to the impact of the play in performance. Only Chadwick notes that Pinchwife's role is virtually the same length as Horner's, and that as much action takes

---

45. Mostly in gesture and movement, but also in the delivery of such speeches as "I wish my Gallant had his person and understanding.—Nay if my honour—" (p. 273) and "I wou'd see him no more, because I love him" (p. 304). If Pinchwife is intimidating, Alithea's dutifulness is more understandable.
46. Beauchamp, p. 324.

place at Pinchwife's quarters as at Horner's. Mr. Pinchwife is universally condemned as a contemptible person and a disgusting husband. This is indisputable but unspecific: it does not address production choices. We know that Pinchwife is an experienced womanizer of forty-nine who has married a country girl because, as he admits, "I cou'd never keep a Whore to my self" (pp. 262–63). He is wealthy enough to give Alithea a dowry of £5,000, jealous to the verge of paranoia, and hot-tempered enough to draw his sword on his wife (p. 330). But is he a blustering clown or a frightening tyrant? Michael Mohun, who created the role in 1675, could play dashing lovers (Rhodophil in *Marriage A-la-Mode*), but had the force and stature to play the Emperor in *Aureng-Zebe*, Maximin in *Tyrannick-Love*, and Ventidius in *All for Love*. He could certainly have made Pinchwife seem threatening, his readiness to use his sword a genuine inclination to violence rather than mere bluster. After the turn of the century the role was taken by George Powell and Barton Booth, either of whom could likewise have made Pinchwife a disturbing threat. If the role is given to someone more like William Bullock (Sir Tunbelly Clumsey in *The Relapse*, Sir Jealous Traffick in *The Busie Body*), that part of the plot would make a very different impression.

Margery Pinchwife is usually taken as a silly innocent, though most critics have a kind word for her "naturalness" and "honesty." Her naïveté is so exaggerated ("Jealous, what's that?" p. 265) that critics have usually seen her as a comic caricature, a hyperbolic travesty of country ladies. The principal exception is Birdsall, who finds her part of "Wycherley's . . . 'right-way' category."[47] This reading is both historically and theatrically implausible. Wycherley's town-oriented audience seems unlikely to have admired a bewildered country bumpkin, and a modern audience is likely to find her too silly to serve as any sort of positive model. Maximillian Novak usefully stresses the degree to which *The Country-Wife* reflects arguments about town versus country and libertinism versus marriage in the seventies, and the sympa-

47. Birdsall, p. 147.

95

thies of Wycherley's circle seem to have been decidedly in favor of town and libertinism.[48] Margery is lucky for the moment but is incapable of keeping up such intrigues. Chadwick rightly objects to the idea that Margery learns "guile" or quickly "develops all the brilliant cunning of a sophisticated townswoman," pointing out that she "accomplishes her coup more by luck than by good judgement" and that in truth "Margery is as simple and disarming at the end of the play as she is at the beginning."[49]

Utter innocence can seem admirable, contemptible, or amusing. In the context of this play Righter seems correct in calling Margery "hopelessly naïve and foolish."[50] A director does have some choices, however. Margery could be cast and played as a bewildered innocent, an incipient slut, or a quick learner who survives only by luck here but who will soon be able to manage her intrigues more skilfully. Her ignorance, we should note, is apparently not (in Wycherley's mind) a matter of social background, since Mr. Pinchwife refers to "the Suit, we are to carry down to her Brother, little Sir *James*" (p. 286). Margery's innocence is the result of upbringing, not social class.

Given an attractive, artless Margery intimidated by Pinchwife, the role has genuinely pathetic possibilities. Most critics have seen her as "simply a pawn" (Fujimura) or as a laughable simpleton, but Chadwick argues persuasively that compassion could be sought for her.[51] Pinchwife is a dreadful husband, and she is a "poor lonely, sullen Bird in a cage" (p. 283). She starts the play reasonably content with her lot, but by the end she has come to "loath, nauseate, and detest" her husband (p. 329). Her fear that Pinchwife "should come home, and pinch me, or kill my Squirrel" (p. 325) is a painfully vivid glimpse into her life. The possi-

48. Maximillian E. Novak, "Margery Pinchwife's 'London Disease': Restoration Comedy and the Libertine Offensive of the 1670's," *Studies in the Literary Imagination*, 10 (Spring 1977), 1–23. Novak makes the good point that by the end of the play Margery has become a kind of comic female convert to libertinism.

49. Chadwick, pp. 112–13 (citing Zimbardo, p. 158, and Vernon, p. 25).

50. Righter, p. 79.

51. Fujimura, p. 143; Chadwick, pp. 113–14.

bilities of domestic violence in this play are numerous. Pinchwife could be quite rough when he locks up his wife (pp. 269, 316, 331), and his threat to take a penknife to Margery (p. 313) need not be played as hyperbole. We should remember Pepys' report of his wife's threat to brand him with hot tongs when he was having an affair with Deb Willet, and other quarrels leading to a black eye, hair pulling, and the like.[52] Most productions stress Margery's sexual awakening, but the possibility of domestic pathos is real and easy to evoke by making Margery physically frightened of her husband.

The staging of the finale

Exactly what happens in the finale? What do we see? Who realizes what? Events have begun to escape from Horner's control by V.iv.185., when Pinchwife arrives to insist that he marry Alithea. Horner besmirches Alithea's name and is challenged by Pinchwife, whereupon Margery makes her untimely appearance to stop the duel ("they'll kill poor Mr. *Horner* . . . I'll not lose my second Husband so"). Pinchwife understands perfectly what has happened. (A few lines later he says to Sir Jaspar, "he has whor'd my Wife, and yours too.") According to the stage direction he "stands doggedly, with his hat over his eyes." He is on the verge of exploding Horner's hoax, and ready to kill either Margery or Horner, when his threat is disrupted by the entrance of the Fidget party. Pinchwife's anger shakes Sir Jaspar's faith, which is restored only by the assurances of the Quack and Dorilant.

But Horner's cover story remains vulnerable to Margery, who will not abide by his hints ("Peace, Dear Ideot"). When Dorilant calls Horner "an errant French Capon," Margery bursts in to contradict ("'Tis false Sir, you shall not disparage poor Mr. *Horner*, for to my certain knowledge—"). The honorable ladies interrupt her revelation, and everyone joins in the effort to distract Pinchwife, except Dorilant. Amid the uproar, this cipher,

52. See *The Diary of Samuel Pepys*, ed. Robert Latham and William Matthews, 11 vols. (London: Bell, 1970–83), IX, 413–14, and index under "Elizabeth, Their Quarrels."

about whom we know almost nothing, manages to convince Margery that she must hold her tongue—and he does so in a conversation that Wycherley chose *not* to write.

What is the audience to assume that Dorilant says? A director could have him mime an urgent explanation (with Margery nodding in muddled comprehension), or have him shake her and mime "SHHHHH!" (with Margery intimidated into acquiescence), or have him learn the truth and offer himself as a replacement for Horner (with Margery quickly indicating enthusiasm).

While Dorilant is whispering with Margery, Alithea has tried to reassure Pinchwife ("Come Brother your Wife is yet innocent"). Does Alithea really believe this? To have her say so with conviction makes her look naïve and foolish, but if she clearly knows the truth, then she is lying—either to protect Margery or to give Pinchwife a way to save face.

Pinchwife does not respond verbally to Alithea's assurance. Does he mime relief and satisfaction? appalled comprehension? While he stands silent, Harcourt expresses eagerness to be a husband; Dorilant says he "will never be one"; Horner says, "And I alass can't be one."[53] Pinchwife laments, "But I must be one," and in his final speech he says "For my own sake fain I wou'd all believe. / Cuckolds like Lovers shou'd themselves deceive." Is he closing his eyes to the truth or biting the bullet? He has enough self-control not to make a spectacle of himself. Does he shrug and join in the festivities or stand aside, brooding? Does Margery make up to him? stand with Alithea? or go flirt with Dorilant?

The play concludes with "A Dance of Cuckolds." In 1675 the dance was probably performed by professional dancers who entered when Horner asks, "Doctor where are your Maskers."[54] A

53. David Vieth (p. 346) reads this "admission" as "a belated recognition that he was capable of something better." We must agree with Harold Weber that in view of Horner's "pervasive irony" this reading reflects "an innocent, literal understanding" (to quote from Horner himself, p. 322). Horner has, after all, been gloating over his "good design that carryes a man on unsuspected" (p. 351) a dozen lines earlier.

54. H. M. Klein, "'Where are your Maskers?' Queries about the *finale* in Wycherley's *The Country Wife*," *Archiv für das Studium der Neueren Sprachen und Literaturen*, 126 (1974), 66–68, suggests that the query should be ad-

modern director might well add some or all of the characters to the dance. We could have Pinchwife stomp off (perhaps dragging Margery) or join in bitterly. What does Horner do? Birdsall suggests that "Horner will stand at the vital center of the circling dancers—the phallic symbol incarnate—and will draw each of the ladies in turn into the center with him to dance a turn, for he represents, in all his impudence, the life force triumphant."[55] From the opposite point of view Matalene thinks the dance "might plausibly be staged as the celebration of the cuckolded Pinchwife and Fidget households at having safely escaped from Horner's involvement with them. The dance could be the means by which everyone but Horner leaves the stage, whereupon, ostracized, in the final couplets, he discovers that maturing as a ladies' man in fashionable London means abandoning homosociality."[56] The staging of the dance is open to almost anything the director wants to do with it. We can put Horner in the center, or we can isolate him. Harcourt and Alithea can join in or stand aloof. Horner can speak his final lines ("he who aimes by women to be priz'd, / First by the men you see must be despis'd") off by himself in isolation or with one arm around Lady Fidget and the other around Dainty. He can address the lines directly to the audience, to his fellow rake Dorilant (busy taking mental notes as he figures out what has happened), or to a fatuously uncomprehending Sir Jaspar, or to each in turn. Since Horner does escape unscathed, it would be almost impossible to make him look worse in the finale than in the rest of the play, but otherwise Wycherley lets us make of the ending almost anything we please.

LIBERTINE COMEDY, FARCE, OR SATIRE?

Critics' views of *The Country-Wife* have been largely governed by their assumptions about sex. Those who believe "that sex is

---

dressed to Sir Jaspar, who has promised to "send in the Banquet and the Fiddles" for a "Masquerade" at Horner's lodgings (p. 337).
    55. Birdsall, p. 156.
    56. Matalene, pp. 409–10. How the Pinchwifes and Fidgets have "safely escaped" we do not see, and we regard this reading of Horner's concluding

fun, that it is pleasurable to sleep with as many attractive women as possible," and that this idea "would not be alien to either Restoration or modern audiences" tend to see the play as a comic celebration of libertinism, or as a cheerful "bed tricks" farce.[57] But if, as Weber observes, "one assumes that a healthy sexuality can express itself only through marriage and an enduring relationship with one partner, then Horner of course appears a perverse figure . . . the pathetic playboy doomed to an eternal round of unsatisfactory affairs."

Our best guess is that in 1675 *The Country-Wife* was staged as a libertine comedy, with Horner as a glamorous rake. Other rakish protagonists from plays in the mid-1670s sex comedies seem designed for audience empathy, and very probably Horner was presented that way.[58] The apparent readiness of the Carolean audience to accept raw sex in such plays as *The Man of Mode*, *The Virtuoso*, and *A Fond Husband* at about the same time argues a majority acceptance of a nonsatiric production of *The Country-Wife*. We would guess that after the turn of the century, when the play remained popular despite greatly diminished audience tolerance for cuckoldry, a more farcical production was the norm.

A director has a number of key choices to make. (1) Should Horner be cast as a scamp, a glamorous libertine, or an aging debauchee? (2) Are the "honourable ladies" attractive, glamorous, or repulsive? (3) Is Pinchwife comic or frightening? A blustering incompetent or a genuine bully who physically abuses his frightened wife? (4) Is Margery sweet or just dumb? (5) Should Harcourt and Alithea's courtship be played as a stock formula, farcicalized, or romanticized? (6) Is Sparkish a blatant fool or should he appear more commanding and plausible? Jo Haynes probably made him an obnoxious ass in the 1675 production, as Cibber

---

speech as downright perverse: the plain sense seems to be that Horner is boasting of his success.

57. W. R. Chadwick, p. 117; Harold Weber, "The Rake-Hero in Wycherley and Congreve," *Philological Quarterly*, 61 (1982), 143–60, quotation from p. 147.

58. On the boom in sex comedy between 1668 and 1678, see Hume, *Development*, Chapter 7.

did for the Triumvirate. William Mountfort's Sparkish—highly commended by Cibber—we would guess to have been less openly ridiculous, and hence appropriate to a romanticized treatment of Harcourt and Alithea.[59] (7) Is the style of performance to be boisterous, glamorous, or more "realistic"? In a farce production the pace will be breakneck, with entrances tripping over exits, and plenty of comic exaggeration in behavior and characterization. In the libertine comedy the presentation will be more urbane. In a satiric production the characters' behavior is probably best made as natural and real as possible: the audience is asked to look at characters and actions with something closer to their real-life standards. The tolerant suspension of judgment permissible in farce and libertine fantasy would subvert the point of a satire.

Throughout this chapter we have implied the possibility of three distinct production concepts—farce, libertine comedy, and satire. A farce production would aim at simple amusement. Given the material, *The Country-Wife* can hardly help being provocative on all sorts of serious issues, but a farce production makes no statement, assumes the unreality of what it shows, and gives the audience little opportunity or encouragement to think about what it sees. The libertine comedy production invites the audience to identify with a libertine Truewit, and ideologically it presumes approval of promiscuous sex for those who can get away with it. No doubt some members of almost any audience would be offended or critical, but most will suspend judgment and allow themselves to enjoy the fantasy of unrestricted sexual opportunity. The satiric production is more complicated. What does *The Country-Wife* satirize? The script by itself is not a satire, though it can be produced that way. The most plausible satiric targets in performance are (a) Horner's mindless quest for all the sex he can get, or (b) the hypocritical society so successfully hoodwinked by Horner. In the first case we need merely make

59. Cibber, *Apology*, I, 128–29. Mountfort "could at once throw off the Man of Sense for the brisk, vain, rude, and lively Coxcomb, the false, flashy Pretender to Wit, and the Dupe of his own Sufficiency: Of this he gave a delightful Instance in the Character of *Sparkish*."

Horner and his conquests repulsive; in the second, Horner functions as a kind of Vice-figure, a "satirical instrument" who exposes "the corrupt world through which he moves."[60]

To debase and ridicule Horner makes a clear moral point about lust and womanizing; in conjunction with a romanticized treatment of Harcourt and Alithea, a director could push the play toward the reading favored by Norman Holland and Anne Righter. How well the play would work as a satire on society is questionable, but probably better in 1675 than today. The society Wycherley shows us is remote enough from ours that to get a modern audience to take it seriously but not reject it outright would be extremely difficult, perhaps impossible. Even for the Carolean audience the play seems unlikely to have worked as a genuine satire, regardless of how it was produced. That most of the characters are ridiculed is clearly true, but Wycherley never goes beyond exposing obvious butts to contempt. The audience is invited to enjoy its superiority, not threatened by the possibility that it must identify with what is attacked. Even in its original context we cannot see *The Country-Wife* as a harsh criticism of the society it presents, though it could certainly have been staged as the semblance of a social satire.

A special difficulty posed by *The Country-Wife* to both critic and director is the degree to which production choices in any one of its three principal plots do not imply parallel production choices in the others. A libertine Horner does not imply a pathetic Margery; a scamp Horner can coexist comfortably with either a farcicalized or a romanticized Harcourt and Alithea. This is much less true in most of the plays analyzed in the rest of this book: in *The Wives Excuse* or *The Beaux' Stratagem* a couple of key choices dictate most of the rest. The astonishing latitude Wycherley leaves his performers makes the exact constitution of any one actual production unusually arbitrary. Nonetheless, granting that a different set of secondary choices (beyond Horner) would be entirely possible, we would like to sketch in tabular form the differences in the three principal productions we have envi-

60. Chadwick, p. 119.

Table 3.1
Various Character Treatments for *The Country-Wife*

Character	Farce	Libertine comedy	Satire
Horner	dashing scamp of 25	glamorous Truewit of 35	debauchee of 40+
Harcourt	moonstruck lover	romance convention lover	serious lover
Dorilant	(parallel to Horner)	(parallel to Horner)	(parallel to Horner)
Sparkish	stupid clothes horse	arrogant courtier	obnoxious ass
Pinchwife	roaring booby	threatening bully	wife-beater
Sir Jaspar	doddering butt	complaisant butt	smug dupe
Quack	cheery accomplice	smooth accomplice	society leech
Margery	silly newly-wed	budding Hoyden	victimized innocent
Alithea	comically blind	romance convention lover	serious lover
Lady Fidget	bored young wife	sexy lady on the prowl	amorous older woman
Dainty	receptive ingenue	easy pickings	amorous spinster
Squeamish	giddy adolescent	younger easy pickings	hypocritical young cow
Lucy	wide-eyed auxiliary	practiced schemer	experienced go-between

sioned. We will assume that the satire is principally directed against Horner's lust, but that it attempts to expose his society as well. Readily agreeing that different combinations of choices are possible and that we are far from exhausting the possibilities of the script, we would suggest that Table 3.1 conveniently demonstrates the reason for the chaotic state of Wycherley criticism:

bringing different assumptions to the text validates radically different production choices.

Some play texts are much more restrictive than others. When we get to *Love for Love*, for example, we will find that an essentially positive view of the protagonists is built into the text in a way almost impossible to defy except by travesty. Wycherley does not establish a definite attitude toward the principal characters in *The Country-Wife*: whether we regard this as profound complexity or bad dramaturgy is another question. The crucial point for the critic is to recognize the essential *openness* of the script Wycherley has given us. The many critics who have quarrelled so long and inconclusively over *The Country-Wife* are for the most part neither stupid nor totally wrong-headed about the play. The problem lies in their essentially unanimous insistence upon trying to establish a "correct" reading of a text that clearly permits a wide range of quite contradictory performance possibilities. We do not believe in unrestricted critical pluralism, as our discussion of *The Country-Wife* should have made clear. But given the wide-open nature of the script, and the broad range of production concepts appropriate to it, to imagine that there is a single "valid" interpretation is madness.[61]

APPENDIX: TIME AND SCENE PLAN

Wycherley is casual about announcing times and locations in the first three acts of the printed text, but a tight and consistent plan is deducible. From the middle of Act III he is careful to tell audience and readers exactly where his fast-shifting action is taking place.

Act

I: [Horner's lodgings]; late morning ("a quarter and a half quarter of a minute past eleven," p. 252).

II: [Pinchwife's house]; early afternoon (most of the characters are about to go to a play, p. 274).

61. We are grateful to Aparna Dharwadker for a helpful reading of this chapter.

III: [Pinchwife's house] late afternoon or early evening (the play is over, but the New Exchange is still open).

"*The Scene changes to the new* Exchange" (p. 286). Time: immediately following the previous scene.

IV: "*In* Pinchwife's *house in the morning*"—i.e., the next day (p. 304). Alithea, "*dress'd in new Cloths*," and Lucy awaiting Alithea's wedding.

"*The Scene changes to a Bed-chamber, where appear* Pinchwife, *Mrs.* Pinchwife" (p. 310). Evidently a discovery scene following immediately upon the previous scene.

"*The Scene changes to* Horner's *Lodging*" (p. 316). The time is early afternoon; the "wedding" has taken place, and Sparkish is collecting a party for his wedding dinner (p. 327).

"*The Scene changes to* Pinchwifes *house*" (p. 329). Probably a discovery scene in the "Bed-chamber" with a table revealed. Time: afternoon.

V: "*Mr.* Pinchwifes *House*" (scene continues, evidently following Pinchwife's return from Sparkish's wedding dinner).

"*The Scene changes to* Horners *Lodging*" (p. 335). The time is immediately after the previous scene.

"*The Scene changes to the Piazza of Covent Garden*" (p. 338). This is a night scene ("*Enter* Alithea *following a Torch*") taking place while Horner beds Margery.

"*The Scene changes again to* Horner's *Lodging*" (p. 340). Horner has finished with Margery but has not yet managed to get her off the premises when the honorable ladies arrive with food and drink for a masquerade.

Schematically, this translates into a straightforward scene plan:

2.3 Bedchamber in Pinchwife's house
2.2 The New Exchange
2.1 Horner's lodgings

1.2 Covent Garden Piazza
1.1 Pinchwife's house

No scene has to be a discovery, but the second and fourth scenes in Act IV would be much more effective that way, as would the final change to Horner's lodgings in Act V. The total time is under thirty-six hours (11:00 A.M. one day to mid-evening the next). In the first three acts Wycherley changes the scene only twice; the six further scene changes in Acts IV and V reflect the increasing complexities of the intrigues and the accelerating pace of the action.

4

All for Love (1677)

IN ITS OWN DAY, *All for Love* was a great and lasting success (holding the stage to the end of the eighteenth century), and some twentieth-century productions have reportedly gripped their audiences.[1] The play has been both highly praised and dismissed with contempt. Moody Prior calls it "the best tragedy of its age." Hazelton Spencer finds its unity "artificial," its "consistent" characterization a "grievous fault," Antony "the merest sentimentalist," Cleopatra a "puppet of a ruling passion."[2]

Modern criticism has been curiously ineffective, though most critics have tried to be sympathetic. Much of the difficulty stems from unconscious importation of Shakespearean expectations and failure to understand what kind of play Dryden was trying to write. Even favorable critics have tended to be apologetic about Dryden's failure to be Shakespeare. Others have seen *All for Love* as a play written to illustrate a tidy moral; as a Racinean attempt to analyze an "identity crisis"; as an embodiment of "Restoration skepticism" illustrated in Antony's "inability to choose"; as a step towards the pathetic drama of Banks and Rowe. Taken on its

1. Frank Hauser's 1977 Edinburgh Festival production was particularly well-received, even in direct comparison with Toby Robertson's *Antony and Cleopatra*. On that production, see Cordelia Oliver in *Plays and Players*, 25, No. 2 (November 1977), 30–31.

2. Moody E. Prior, *The Language of Tragedy* (1947; rpt. Bloomington: Indiana Univ. Press, 1966), p. 192; Hazelton Spencer, *Shakespeare Improved* (1927; rpt. New York: Ungar, 1963), p. 220.

own terms, however, we will find that *All for Love* is a carefully wrought and splendidly stageworthy tragedy.

A large part of our task must be to get away from the clutter of false expectations in order to see what the play itself actually offers us. Dryden has been criticized for starting his play so close to the end of Antony's life, after his ruin has been accomplished and his death is inevitable. We are going to argue that the key to understanding *All for Love* is the recognition that it is a play not about choice but about discovery of self. Antony has no choices he can accept; when he has come to understand this fact—to discover his own feelings and values—he realizes that he would rather die than live on the terms available to him.

All for Love is unique among the plays analyzed in this book in the fixity of the authorial conception embedded in its text. Dryden's position is unambiguously stated in his subtitle: *The World Well Lost*. Because this makes the play essentially untragic by most critical formulas, the implications of the subtitle have often been evaded or downplayed. We must, however, remember the obvious. By 1677 Dryden was a highly professional playwright and an exceptionally self-conscious craftsman, well aware of current critical theory and the conflicting demands of classical, Shakespearean, and French neoclassical practice. *All for Love* shows every sign of mature ratiocination. We need to ask, therefore, both what Dryden was trying to do in the play and how his apparent aims can best be made effective in performance.

DRYDEN'S CONCEPT OF TRAGEDY IN 1677

All for Love represents a major departure in Dryden's dramatic practice. After a dozen years of writing rhymed heroic plays— from *The Indian Queen* (1664) to *Aureng-Zebe* (1675)—Dryden announced his weariness of rhyme and his veneration for Shakespeare and proceeded to set off in quite a different direction. So runs the cliché, and as far as it goes it is quite true. Exactly what this new direction was, however, has not seemed altogether clear. Some points are obvious. In *All for Love* Dryden abandons rhyme for blank verse, narrows his focus drastically and concentrates on fewer characters, and adopts the unities from French neoclassical practice. The heroic plays (with the exception of *Tyrannick-Love* in 1669) are not really tragedies. All of the rhymed plays reflect Dryden's fascination with the epic, and this predisposition carries over to *All for Love* in its love and honor themes and in the "Herculean" facets of Antony's character.[3] Viewed from the vantage point of *The Conquest of Granada* (1670–71), *All for Love* is a shrunken heroic play—testimony to Dryden's failing confidence in superhuman heroes and heroic ideals. Seen against the background of French neoclassical practice, *All for Love* is an imitation of Racine. Regarded as an attempt to return to the verities of Shakespeare, *All for Love* is a second-rate homage to the English tradition, made timid by needless obeisance to prissy French rules.

Dryden would have been startled by any of these readings. The play is first and foremost an attempt to write tragedy rather than quasi epic.[4] This point tends to be obscured by our modern view of what constitutes tragedy. Dryden further confuses matters with his title page description: "Written in Imitation of Shakespeare's Stile." This statement has exacerbated the inevitable tendency to treat the play as an "adaptation" of *Antony and Cleopatra*, which it most decidedly is not. Numerous critics have understood (and loudly said) that Dryden wrote an independent play from scratch, that the story is drastically different, and that Dryden drew much more heavily on other sources than he did on Shakespeare. But Dryden himself pointed to the Shakespearean

3. The epic/heroic side of *All for Love* is best discussed by Eugene M. Waith in *The Herculean Hero* (New York: Columbia Univ. Press, 1962), Chapter 6, and *Ideas of Greatness: Heroic drama in England* (New York: Barnes and Noble, 1971), pp. 231–35.

4. For the best account of the essential differences between *All for Love* and the rhymed heroic plays in both concept and ideology, see Alan S. Fisher, "Necessity and the Winter: The Tragedy of *All for Love*," *Philological Quarterly*, 56 (1977), 183–203. Roberta F. Sarfatt Borkat does an excellent job of tracing the change in Dryden's concept of tragedy in the 1670s, but she is so hostile to "sentimental" tragedy of the sort Dryden experiments with in this play that her comments on *All for Love* itself are almost entirely dismissive. See "Dryden's *All for Love*, the Critics, and the Idea of Tragedy," *Moderna språk*, 73 (1979), 209–20.

connection. What did he mean? Probably little more than the obvious: the play is in blank verse.[5] Novak rightly observes that "Dryden abandoned Shakespeare's fable, characters, manners, and thoughts as unsuitable for the kind of tragedy he was writing," but "did make an effort to draw on Shakespeare's language."[6] As we shall see, in 1677 Dryden ranked language ("words") as the most crucial part of an effective tragedy. The blank verse of *All for Love* does not strike us as terribly Shakespearean; Dryden would not want it to. He firmly believed in the linguistic "refinement" of his own age, and as Novak suggests, he evidently tried to write as he believed Shakespeare would have written "had he been so fortunate as to have been born into a more refined age than his own." *Antony and Cleopatra* is just about the last place we should look for an understanding of what Dryden was up to in *All for Love*.

The second great red herring for critics of *All for Love* has been Dryden's statement in the preface that he, like many other writers, has been attracted to the story by "the excellency of the moral."[7] Critics have been variously baffled, annoyed, or misled by this peculiar assertion. Bruce King dismisses the statement as a confusion engendered by Dryden's changing "idea of drama." Earl Miner says more bluntly: "The description of the play is inaccurate. It accords with the sort of tragedy that Thomas Rymer might have written."[8] The inappropriateness of Dryden's praise of "the moral" is underlined by his subtitle. As King suggests, "We do not judge the hero and the heroine; rather at the play's

5. The two best accounts of the genesis of the play are Howard D. Weinbrot, "Alexas in *All for Love*: His Genealogy and Function," *Studies in Philology*, 64 (1967), 625–39, and Maximillian E. Novak, "Criticism, Adaptation, Politics, and the Shakespearean Model of Dryden's *All for Love*," *Studies in Eighteenth-Century Culture*, 7 (1978), 375–87. Following quotation from p. 383.

6. For a contrary opinion, see the anonymous *A Review of the Tragedy of Jane Shore* (London: J. Roberts, 1714), p. 12: "Mr. *Dryden*, in his *All for Love*, seems to have taken the contrary Method, and to have endeavoured to Copy the Spirit and Fancy of his Predecessor, rather than his Words."

7. All references are to *All for Love*, ed. N. J. Andrew (London: Benn, 1975).

8. Bruce King, *Dryden's Major Plays* (Edinburgh: Oliver and Boyd, 1966), p. 140. Earl Miner, *Dryden's Poetry* (Bloomington: Indiana Univ. Press, 1967), pp. 38–39.

conclusion they receive our pity, and because of this their passion seems inevitable, correct, and vindicated." Why then did Dryden make his comment about "the moral"? Confusion seems less likely than ironic defensiveness. A play that glorifies illicit love is open to moral question, and Dryden may well have been trying to throw up a smoke screen. Alternatively, he may simply have meant that he wanted a story with an "unfortunate" end that was in some sense deserved, not merely pathetic.

We can get a sense of Dryden's possible aims in *All for Love* by considering a pair of new plays that almost undoubtedly influenced him when he set out to write in the spring of 1677. Nathaniel Lee's highly popular *The Rival Queens*, premiered by the King's Company in mid-March, was a blank verse tragedy (subtitled *The Death of Alexander the Great*) full of rant and flummery, but with a tragic action genuinely stemming from Alexander's character. Novak rightly reminds us that Lee glorified homosexual love and gave a "half sympathetic portrayal of polygamy." Dryden's choosing to glamorize (if not justify) "unlawful love" follows Lee's lead, and moves decisively away from tidily moral tragedy. His interest in the subject may well stem from Sir Charles Sedley's *Antony and Cleopatra* (premiered by the Duke's Company in early February 1677). Sedley's wretched play is a standard exercise in rhymed heroic guff, but was evidently a success—"acted often," according to a contemporary letter.[9] We may guess that Dryden was irritated by this sorry use of the rhymed heroic drama he had championed and irked by the rival company's success with it. At any rate, he chose the Antony and Cleopatra story as the basis for his first public display of his new dramatic ideals.[10]

Dryden's long preface is less help than we could wish, but it does offer an important hint.

> The hero of the poem ought not to be a character of perfect virtue, for then he could not, without injustice, be made unhappy; nor

9. Marquis of Worcester to his wife, 17 March 1677, cited in *The London Stage*, Part 1, p. 255.
10. For a discussion of specific parallels, see Peter Caracciolo, "Dryden and

yet altogether wicked, because he could not then be pitied: I have therefore steered the middle course, and have drawn the character of Antony as favourably as Plutarch, Appian, and Dion Cassius would give me leave; the like I have observed in Cleopatra. That which is wanting to work up the pity to a greater height was not afforded me by the story: for the crimes of love which they both committed were not occasioned by any necessity or fatal ignorance, but were wholly voluntary. (p. 10)

Dryden says he aimed at *pity*; he has drawn his protagonists as "favourably" as history would permit; he has tried to elicit a pity beyond that inherent in the story itself. To get a better sense of why he did this, and what he hoped to achieve in *All for Love*, we should turn to the marginalia known as "Heads of an Answer to Rymer," written circa August 1677.

The "Heads" are scrappy and unsystematic, a sometimes cryptic response to Rymer's new book, *The Tragedies of the Last Age*.[11] They cannot be taken as an expression of a formal, fully worked-out position on Dryden's part, but they do offer us helpful clues to his views of tragedy at about the time he completed *All for Love*.[12] Dryden's basic object in the "Heads" is to refute Rymer's claim that English authors should adopt Greek models, though his interest in justifying what he had just written seems obvious throughout. For our purposes here, Dryden makes seven main points.

1. "Fable" is not central to a tragedy, even "tho' it be the Foundation of it" (p. 185).[13] In other words, plot is not the vital feature.

---

the 'Antony and Cleopatra' of Sir Charles Sedley," *English Studies*, 50 (1969), 1–lv [Anglo-American Supplement].

11. For an analysis, see Robert D. Hume, *Dryden's Criticism* (Ithaca: Cornell Univ. Press, 1970), Chapter 4.

12. Dryden says "my Tragedy . . . is already written" in a letter written ca. July 1677, and comments on Rymer's book in another, ca. August. See *The Letters of John Dryden*, ed. Charles E. Ward (Durham: Duke Univ. Press, 1942), Nos. 5, 6.

13. All references are to "Heads of an Answer to Rymer," in *The Works of John Dryden*, Vol. XVII, ed. Samuel Holt Monk et al. (Berkeley: Univ. of California Press, 1971), pp. 185–93.

2. "Love, being an Heroique Passion, is fit for Tragedy" (p. 186). Dryden finds display of "Passions" crucial to tragedy, and argues that English dramatists have surpassed the Greeks in the addition of "new Passions; as namely, that of Love."

3. Tragedy is to render virtue amiable and vice detestable, and to this end "Pity and Terror, tho' good Means, are not the only" (p. 186). Dryden insists that all passions—including joy, anger, love, and fear—are appropriate "means" to the end of tragedy.

4. "Poetique Justice" should be observed (p. 189).

5. The dramatist should aim to raise the passions of the audience as high as possible (p. 191), a purpose to which the sufferings of lovers are especially well suited.

6. "The Pity which the Poet is to Labour for, is for the Criminal. . . . The Terror is likewise in the Punishment of the same Criminal" (p. 192).

7. "*Rapin*'s Words are Remarkable: 'Tis not the admirable Intrigue, the surprizing Events, and extraordinary Incidents that make the Beauty of a Tragedy, 'tis the Discourses, when they are Natural and Passionate. So are *Shakespear*'s" (p. 193).

Looking at *All for Love* in conjunction with the "Heads" helps clarify Dryden's aims in the play. It is "affective" rather than "fabulist" in design.[14] Dryden's comment about imitating Shakespeare's style ties in with his citation from Rapin: for him, words are as important as action and character. The plot is conformable with the demands of poetic justice, but the central object is to rouse *admiration* for the love of Antony and Cleopatra; only secondarily are pity and terror appropriate.[15]

---

14. See Rothstein, *Restoration Tragedy*, Chapter 1. "The 'fabulist' hypothesis . . . held that the value of a play is in the moral of its story. . . . The 'affective' hypothesis . . . interpreted Aristotle to support the idea that the exercise of the passions, especially those of pity and fear, was itself a desideratum" (p. 22). The one assumes the primacy of an instructive plot, the other holds that arousing the emotions of the audience is an end in itself. Dryden makes significant concessions in the "Heads" to Rymer's fabulist position, but his inclination toward "affective" tragedy is plain.

15. In the preface to *All for Love* Dryden suggests that pity was his primary goal. We suspect that he was being careful about possible moral objections, a caution quite unnecessary in marginalia not intended for public dissemination.

113

Dryden's aims may be clarified by considering what he chose not to do. Unlike Shakespeare, Dryden gives Antony no genuine choices. *All for Love* opens after the battle of Actium, when the world is already lost. We watch Antony gradually comprehend that fact and try to deal with it. Antony's major choices are behind him; all conflicts between love and honor merely reenact past choices. Similarly, Dryden does not present and juxtapose the Roman and Egyptian worlds. Ventidius and Octavia emblemize Roman outlook and values, but Caesar never appears. Nor is Dryden writing a tragedy of character. The point is not that a flaw has brought about the hero's ruin: rather, this play shows the world "well lost."

Dryden's Antony is a great leader who throws everything over for passion; Cleopatra is his faithful lover. This is far from what we would expect from reading Shakespeare, Thomas May, Sedley, or Plutarch and other historians, but Dryden tries to make us believe that "losing the world for Cleopatra is an act worthy of a hero," as Novak phrases the point. Dryden would not argue that Antony should have done what he did, or that he is a fit object for imitation. Rather, Dryden shows us a transcendental passion that ultimately outweighs everything else. This is certainly not tragedy as we usually conceive it, demise of the protagonists notwithstanding. *All for Love* is an odd hybrid: an affective display piece aimed at eliciting admiration for its doomed lovers. Generically, it is a cross between French neoclassical tragedy and English heroic drama. How to produce the play to make it work as Dryden evidently wished is an interesting challenge indeed.

CHARACTER ANALYSES

Dryden's attitude toward Antony and Cleopatra is absolutely unambiguous. One could stage a production in which they were negatively presented, but only by playing against the obvious sense of the text. Even so hostile a critic as John Dennis is in no doubt that we are meant to view the lovers with admiration and pity. The question a director must ask is how to elicit this response. The problems are obvious. Dryden is not writing pathetic tragedy: Antony and Cleopatra are hardly persecuted innocents. "Criminal passion" (in Dryden's phrase) is the basis of the relationship, and Dryden is at pains to display the obligations of military honor and family duty through Ventidius and Octavia.

We must keep a firm grip on a crucial fact: the audience knows from the outset that Antony and Cleopatra will die. In some ways, this knowledge is a problem, especially since the play starts where it does. Shakespeare shows us a series of fatal choices; Dryden (possibly for the dubious sake of the unities) gives us what R. J. Kaufmann has called "terminal tragedy," in which all possibilities are closed out and we are left to concentrate on the catastrophe.[16] To the critics who insist that we ought to see the protagonists before fatal decisions are made, Dryden's design seems frustrating and unsatisfactory. But instead of concentrating upon choices and their results, Dryden focuses on the characters as they try to come to terms with the realities of their situation.[17] The audience knows that actual choices are a thing of the past and that Antony is doomed; but Antony does not, and nor is his fate clear to the other principals. Dryden presumes that Antony could retreat to lower Syria and fight on, or that Octavia could patch up a compromise between Antony and Caesar. The play is set up to show us why neither happens.

The key to *Antony* is his failure to understand himself. For ten years he has been able to maintain the illusion that he is still a great Roman general, even though (from the Roman point of view) his affair with an Egyptian siren ruinously compromises that claim. Following Cleopatra, he has fled from the battle at Ac-

16. "On the Poetics of Terminal Tragedy: Dryden's *All for Love*," rpt. in *Dryden: A Collection of Critical Essays*, ed. Bernard N. Schilling (Englewood Cliffs, N.J.: Prentice-Hall, 1963), pp. 86–94.

17. Frank J. Kearful makes the sensible observation that "Through the first four acts of *All for Love* the audience has been empathetic, embarrassed, and piteous witness of Antony's attempts to overcome the knowledge, which it shares with him, that ''tis past recovery.'" See "''Tis Past Recovery': Tragic Consciousness in *All for Love*," *Modern Language Quarterly*, 34 (1973), 227–46. Quotation from p. 243. We would say that Antony struggles to *resist* the knowledge of his doom, but Kearful is absolutely right in stressing the degree to which all apparent choices are illusory.

tium (Act I, lines 287–88). Now even he must face questions about his status as a hero. Moreover, he is astounded to find himself besieged by Octavius Caesar, whom he despises (Act II, lines 110–43). The loss of a comfortable status quo has come as a dreadful shock to him. His response, as we see in Act I, is a highly unrealistic fantasy of pastoral retreat.[18] Antony is emotional, hot tempered, and at best not much of a thinker. Throughout the first four acts he is in a manic-depressive state that renders him vulnerable to manipulation by anyone who seems to offer a way out of his predicament. Antony is always likely to act on his emotional impulses. He attacks the Roman camp in Act II suicidally unprepared; the attack succeeds only because it is strategically pointless and the Romans are off guard. He does it in the heat of the moment to prove to Ventidius that Cleopatra has not unstrung him (Act II, lines 454–56). Banishing Dollabella and Cleopatra in Act IV (lines 543–48) and raging at the desertion of the Egyptian navy in Act V (lines 100–104) are similar outbursts.

Antony responds electrically, galvanically, to Cleopatra, but he is not just besotted. Like Edward VIII, he cannot fathom the reluctance of his countrymen to accept the lady of his choice. In the play, however, Antony spends much of his time resisting his choice, trying to obey the dictates of reason and Roman duty. He has trouble realizing the potency of Cleopatra's hold: in Act II he agrees to see her despite Ventidius' almost superstitious warning not to (lines 226–28). In Act IV, having acknowledged Octavia as his wife, Antony dares not face Cleopatra, and so sends Dollabella in his stead to say goodbye.[19] Prepared for doubt by Ventidius, Octavia, and Alexas, Antony sees Dollabella emerge from

18. Antony imagines himself "Of all forsaken" living "in a shady forest's sylvan scene, / Stretched at my length beneath some blasted oak" (Act I, lines 230–44).

19. Antony's three returns to the stage to add injunctions and further instructions before he finally lets Dollabella go ("Goes to the door and comes back. . . . Antony goes again to the door and comes back. . . . Goes out and returns again"—lines 26–35) run some risk of seeming funny. They must be played as evidence of his anguish, and his profound reluctance to carry out the plan he has agreed on.

Cleopatra's palace (line 440.1) and takes this as proof of an assignation, causing him to doubt Cleopatra for the first time.

Bereft of love and deserted by the Egyptian navy, Antony resolves to die fighting with Ventidius at his side (Act V, lines 185–88). He still hopes that against all odds "we may pierce through all their troops, / And reach my veterans yet." But when Alexas reports Cleopatra's death we see an instantaneous reversal, a potent and moving climax to Antony's part of the play. In that moment all his doubts and turmoil resolve into serene clarity. We have seen Antony rant and posture, unable to control his temper or his destiny. We now see him restored to his full stature, a man who finally understands himself and who knows exactly what he means to do. For the first time he takes the blame upon himself.

> Then art thou innocent, my poor dear love?
> And art thou dead?
> . . . .
>   . . . Then what am I,
> The murderer of this truth, this innocence?
> Thoughts cannot form themselves in words so horrid
> As can express my guilt! (Act V, lines 236–44)

Antony is oblivious or indifferent when Ventidius responds to Cleopatra's reported demise ("Heaven be praised. . . . Would she had died a little sooner, though, / Before Octavia went: you might have treated"). Instantly sure of his own mind, Antony declares, "I will not fight: there's no more work for war. / The business of my angry hours is done." He will die,

>   but not by fighting. O Ventidius!
> What should I fight for now? My Queen is dead.
> I was but great for her; my power, my empire
> Were but my merchandise to buy her love,
> And conquered kings, my factors. Now she's dead,
> Let Caesar take the world.

This scene restores the stature Antony's extended flounderings and false starts have called in question. He is a hero, and his death is a triumph.

The suicide itself is tricky. A daring actor (an Olivier) might risk inviting laughter at "I've missed my heart." The brief final love scene (Act V, lines 357–402) is tender, and mercifully underwritten, though the exaggeration in Antony's last line ("This one kiss—more worth / Than all I leave to Caesar") could easily seem silly. Antony must not enjoy a conveniently lingering demise while Dryden works in fine sentiments. To counteract any sense of bathos, the actor might either play Antony as having already arrived at a state of serene transcendence, oblivious of all but Cleopatra, or alternatively he could show us the effort it costs Antony not to succumb to pain and loss of blood.

Cleopatra is a problem because of extraneous expectations. Almost anyone familiar with Shakespeare will tend to look for the serpent of old Nile, though what Dryden gives us is a simple, honest woman who wishes only to be a loved wife. Early in Act IV Alexas advises her to make Antony jealous by flirting with Dollabella, and she replies:

> Can I do this? Ah, no; my love's so true
> That I can neither hide it where it is,
> Nor show it where it is not. Nature meant me
> A wife, a silly, harmless, household dove,
> Fond without art, and kind without deceit;
> But Fortune, that has made a mistress of me,
> Has thrust me out to the wide world, unfurnished
> Of falsehood to be happy. (Act IV, lines 89–96)

The "household dove" has occasioned some ridicule, but this Cleopatra is a woman both passionate and mothering, with whom Antony has lived for ten years (Act V, lines 391–93).

Dryden does not try to explain Cleopatra's attraction, which means that it must be reinterpreted for each production. Her charms are potent enough to have conquered Julius Caesar and Antony, and to overwhelm Dollabella's judgment, but they are not universal. Ventidius is immune to her appeal, whatever it may be. Cleopatra is regal, but not extravagantly so. She talks as an equal with Antony, but is submissive to him when he gets angry or upset. She considers him her "Lord" (Act II, lines 338, 353), and her overriding concern is to keep him from leaving her. The focus of the play is principally on Antony, but Dryden's prologue reference to "a tale . . . As sad as Dido's" is appropriate to what befalls Cleopatra in the play. But unlike Aeneas, Antony does not abandon the African Queen who has staked kingdom, life, and honor on their love.[20] Dido's story is pathetic; Cleopatra's is ultimately triumphant.

Dryden gives us no reason to doubt the authenticity of Octavius Caesar's offer to give Cleopatra Egypt, plus Syria as a present, if she will betray Antony to him (Act II, lines 397–400). But she never wavers from her passionate declaration in Act II:

> You leave me, Antony, and yet I love you,
> Indeed I do. I have refused a kingdom;
> That's a trifle:
> For I could part with life, with anything
> But only you. Oh, let me die but with you!
> Is that a hard request? (lines 401–6)

Against her better judgment she momentarily allows herself to be persuaded to try to make Antony jealous, but never at any time in the play are her honesty and love called in question except by Ventidius.

Cleopatra's faint in Act IV is genuine, testimony to her devotion to Antony. She has nothing to gain from Dollabella by fainting, and her doing so is directly counter to the policy Alexas has persuaded her to adopt (lines 70–88). Her attempted suicide at the beginning of Act V (line 10.1) might be regarded as emotional blackmail of the sort popular among Racine's characters. She is straightforward elsewhere, however, and we interpret the scene as her despairing response to Antony's apparent abandonment of her for Octavia. By this time Cleopatra has every reason to be frantic. She should be appropriately frazzled—hair beginning to come down, clothes disarranged. Having learned that she

---

20. For an interesting and persuasive account of the parallels, see Carol Freed Levine, "*All for Love* and Book IV of the *Aeneid*: The Moral Predicament," *Comparative Literature*, 33 (1981), 239–57.

will have one last chance to see Antony (lines 115–21), she goes offstage. We would suggest that she spends the time doing her hair, fixing her makeup, perhaps changing her gown. When she comes back, she should look as good as we have ever seen her. As nearly as possible, she should look the way she did when Antony first saw her. To reinforce the positive impact of the double suicide, she needs to be calm, collected, and lovely.

When Cleopatra finds Antony dying, she utters not a word of reproach. Their brief reprise of their Act III love scene is just enough to suggest for us their tenderness and passion. Their magnetic attraction must be made evident in this scene, when Antony wants to move, and can't.[21] Cleopatra goes about her final preparations happily. She wants to die: death with Antony is marriage with Antony, placing them beyond the power of Roman law—and so she says. This ending is a triumph for Cleopatra, and should be played with serenity and utter confidence: she knows exactly what she wants to do and does it. The conclusion is every bit as ecstatic as Aida's: "Di morte l'angelo / radiante a noi s'appressa . . . ivi comincia l'estasi / d'un immortale amor."[22]

Ventidius is generally treated as a hero and a walking embodiment of Roman virtues. Even the grumpy John Dennis commended the first act, in which Ventidius temporarily recalls Antony to his martial duty. Sublimely confident of his own rectitude, Ventidius is intensely loyal to Antony, and an old campaigner with a much cooler strategic head. As commander of an Empire outpost, he has reached the limits of promotability. We cannot find him quite as flawless as Howard Weinbrot, who calls him "the instigating hero" (in opposition to the "instigating villain," Alexas). Contrary to Weinbrot's assertion, Ventidius does not learn deceit from Alexas. The first thing we see him do in Act I is eavesdrop for forty lines, and even cursory reflection on his motives suggests some self-interest. Yes, he loves Antony; but he

21. The contrast is particularly effective because Antony has been dashing about in a hyperactive way for four and a half acts. His sudden immobility is a visual confirmation of his quitting the world and coming to rest.

22. Aida: "The angel of death, radiant, approaches us . . . there begins the ecstacy of an immortal love."

is too much Antony's man to have much future without his general in power.

Ventidius arrives hoping to get Antony to return to Syria and fight on there. When Plan A fails (Cleopatra wins Antony back in Act II), we find that Ventidius has already set up Plan B, which is to use Octavia to reconcile Antony to Rome. He needs no lessons in court intrigue from Alexas. When Plan B comes unstuck, Ventidius has no honorable options, and we can certainly admire his unflinching willingness to die with his leader.

What sort of man is Ventidius? A blunt old soldier; loyal; brave; hostile to women (Act II, lines 451–53); extremely chauvinistic about anybody and anything not Roman. If he were a British civil servant in the Indian empire, he would wear a dinner jacket every night. Many critics rightly stress his embodiment of the Roman and military virtues Antony has betrayed. Within the action of the play, however, Ventidius has a second, equally important function: he is utterly blind to Cleopatra's appeal. From beginning to end he cannot understand what Antony sees in her, and his incomprehension helps make Antony's love special. If Ventidius could feel Cleopatra's pull and spurn it, Antony would seem weak, a bad Roman. Dryden goes to considerable lengths in Act V to show us Ventidius' failure to recognize, let alone understand, Antony's feelings when Cleopatra's death is reported. This insensitivity leaves him brave and loyal, but something of a clod.[23]

Octavia is a female Ventidius. Dryden's presentation of her is plainly calculated to limit audience empathy for a character whose position invites sympathy. She has a hard row to hoe. Antony cannot bring himself to be more than polite to her, and she, understandably but unreasonably, wants him to love her. She is not loveable, even in Roman terms, let alone to the sybarite Antony has become. She is a wife to be proud of; a great political asset; no doubt a fine housekeeper and an admirable mother. She is not, however, emotionally responsive to Antony. She can lose her temper, but as Dollabella points out (Act III, lines 332–35)

23. There is, however, no evidence in the text to suggest that Ventidius might be homosexual.

she cannot show love. She is as emotionally self-contained as Cleopatra is expressive toward Antony, a difference easy to make almost palpable in the theatre.

Octavia needs the children to move Antony to do his duty. He will live with her; he cannot love her. Was she ever anything more than a political gesture on Antony's part? If he only gradually discovered that he had made a mistake, her suffering may well be genuine. If the match was strictly political on both sides, then Antony's abandonment of her is much less reprehensible, and her distress is more a matter of offended dignity and pride of place. Octavia can be played either as yearning hopelessly for Antony or as a mortified grande dame. The former is more interesting; the latter, safer.

Dryden uses the catfight in Act III (probably inspired by the Statira-Roxana scene in *The Rival Queens*) to make Octavia "change places" with Cleopatra in more ways than she realizes. Octavia first appears in the play as a victim, the abandoned spouse. If she could draw Antony back and refrain from gloating, she would be the right-way choice. But she comes back for no reason other than to flaunt her triumph. Octavia leaves Cleopatra as devastated as ever she was herself when abandoned—and Cleopatra does not have an Octavius Caesar to fend for her. By the end of this scene Cleopatra should collect much of the sympathy we may have developed for Octavia in the scene with her children.

Like Ventidius, Octavia simply cannot see Cleopatra's attraction (or at least cannot admit it). Far worse, she cannot understand that Antony might legitimately retain some feeling for Cleopatra even after he has agreed to return to his lawful wife. Octavia's insensitivity to Antony's feelings is underlined in the scene in which she finally walks out. If she really loved Antony she would stay, in spite of learning that he still cares for Cleopatra (Act IV, lines 375, 386–89). She believes, after all, that Dollabella is cutting Cleopatra out for himself. What is her hysterical response to Antony's distress but sheer pique?

Various critics (especially Reinert) have seen this play as a contrast between Roman reason and Egyptian passion.[24] This is an oversimplification. If *All for Love* is to work as more than a morality play upside down, we need to see Antony regain the advantages of being Roman (friends, wife, military heroism, official place) and then lose them again for reasons that he does not fully understand and cannot control. An important part of the play's complexity depends on our coming to understand that in her chilly way the Roman Octavia is just as passionate and unreasonable as the fallen Antony.

Dollabella has attracted rather little analysis. Dryden never tells us much about the relationship between Antony and Dollabella. It could be played as Achilles-Patroclus or more simply as Julius Caesar-Brutus. Mentor-protégé makes good sense. So does the notion that Dollabella has been the son Antony never had. Especially in the latter role, Dollabella is a threat to depose his "father," as indeed Antony feared the last time he, Dollabella, and Cleopatra were together. Whatever the past relationship with Antony, Dollabella is now a diplomat, a polished courtier who contrasts with Ventidius the soldier.

Dollabella fulfills three major functions in the mechanics of the play. First, he illustrates what Antony has lost by dallying in Egypt. Dollabella is now Octavius Caesar's man, not Antony's—which Alexas knows from the start (Act I, lines 55–56) but which Antony would like to forget. Second, Dollabella, cool envoy though he is, finds himself completely unable to keep his head in Cleopatra's presence. Antony is not the only susceptible Roman, and in Dollabella, Dryden lets us see just how potent Cleopatra's charm can be. If Dollabella can succumb, then Antony's doing so seems much less a matter of personal weakness. Third, Dollabella's participation in the rescue-Antony movement lends credibility to the idea that he could retrieve his Roman standing, that this is not just a pipe dream fed by Ventidius.

Dollabella's exit, after Antony has denounced him at the end of

24. Otto Reinert, "Passion and Pity in *All for Love*: A Reconsideration," in *The Hidden Sense and other essays*, by Maren-Sofie Røstvig et al. (Oslo: Universitetsforlaget, 1963), pp. 161–95.

Act IV, gives the director a chance to make a telling comment. The actor might leave reluctantly, hoping that Antony will calm down and see reason. He might pay silent tribute to the ruins of the emperor Antony could have been and exit sadly. Or he might draw back from the childish tantrum, give up on Antony in obvious disgust, and head briskly for Caesar's tent with his report. The occasion can either leave the future seemingly open or serve as a hint that the end is near. If Dollabella visibly chooses Caesar, Antony has lost not only this hope for the future but another part of his past.

Cleopatra's eunuch *Alexas* can be played either as the harsh voice of common sense (Egyptian version) or as a slimy villain. He serves two principal functions. First, as Howard Weinbrot points out, "in all four of the [non-Shakespearean Antony and Cleopatra] plays which Dryden definitely knew, the eunuch Photinus is a catalytic agent who originates and complicates much of the action." Dryden uses him to forward the plot in opposition to Ventidius' effort to recall Antony to his Roman duty. We cannot, however, agree with Weinbrot that "the movement of the play depends upon the battle of Ventidius (Rome) and Alexas (Egypt) for Antony." In fact Alexas has no use for Antony. Early in Act I he tells Serapion that Cleopatra has refused his advice to save them all by yielding Antony to Caesar (lines 77–81). In Act II he tries hard to turn her against the "vanquished" warrior. But Alexas is Cleopatra's creature, and he will use his wits to keep Antony from leaving if she will have it so, even while lamenting her folly. As late as Act V Alexas is all for making a deal with Caesar: "haste you to your monument, / While I make speed to Caesar. . . . I can work him / To spare your life, and let this madman perish" (lines 106–9). Alexas is a professional court intriguer forced to work against his own counsel and interest throughout the play.

Alexas' second function is to serve as a foil for Cleopatra. He is the consummate schemer; she is simple and straightforward. He is frightened for his skin (Act V, lines 131–39) and quite prepared to sell Antony; she is serenely faithful unto death. Alexas is what Ventidius imagines Cleopatra to be—selfish, devious, and totally untrustworthy. Alexas represents the self-interest Cleopatra entirely rejects. If she were what Ventidius imagines her, she would do exactly what Alexas advises. Although critics seem largely unconscious of the fact, Alexas' most crucial function is to remind us what Cleopatra is not.

ASSUMPTIONS AND PRODUCTION CHOICES

Beyond the text certain assumptions and production choices determine the impact of the play in performance. Given the fixity with which Dryden aims his text, production variation will come largely in these realms.

Rhythm

Because *All for Love* presents only the last day or so of the story, critics often assume that it is "one long catastrophe," in R. J. Kaufmann's phrase. Diagramatically, this view looks like Figure 4.1. Other critics see the play as a kind of tennis match, with Antony as the ball being bounced back and forth between the demands of Rome and Egypt (see Figure 4.2). If, however, we consider Antony's emotional state rather than the apparent solutions at which he keeps grabbing, we see the play in quite different terms. Antony starts Act I terribly depressed. Ventidius revives him and gives him hope, which he promptly transfers to Cleo-

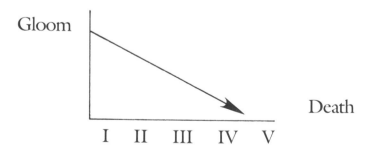

Figure 4.1. Diagrammatic view of *All for Love* as "one long catastrophe."

125

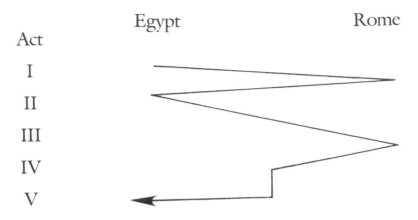

Figure 4.2. Diagrammatic view of Antony's vacillations
in *All for Love*.

patra. Antony attacks the Roman camp and wins—a meaningless
victory, but one which gives him an enormous psychic boost.
The Act III victory celebration is the high point of the play so far,
both visually for the audience and emotionally for Antony and
Cleopatra. But during Act III Antony allows himself to be reconciled with Octavia, a reversal and an emotional letdown. The farther he goes with this policy, the more depressing it becomes, until by the end of Act IV Antony has not only alienated Octavia
but banished Dollabella and Cleopatra. His nadir is the naval mu-
tiny in Act V. The loss of Egypt puts Antony against the wall: he
is trapped, but he is a fighter and will not die passively. Before he
can go off to battle, he is stopped cold by Alexas' false report of
Cleopatra's suicide. His acceptance of blame and renunciation of
the world lead to his falling on his sword. Like Hedda Gabler's
suicide, this is a positive act. Antony's emotional curve is on the
way up from the time he hears of Cleopatra's alleged death. She
makes clear her determination to join him, and both die happier
than they have been at any time during the play. Diagramatically,

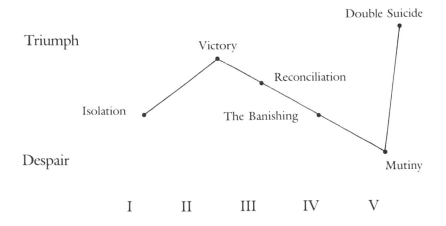

Figure 4.3. Diagrammatic view of emotional polarity
in *All for Love*.

the emotional temperature looks like Figure 4.3. To see *All for Love* as a downward progression to death, or as a prolonged vacillation between Roman and Egyptian values, is to miss the emotional structure of the play, and with it much of Dryden's point. The beginning of Act III takes us to a false high that quickly evaporates. The nadir of Act V leads quickly to the serene affirmation of the double suicide.

Location

Dryden is quite unspecific about location. The "Persons Represented" page of Q1 says "Scene Alexandria," and Act I specifies "Scene, The Temple of Isis"; for the rest the director is left to deduce what is appropriate. Where we are is less important than a sense of direction: the audience needs to be clear where people come from and where they are going when they leave. *All for Love* could be staged as a one-set show if this sense of direction is

clearly established. The four necessary exits are (1) the Temple
of Isis (or Inner Temple in Act I); (2) the City of Alexandria;
(3) the Roman camp; and (4) Cleopatra's palace (or Inner Palace
in Acts IV and V). On stage they are probably best placed as indicated in Figure 4.4.[25] Because the play is supposed to convince
us that Antony and Cleopatra make the right choice (for them,
not necessarily for us), Egyptian territory should be located
closer to the audience, Roman-occupied ground farther away.
Otherwise the Romans are literally between the audience and
Antony and Cleopatra. Such distancing, though slight, would be
psychologically important. It could be used effectively by a director who wanted to "display" the protagonists rather than let us
empathize with them.[26]

The reader who takes the trouble to review entrances and exits
throughout the play will find that Dryden establishes a consistent
pattern. (For a detailed account of Dryden's use of place conventions in *The Spanish Fryar*, see the next chapter.) Only after a major change does a principal character go off some way other than
he or she came on. (For example, in Act I Antony enters from the
inner temple and exits with Ventidius toward the city.) This pattern allows Dryden to reinforce character allegiances and to signal changes in a way that subtly but clearly underlines them. At
the end of Act IV, for example, "Exeunt severally" means that
Antony goes back toward the city, Cleopatra into the palace, and
Dollabella toward the Roman camp—ocular demonstration of
their breakup. Perhaps the weakest spot in the whole pattern is

25. Dryden's stage direction at the opening of Act III implies use of the four
ante-proscenium doors for the four "directions" rather than two doors and two
exits through the wings. Either would work: we have chosen the latter because
of its more decisive differentiation.

26. For a well worked out interpretation along these lines, see Derek
Hughes, "Art and Life in *All for Love*," *Studies in Philology*, 80 (1983), 84–107.
Hughes sees the play as a demonstration of the inevitable failure of the characters' "dramaturgic attempts to resurrect and perpetuate a dying order" imposing "the permanence of art" on "the transient, ever-changing patterns of life"
(p. 96). We regard the interpretation as producible, though it seems to us to
overstress the flounderings of the first four acts at the expense of the finale.
Hughes' reading would force the actors to play against the sense of affirmation
and serenity implicit in Act V and suggested in Dryden's subtitle.

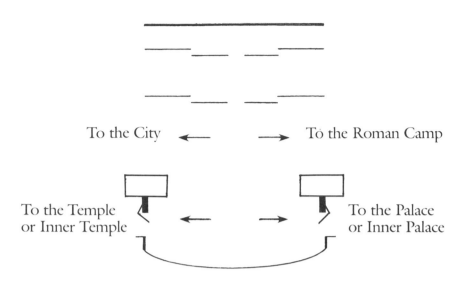

Figure 4.4. Sense of direction in *All for Love*.

Octavia's final exit (Act IV, line 428), which is toward the city to pick up her children. It would be iconographically stronger if toward the Roman camp, but Dryden must get Ventidius off at this point (he follows to try "to win her back"), and he cannot follow her to the Roman camp.

Although a single exterior set would suffice, we would hypothesize that the Drury Lane company originally used at least three, probably four sets, all of which could have been pulled from stock. For the Temple of Isis in Act I any pagan temple set would do. Acts II and III clearly take place outdoors, some place where official farewells and triumphal processions can fit comfortably— a palace square. Act IV could continue there, but the eavesdropping scenes (especially Ventidius "above"—line 52.1) would probably go better indoors. A great hall in Cleopatra's palace seems plausible. Act V could continue in the great hall (it clearly ought to be indoors—Cleopatra's suicide would come awkwardly in the palace square). We would, however, favor a more intimate interior—a private room in the palace, or even Cleopatra's state

129

2.3	Palace Square	(Acts II, III)
2.2	Temple of Isis	(Act I)
2.1	Great Hall	(Act IV)
1.1	Cleopatra's Bedroom	(Act V)

Figure 4.5. Scene plan for *All for Love*.

bedroom. The smaller room should give a sense of closing in, of the broader world gone, no choices left. The bedroom is where the lovers have been happiest, and for them to wind up there at the crisis seems natural. Schematically, the scene plan is simple (see Figure 4.5).

Time

The text of the play says almost nothing about the passage of time. Dryden says in his preface that "the unities of time, place, and action [are] more exactly observed than, perhaps, the English theatre requires." Critics interested in the matter generally assume that this implies a duration of a single day, which is possible though not essential—or even particularly apparent to the audience.

Act I begins with Serapion recounting portents and prodigies of "Last night." Ventidius convinces Antony to leave (ca. 9:00 A.M.?). In Act II Cleopatra persuades him not to, and he dashes off to attack the Romans. Act III opens with the triumphal procession (ca. 2:00 P.M.?). Ventidius meanwhile has managed to get in touch with Dollabella and Octavia and to arrange to have them on hand, along with the children. Fresh from victory Antony encounters these unexpected ambassadors and decides to accept amnesty (4:00 P.M.?). Act IV must begin late in the afternoon. Antony has Dollabella tell Cleopatra goodbye while he writes letters. Ventidius sees what he thinks is an assignation, and uses it; Antony mortally offends Octavia and banishes Cleopatra and Dollabella (6:00 P.M.?). In Act V Antony has gone off to the Pharos lighthouse (line 78), where he watches the fleet defect. The double suicide would thus take place circa 8:00 P.M., as night falls.

A director could choose to assume that time passes (say 24 hours) between Acts II and III, and again between III and IV. Such a stretching out affects our conception of character. In the one-day version we must assume that Ventidius set both his plans in motion simultaneously. With an extra day following Cleopatra's winning Antony back in Act II he could plausibly regroup and start Plan B from scratch. Likewise, we may wonder if Octavia gets Antony back for a night between Acts III and IV. A single day gives a sense of onrushing doom; three days strengthen plausibility and make the whole business less frenetic. But in performance, time will be little noticed unless the director chooses to emphasize it.

Costumes

Costume will underline the difference between Romans and Egyptians. Antony should appear in Act I in an Egyptian lounging robe and change to Roman armor for Act II. We may deduce that he appears in armor for the triumphal procession at the start of Act III but quickly sheds it in favor of the (Egyptian) "robe" on which Ventidius tugs to catch his attention (line 38). Dollabella, a diplomat, presumably wears senatorial robes for the Act III confrontation with Antony—a significant contrast to the "Egyptian" Antony. For Act IV Antony presumably switches back to Roman dress (though probably not to armor—he is not proposing to fight). In Act V he is on his way to do battle, and armor is again appropriate.[27]

Much could be done with contrasts between Cleopatra and Octavia, depending in large part on what one wants to say about Octavia. Cleopatra should be glamorous and expensively dressed, but not revealingly so. Though Cleopatra is queen, she is also at home, not on public display, save perhaps in the victory celebration in Act III. Octavia might be very plainly (but not dowdily) dressed, her clothes reflecting her severity. Alternatively, she

27. Do Ventidius and Antony wear essentially identical Roman uniform? Not necessarily. A point can be made by presenting Ventidius in battered armor that shows obvious signs of hard use, while Antony's is elegantly new and dressy.

might be given elegant but very formal clothes reflecting her official status as ambassadress. Octavia's "train" (Act III, line 416.1) presumably includes a couple of maids, whose behavior and dress can contrast with Cleopatra's women.

Serapion's dress should signal "priest" and Alexas' "court eunuch."[28] The triumphal procession contrasts Cleopatra's Egyptians and Antony's Romans. This is an opportunity to underline how exotic Egypt is: we need merely parade some native guards and belly dancers. There is nothing subtle about any of this, but just doing the obvious will reinforce the basic contrast in the play and provide visible evidence of Antony's flounderings.

Casting possibilities

A convenient way of getting some sense of the effect of different casting choices is to look at three major early productions (see Table 4.1). Some of the original 1677 cast is surprising. Hard times and internal dissention racked the company this season, which may account for some oddities, but they are certainly thought provoking. Charles Hart is the obvious choice for a soldier-hero. Elizabeth Bowtell, however, is hardly what most of us would expect as Cleopatra, though we would argue that she is entirely appropriate to the character as Dryden delineates her. Edmund Curll describes her as "a very considerable Actress; she was low of Stature, had very agreeable Features, a good Complexion, but a Childish Look. Her Voice was weak, tho' very mellow; she generally acted the *young Innocent Lady* whom all the Heroes are mad in Love with; she was a Favourite of the Town."[29] She had scored a great success earlier the same year as the loving and trustful Queen Statira in *The Rival Queens*. A survey of her roles shows a large number of breeches parts and a high propor-

28. The conventions of history painting suggest that robes and a pagan priest's mitre would have identified Serapion to the audience in 1677, but how "eunuch" was signaled we do not know. A modern designer would probably give Serapion robes and mitre, and might well give Alexas the body-type and costumes conventional in present-day harem cartoons.

29. "Thomas Betterton" [Edmund Curll], *The History of the English Stage* (London: Curll, 1741), p. 21.

Table 4.1
Casts for Three Major Early Productions of
All for Love

Role	Drury Lane 1677	Lincoln's Inn Fields 1704	Drury Lane 1718
Antony	Charles Hart	Thomas Betterton	Barton Booth
Cleopatra	Elizabeth Bowtell	Elizabeth Barry	Anne Oldfield
Ventidius	Michael Mohun	John Verbruggen	John Mills
Octavia	Katherine Corey	Anne Bracegirdle	Mary Porter
Dollabella	Thomas Clarke	Robert Wilks	Robert Wilks
Alexas	Cardell Goodman	Barton Booth	Colley Cibber

tion of "innocent" roles—Benzayda, Fidelia, Desdemona (as well as Margery Pinchwife). Bowtell played ingenues and innocent victims, not femmes fatales, and as Novak rightly remarks, the much-maligned "household Dove" speech, from her lips, "is only announcing what the audience would have known from her appearance on the stage and her first speech."[30] John Harold Wilson has speculated that Dryden originally intended the part for Rebecca Marshall, who took such roles as Lyndaraxa, Nourmahal, and the stormy Roxana in *The Rival Queens*.[31] There is no hard evidence: she worked with the King's Company as late as March 1677, but had decamped to the Duke's Company by May. Dryden could certainly have conceived Cleopatra with Marshall in mind, though as he wrote the role—honest, constant, rather passive—it seems more appropriate to Bowtell.[32] Whatever the facts of the matter, Bowtell's presence in the original cast serves as a reminder that we are dealing with Dryden's play, not Shake-

30. Novak, p. 381.
31. *Mr. Goodman the Player* (Pittsburgh: Univ. of Pittsburgh Press, 1964), p. 58.
32. For a helpful analysis of Dryden's changes in the "barge" description (changes that make Cleopatra a passive and ingenuous heroine), see Derek Hughes, "*Aphrodite katadyomene*: Dryden's Cleopatra on the Cydnos," *Comparative Drama*, 14 (1980), 35–45.

speare's. Wilson finds it hard "to picture blue-eyed Betty Bowtell as Cleopatra, the serpent of the Nile." True—but that Cleopatra is Shakespeare's, not Dryden's.

The original Octavia was Katherine Corey (then aged ca. forty-five to Bowtell's ca. twenty-seven), a specialist in unpleasant or comic older women. She had created the part of the Widow Blackacre in *The Plain-Dealer* one year earlier. Even supposing that her propensity for the shrew and the battle-ax were minimized, one can hardly imagine her diverting much sympathy away from Bowtell's Cleopatra. Dryden was afraid that "the compassion she [Octavia] moved to herself and children" in Act III would prove "destructive to that which . . . [he] reserved for Antony and Cleopatra" (preface), so perhaps casting Mrs. Corey as Octavia was a way to guarantee that audience sympathy would not get out of hand. Other, younger actresses were available.

Elizabeth Barry and Anne Oldfield are both much more thinkable than Bowtell as Shakespeare's queen. We would guess that they played Dryden's Cleopatra in a much more energetic and aggressive style, more overtly sensual and passionate. Such information as we have suggests that they were both highly effective in the role, but they were not necessarily more appropriate to the largely passive character Dryden created. Statira was probably closer to Dryden's idea of his character than Shakespeare's Cleopatra.

The later Octavias represent much more interesting choices than Corey. Anne Bracegirdle doubtless played outraged virtue, but she was beautiful—a glamorous if chilly wife. Mary Porter was likewise good-looking, though less a specialist in virginity. We suspect that the original cast considerably overdid the contrast. Antony's preference for Cleopatra is more interesting and impressive if he is merely indifferent to Octavia, not actively repelled by her. She should be Verdi's Princess Eboli, not Gilbert and Sullivan's Katisha.

Casting Thomas Clarke as Dollabella in the original production was probably a stopgap. Dollabella is the sort of role in which Edward Kynaston specialized, but he seems to have sat out the 1677–78 season in a huff. Clarke had created Alexander's "favorite," Hephestion, in *The Rival Queens*, an interesting background for this role. Wilson finds Cardell Goodman "atrociously miscast" as Alexas, an opinion with which we would respectfully disagree. Though young, Goodman was forceful. If he was miscast, so would Barton Booth have been in 1704. Colley Cibber, who took the part in 1718, was doubtless a splendidly slimy villain, but as we have tried to suggest, that is not the only way to conceive the part.

Ventidius is routinely typecast as the rugged, honest old soldier; Dollabella, as a handsome young man—someone whose sexual rivalry Antony can legitimately fear. This brings us to the question of relative ages. Ventidius is unquestionably the oldest. Antony calls him "father," and he refers to his own age (Act I, lines 273, 395). If Serapion is nearly as old, the play is more strongly framed. If Antony is a somewhat battered thirty-eight or forty (and Ventidius about fifty) he appears to have more future than if he is circa fifty with Ventidius pushing sixty. Especially if Dollabella and Alexas are under thirty, as in the original cast, Antony's apparent age is critical. The unseen Octavius (described again and again as a "boy") plus a young Dollabella and Alexas weight the play heavily toward Time's attack on Antony. Dollabella can be played as a renegade son (Clarke in 1677) or renegade friend (Robert Wilks in 1718—in actual years older than Booth as Antony). The first production notwithstanding, Octavia might logically appear younger than Cleopatra—say twenty-seven to Cleopatra's thirty-five. In this respect Barry and Bracegirdle would be in just the right balance.

If we may indulge in the concoction of an "ideal cast," we would choose as follows: For Antony, Thomas Betterton (ca. 1690)—greater emotional variation than Charles Hart, and perhaps less tendency to overinflate the heroic side of the role. For Cleopatra, Elizabeth Bowtell—absolutely appropriate to the innocence and purity of Dryden's character. For Ventidius, Michael Mohun—more stature than John Verbruggen, more variety than John Mills. For Octavia, Anne Bracegirdle—giving Antony a genuine choice. For Dollabella, either Robert Wilks or Edward Kynaston at age forty—polished courtiers and genuine sexual rivals to Antony. For Alexas, Colley Cibber—or perhaps even better, William Mountfort, who played Friendall in *The Wives Excuse*. We want a practiced politician, a coward who is not instantly recognizable as a villain. If Alexas is too obviously a skunk, he contaminates Cleopatra by association. Ventidius' scorn notwithstanding, Alexas needs to seem plausible in the world he inhabits, even if creepy from the Roman point of view.

AIMS AND EFFECTS

Critics have tended to see the character configuration of *All for Love* as a tug-of-war with Antony in the middle (see Figure 4.6). In such a reading one might see Ventidius and Cleopatra as the good and bad angels in a misbegotten morality play that becomes a tragedy when the bad angel wins. But as we have tried to suggest in the last few pages, this reading is at best a distortion of a more complex set of interactions.

Despite the unusually tight confines of Dryden's text, critics have suggested or implied a variety of production concepts. Except for the first three, all of the following views are more or less producible.

Illustration of a moral. This reading is presumed by Everett H. Emerson, Harold E. Davis, and Ira Johnson in a denunciation of Dryden's failure to make the moral work effectively.[33] The play is distorted by such an assumption, though a production could certainly be set up to display and condemn Antony and Cleopatra. But why bother? The obvious "moral" reading is voiced by John Dennis, who finds *All for Love* "pernicious," "immoral," and "criminal," and cannot see why Antony would "turn away his . . . young, affectionate, virtuous, charming Wife . . . to take to his Bed a loose abandon'd Prostitute."[34]

Political statement. Might Dryden have been offering an ambiguous comment on Charles II via Antony? Alternatively, as

33. Everett H. Emerson, Harold E. Davis, and Ira Johnson, "Intention and Achievement in *All for Love,*" *College English,* 17 (1955), 84–87.
34. *The Critical Works of John Dennis,* ed. Edward Niles Hooker, 2 vols. (Baltimore: Johns Hopkins Univ. Press, 1939–1943), II, 163 (letter to Steele, 26 Mar. 1719).

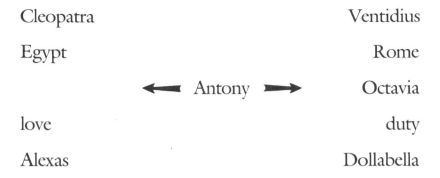

Cleopatra		Ventidius
Egypt		Rome
← Antony →		Octavia
love		duty
Alexas		Dollabella

Figure 4.6. Character configuration in *All for Love*.

Novak inquires, was Dryden "inculcating a message of libertinism and absolutism"? This question follows from Dennis' charge in 1719 that *All for Love* was designed to "square . . . exactly with the Design of *White-Hall* . . . which was by debauching the People absolutely to enslave them."[35] We agree with Novak, however, that in comparison with other Antony and Cleopatra plays, *All for Love* seems exceptionally apolitical.

Rejection of a threat to the "new order." Timothy J. Reiss reads the play as Dryden's condemnation of "a threat to . . . the order being created by Caesar."[36] This interpretation seems to us both unproducible (*what* order?) and contrary to Dryden's obvious sympathy for his protagonists.

Freudian psychodrama. R. E. Hughes sees the play as "an account of Antony's attempts to prove his manhood," his inability to choose a sign of "impotence" figuratively announced by Ventidius ("I tell thee, eunuch, she has quite unmanned him"—Act I, line 174) and symbolized in Alexas. This pop-Freudian reading seems producible if overreductive.[37]

35. Dennis, ibid. See Novak, especially pp. 378–80, for a useful discussion.
36. Timothy J. Reiss, *Tragedy and Truth* (New Haven: Yale Univ. Press, 1980), Chapter 8. Quotation from pp. 217–18.
37. R. E. Hughes, "Dryden's *All for Love*: The Sensual Dilemma," *Drama Critique*, 3, No. 2 (1960), 68–74.

Identity crisis. This reading was popularized by R. J. Kaufmann, and it makes excellent sense within the limits of Dryden's rather scanty psychological analysis.

Celebration of the passional life. The phrase is Otto Reinert's, whose reading supposes a fundamental reason/passion dichotomy in the play. Jean Hagstrum has likewise emphasized Dryden's glorification of tender and passionate love.[38] This production concept works very well, though we would caution against seeing the play as an endorsement of passion at the expense of reason.

Pathetic tale à la Dido. Carol Levine's stress on the Dido parallel gives a particular focus to the widespread assumption that Dryden was in the process of moving from heroic to pathetic tragedy. While perfectly true as far as it goes, this view does not account very fully for Antony.

Vision of mutability. This reading was proposed by Derek Hughes on the basis of a close analysis of imagery.[39] Hughes' article is valuable for its implicit refutation of Kenneth Muir's derogatory conclusions about Dryden's poetic technique.[40] All considered, however, we must agree with the rejoinder of J. Douglas Canfield, who argues that Dryden stresses mutability because it provides a setting in which the constancy of Antony and Cleopatra can be glorified.[41]

Exploration of "tragic consciousness." We borrow this phrase from Frank Kearful, who emphasizes that the focus of the play is on Antony and that the "action" of the first four acts is simply a way of letting us see his struggles to deal with an untenable position.

On the whole, our preference is for a production that displays

38. Jean H. Hagstrum, *Sex and Sensibility: Ideal and Erotic Love from Milton to Mozart* (Chicago: Univ. of Chicago Press, 1980), pp. 61–62.

39. Derek W. Hughes, "The Significance of *All for Love*," *ELH*, 37 (1970), 540–63.

40. Kenneth Muir, "The Imagery of *All for Love*," *Proceedings of the Leeds Philosophical and Literary Society*, 5 (1940), 140–47.

41. "The Jewel of Great Price: Mutability and Constancy in Dryden's *All for Love*," *ELH*, 42 (1975), 38–61. Hughes has replied, correcting Canfield on a number of matters of fact, in "Art and Life in *All for Love*" (note 26, above).

Antony's "tragic consciousness," but several of these readings are essentially compatible with Dryden's aims as we understand them.

Dryden gives us something disconcertingly different from other Antony and Cleopatra plays, and from what we might expect on the basis of his earlier work. His focus is almost entirely on Antony, and Cleopatra is anything but a femme fatale. For Dryden's Antony nothing matters but Cleopatra, and when he comes to understand this, he is ready to die. One cannot say that Antony chooses death in preference to separation from Cleopatra: he commits suicide only when he believes that she is dead. He has (he thinks) discovered her faithlessness, and he is heading off with Ventidius to be a Roman warrior when the false report of Cleopatra's death abruptly clarifies for him his true feelings and priorities. Cleopatra has tragic self-knowledge from the outset of the play; Antony gains it when he finally comes to understand himself in Act V.

The point of the play as Dryden designed it is that it must elicit both admiration and pity from the audience—hardly the objective of most plays we think of as tragedies. We must sympathize with Antony, but we know from the start that he will die: Dryden shows us Antony's fevered attempts to resist the knowledge that his position is hopeless. He can save his neck and even his position in Rome, but only by leaving Cleopatra, and this he proves incapable of doing. Antony is doomed not by his losing a battle or by the enmity of Caesar but by a passion so overwhelming that it renders everything else insignificant for him.

The great danger in any production of *All for Love* is that Antony will seem weak, too easily manipulated by others.[42] An Antony without force and heroic credibility could turn the play into an unsatisfactory pathetic tragedy. For Antony to make and quickly abandon a series of definite choices would seriously undermine his stature. We would advocate stressing Antony's manic-depressive response to his predicament: for Antony to snatch at successive

42. For a statement of this position (hereby recanted) see Hume, *Development*, pp. 203–4.

straws is entirely comprehensible, but neither he nor the audience should really believe in the viability of these possibilities for him. Starting after Actium, the play should keep us conscious of inevitable disaster, of the ending foretold by Cleopatra's long string of death-related images. Whatever production variations the director may choose to introduce, the central focus of the play is always on Antony's confused and tortured state of mind, and the audience should be steadily reminded that it is watching a terminal tragedy: all choices will turn out to be illusory.

5

The Spanish Fryar (1680)

The Spanish Fryar has gone largely unstudied, despite Dryden's own praise for it and its long success in the theatre. In truth, it is not a very literary play, and it offers few of the ambiguities and interpretive complexities that invite literary explication. Critics have tended to contemplate the split plot with dismay, the anti-Catholic smears with disdain, and the political moral with indifference. We have chosen to include the play in this book for three reasons. First, the double plot offers a special challenge in production. Second, the play serves as a particularly vivid and significant illustration of place and direction conventions as they are to be found on the late seventeenth-century stage. And third, the meaning of the play is pretty obvious. Unlike *All for Love*, for which critics have proposed a wide variety of disparate readings, *The Spanish Fryar* offers us a substantially self-evident meaning. No one doubts that Dryden was in favor of the legal succession and against libertinism. The challenge for the interpreter is to find a viable production concept that unites the apparently disparate pieces of the play.

The Spanish Fryar could certainly be given a "literal" production, in which case the comic plot serves merely as relief and variety, and the play amounts to a Tory fable with popular sugarcoating. But a production that takes the play seriously and attempts to meet Dryden's claim that he has made the plots "of a piece" must offer and communicate a view of the relationship between the two plots. We will try to show that at least two distinct production concepts meet this demand. The first we might call a "sympathetic" production, with stress on the emotions of the characters, and sin luckily prevented by thwarted intention in both plots. An alternative is an "ironic" production, in which the comic plot is used to question the values of the serious plot.

THE POSSIBILITIES OF SPLIT-PLOT TRAGICOMEDY

Dryden's predilection for split-plot tragicomedy is notorious, extending from *Secret-Love* (1667) and *Marriage A-la-Mode* (1671) to *Love Triumphant* (1694). The crucial problem for any interpreter of *The Spanish Fryar* is obvious: Why did Dryden yoke two seemingly unrelated plots? In the dedication he says, "I satisfied my own humour, which was to tack two Plays together; and to break a rule for the pleasure of variety."[1] But Dryden's fondness for the genre is hardly an explanation for his use of it.

The simplest explanation of the split-plot form is ruthlessly pragmatic: Dryden thought it would appeal to his audience. Or as he explains, "The truth is, the Audience are grown weary of continu'd melancholy Scenes: and I dare venture to prophesie, that few Tragedies except those in Verse shall succeed in this Age, if they are not lighten'd with a course of mirth." We can imagine Dryden cold-bloodedly deciding that he needed to "lighten" his Tory fable about divine protection of monarchs. And what better devices to employ than a safely abortive seduction plot and a rogue priest? Writing less than two years after the start of the Popish Plot furor, Dryden may well have regarded anti-Catholic sentiments as the ideal counterbalance for his royalist tract. If that was Dryden's thought when he put the play together, he calculated dead right. How many people noticed the Tory propaganda

1. All page references are to Volume V of *Dryden: The Dramatic Works*, ed. Montague Summers (London: Nonesuch, 1932).

142

we have no way to tell, but the play was a great success. As Downes tells us, "'twas Admirably *Acted*, and produc'd vast Profit to the Company."[2]

Without challenging this crass interpretation of Dryden's motives, we need to consider his claim that there is a serious aesthetic basis for his joining of the two plots. At the outset of the dedication he says, "When I first design'd this Play I found or thought I found somewhat so moving in the serious part of it, and so pleasant in the Comick, as might deserve a more than ordinary Care in both: Accordingly, I us'd the best of my endeavour, in the management of two Plots, so very different from each other, that it was not perhaps the Tallent of every Writer, to have made them of a piece. Neither have I attempted other Playes of the same nature, in my opinion, with the same Judgment; though with like success" (p. 119). What exactly does Dryden mean by "of a piece"? He uses the phrase again in the preface to *Don Sebastian* (1689), but with no clearer hint of its meaning. Our best guess (and it is no more than that) is that Dryden means to distinguish between split-plot plays whose object is simply variety and those in which the combination is designed to affect the impact of one or both plots. Thus *Secret-Love* seems to do little more than present a pleasant "juxtaposition of love plots in different moods,"[3] while *Don Sebastian* is much more tightly integrated in theme and effect.[4] The tone and subject matter of the two plots in *The Spanish Fryar* are glaringly dissimilar, but they do exhibit some obvious parallels. Both display violent male passion for a female; both present questions about "authority"; both turn on plots and stratagems; both discuss the justification of rebellion. What these parallels add up to, however, is not easy to say.

As a convenient way of surveying the possibilities open to Dryden, let us consider the varieties of multiple plots identified and

2. *Roscius Anglicanus*, p. 37.
3. *The Works of John Dryden*, Vol. IX, ed. John Loftis and Vinton A. Dearing (Berkeley: Univ. of California Press, 1966), 335–36.
4. For a good analysis and demonstration, see Rothstein, *Restoration Tragedy*, pp. 147–52.

analyzed by Richard Levin in Renaissance drama.[5] Table 5.1 lists and illustrates the options.[6]

Direct-contrast plots generally show us a right way/wrong way comparison in fairly unmistakable terms, as in *Rule a Wife*, *The Second Maiden's Tragedy*, and *The Changeling*. Three-level hierarchies may present such a contrast, but add to it what is often a comic level of action, and such plays tend to be less overtly judgmental. Plays with clown subplots use the low plot either as a foil to glorify the action and ethos of the upper plot (as Levin reads *Henry V*), or parodically to debase or question what is presented in the upper plot (*Dr. Faustus*). Plays comprising equivalence plots display significant common values and problems in seemingly disparate actions and characters—usually analytically more than judgmentally.

Dryden would certainly have been acquainted with all five kinds of multiplot plays. *Rule a Wife* was one of the perennial favorites on the Carolean stage, and Dryden had brought out his own adaptation of *Troilus and Cressida* in the spring of 1679—a year before he was to write *The Spanish Fryar*. About Levin's other examples there is some doubt. Marlowe's *Faustus* was a Red Bull play in the early 1660s and was in the Duke's Company's repertory in 1675; we have no performance records for *Henry V* or *The Atheist's Tragedy*. But Dryden had collaborated with Davenant on a revision of *The Tempest* (1667) in three-level hierarchy form; his *Marriage A-la-Mode* is probably best viewed as a "foil" play; and Dryden's *Secret-Love* is evidently patterned in part after his brother-in-law James Howard's parodic *All Mistaken*.[7] Dryden was unquestionably familiar with the full spread of possibilities outlined by Professor Levin.

5. Richard Levin, *The Multiple Plot in English Renaissance Drama* (Chicago: Univ. of Chicago Press, 1971). We have not found much help in Laura S. Brown, "The Divided Plot: Tragicomic Form in the Restoration," *ELH*, 47 (1980), 67–79.

6. In giving late seventeenth-century examples we have drawn freely on post-1680 plays, since our object is to illustrate types for the modern reader. Examples of the types known to Dryden are discussed below.

7. See Robert D. Hume, "Dryden, James Howard, and the Date of *All Mistaken*," *Philological Quarterly*, 51 (1972), 422–29.

Table 5.1
Varieties of Multiple Plots

Type	Renaissance Example	Late 17th-Century Example
Direct Contrast	*Rule a Wife*	*The Disappointment* (1684)
Three-level Hierarchy	*The Atheist's Tragedy*	*The Widdow Ranter* (1689)
Clown Subplot		
Foil	*Henry V*	*Oroonoko* (1695)
Parody	*Dr. Faustus*	*All Mistaken* (1665)
Equivalence Plots	*Troilus and Cressida*	*Don Sebastian* (1689)

We cannot readily conceive *The Spanish Fryar* as either a "direct contrast" or a "three-level hierarchy." The possible alternatives (beyond "no meaningful relationship") are therefore (a) foil, (b) parody, and (c) equivalence plots. We are not prepared to rule "foil" out of account, though we have difficulty in seeing how to stage the play to make it work this way. Torrismond's heroism and nobility are not enhanced by the juxtaposition of the Lorenzo-Elvira-Gomez-Dominic plot, though we can imagine that given the right production some viewers might take the play this way.

The likeliest possibilities are what Levin calls equivalence and parody plots. Abandoning his terms for our own, we would say that Dryden intended either to make the plots parallel (as an intellectual display of connections and contrasts) or to make them antagonistic (to use the low plot as ironic commentary on the high plot). Given Dryden's comment about making the plots "of a piece," we would suggest that he had parallelism in mind. Such a production would seek a not uncritical sympathy for the characters in both plots, with the exception of Dominic, who would be amusing but entirely unthreatening. Whether Dryden intended it or not, however, the low plot could be played as parodic counterpoint. There are differences enough in tone, action, and social level to let the plots function in a sharply contrastive way, and if they do, the blunt physicality of the low plot will almost inevitably deflate the heroic ethos of the upper one.

POLITICAL IMPLICATIONS IN 1680—AND LATER

Before we plunge into the specifics of the play, a historical question requires attention. How political was *The Spanish Fryar*? Dryden himself refers to it in the dedication as "a Protestant Play," a claim which seems disingenuous. Dryden's picture of Dominic is unquestionably anti-Catholic, but by 1681 "Protestant" was a Whig codeword implying support for the parliamentary move to exclude the Catholic duke of York from the succession. Some scholars (overly anxious to see Dryden as an inconsistent time-server) once read *The Spanish Fryar* as Whig propaganda, evidence of a temporary alliance that Dryden soon betrayed. This reading was demolished in 1932 by Louis Bredvold.[8] As recently as 1963, however, John Loftis was able to speak of "the change observable in Dryden's progress from satire on the Catholics in *The Spanish Friar* to defence of the King's position in the non-dramatic *Absalom and Achitophel* and the plays *The Duke of Guise* and *Albion and Albanius*."[9] Did Dryden's position change? In what sense and to what degree is *The Spanish Fryar* a political play?

In fact, the political meaning of *The Spanish Fryar* resides almost entirely in the serious plot and has nothing to do with Catholicism. As Bruce King points out in an excellent analysis of the play, Dryden presents us a fable about the evils of tampering with the legitimate succession.[10] In this respect the play is right in line with the last words of Dryden's *Troilus and Cressida* ("Then,

8. Louis I. Bredvold, "Political Aspects of Dryden's *Amboyna* and *The Spanish Fryar*," *Univ. of Michigan Studies in Language and Literature*, 8 (1932), 119–32.

9. John Loftis, *The Politics of Drama in Augustan England* (Oxford: Clarendon Press, 1963), p. 15.

10. Bruce King, *Dryden's Major Plays* (Edinburgh: Oliver and Boyd, 1966), Chapter 9.

since from homebred Factions ruine springs, / Let Subjects learn obedience to their Kings"), *Absalom and Achitophel* ("And willing Nations knew their Lawfull Lord"—line 1031), *The Medal* ("Reclin'd us on a rightfull Monarch's Breast"—line 322), and on to *The Duke of Guise*, a "parallel" play which elicited furious pamphlet denunciations from the Whigs. Dryden's characterization of Dominic may camouflage his fable, but his support for Sancho (the deposed King) and his sour view of Raymond's rebellion against authority are beyond dispute.

As first conceived and staged, *The Spanish Fryar* was unquestionably a political play. But to understand it as a political document, we need to be clear on the circumstances that engendered it. Most critics have assumed that it was premiered in February or March 1680, which has confused the issue. The correct date is circa 1 November 1680, and the difference is important.[11] If Dryden had written the play in the fall of 1679 (as Bredvold and others believed), we could assume a rather general Tory meaning, and deduce a desire to capitalize on topical events, especially the famous Pope-burning procession of November 1679. The first Exclusion Bill was introduced in May 1679, but was not regarded as much of a threat. By the spring and summer of 1680 the battle lines were very much clearer. Shaftesbury "presented" James as a popish recusant to a Grand Jury in June, and a concerted effort at exclusion was begun. The second Exclusion Bill was introduced 4 November 1680 and defeated in the Lords 15 November. Dryden's play came out right in the midst of the hullabulloo—a blunt and timely warning against rebellion and usurpation.

Dryden's political message is at least tripartite. First, in references to King Sancho he reminds us of the imprisoned Charles I —a shrewd move, since few Whigs wanted to be equated with the regicides. The parallel is remote but significant: Dryden firmly believes that a legitimate monarch should not be put aside for any reason, and that if he is, only trouble, civil instability, and danger from abroad can follow. Second, his hostile treatment of Raymond's "plot" suggests the impropriety of rebelling against

11. *The London Stage*, Part 1, p. 292.

authority even on a seemingly good pretext. And third, Dryden uses blatant satire on Dominic to dissociate the Tories from Catholicism. Or as Loftis observes, "there would have been political advantages in indicating that the Tories as well as the Whigs could be critical of Catholic duplicity."[12]

During 1681 the authorities started to get extremely nervous about anti-Catholic satire, regardless of context. Crowne's staunchly Tory *Henry the Sixth* was quietly suppressed, and Shadwell's very Whiggish *The Lancashire Witches* was cut to ribbons by the censor because of its presentation of a priest, Teague O'Divelly. By the time of the Oxford parliament and the Third Exclusion Bill (March 1681), anti-Catholic sentiment tended to be seen as Whig propaganda, context notwithstanding. But in 1680, somewhat in defiance of logic, the Tories were still loudly maintaining both their loyalty to James and their hatred of popery. Dryden must have surmised that crude satire would sit well with an audience that had flocked to see Elkanah Settle's *The Female Prelate* (June 1680). In *The Spanish Fryar* Dryden loudly reaffirms legitimacy, while firmly underlining his "Protestant" loyalty.

Dryden evidently wrote *The Spanish Fryar* as a topical partisan document, though it is not a "parallel" play like *The Duke of Guise* two years later. Its very generality, however, made it applicable in a variety of situations. We can scarcely be surprised that James II saw fit to ban the work in 1686.[13] What Dryden conceived as a pious allusion to the martyred Charles I became after 1688 a reference that could be "applied" to the exiled James II and his heirs.[14] Thus Queen Mary found herself acutely embarrassed at a command performance in May 1689. No doubt the play seemed

12. John Loftis, "Dryden's Comedies," *John Dryden*, ed. Earl Miner (London: Bell, 1972), pp. 27–57; quotation from p. 48.
13. "That y[e] play called y[e] Spanish Friar should bee noe more Acted" (PRO LC 5/147, p. 239).
14. For helpful discussion of this sort of "application" as practiced by seventeenth-century readers and audiences, see John M. Wallace, "Dryden and History: A Problem in Allegorical Reading," *ELH*, 36 (1969), 265–90, and "'Examples Are Best Precepts': Readers and Meanings in Seventeenth-Century Poetry," *Critical Inquiry*, 1 (1974), 273–90.

a safe choice, but according to a contemporary letter, "Some un-happy expressions" led the audience to identify Queen Mary with Leonora and the deposed Sancho with her father, James II, and their response "forc'd her to hold up her fan, and often look behind her, and call for her palatine and hood, and any thing she could think of."[15] As late as February 1716 a playgoer noted "most of the clappings were upon party accounts. There hap-pened to be some reflections upon the priests which the Whigs clapped extremely and the Tories made a faint hiss."[16]

The degree to which *The Spanish Fryar* was originally a party play has been insufficiently realized, probably because the anti-Catholic sentiment seems inconsistent with fervent Tory support for the duke of York. In fact, we should admire the skill with which Dryden achieved his ends. He made his point without tying himself to the sort of specific parallel that might quickly date and would certainly have inflamed the opposition. And he made his "Protestant" point without involving his rogue priest in politics. This may, in fact, have something to do with his choice of the split-plot form. To dream up a plot in which a priest served as villain and political schemer would have been easy enough, but would have tended to remind the audience of popish plots in a most unfortunate and counterproductive way, making a Whig point Dryden clearly wished to avoid. Regarded in this light, *The Spanish Fryar* is a first-rate piece of Tory propaganda, and one cleverly calculated to resist Whig objections or reinterpretation.

SCENE PLAN AND PLACE CONVENTIONS

As we have already seen in *All for Love*, Dryden has a strong sense of place-consciousness of the sort explored by Barthes in *Sur Racine*. All of Dryden's serious plays are susceptible to analy-sis of implied location, and the results can be extremely helpful in clarifying for us the nature of the oppositions and changes Dry-den presents. Dryden is not the minimalist Racine is, but he is

15. Quoted in *The London Stage*, Part 1, p. 371 (28 May 1689).
16. *The London Stage*, Part 2, I, 389.

149

exquisitely conscious of placement in relation to power, and he is demonstrably concerned to manipulate the flow of events around centers of power. Unlike Racine, Dryden shows throne rooms, and his characters can do much more than Racine's. Writing in an English tradition, Dryden presents action rather than concentrating on the analysis of "the moment of decision" that Barthes finds central in all of Racine's plays.[17] The differences notwithstanding, we should be conscious of Dryden's simple, vivid place-iconography.

Scenic requirements are straightforward, as usual with Dryden. We need a "City" setting (not specified) for Act I, with Gomez' house part of it. Presumably this is identical with "Before Gomez' door" in Act IV. Dryden specifies the "Queen's Antichamber" in Act II, with a subsequent discovery of "the Queen sitting in state" (p. 141). We need a general purpose "Chamber" that can serve for Lorenzo to meet Dominic (p. 152) and also for Elvira to occupy ("Enter . . . in her Chamber"—p. 153). Beyond this Dryden specifies the Queen's "Bed-Chamber" (pp. 159 and 184) and a "Palace-yard" for the finale. We will need to use the proscenium front for the "Street" at page 152. All this translates into a straightforward shutter plan.[18]

As we will see, the whole ideological basis of the play is grounded in the iconic opposition of palace and city.

The unspecified setting for Act I evidently shows us the "City." We can deduce that the palace is to one side (either visible, or merely in that direction); private houses of wealthy citizens are in view on the other, with Gomez' house at the "Corner." Arbitrarily, we will say that the palace is stage left (SL), Gomez' house, stage right (SR). Exits SR lead to the cathedral, to the city

17. Roland Barthes, *On Racine* (orig. French, 1960; trans. Richard Howard [New York: Hill and Wang, 1964]). For an effective contrast of the French and English traditions, see Elder Olson, *Tragedy and the Theory of Drama* (Detroit: Wayne State Univ. Press, 1961).

18. The only minor infelicity occurs at page 145, where we must move from the throne room to "A Chamber. A Table and Wine set out." The table must be carried on in full view.

2.3 City
2.2 Palace Yard
2.1 Court/Throne Room

1.3 Queen's Bed Chamber
1.2 Queen's Antechamber
1.1 A Chamber

Figure 5.1. Scene plan for *The Spanish Fryar*.

(where Lorenzo goes looking for whores), and to the city walls, beyond which the besieging Moorish army is encamped (see Fig. 5.1).

When Alphonso challenges Pedro to give the watchword (p. 127) Alphonso has come from the palace. He knows that the queen has been praying in her private chapel, while Pedro has been with the troops on the walls and has information about their morale (p. 128). Bertran comes from the palace to give orders as commander in chief—he has to ask about morale. The queen's "Procession of Priests and Choristers . . . goes over the Stage" (p. 130) from the palace toward the "cathedral" somewhere in the city. The captains who report on the battle come from the walls, as do both Lorenzo and Torrismond. Bertran intercepts Torrismond at pages 131–34 and tries to turn him away from the palace, determined to deliver good news himself. Throughout the play we will see Torrismond go back and forth from city to palace, eventually displacing Bertran there. Bertran's reacceptance in Act V is signaled by Torrismond's welcoming him back to the palace as a "Brother" (p. 200). At the end of the first scene Bertran and Alphonso both return to the palace, followed by Pedro, who will not have to spend the day fighting after all (p. 135). Lorenzo returns from the city sans whore at page 135 and watches Pedro go into the inner palace, where he will try to intercede with the queen for Torrismond. Elvira slips out of Gomez' house and calls Lorenzo from behind ("Face about, Man"). If the house door is a proscenium door with a balcony

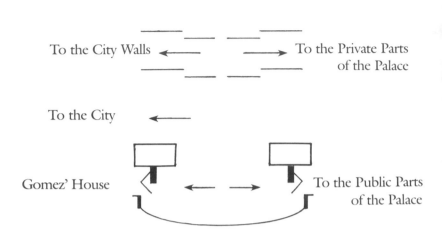

To the City Walls ⟵—   —⟶ To the Private Parts
                                          of the Palace

To the City   ⟵

Gomez' House   To the Public Parts
                                          of the Palace

Figure 5.2. Sense of direction in Act 1 of *The Spanish Fryar*.

above it, Elvira can have watched part of the preceding scene, and her duenna can be posted there to serve as lookout while her mistress flirts (pp. 135ff). Gomez evidently enters from the city way upstage—giving the duenna time to warn Elvira with a few seconds to spare for her to slip back into the house (p. 137). After talking with Lorenzo, Gomez enters his "Corner House," and Lorenzo goes off into the city.

This palace/city dichotomy should be preserved throughout the play.[19] Thus in the antechamber in Act II Bertran clearly ought to enter SL (from the inner palace); Torrismond, SR from

19. The discussion which follows focuses on the serious plot. Sense of place and direction is much less important in the comic plot, but Dryden's entrances and exits continue to fit a systematic plan. In the scenes confined to the comic plot, we would recommend treating SL as toward the street, SR as further into the house. (Gomez' house is to the left of the stage as seen by the audience; hence when we are "in" the house the street ought to be to the audience's right.) Thus, for example, in Act II Elvira should enter the "Chamber" SR from elsewhere in the house (probably through a proscenium door—p. 153). Lorenzo and Dominic enter SL (from the street, probably through a proscenium door). Dominic exits SR upstage toward a "Garden." Gomez enters SL from the street

the outside (p. 140). The mass exit at page 143 is SR; Torrismond is then called back into the queen's presence. When they part, it must be severally—the queen into her private chambers SL, Torrismond to more public places SR. The queen's "Bed-chamber" in Act III (p. 159) is a highly charged place from which to send Bertran to kill the old King, and likewise a signifi-cant place to receive Torrismond, whom the queen had hardly noticed until the previous day. Here SR exits are to public parts of the palace; SL exits to still more private chambers. In the course of this long scene (pp. 159–66) Torrismond displaces Bertran, and we need to see this happen. Both enter SR, and Bertran exits that way; but when Leonora and Torrismond agree to marry, he should lead her off SL into an inner sanctum.

In Act IV Raymond returns from his embassy and enters "The Court" with Alphonso and Pedro—SR from the outside (p. 173). The queen and Bertran enter together SL from her private apart-ments, where he has been making his report (p. 174). When she disavows the murder of Sancho and banishes him, he obviously must make his exit SR toward the "outside"—visual confirma-tion of his banishment (p. 176). If he leaves by the same door he came in, there is no meaning, no development, behind the stage movement. Alphonso and Pedro exit SR when the queen tells them to go raise the city mob (p. 178), and the queen retires SL toward her bedroom to prepare for her wedding night (p. 180). When Torrismond enters to greet Raymond, the director has a choice. Torrismond can enter SR (as might be expected) or SL—from the proscenium door—so as not to encounter the queen. If Torrismond enters SL, Raymond should probably appear visibly startled by his apparent intimacy with the usurper (p. 180). At the end of the act Raymond departs SR to work up the mob, and Torrismond goes off SL toward the queen's bedroom (upstage) to spend his wedding night with the woman he now believes is his father's murderer (p. 184).

(p. 155). Dominic reenters from the garden (SR, upstage—p. 157). Elvira is sent off SR to her "Appartment" before Gomez evicts Lorenzo and Dominic (who exit SL to the street) and follows his wife off SR.

Act V opens the next morning with Torrismond and the queen moving SL in and out of the bedroom from the inner rooms. Lorenzo enters SR to warn Torrismond that "the City Bands are up" (p. 188). He goes off SR toward the city to face the threat, followed by Torrismond. The confrontation takes place in "The Palace-yard" (p. 190). "Raymond, Alphonso, Pedro, and their Party" enter SR from the city; "Torrismond and his Party" appear "on the other Side"—i.e., SL from the inner palace. Lorenzo enters with "his Party" SR, having routed the rest of the city bands, and flanks his father's insurrectionaries. The rebels retire quietly SR to the city, leaving Raymond to argue with Torrismond and the queen (who has come out of the palace, SL).[20] Torrismond goes off SL into the palace with the queen, leaving Raymond to encounter Alphonso and Pedro, who bring Bertran's request for a "safe Conduct" (p. 196).

Gomez, Elvira, Dominic, and a crowd then enter SR from the city (we are still in the palace yard), and Gomez complains to Alphonso, who turns out to be his father-in-law (p. 196). Lorenzo enters "unseen" and overhears. We would favor having him make his previous exit into the palace, letting him notice the gathering from the proscenium balcony, and hasten out to investigate. The alternative is an unmotivated entry SR from the city.

At the end of this scene Dominic is run offstage SR by "a Rabble" (p. 200), and Torrismond, Leonora, Bertran, and Raymond rush onstage for the announcement that "King *Sancho* lives!" delivered by Torrismond. This final entry presents something of a problem. For the first time in the play Dryden's stage directions appear to violate the place convention he has been following. Torrismond and Leonora ought to be in the palace, Bertran and Raymond in the city. Dryden may simply have overeconomized here to make a quick end. Many years later he commented that "when the discovery was made that the king was living, which was the knot of the play untied; the rest is shut up in the compass

20. The director has the option of sending Lorenzo into the palace SL at this point—visibly supplanting his father, who as a beaten rebel has to go off SR toward the city.

of some few lines, because nothing then hindered the happiness of Torrismond and Leonora."[21] There is no plausible way to get Bertran and Raymond into the palace unseen, and no explanation of why Torrismond and Leonora would cross the stage to meet them and get the news so as to enter with them from SR. A director can either play over the problem on the theory that the rush of the happy ending will blot it out or alternatively can tinker slightly with the entry as described for the sake of logic and consistency. A messenger could fetch Torrismond and Leonora from the palace shortly before the end of the Gomez-Elvira-Alphonso-Dominic scene. Alternatively, a trumpet or a shout of joy from guards off SR could bring Torrismond and Leonora rushing out of the palace to meet Raymond and Bertran entering from the city.

Like Homer, even Dryden nods, though this slip presents no major problem for the director. But this small contretemps illustrates how careful Dryden generally is with locations and sense of direction. Obviously, the text does not specify such matters, but its near-perfect compatibility with "French" place assumptions is clear proof that Dryden took pains over the matter. Consistent treatment of place and direction does not happen by accident.

CHARACTERS AND CASTING

Do we accept Torrismond absolutely straight as hero? Or, put another way, does the comic plot undercut the values of the heroic plot? This is the key question for any interpreter of *The Spanish Fryar*. Critics differ. Bruce King finds no deflation of the heroic plot, despite the "ironic" reflection of the "comic subplot" on "patriarchal ideas."[22] William Myers believes that the comic plot "sharply qualifies the idealism of the main plot, especially as

---

21. "A Parallel of Poetry and Painting" (1695), *Of Dramatic Poesy and Other Critical Essays*, ed. George Watson, 2 vols. (London: Dent, 1962), II, 207.

22. Bruce King, p. 157. King believes that "the debasement of the comic characters' moral values . . . shown by their crude naturalistic and libertine assumptions" prevents any ironic deflation of the values of the heroic plot.

it is Lorenzo who finally rescues the kingdom's lawful heir, Torrismond."[23] But in fact, either view could be valid, depending on the way the play was cast and directed, and either interpretation can be supported from the text.

To understand the nature of the play's unity and the potential interconnections Dryden sets up, we must be clear on the family relationships, this being a play in which family and patriarchal obligations are of considerable importance. The character interconnections are clearest in genealogical form (see Fig. 5.3). Raymond and Alphonso are brothers, and so Torrismond and Lorenzo (the "lovers" of the two plots) are apparently cousins. Lorenzo and Elvira are brother and sister, which is vital to breaking off their intrigue when they discover the fact. The only "unattached" characters are Pedro, Bertran (originally betrothed to Leonora), and the friar, Dominic.

All signs suggest that the original 1680 production was sympathetic to the characters in both plots, presenting the heroic ethos without irony. Certainly this is what we would deduce from the original cast (see Table 5.2).[24] Some comments are in order.

Torrismond is a hero—the conquering general. He is devoted to King Sancho, whom he visits in prison (p. 163); a good son to his supposed father, Raymond (p. 180); a passionate lover. Torrismond is a life-size Almanzor, and his rhetoric is rigorously restrained. ("I remember some Verses of my own *Maximin* and *Almanzor*, which cry, Vengeance upon me for their Extravagance," Dryden admits in his dedication.) Torrismond has several high-voltage scenes—his first confrontation with the queen (pp. 143–45), his discovery that she has authorized Sancho's murder (pp. 163–66), his admission that "The Murtherer of my Father, is my Wife" (p. 183)—just before he goes to his marriage bed. Betterton would certainly have invested the role with appropriate pas-

23. William Myers, *Dryden* (London: Hutchinson Univ. Library, 1973), p. 85.
24. Table 5.2 compares the cast given in the edition of 1681 for the original production with those advertised for 13 November 1706 at the Haymarket and 9 October 1711 at Drury Lane.

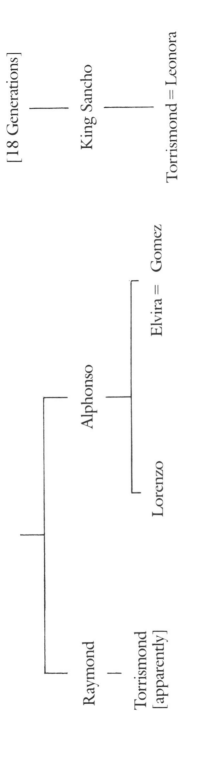

Figure 5.3. Interconnection of characters in *The Spanish Fryar*.

Table 5.2
Casts for Three Productions of
The Spanish Fryar

Role	1680	1706	1711
Torrismond	Thomas Betterton	Betterton	George Powell
Bertran	Joseph Williams	John Mills	Mills
Alphonso	John Wiltshire	?	?
Lorenzo	William Smith	Robert Wilks	Wilks
Raymond	Thomas Gillow	Theophilus Keen	John Boman
Pedro	Cave Underhill	?	George Pack
Gomez	James Nokes	Henry Norris	Norris
Dominic	Anthony Leigh	William Bullock	Richard Estcourt
Leonora	Elizabeth Barry	Barry	Frances Knight
Elvira	Mary Betterton	Anne Oldfield	Oldfield

sion and heroic dignity. It is a fine vehicle for the actor, but not one susceptible of much interpretation.

Queen Leonora's function in the plot is equally clear, but provides the performer with more variety of situations. The queen is beautiful, greatly smitten with Torrismond, and visibly unfitted to rule. She cannot be evil, but she must be sufficiently implicated in bad decisions that we are relieved to see her supplanted by the legitimate ruler. Her self-serving decision to let Bertran murder Sancho does not make terribly good sense and should be played as the result of impulse and muddled thinking. We see her inept scheming again when she authorizes Raymond to raise the city mob (p. 178). Act V relies heavily on her ability to project distress and regret. When she kneels to Torrismond (p. 187), and when she agrees to accept banishment and divorce, we need to feel enough sympathy to make us rejoice in the prospect that Sancho will pardon her and bless the marriage. The passionate Elizabeth Barry was probably ideal for the part—a much more demanding one than Torrismond because it is less monolithic.

The three older men are sharply differentiated and serve entirely separate functions. The brothers *Alphonso* and *Raymond* stand in sharp contrast. Alphonso is a soldier (p. 128), but probably more a palace guard administrator than an active campaigner. He is decent, loyal, and rather ineffectual (p. 135). He readily agrees to join his brother in seeking revenge for Sancho but can still say, "I pity *Leonora*'s case; / Forc'd, for her Safety, to commit a Crime / Which most her Soul abhors" (p. 174). Alphonso's essential unimportance in the play is reflected in the part's being given to Wiltshire in 1680 and not even being advertised in 1706 or 1711. Raymond, the dominant brother, is evidently a courtier-ambassador rather than a soldier (p. 135). He is a hardheaded power politician who manipulates people as he sees fit, easily tricking Leonora into letting him raise the city mob (pp. 177–78) and making every effort to force Torrismond to abandon and punish the queen (pp. 181–83). Raymond is Dryden's picture of a loyal and competent courtier who goes too far and determines to serve his king even against the king's will (p. 191). Dryden uses his tears of distress at Leonora's contrition (pp. 195–96) to indicate that even her principal accuser pities and forgives her. The original Raymond was Gillow, an actor of no great force or distinction.

Pedro is altogether different. Unlike Alphonso, he is a colonel who has been out with the frontline troops (p. 128). But where Raymond is a power politician and Alphonso a company man, Pedro is a sour realist, a cynic who stands back and comments sardonically on Lorenzo and Torrismond alike. He equates religion with roguery (p. 130) and courtiers with dogs. He takes a dour view of "the Arts of Court." He is a Sancho loyalist (p. 140) and gives both Alphonso and Lorenzo tough, practical advice about coping with a political crisis at court (p. 135). His view of Torrismond's great love is cutting:

> Now Plague and Pox on his Smock-loyalty!
> I hate to see a brave bold Fellow sotted,
> Made sour and sensless; turn'd to Whey by Love:
> A driveling Hero; fit for a Romance. (p. 140)

159

A few lines later he responds to Torrismond's plea for "pity" with sarcasm to the great general's face. To introduce such a character into a heroic plot is highly unusual, and we have to wonder how much air Pedro lets out of Torrismond's balloon. In the original production Pedro was played by Cave Underhill, a specialist in comic roles who would probably not have carried much satiric weight.[25]

Bertran is a difficult and thankless part. He is quintessentially the slippery court politician, a textbook general, and a self-serving intriguer—but he must not seem wholly evil, or else his preserving Sancho's life and his acceptance as a "Brother" by Torrismond (p. 200) will seem entirely implausible. He is quite smart enough to see right through the queen's plot to discredit and dispose of him (pp. 160, 163), and he can accept her denial of authorizing the murder calmly—because he has in fact not carried it out. Dryden develops Bertran almost not at all. We may infer that he would like to be royal consort but is too conscious of his own limitations to take great risks toward that end. He resents Torrismond but recognizes his own inability to compete—as general or as lover. The casting of Joseph Williams in this part is a clear hint that the audience was meant to take him seriously, and that it would not automatically have seen him as a villain. Williams took such parts as Cassio, Mellefont, the Prince of Cleve, Sebastian (in *Don Sebastian*), Amphitryon, and Polydore (in *The Orphan*). John Mills, who succeeded him in the role, likewise specialized in secondary leads and by no means in villains.

Reflecting on the characters of the heroic plot, one finds remarkably little room for variant presentation, short of travesty. Torrismond is heroic; Leonora passionate and impulsive; Alphonso colorless. Bertran could be made an obvious villain by the simple expedient of casting Samuel Sandford for the part, but to what end? The two characters susceptible of major change are Raymond and Pedro. The consistent casting of second-rank

25. Underhill took such roles as Diego in *The Adventures of Five Hours*, the coward Daredevil in *The Atheist*, the first grave digger in *Hamlet*, Feste in *Twelfth Night*, Thersites in *Troilus and Cressida*, and Wiseacre in *The London Cuckolds*.

actors as Raymond (Thomas Gillow, Theophilus Keen, John Boman) suggests a deliberate attempt to minimize the threat posed by his insurrection. Casting William Smith for the part (instead of as Lorenzo) would lend Raymond's arguments substantially more force. Even more interesting are the possibilities for Pedro. Underhill was followed in the role by George Pack, another low comedian. There is nothing in the part, however, to dictate its assignment to a comedian. Using Smith as Pedro (or at a later date the likes of Verbruggen or Booth) would entirely change the impact of his cynical observations on the court and more especially on Torrismond as lover. They would become not just a comic point of view but potentially devastating and deflationary. George McFadden comments that "the action of the serious part, and even more its characterization, is constantly undercut by the cynical, anti-heroic jibes of Pedro (a sort of honest cynic *raisonneur*)." [26] We believe that this is true if the part is cast for that sort of effect. In Underhill's hands Pedro is merely a comic alternative; with Smith or Verbruggen in the part it could significantly alter the impact of the heroic plot.

The four principals in the comic plot are all open to a wider range of interpretation. As in the heroic action, the gist of this plot is a contest between two men for a woman:

Leonora   Elvira

Torrismond △ Bertran   Lorenzo △ Gomez

In each case the woman makes the choice, opting for a mettlesome young soldier. In neither case do we have a great deal of sympathy for the fiancé/husband, though Bertran is a Machiavellian figure; Gomez, basically a comic one.

Lorenzo is a dashing young colonel, a friend and ally of his cousin Torrismond, and a would-be womanizer with some of the qualities of the "extravagant rake." [27] "Good store of Harlots, say

26. George McFadden, *Dryden the Public Writer, 1660–1685* (Princeton: Princeton Univ. Press, 1978), p. 219.

27. For discussion of rake types, see Robert Jordan, "The Extravagant Rake

you, and dog-cheap? . . . they must be had, and speedily: I've kept a tedious Fast. . . . I leave the choice to you; Fair, Black, Tall, Low: Let her but have a Nose" (p. 131). He is pleased to learn that Elvira is married (p. 137): he wants sex without complications. As played by the versatile William Smith in 1680, Lorenzo probably came across as a gay blade who had not yet settled down, rather than as a hard-bitten whoremonger. He took such roles as Pierre in *Venice Preserv'd* and Carlos in *Don Carlos*, but also such dashing libertines as Rashley in *A Fond Husband*, Ramble in *The London Cuckolds*, and Willmore in *The Rover*. He was frequently cast as "friend" to Thomas Betterton, as he is here. Wilks, who followed Smith in the role, is probably the best archetype for it—the high-spirited, attractive young scapegrace who will grow up in due course and who can be taken seriously as a soldier and friend to Torrismond. We must grant, however, that nothing in the role would prevent us from presenting Lorenzo as a debauched and unpleasant character. Played by a sneering sensualist like Cardell Goodman,[28] Lorenzo would remain a credible soldier, but his pursuit of Elvira would seem much less a game played with gusto and much more genuinely a case of a horny soldier stalking a punk into whom he could untap, to borrow Nat Lee's unlovely terminology. Lorenzo can be a Sir Harry Wildair or he can be a Woodall (in Dryden's *Mr. Limberham*).

Elvira. How Alphonso's daughter has come to marry old Gomez we are not told; presumably her father considered the match financially advantageous. She has many characteristics of the young wife anxious to cuckold an elderly and unwanted husband—like Lady Dunce in *The Souldiers Fortune* or the three wives in *The London Cuckolds*. But what she really wants is rescue: "deliver me from this Bondage . . . and I'll wander with you as

---

in Restoration Comedy," *Restoration Literature*, ed. Harold Love (London: Methuen, 1972), pp. 69–90; and Robert D. Hume, "The Myth of the Rake in 'Restoration' Comedy," *Studies in the Literary Imagination*, 10 (Spring 1977), 25–55.

28. Then a member of the King's Company and hence unavailable in 1680.

far as Earth, and Seas, and Love can carry us" (p. 154). Is she prepared to become a kept woman? Dryden does not explore the possibilities. Her husband is jealous, exacting, and impotent. (Gomez attests to her virginity, so far as he is concerned—p. 196.) She is quite prepared to steal his money and run off with a handsome soldier (p. 171)—a pretty serious business if not treated so farcically. The role was created by Mary Betterton, by this time staid and middle-aged, though she still played the occasional wanton wife (Elianor in *The Princess of Cleve*). Dryden may have cast her because of seniority, personal preference, or a desire to keep the subplot from becoming dangerously seamy. Had he wanted to play up the smut he might have turned to Charlotte Butler or to Elizabeth Currer, who was to create Aquilina in *Venice Preserv'd*.

Gomez, the old cit moneylender/husband, is one of a long series of such roles written for the great James Nokes.[29] Barnaby Brittle in *The Amorous Widow*, Sir Davy Dunce in *The Souldiers Fortune*, Doodle in *The London Cuckolds*, Peregrine Bubble in *A Fond Husband*, and Poltrot in *The Princess of Cleve* come readily to mind. Anyone familiar with his line will agree that Dryden has given him a marvelous comic vehicle—but with a difference. Gomez is nobody's fool. Amusing though he is, he displays brains and resource, and he has the best of every argument (whether his opponents realize this or not). Unlike practically all other such figures in late seventeenth-century drama he wins, remaining uncuckolded.

Dominic was plainly written both as anti-Catholic window-dressing and as a vehicle for Anthony Leigh. Downes mentions it as one of his great roles. Leigh excelled in such parts as Antonio (*Venice Preserv'd*), the homosexual pimp and voyeur Sir Jolly Jumble (*The Souldiers Fortune*), Mercury (*Amphitryon*), and Pandarus (*Troilus and Cressida*). Copies after the Kneller portrait of Leigh as the Spanish Fryar are among the best known theatrical

29. The role was later taken by Jubilee Dicky Norris and became one of his best vehicles.

illustrations of the time.[30] Dryden's choice of title and the enormous popularity of the play through the eighteenth century are sufficient indication that Dominic amused several generations of audiences, despite the grossness of the satire and his essential irrelevance to the rest of the play. Dominic serves as bribed go-between in the comic plot, but there is really no need for him to do so. The duenna could have managed the intrigue perfectly well without him. Dominic is venal, hypocritical, ready to justify either adultery or murder, and marvelously slippery. As written, the part is so much a caricature that it is hard to take seriously as satire, except perhaps by Whig fanatics in 1680. Dominic is really a comic creation, and so exuberant a sinner that he is funny rather than disgusting. Both William Bullock and Richard Estcourt (who followed Leigh in the role) probably stayed with the original concept. But could Dominic be made a Tartuffe rather than a Foigard?[31] The possibility seems real. When Betterton took the role in 1707 he probably just worked with the concept he was used to, but he had played plenty of genuine villains and would have been able to make Dominic repulsive and disturbing. To put this concept of Dominic across would require a noncomic actor; studied avoidance of the high spirits implicit in the part; a slow, cold delivery of harsh lines; and no mugging.

The characters of the comic plot are considerably more susceptible to variant presentation than are those of the heroic plot. In Lorenzo and Elvira lies the flexibility that permits a director to leave the plots essentially distinct in parallel or to swing them into ironic collision. Torrismond et alia are what they are, and how we regard them depends largely on the context in which they are presented. At this point, then, we need to consider exactly how the comic plot can be kept distinct (but not unrelated), or, alternatively, how it can be used to comment on the heroic plot.

30. One of them is reproduced opposite page 401 in Part 1 of *The London Stage*.
31. Dominic has often been linked with Falstaff—rather misleadingly, in our opinion, although their gusto has something in common. We find Farquhar's comically scoundrelly priest in *The Beaux' Stratagem* a better comparison.

PARALLEL PLOTS OR ANTAGONISTIC PLOTS?

At this time in his career Dryden was significantly influenced by both Le Bossu and Rapin.[32] Le Bossu stresses "moral fable"; Rapin is primarily concerned with "compassion" to be raised for the characters. In his "Grounds of Criticism in Tragedy" (1679) Dryden says that "the first rule which Bossu prescribes . . . is to make the moral of the work, that is, to lay down to yourself what that precept of morality shall be, which you would insinuate into the people."[33] King glosses this with the comment that Dryden does not mean a "didactic message" but rather a symbolic significance deducible from the fable. Rapin—well known to Dryden from Rymer's translation of 1674, and perhaps also from the original—emphasizes the need to create compassion and sympathy for the hero and heroine. Two very different concepts of tragedy are involved, dubbed "fabulist" and "affective" by Eric Rothstein.[34] Dryden tries to make his plays effective on both levels.

The point of the "fable" in the serious plot of *The Spanish Fryar* would be hard to miss: "let the bold Conspirator beware, / For Heaven makes Princes its peculiar Care" (p. 201). The fabulist point of the comic plot is much less explicit, but we would agree with John Loftis that one can see an "analogous" message, in that Providence thwarts intended sin and prevents incest. Bruce King seems correct, however, in saying that the "main interest" lies in "the intense emotional involvement of Torrismond with Leonora" (and, we would add, in the intrigues of the comic plot), not in the moral fable.

The serious plot presents the heroic ethos in conventionally positive terms, save for the presence of Pedro. The values of the comic plot are ambiguous. Are we seeing lively young people playing a game? Or are we watching base appetites foiled? Dryden offers no resolution of the comic plot. Has Lorenzo learned

---

32. A point well made by Bruce King.

33. "The Grounds of Criticism in Tragedy," *Of Dramatic Poesy and Other Critical Essays*, I, 248.

34. *Restoration Tragedy*, Chapter 1.

anything? Has Elvira? Her virginity might have been used to justify an annulment, but Dryden does nothing of the sort. The director has a choice at the end. He can show Elvira making eyes at
the guards in the palace yard, or he can show her resigning herself
to life with Gomez. Here the stage picture will be all-important.

Unlike some of Dryden's earlier plays, the heroic plot is not
readily susceptible to overplaying for comic effect. Torrismond's
values are never questioned. But the comic plot can be either (a) a
lively game, in which Dryden teases us with intellectual parallels
to the other plot—love, plots, rebellion, and so forth, or (b) an
ugly demonstration of human nature as it really is.

The parallel plot production

Aim: Sympathy for all characters save Dominic.
Values: The heroic ethos.
Spokesman: Torrismond.

The "sympathetic" or "parallel plot" production is relatively
simple to stage. From the original cast we would hypothesize
that it was pretty much what Dryden had in mind. In the heroic
plot Torrismond and Leonora should be presented absolutely
straight, and their emotions projected with great intensity. Pedro
is strictly comic variety, an emotional safety valve who constitutes
a foil, and whose mocking remarks about love and romance are
not to be taken seriously. As a parallel we might adduce the comic
servant Diego in Tuke's popular *The Adventures of Five Hours*, another of Underhill's roles. The comic plot could be played either
sedately and self-consciously as formula (which Smith and Mary
Betterton might well have done in 1680) or "extravagant rake"
style (as Wilks and Mrs. Oldfield probably did it in 1706).

The parallels between plots hardly need underlining. Both
Leonora and Elvira want to change their male partners. In both
plots we see rather ugly stratagems to get rid of the unwanted
man—Bertran is told to kill King Sancho and then is banished
for supposedly doing so; Gomez is abducted and then accused of
complicity in the murder. Both plots show us rebellion against
legitimate authority, and both ultimately uphold a patriarchal

view of government and society. The most obvious difference is the lack of any moral restraint in the comic plot. Torrismond is a normative figure; Lorenzo is not. The low plot is basically a game, carried on with little concern for the outcome—so much so that there is no outcome. We assume that Lorenzo will some-day settle down and achieve high rank; in this production Elvira shrugs and rejoins her husband, who is not such a bad sort. Dominic is exuberant and no serious threat to anyone.

In essence Dryden shows us the standard protagonists of both heroic tragedy and Carolean sex comedy. In this production we are allowed to be sympathetic to both sets of characters. Only at the end will the intelligent viewer realize that Dryden's conclu-sion implies a sharp differentiation. Torrismond's heroic values are endorsed, but the libertine values of the rake hero, however entertaining, are not. Only good fortune has averted accidental incest. The audience should depart well entertained, secure in its admiration for the hero, and a bit chastened by its readiness to enjoy cuckolding plots.

The antagonistic plot production

Aim: Skeptical reconsideration of the heroic code.
Values: Cynical realism.
Spokesman: Pedro.

As in the "parallel plot" production, the heroic action should be presented straight, though the actors should be instructed to shade their performance toward the stiff and artificial, for in this production we want the world of sensual appetite in the comic plot to be accepted as "reality." The principal difference between the two productions, however, lies in the comic plot, where an ironic production will present the characters much less sympa-thetically and will attempt to link them more closely with their counterparts in the upper plot. Pedro should be cast for force and conviction—a Booth, not an Underhill. The seduction plot ought to be overtly seamy, with Lorenzo a genuine debauchee (not an "extravagant rake") and Elvira clearly a scheming slut. Cardell Goodman and Elizabeth Currer would serve the needs of this production very well. The finale will leave Lorenzo entirely unpenitent ("What a delicious Harlot have I lost! Now, Pox upon me, for being so near akin to thee!"—p. 200) and Elvira looking about for a lover. The director can also choose to make Dominic as disgusting and disturbing as possible. If the hits at religion are serious, they call into question the religious and providential assumptions of the heroic plot—and we have only to put a couple of silent friars in the rejoicing crowd at the end to underline that parallel very heavily indeed.

The crux in an effective antagonistic-plot production is making the audience associate the "lovers"—Torrismond and Lorenzo. Casting and costume are essential here. The more alike the two look and act, the easier it is for the audience to compare them. Costuming is of special importance in a multiplot play, where the director may wish either to encourage or to minimize parallel drawing. Costume is always a way of pointing up identifications, discouraging unwanted associations, and clarifying distinctions, especially in an unfamiliar play.

In *The Spanish Fryar* we have four (arguably five or six) soldiers. To dress Torrismond, Lorenzo, Alphonso, and Pedro (and perhaps Bertran and Raymond) identically would cause great confusion. The older men, Pedro, Alphonso, and Raymond, can readily be distinguished by costume. We can put Pedro in a relatively simple field uniform, Alphonso in something showy and appropriate to the Palace Guard, Raymond in the dress of a diplomat/courtier. Bertran, commander-in-chief or no, should appear in court dress: he is not really a soldier, and we can visually underline that fact. (If we want to jaundice the audience's view of Raymond, we can give him a costume reminiscent of Bertran's.) Torrismond, a general rather than a colonel, could be made very showy indeed—lots of plumes. What do we do with Colonel Lorenzo? If we want to minimize comparisons and stifle ironic commentary, then Lorenzo should be dressed in an active-duty uniform remote from Torrismond's gaudy togs. But if Lorenzo is a young dandy, twinned with his cousin Torrismond, the parallels between the two lovers can become disturbingly obvious, especially if we echo the queen's clothes in Elvira's.[35] Ultimately, the key to the impact of *The Spanish Fryar* in performance is whether we use physical type and costume to associate Torrismond and Lorenzo or to keep them distinct.

Some functional ambiguities

As we read *The Spanish Fryar*, Dryden set out to make a political point, employing (a) a Tory fable demonstrating divine protection of legitimate monarchs and (b) a negative depiction of Raymond's city mob uprising. The comic plot allowed him both "variety" in response to audience preferences and a chance to ridicule a priest. In political terms, the split plot is highly advantageous, letting Dryden capitalize on anti-Catholic sentiment and demonstrate his "Protestant" loyalty while leaving the priest safely insulated from the political parts of the play.

Critical disagreement over the relationship between the two plots quickly evaporates if we admit that the play is suited to strikingly different production concepts. Staged as we suspect the work was in 1680, the play supports Torrismond's heroic ethos and comments negatively if unobtrusively on the libertine values of the comic plot. At the other extreme (in the "antagonistic plot" production) the heroic values can be made to seem artificial and unreal when juxtaposed with the raw appetite and insistent sensuality of the comic plot. But though production choices make a major difference to the play's meaning and impact, so do the predispositions of the individual viewer. Someone firmly committed to the heroic ethos (a John Evelyn) will not accept Lorenzo and Elvira as "reality," production concept notwithstanding. Likewise a cynic or a determined libertine (a Sir Charles Sedley) is not going to accept Torrismond straight and will be inclined to find ironic implications in the comic plot, regardless of the way the production is designed.

---

35. To dress the two women too similarly would be inappropriate, one being a queen and the other merely the wife of a wealthy citizen. But if their clothes are reminiscent in line and color, a point is made.

A production slanted to either extreme would certainly influence the responses of a substantial middle-of-the-road group in the audience. But canny professional playwright that he was, Dryden set up his split plot so that it can "mean" pretty much what any member of the audience wants it to. Like Farquhar in *The Beaux' Stratagem*, Dryden presents us an ending heavily dependent upon the imagination of the audience. Bruce King waxes somewhat indignant over the "arbitrary" solution of the serious plot and the nonresolution of the comic one. But to regard these features as proof that "something is basically wrong with *The Spanish Friar*"[36] asks Dryden's play to be something he never tried to make it. The "arbitrariness" is part of Dryden's "Providential" point: if Torrismond could control the outcome with "significant action" (as King demands), we could hardly see the ending as proof of divine providence. And strange though the dangling seduction plot may seem, consider the alternatives. Dryden's dislike of libertine sex comedy is well documented (*Mr. Limberham* notwithstanding), but to take an openly negative position would be to offend a significant part of the audience. Dryden lets us sympathize with the would-be adulterers until we discover that they are brother and sister. That development should leave the more thoughtful members of the audience reconsidering their facile sympathy for the lovers' tricks and schemes—but without the sort of preachment that would offend or irritate that part of the audience panting for consummation. Dryden's point about adultery is clear but exquisitely tactful. The failure of Lee's *The Princess of Cleve* two years later suggests that Dryden was a wise judge of his audience. Lee uses repulsive cuckolding games as parodic commentary on the heroic love in his serious plot, but brilliant though the play is, it did not succeed in the theatre.[37] Dryden was realist enough to let people see what they wanted to see.

By modern critical standards, *The Spanish Fryar* is a very odd piece of work, neither tragedy nor comedy. We have tried to sug-

36. King, p. 161.
37. See Robert D. Hume, "The Satiric Design of Nat. Lee's *The Princess of Cleve*," *Journal of English and Germanic Philology*, 75 (1976), 117–38.

gest, however, that both as a political document and as a theatrical vehicle it is expertly contrived to do exactly what Dryden wanted it to. In the "fabulist" terms applied by most modern critics, the two plots are insufficiently related. But if we look to the affective possibilities in performance, we arrive at a very different verdict. The play is eminently producible as either a celebration of the heroic ethos (together with an implicit repudiation of libertine comedy) or as an ironic reconsideration of the heroic drama code.

6

Venice Preserv'd (1682)

No "Restoration tragedy" had a longer or more successful
stage history than *Venice Preserv'd*. Critics, however, have
generally felt less than comfortable with Otway's play. Was it
written as a topical political piece, as John Robert Moore believes, or was it as essentially apolitical as John Harold Wilson
finds it when he calls it a pathetic vehicle for Elizabeth Barry? Jaffeir's lack of stature troubles A. H. Scouten; Aline Taylor apolo-
gizes for the "undistinguished" verse; Bonamy Dobrée admires
the political intrigue but regrets the intrusion of "unfortunate
love." Careless plotting is lamented on all sides. We know that
Venice Preserv'd was a great success in the theatre, and long remained so—but why? Wherein lay its appeal, and what sort of
impact did it have in the theatre?

Our analysis suggests that the play has four basic production
potentialities. (1) Topical political commentary: what was probably central to the original 1682 production is now completely
unrecoverable in performance. (2) Pathetic vehicle: the blood
and thunder potentialities, emphasizing Jaffeir and Belvidera, are
obvious. (3) Political manifesto: suitably cut, and with Pierre
made the lead character, *Venice Preserv'd* was turned into a liber-
tarian tract in the mid-eighteenth century. (4) Pessimistic satire:
the "bitter pessimism" remarked by Thomas B. Stroup could be
emphasized to qualify or undercut the heroic/pathetic surface of

172

the play. Our guess is that Otway's original idea was a combination of number 1 and number 4, but he provided such good material for Belvidera, Jaffeir, and Pierre that the play was quickly cut and reconceived essentially as a vehicle for emotional display by the protagonists. If, however, we take the whole text—including Antonio and the Nicky-Nacky scenes—then Otway's complex ironies are hard to ignore. To produce the play today as more than a flaming melodrama would not be easy but is by no means impossible.

POLITICAL IMPLICATIONS IN 1682

Whether or not we agree that politics are central to *Venice Preserv'd*, we can scarcely deny that the original production was seen in partisan political terms. The subtitle—*A Plot Discover'd*—invited topical interpretation. In the three and a half years since the "discovery" of the supposed "Popish Plot," England had thought of little but plots and monarchical succession. Otway's prologue is replete with unmistakable topical references—"these distracted times," "Witnesses" rotting in jail, "a Plot," "all our Swearers," a "murther'd Magistrate" (Sir Edmund Berry Godfrey), "a Traitour . . . that's very old, / Turbulent, subtle, mischievous and bold" followed by a reference to Poland which underlines the connection to Shaftesbury. That any member of the audience in 1682 would not have been looking for topical allegory is inconceivable. Moreover the first line of Otway's epilogue says, "The Text is done, and now for Application," and concludes with an overt reference to Whig opposition to the duke of York. The play's Tory appeal is well-documented. Charles II came to the third day of the initial run, and the play was attended first by the duke of York and then by his wife later that spring when they returned from exile in Scotland.[1] Dryden and Otway provided special "loyal" prologues and epilogues for the latter occasions.

---

1. See *The London Stage*, Part 1, pp. 306–9 (11 February, 21 April, 31 May 1682).

That *Venice Preserv'd* was originally seen as a Tory manifesto can hardly be doubted. Why this was so, however, is not easy to explain.

While certain identifications seem beyond question, other applications are puzzling. The earl of Shaftesbury appears both as Antonio and as Renault. But what does Bedamar's conspiracy parallel? And since Otway makes the plot corrupt and despicable, why does he make the government of Venice equally contemptible? Here is the nub of the problem. If Venice is England, then Otway appears to be attacking Charles II almost as harshly as he is attacking the Whigs. Several critics have read the play this way—"a plague on both your houses"—but such a reading seems historically implausible.[2] Any Tory who took the play as a simple parallel (Venice is Charles II's government beset by devilish Whig plots) would certainly have found it violently objectionable. In light of the play's success, we may deduce that the audience did not see *Venice Preserv'd* in these terms. It is not a "simple parallel" play of the sort we find in Southerne's *The Loyal Brother* the same spring.

The complexity of Otway's political references was recognized by John Robert Moore as early as 1928.[3] Moore noted six sorts of topical allusion. (1) Otway's extensive introduction of formal swearing, not in his source, alludes to the Popish Plot trials and parliamentary investigations. (2) Shaftesbury appears as the conspirator Renault, aged sixty-one. (3) Shaftesbury appears as the speechmaking senator, Antonio. (4) Explicit reference to contemporary politics occurs in prologue and epilogue. (5) Bedamar's conspiracy is made ineffective and unthreatening, merely a "bubble"—parallelling the Tory view of Titus Oates' alleged Popish Plot. (6) The "scornful presentation of the Senate" is

---

2. See especially Aline Mackenzie Taylor, *Next to Shakespeare: Otway's Venice Preserv'd and The Orphan and Their History on the London Stage* (1950; rpt. New York: AMS, 1966), Chapter 2; and W. Van Voris, "Tragedy through Restoration eyes: *Venice preserv'd* in its own theatre," *Hermathena*, 99 (1964), 55–65.

3. "Contemporary Satire in Otway's *Venice Preserved*," *PMLA*, 43 (1928), 166–81.

made "apparently with reference to Parliament." On all but the last point Moore seems dead right, but his misidentification of Venice and the senate has proved a most troublesome red herring.

The central problem with "direct parallel" readings is cogently stated by David Bywaters. "Since neither the senate nor the conspiracy against it is politically respectable, neither can be Tory; yet since the two factions are violently opposed, both cannot be Whig."[4] The key to this puzzle was supplied by Zera S. Fink in 1946, though he unfortunately succeeded simultaneously in obscuring as much about the conspiracy as he clarified about Venice.[5] Fink makes this vital point: Venice is Venice. If there is an English analogue, it is the City of London (a Whig stronghold run by an elective oligarchy), not England more generally. Hence there is no parallel between the corrupt government of Venice and that of Charles II. Otway offers Venice as a representation of the Whig ideal of government, a corrupt and unstable system whose introduction into England should be resisted at all costs.

In some other identifications, Fink is unconvincing. As he reads the play, the conspirators are Whigs plotting against Charles II, even though the senate cannot be equated with the English government. There are, however, difficulties with this interpretation. The original Popish Plot scare was three and a half years old at the time of the premiere, so there is some plausibility to the idea that "Whig conspiracies" were Otway's satiric target. But which conspiracies? A Whig plot might well be seen by the Tories as a genuine threat, but Otway takes a serious conspiracy from his source and reduces it to unthreatening fatuity. And second, as Bywaters asks, how are we to explain "the considerable sympathy with which Otway treats Pierre, a sympathy never accorded any member of the Venetian senate?" If the conspiracy represents a genuine Whig threat to Charles' government, then how are Jaffeir and Pierre to be allowed any sympathy and stature at all? By-

4. "Venice, Its Senate, and Its Plot in Otway's *Venice Preserv'd*," *Modern Philology*, 80 (1983), 256–63.
5. *The Classical Republicans* (Evanston: Northwestern University, 1945), esp. pp. 144–48.

waters concludes that the Venetian conspiracy is a parody of the old 1678 Popish Plot, not "actual and dangerous" but "hollow and silly, a sort of Whig nightmare."[6]

Viewed this way, *Venice Preserv'd* makes perfect sense as a political document in the context of 1682. Otway satirizes the Whig theory of government in his presentation of the corrupt and ineffectual Venetian Senate, and by presenting a comically ineffective version of the Popish Plot he ridicules the claim that the Whigs were trying to avert a real danger. There is nothing very Whiggish about the conspirators, but according to this reading they are riff-raff in cahoots with—significantly—the Spanish ambassador, who is, of course, a Catholic. The sheer silliness of the alleged Popish Plot was a point the Tories never tired of reiterating, and that is exactly what Otway chose to insist upon in *Venice Preserv'd*.

Because Otway shows us what amounts to a foreign-inspired Catholic plot against a contemptible Whig government, he is free to develop as much admiration and sympathy as he chooses for his fatally deluded protagonists. Jaffeir and Pierre can be thoroughly noble and heroic, if misguided, as long as they are not participating in what amounts to a rebellion against Charles II. Seen in this light, *Venice Preserv'd* is a clear and consistent attack on the seriousness of the Popish Plot and on the kind of government the Whigs wanted to bring to England.[7]

6. In a forthcoming study John M. Wallace argues persuasively that the conspiracy is a hostile comic depiction of the "Whig association" as the Tories perceived it in 1681–82. The proposed "Association of all his Majesty's Protestant Subjects" was designed to accomplish much the same thing as the exclusion bills. The impact is softened somewhat by the corruption of the senate, which allows Otway to grant Jaffeir and Pierre a reasonable amount of stature and sympathy. We are grateful to Professor Wallace for allowing us to see an advance copy of his article.

7. An interesting hypothesis should be noted and dismissed. In a long and carefully argued article not included in her 1950 book, Aline Mackenzie [Taylor] argues that Otway started the play in 1680 as a republican document, and later imposed an orthodox Tory outlook by adding Antonio and the Nicky-Nacky "subplot." See "*Venice Preserv'd* Reconsidered," *Tulane Studies in English*, 1 (1949), 81–118. The theory is ingenious but ultimately implausible. She starts from the premise that the play is badly flawed because Otway "equates the

THE LESSONS OF STAGE HISTORY

The original political significance of *Venice Preserv'd* became a dead issue in 1685. The play's long popularity must therefore derive from other kinds of appeal, and we can learn a good deal about it from its eighteenth- and nineteenth-century productions, a subject on which we are much indebted to Aline Mackenzie Taylor's researches in *Next to Shakespeare*. Taylor speaks of "the chameleon-like quality of the fable" when she calls attention to the remarkable diversity of the major interpretations. "That the same play should be received at one time as a manifesto of monarchists and at another time as a manifesto of republicans is a phenomenon of stage history which suggests an ambivalence in the structure of the play."[8] True, though between about 1700 and 1895 nothing like the full text of 1682 was ever performed, a point we should remember when analyzing celebrated eighteenth-century interpretations. Between 1682 and 1805, we find six distinctive concepts of the play on the London stage.

1. The Tory manifesto of 1682. The essence of this production is described in the discussion of "Political Implications in 1682," above. Without contemporary commentary, we are merely guessing about the rest of this interpretation, but simple logic and some knowledge of the original cast give us plausible conjectures. Heavy emphasis must have been laid on ridicule of Shaftesbury via Antonio and Renault. Betterton was presumably a strong and dignified Jaffeir, neither a ranter nor a sighing lover. Mrs. Barry's Belvidera would have provided an active and fascinating heroine to unseat his judgment. Smith's Pierre would probably have been a genuine if misguided friend, played with elegance and dash. This production seems to have featured a Jaffeir drawn blindly into an evil conspiracy from which he proved unable to salvage either his friend or himself. The audience would have been in-

---

conspirators . . . with the government they seek to overthrow." But as we have seen, this is a misreading, and hence there is no reason to hypothesize that Otway underwent "a political *volte-face*" requiring him to abandon a design that glorified the conspirators.

8. *Next to Shakespeare*, p. 144; "*Venice Preserv'd* Reconsidered," p. 81.

vited to lament his fate (and Belvidera's) while deploring both the conspiracy and the government of Venice.

The second and third production concepts treat the play as a showcase for different Jaffeirs. We have no definite evidence of revival until Gildon's comment in 1699: "an incomparable Play, and often acted of late Days."[9] At what point the Nicky-Nacky scenes were dropped we do not know, but in 1718 Gildon says that the "miserable Farce *under Plot* . . . has been left out [in performance] for many Years."[10] Aquilina was still part of the play in June 1703,[11] but as Genest observes, her name is nowhere to be found in the eighteenth-century bills.[12] Dropping the "under Plot" expunges much of the malaise and dirt, and the three principal characters loom even larger in what remains.

2. A vehicle for the plaintive Jaffeir. By 1707 Robert Wilks was playing Jaffeir. We have little specific commentary on Wilks' concept of the role (though it was highly praised), but Taylor's hypothesis about it is persuasive. We may guess that Wilks "brought out the amorous pathetic quality of Jaffeir as the more robust Betterton would not have done."[13] Wilks' strength in tragedy was "manly sorrow," tenderness, and resignation. Opposite Mrs. Barry's forceful Belvidera, Wilks probably would have been wise to avoid direct competition by sounding "the plaintive note in the role," in Taylor's words. Conceived this way, the play becomes a showcase for the pathetic dolors of a hero bewitched by love and unluckily ensnared in a doomed conspiracy.

3. A vehicle for the violent Jaffeir. When Barton Booth took over the role in 1713, he almost certainly rethought it. As Taylor

9. Charles Gildon, *The Lives and Characters of the English Dramatick Poets* (London: Leigh and Turner, [1699]), p. 108. Unfortunately, Gildon does not specify which company—Drury Lane or Lincoln's Inn Fields. Betterton, Verbruggen, and George Powell could all have played Jaffeir in the nineties.

10. Charles Gildon, *The Complete Art of Poetry*, 2 vols. (London: Charles Rivington, 1718), I, 237.

11. A manuscript cast in the British Library copy, 841.c.8(3), lists Mrs. Boman as Aquilina for a performance in June 1703.

12. Genest, III, 138. On a command performance of the complete text ca. 1716 ordered by the Prince of Wales, see Taylor, *Next to Shakespeare*, p. 148n.

13. Taylor, *Next to Shakespeare*, pp. 151–52.

observes, "plaintive distress was not his forte"; his penchant was "for the more violent passions of tragedy." Writing in *The Prompter* (20 June 1735), Aaron Hill describes "Violences," "Starts," and "Frenzies" in Booth's Jaffeir. Approached this way, the play displays the stormy emotions of an idealistic but impractical man swept into a disastrous plot by blind trust in an equally befuddled friend and destroyed by circumstances beyond his control. In this production Belvidera was evidently a sounding board: her principal function was to react sympathetically to Jaffeir. Thomas Davies reports that Booth found an ideal match in his Belvidera, Mary Porter. David Garrick seems to have carried on the Booth tradition: his Jaffeir expressed agonizing conflicts and radical transitions of mood, put across with electrifying energy.

4. A vehicle for Pierre as republican idealist. The Lincoln's Inn Fields production of *Venice Preserv'd* was first mounted in 1721, but was not competitive with Drury Lane's until the end of the decade when Booth retired. Lacy Ryan was a "soft" Jaffeir in the style of Wilks; Belvidera (various actresses, principally Mrs. Seymour and Hannah Pritchard) seems to have stressed dignity more than pathos. The mainstay of this production was James Quin as Pierre—a characterization which became so popular that David Garrick could not compete with him in the role when he tried it in 1742. Quin made Pierre the "first part," interpreting him as the hero of the play. Quin's Pierre was a patriot fired by genuine opposition to corrupt government, not merely by personal grievance or revenge. Whatever the audience might think of the Jacobites, in the 1730s and early 1740s any opponent of Walpole could see the senate as his government, and Pierre as a noble opponent of corruption. Of course this drastic reinterpretation was made possible by cutting: Pierre can be a noble hero only if the Nicky-Nacky scenes are gone, and preferably Aquilina with them. A Pierre bent on avenging the loss of a Greek courtesan to a sleazy masochist and foot fetishist does not qualify as a Tory hero.

5. A vehicle for Pierre as cynical traitor or stage villain. The opposite to Quin's noble but misguided patriot was Pierre as

tempter and villain. Henry Mossop seems to have been the first actor to play him this way. Taylor paraphrases John Hill's description of 1755: "a cynical traitor of force and understanding" who successfully seduced Jaffeir to treason. Mossop can hardly have made Pierre the center of attention against Garrick's Jaffeir, but his interpretation was picked up by a number of actors who made Pierre the principal character, notably William Barrymore (a specialist in stage villains), George Frederick Cooke in 1802, and J. P. Kemble in 1805. The impetus for the later evil Pierres was undoubtedly the fiasco of 1795, when Robert Bensley's revolutionary fervor attracted such enthusiastic support that *Venice Preserv'd* was banned for sedition. Kemble's deep-dyed Machiavellian villain was certainly the safest way to present Pierre in politically troubled times.

6. A pathetic vehicle for Belvidera. Many productions must have made much of Belvidera's woes, probably starting with the first. One can hardly imagine Elizabeth Barry failing to pull out all the stops. By all accounts Susanna Cibber's delicate and adoring Belvidera made the perfect complement to Garrick's stormy Jaffeir, and we may be sure that it was calculated to "Call Tears of Pity from the melting Heart," in the words of George Keate's poem to her memory. But only with the appearance of Sarah Siddons as Belvidera in 1782 did the role come to outweigh both Jaffeir and Pierre. Extensive descriptions of this celebrated characterization make plain that she brought a self-centered vehemence to the part quite different from the eighteenth-century norm. Physical violence, stridency, despair, shrieks—such were the features of her performance. Earlier Belvideras worked from the assumption that she was an innocent bystander dragged down in general ruin. Siddons adopted the idea that she was the cause of the whole catastrophe, and her mad scene (played at hysteric pitch) reflected her sense of responsibility and despair. The text does not say this, but it is a valid production concept, and by numerous accounts it seared itself in the memories of shocked and sympathetic audiences.

From this survey we learn that the play's innate potentialities allowed radically divergent production concepts within the limits

of a text free of the original political context and shorn of the
"under Plot." Few plays have three parts equally capable of domi-
nating and redirecting the whole show, but *Venice Preserv'd* does.
Otway is unlikely to have foreseen Pierre the republican hero,
and given his political purposes he had no need of a villainous
Pierre. But bearing in mind the widely divergent potentialities
of the three principal parts, we need now to inquire what con-
straints the Nicky-Nacky scenes would impose, and how the principals might best be balanced and set off against one another.

CRUXES AND KEY SCENES

Venice Preserv'd shows us the agony of Jaffeir and Belvidera
caught in a hostile and degraded world. Emphasizing their torment gives us a pathetic production; emphasizing the Venetian
world moves a production toward pessimistic satire. The director
needs to find motivations for the characters that are consistent
with one view or the other. The plot is no problem, since the
structure of events, act by act, is simplicity itself.

I   Jaffeir, broke, is refused help by Priuli.
II   Jaffeir joins the conspiracy.
III   Jaffeir becomes disillusioned with the conspiracy.
IV   Jaffeir betrays the conspiracy.
V   Catastrophe ensues.

The searing passions of Jaffeir and Belvidera must certainly loom
large in any production, and they offer splendid opportunities
for performers ready to indulge in extravagant emotional display.
But why does the tragedy happen? And how uncritically are we
to sympathize? Otway does not give us explicit answers to either
question. As Dryden justly observes, "the passions are truly
touched" in *Venice Preserv'd*, "though perhaps there is somewhat
to be desired . . . in the grounds of them."[14] The grounds will
bear investigation: they have to be decided on to control a
production.

14. "A Parallel Between Poetry and Painting," *Of Dramatic Poesy and Other
Critical Essays*, ed. George Watson, 2 vols. (London: Dent, 1962), II, 201.

The basis of the tragedy. What causes the events of the play? (a) Priuli's hard-heartedness? (b) A reckless elopement? (c) Jaffeir's prodigal inability to live within his means? (d) Jaffeir's bad judgment in joining the conspiracy? (e) A false (or deluded) friend who involves Jaffeir in ruin? (f) A corrupt society in which Jaffeir is a helpless victim?

Once Jaffeir has joined the conspiracy, he feels torn between his obligations to Pierre and his obligations to Belvidera. The play has, therefore, often been treated as an embodiment of the love versus honor dilemma central to so many of the rhymed heroic plays of the 1660s and 1670s. Eugene Waith reads the play this way. "The tragedy is finally a personal one [i.e., not political or social], in which the lives of the three chief characters are destroyed by conflicting loyalties. Otway is extraordinarily adroit in the management of Jaffeir's dilemma, balancing Belvidera . . . against Pierre, as the spokesmen for order and revolution, respectively, and the embodiments of love and friendship."[15] Jaffeir is certainly torn between the claims of friend and wife. But he is not simply a latter-day Orrery protagonist, weighing the niceties of two valid ethical obligations. The conspiracy is foul, and Pierre is far from lily-white. And while our attention is largely taken up with Jaffeir's immediate problems, Otway is at pains to see that we ask ourselves how he got into this mess.

Jaffeir certainly believes that Priuli has driven him to rash action, and the lines with which Priuli ends the play ("Sparing no Tears when you this Tale relate, / But bid all Cruel Fathers dread my Fate.") suggest that he ultimately blames himself. But Otway is not just giving us a tidy little moral about parental obduracy, and this play does not reduce to the usual formulas. Unlike Maximin, Jaffeir does not succumb to ambition or temptation; he is not an Alcibiades; he is not, like Don Carlos, a victim of intrigue; and nor is he, like Castalio in *The Orphan*, a victim of unlucky circumstance. We are not shown the folly of Lear, the ambition of Macbeth, the flawed character of Dryden's Antony, or the

15. Eugene M. Waith, *Ideas of Greatness: Heroic Drama in England* (New York: Barnes & Noble, 1971), p. 251.

182

hubris of Dryden and Lee's Oedipus. Otway does not give us a neat explanation of why this tragedy must happen—a crux in any analysis.

The impact of the opening scene. Jaffeir would presumably not appeal to Priuli for help unless he were desperate. Three years have passed since the elopement,[16] but Priuli does not know he has a grandson. His sneering advice ("Home and be humble, study to retrench . . . Get Brats and Starve"—p. 207) consigns Jaffeir to penury. Is Priuli harsh and intractable, or hurt and pained? Is Jaffeir arrogant and demanding, or pleading and expostulatory? Is Jaffeir shabby and humbled? Or is he (as Garrick played him) gorgeously dressed, a foolish spendthrift? This scene is crucial in establishing our sense of responsibility for subsequent events, and Otway gives us plenty of negative information about both men. Priuli is rigidly unforgiving; Jaffeir has recklessly eloped and lived far beyond his means. Priuli wants to punish Belvidera for eloping; he even claims he would be pleased to see her weep "in bitterness of want." Priuli is trying to deny his love for his daughter: "Once she was dear indeed . . . But she is gone, and if I am a man I will forget her." Jaffeir's response is terribly revealing: "Would I were in my Grave" (p. 207). Jaffeir is unable to cope with the situation, and is already voicing a death wish. He is too proud to keep Belvidera in less state than she enjoyed with her father: competition for Belvidera between Priuli and Jaffeir is quite explicit. A director could make Jaffeir seem more sinned against than sinning (a sincere plea on Belvidera's behalf is contemptuously refused), or could make him an improvident wastrel dumbfounded to discover that Priuli will not respond to a demand for help.

Jaffeir's friendship with Pierre. Refused by Priuli, Jaffeir meets Pierre, who tells him that bailiffs have turned Belvidera into the street. Their responses to poverty and misfortune are tellingly different. Jaffeir weeps ("I play the Boy, and blubber in thy bosome"); Pierre is all for action ("First burn, and Level *Venice* to

16. See *The Works of Thomas Otway*, ed. J. C. Ghosh, 2 vols. (Oxford: Clarendon Press, 1932), II, 206. All references will be to this edition.

thy Ruin!"). Overwrought, Jaffeir is easily persuaded to consider "revenge" against Priuli (pp. 212–13). When he then encounters Belvidera, her distress and her devotion to him throw Jaffeir into fits. Their highflown emotional scene is followed at the beginning of Act II by one between Pierre and Aquilina. Otway is making a point: both Jaffeir and Pierre are in great distress over a woman because of money—but Pierre's "love" is a courtesan.

How well do Jaffeir and Pierre know each other? In Act I the conspiracy is only two days away from overt rebellion, but Pierre has not even sounded "the honest Partner of my Heart" (p. 207) on the subject. Pierre twice implies that their closeness is recent, dating since Jaffeir's marriage (pp. 259, 262–63). Are they really bosom friends? Pierre even has to tell Jaffeir about his censure by the senate (pp. 209–10). Why does Pierre want Jaffeir to join the conspiracy? He quite consciously sets out to recruit his "friend" ("Sure I have stay'd too long . . . I may lose my Proselyte"— p. 218). Late in Act IV Jaffeir refers to Pierre as "my father, friend, preserver" (p. 263). Are they on an equal footing? Does age or experience give Pierre a natural dominance?

If Pierre is a villain, then he may be inveigling Jaffeir into ruin, which would make Jaffeir's concern with the code of friendship an ugly irony. The midnight scene in which Pierre persuades Jaffeir to join the conspiracy is explicitly treated as a temptation. "No Minister of Darkness cares to Tempt me. / Hell! Hell! why sleepest thou? . . . I but half wisht / To see the Devil, and he's here already." Pierre gives Jaffeir money ("here's something to buy Pins"), and his response confirms the *topos*: "What must this buy, Rebellion, Murder, Treason? / Tell me which way I must be damn'd for this" (pp. 218–19). Jaffeir half understands that desperation is driving him to folly. Nonetheless, fine words about "Liberty," a chance at "revenge," and the lure of having his "sequestred Fortunes heal'd again" (p. 221) draw him into the conspiracy.

Jaffeir takes the claims of friendship with enormous seriousness. For us to respond sympathetically to Jaffeir's love versus honor conflict, Pierre must be a true if misguided friend, not a villain. One might play Pierre as so fired by his own resentments that he ignores the true nature of the conspirators. The first time Jaffeir sees them he is overwrought, and they are presumably alarmed about being recognized. Hence when a stranger appears they probably move back and cover up, and they soon depart (p. 227). The second time Jaffeir sees the group they have no reason to hide themselves—and of course the attempted rape has given Jaffeir a different outlook. What do the conspirators look like? Are they ugly scoundrels? desperate scum? However portrayed, they plainly horrify Jaffeir when he sees them in Act III. Pierre, in sharp contrast, continues to identify with them. Is he deeply deluded? Pierre can be a self-serving villain, in which case Jaffeir is fearfully misguided in treating the obligations of friendship as binding. Or Pierre may be sincere and self-deluded, a man who "confuses personal injury . . . with universal justice."[17] In the one case Otway may be showing us the folly of living by a heroic code in a fallen world; in the other we can endorse the code, even though it leads to catastrophe. A production needs to take a stand on this point. Heroic friendship is either a transcendental virtue or utter folly. In the world of Otway's *Don Carlos* it is the former; in the world of his *Friendship in Fashion*, the latter.[18] And Venice as presented here seems an unpromising venue for heroism.

Point of view. By what standards are we to judge the characters and events? Otway gives us singularly little help in this respect, which is decidedly uncharacteristic of late seventeenth-century tragedies. No one is in any doubt about how to judge the events of *All for Love*, or *The Rival Queens*, or *Don Sebastian*. Aline Taylor comments that "For the modern reader, the first great difficulty lies in finding a point of view from which the principal characters may be seen in just perspective against the background of the Spanish conspiracy and the Venetian Republic."[19] Indeed, we may wonder whether Otway establishes point of view in such

17. See A. H. Scouten's analysis in *The Revels History of Drama in English*, Vol. V (London: Methuen, 1976), pp. 274–75.

18. See Robert D. Hume, "Otway and the Comic Muse," *Studies in Philology*, 73 (1976), 87–116.

19. Taylor, *Next to Shakespeare*, p. 40.

a way that we can have any confidence in our judgment of what he presents us. Eric Rothstein suggests that the whole play is a projection of Jaffeir's point of view.

> Our perceptions of [the conspirators'] actions cannot be divorced from Jaffeir's state at the moment: all actions in the play are functions, in a quasi-mathematical sense, of Jaffeir's suffering. The conspirators must be unpalatable in Act III, gallant in Act V, because their virtue and vice are contingent, not absolute. . . . When Jaffeir's world writhes in hostility about him, a new reciprocity has arisen in which world and character seem to shape each other and generic patterns seem to have faded before more lifelike and less univocal kinds of order. In one sense, of course, the environment of the pathetic hero is very much like that of his heroic counterpart, for it is designed to show off the captivating prowess of the hero. His feelings are fanned out like a peacock's tail.[20]

"The pathetic world," says Rothstein, shows itself "singly from the hero's point of view." "Empathy makes public the hero's subjectivity, and becomes a principle of form." This is certainly a stageable concept; it is one way of conceiving the sort of pathetic production discussed below. But Rothstein does not claim—and we would not agree if he did—that this view is built ineluctably into the text.

Any political or satiric production, in our view, would tend to push the audience toward an attempt to settle the problem of point of view, if only to try to decide what is "right." As Taylor asks, "are one's sympathies to lie with the bloodthirsty conspirators whom Jaffeir and Pierre join, or with the perfidious senate that Belvidera saves?"[21] Her answer is that "the plot . . . is so contrived that the audience's ill wishes for both the senate and the conspiracy sway back and forth with the alternate triumph of love or friendship or filial affection." This is an ingenious idea, but hard to conceive in theatrical practice. In performance our attention will be primarily on the three principals, and we must either

20. Rothstein, *Restoration Tragedy*, pp. 103–4.
21. Taylor, *Next to Shakespeare*, p. 41. Following quotation from p. 59. Taylor uses the spelling "Jaffier" throughout. We have silently corrected to the standard form.

sympathize with them, or evaluate them more critically. We see little ground for "alternation" of ill will. Since we cannot sympathize with either conspiracy or senate, we are left with the possibility of identifying with Jaffeir's "heroic" ethos—upholding a code in the midst of evil. The director then has a choice. Personal merit can be upheld and glorified (though unfortunate). Alternatively, the corruption of society can render personal good ineffectual.

The key to any production must rest on the director's decision about point of view. And we must emphasize that it is the director's decision: the play itself does not force values and judgments upon us.[22] This is, obviously, why it has been amenable to such a wide variety of production concepts. One can scarcely imagine legitimate productions of *Aureng-Zebe* or *Don Sebastian* as remote from each other as those *Venice Preserv'd* has spawned. For the twentieth-century critic, the obvious possibilities are mostly pathetic. But as we will show in our discussion of pessimistic satire, the play's lack of an ideological center makes it peculiarly suitable to more subtle and subversive production concepts.

PATHETIC VEHICLE

A pathetic production must concentrate our attention on the psychological torments of Jaffeir and Belvidera in an impossible situation, not invite us to ask how Jaffeir got there, or stimulate any real curiosity about the world of Venice. For obvious reasons Priuli is to be made harsh and Pierre noble. Good and evil are clearly differentiated in this production. The obligations of friendship are vitally important, and to honor them is admirable. The leaders of the conspiracy (Bedamar and Renault) are self-serving villains, but most of the conspirators are misguided idealists, which makes it easy for us to admire their stoic heroism in Act V. The senate is imperfect, but Antonio notwithstanding, it is no more corrupt than most governments. Unlike the satiric

---

22. For an essentially abstract and literary reading which treats "Nature" as a touchstone value for the play, see Ronald Berman, "Nature in *Venice Preserv'd*," *ELH*, 36 (1969), 529–43.

production to be discussed in the next section, this one plays over various chances to bring authority into question. The pathetic production is a showcase for the emotions of the protagonists.[23]

The most effective way of outlining the two productions we envision is simply to describe the principals as we would cast them, adding enough psychological analysis that the actor would know "who" he or she really was. Obviously, we are not just reading the text; rather, we are reading into the text a set of characterizations that we believe are consistent with each production concept of it. The results are a somewhat formalized version of the instructions a director might give performers when the text does not make explicit either motivation or designed effect.

Jaffeir is about twenty-five, an attractive, privileged young man whose idealism is real but who has never had to work for a living. He has always gotten (or taken) what he wanted, not out of greed, but out of unwitting selfishness. He is handsome, innocently fresh-faced, and middle-sized. He wears clothes that were expensive and well-tailored when new but now show three years of wear. His shoes are soft-soled: unlike Pierre, he has not led a life in which boots are necessary. In modern terms, we might say that his games are golf and doubles tennis.

Jaffeir enjoys the idea that he is protecting Belvidera. He wants to believe he can provide for her, does not tell her his plans, does not let her know the full extent of his troubles. He is given to exaggerated posing and inflated language as friend, husband, and conspirator. None of his rhetoric is very real to him when the play begins, but it gains reality for him (and for us) as the play proceeds, until it becomes genuinely horrifying. Jaffeir thinks quickly only in predictable patterns; outside them he thinks slowly and uncertainly. He accepts the conspiracy on Pierre's word, and then has trouble assimilating the corruption he stumbles into. Unable to cope with the situation in which he finds himself, he escapes all conflicts and practical problems by returning to Idealism to die. His suicide affirms the heroic code by

23. For an odd, largely unstageable, antiemotional interpretation, the curious reader can consult Bessie Proffitt, "Religious Symbolism in Otway's *Venice Preserv'd*," *Papers on Language and Literature*, 7 (1971), 26–37.

demonstrating that resistance to corruption is possible. He never doubts that Priuli will look after Belvidera, and he has no idea that his abandonment of her will drive her to madness and death. He is guilty of her death, but had not intended to cause it. We accept him finally as an idealistic man destroyed by circumstances beyond his control who makes what affirmation he can by upholding the claims of friendship and the heroic ethos.

Belvidera is about twenty (having been seventeen when she eloped), fragile but resilient. Child-bearing has not affected her figure. She is unconscious of her physical appeal, though she chooses flattering clothes. She dresses expensively but not revealingly or assertively: classic lines, conservative colors, rare fabrics. (What attracts Renault is her vulnerability, not her body, her class, or her manner.) Belvidera thinks little and does not try to analyze or predict. She reacts submissively, lets Jaffeir speak first; and blames herself for anything he does not like. She accepts his orders and reproaches; ignorance of his affairs is normal for her. She and Jaffeir never quarrel, because she always gives in. Belvidera has substituted husband for father as authority figure. When she uses a quasi-incestuous ploy to soften Priuli (pp. 270–73), she does so by instinct, not as a deliberate manipulative choice. This Belvidera listens more than she responds. The actress should perfect the timing of a few simple reactions: she can let herself go only when responding to rejection and abandonment. Belvidera has committed herself totally to Jaffeir, and all her responses are keyed to him.

Pierre is about the same age as Jaffeir, but is from a less privileged background. Unlike Jaffeir, he has always had to work, and lack of recognition for his military service turns him violently against the status quo. He is genuinely an idealist, though much misled about the conspiracy. (He can rally the other conspirators against Renault in Act III because most of them are, like Pierre, bruised young idealists.) He is physically impressive (though not enormous), and used to enforcing his decisions with his size. His games are rugby (a team sport with plenty of contact) and pool. He is wearing shabby civilian clothes, and unlike Jaffeir he wears boots—he rides and walks a lot on business. Again unlike Jaffeir,

Pierre does little posing and orating: he says much less because he does much more. Aquilina is a recreation, not a great love. Pierre lives out an uncomplicated code of friendship and honor (ranking far above love in his life). Faced with a felon's death all too vividly horrible in his imagination, he has no plan except to send for Jaffeir. Once reconciled, they see their way out almost simultaneously and need not discuss it. Glorious death in each other's arms is the climax of the play: in this production Belvidera is a pathetic coda.

Priuli is fifty or more, a rich man probably self-made and certainly not more than the second generation with money. He dresses well, but not excessively so (expensive off-the-rack suits, not bespoke, in modern terms). He is not evil, but he is a pigheaded man with obvious high blood pressure. Having transfered all his emotional attachment from dead wife to young daughter, he reacts harshly and excessively to her elopement. We may guess that he always overprotected his only child because he was well aware of the corruption all around him. Priuli is a hardheaded realist. He and Jaffeir are much alike in their attitudes toward women and the use of money, though Priuli has worked for his money and has practical knowledge Jaffeir lacks. If he had accepted Jaffeir as son-in-law he could have taught him a lot. Priuli's game is poker, and he wins at it. Unlike almost all the other characters, Priuli has learned something by the end of the play— a fact underlined by his both opening and closing it.

Antonio is sixty-one years old, visibly senile, fat, overdressed, perhaps wearing a toupé. He is used to being obeyed, and as a senator still visibly retains some power. As occasionally happens to senators and congressmen today, he has lost control of his sexual appetites: we know what games he plays. He is a loser at poker, though still a dangerous nuisance in the senate. His function in this production is gross comic relief and contrast. He represents a sordid world transcended by the heroic ethos.

Renault is a malcontent of forty or forty-five, obviously a selfseeker rather than a befuddled idealist. His ambition has been long frustrated, perhaps because he lacks the discipline to resist irrelevancies like Belvidera.

Bedamar must be visibly foreign and old enough (forty-five to fifty) to be a thoroughly experienced intriguer. As ambassador and ringleader, he should be unmistakably well-to-do, a cagey character who knows just how to play on the sympathies of the young idealists he is manipulating. To make anything of his escape from the fate of the rest would be an error. In this production, it would simply distract attention from the protagonists.

The Duke is a veteran power politician, perhaps fifty, and much like Priuli; authoritative; neither handsome nor ugly; no better or worse than one might expect of a man successful in the harsh world of Venice.

Aquilina is recognizably foreign (Greek rather than Spanish like Bedamar). Skin color, dress, and accented English should set her off from everyone else. She is not a hard-bitten slum kid, but a woman of decent background who has had to cope with an unexpected comedown. Part of her bond with Pierre is the degradation they have both experienced. Unlike Belvidera (who would have died immediately of mortification in such circumstances) Aquilina is a survivor. She is toughminded and a quick thinker. Though she does not like what she has to do, she is not much corrupted by it. She is twenty-two or twenty-three, decidedly good-looking and aware of it, revealingly but not tastelessly dressed. (She is an expensive courtesan, not a streetwalker.) She has been foolish enough to fall in love with Pierre, but not to the point of refusing Antonio's business. We may imagine that she will grow up like Shaw's Mrs. Warren. With any luck, she will prevail over her present condition.

What are we left with at the end? Jaffeir and Pierre have stuck to their code; poor Belvidera necessarily goes mad and expires; Priuli recognizes his mistake too late. As "tragedy" this is more than a bit suspect: the "grounds" are flimsy. But given the opportunity to sympathize freely with Jaffeir and Belvidera, the audience should leave well wrung-out emotionally. We should, however, understand that Otway is not trying to pull a John Banks on us, and even a deliberately pathetic production needs to make this distinction. Otway does not, for example, introduce Jaffeir and Belvidera's child on stage (an omission noted with some scorn by

191

Clifford Leech). Nor are we given a family reconciliation just before the Act V catastrophe. Belvidera persuades Priuli to try to save the conspirators (pp. 272–73), but neither then nor later (p. 281) does Otway have Priuli indulge in the "all is forgiven" bathetics that Banks or Rowe would have supplied in full measure. We may fairly say that *Venice Preserv'd* is abundantly provided with pathetic potentialities, but in contrast to *The Orphan*, for example, it is essentially a psychological rather than a pathetic play.

PESSIMISTIC SATIRE

Critics of *Venice Preserv'd* tend to fall into sharply distinct categories. There are those who condemn it for sentiment, poetic flatness, and its failure to provide purgation and restoration of moral order (Leech, Dobrée, Prior).[24] Some try to find satisfactory resolution and order in the heroic code affirmed by Jaffeir's suicide (notably Hauser).[25] Others regard the pathetic (or "sentimental") elements as the basis of an effective play, if not of a "tragedy" in the Shakespearean sense (notably Rothstein). But a number of critics have also found unsettling elements in the play, elements that significantly undermine any ordinary sense of the play as a tragedy. William McBurney has commented at length on the play's "pervasive erotic element," "insistent physicality," and concomitant "misanthropy and disillusion."[26] Derek Hughes finds that the play "questions Restoration heroic ideals by suggesting that they are both generated and belied by the animal and primitive aspects of human nature. . . . Reason is powerless in the face of physical impulse." The "central motif," as Hughes reads

24. See Clifford Leech, "Restoration Tragedy," *Durham University Journal*, 11 (1950), 106–15; Bonamy Dobrée, *Restoration Tragedy* (Oxford: Clarendon Press, 1929), Chapter 7; Moody E. Prior, *The Language of Tragedy* (1947; rpt. Bloomington: Indiana Univ. Press, 1966), pp. 186–92.

25. David R. Hauser, "Otway Preserved: Theme and Form in *Venice Preserv'd*," *Studies in Philology*, 55 (1958), 481–93.

26. William H. McBurney, "Otway's Tragic Muse Debauched: Sensuality in *Venice Preserv'd*," *Journal of English and Germanic Philology*, 58 (1959), 380–99.

the play, is "man reverting to a primitive and animal state."[27] Anne Righter finds *Venice Preserv'd* "nihilistic." "Both the Venetian establishment and the conspirators . . . are hopelessly corrupt. There is nothing to choose between them, and no other alternative. . . . Any possible society is rotten to the core. The good cannot prosper."[28] We find ourselves very much in sympathy with these critics, and yet these readings are at odds with a long and well-documented production history. Some further investigation is in order.

The critic who has developed this negative reading most fully is Thomas B. Stroup in a general account of Otway.[29] Stroup finds "cynicism" and a special "quality of frustration and futility" the basic characteristic of Otway's plays. Discussing *Venice Preserv'd* in particular, he stresses the large number of broken oaths and curses: "moral order is an illusion; the original chaos prevails." For Stroup, "Jaffeir's stabbing of Pierre and himself. . . may save face for them and satisfy a code of honor," but fails to provide redemption, purgation, or reestablishment of moral order. "The audience are not purged of pity or fear, but left to stew in them." This is an impressive and persuasive reading, the more so for being grounded in a broader consideration of Otway's work and outlook. That a production can play over the negative and stress the heroic code is amply proven by the production history. What about the converse? Is the Stroup reading playable, and if so, how?

The difference between the pathetic and satiric productions we are envisioning lies in directorial point of view. The pathetic production shows us noble innocents who live up to the heroic code of friendship and in so doing transcend the world of Venice.[30]

27. Derek W. Hughes, "A New Look at *Venice Preserv'd*," *Studies in English Literature*, 11 (1971), 437–57.

28. Anne Righter, "Heroic Tragedy," in *Restoration Theatre*, ed. John Russell Brown and Bernard Harris (London: Arnold, 1965), esp. pp. 156–57.

29. "Otway's Bitter Pessimism," *Essays in English Literature of the Classical Period presented to Dougald MacMillan, Studies in Philology*, Extra Series, No. 4 (1967), pp. 54–75.

30. For interpretations of this sort see R. E. Hughes, "'Comic Relief' in Ot-

The satiric production displays the helplessness of the individual and the ineffectuality of the heroic code. The pathetic production aims at sympathy for the protagonists; the satire is contrived to condemn the circumstances in which the action occurs.

Blocking and the use of extras can help us visualize the difference between the two productions. The pathetic production focuses attention unremittingly on Jaffeir and Belvidera. Since the world of the play is to intrude as little as possible, we should see an absolute minimum of servants and passers-by. A satiric production needs to insist upon the context, and consequently even tête-à-tête scenes ought to be conducted with the busy world going about its business in full view. Most of the scenes are public (see the scene plan in the appendix): Jaffeir's interview with Priuli, for example, takes place in the street, and could very reasonably proceed in the midst of the indifferent bustle of the city. Even the first Nicky-Nacky scene (in Aquilina's house) could take place before a watchful but impassive lackey. Likewise in a pathetic production the blocking ought to put Jaffeir and Belvidera squarely at the center of attention in every scene, whereas the satiric production would often relegate them to comparative obscurity. Thus in the Senate House scene in Act IV, Jaffeir's importance can be diminished by filling the stage with guards, prisoners, and messengers, keeping him off to one side and giving the audience plenty of activity to occupy its attention.

A director setting out to stage the satiric reading would depart from pathetic practice at a number of obvious points. For example: (1) The Nicky-Nacky scenes, played as low comedy in the pathetic production, become much more central here. As Goethe once said, "the comic scenes are particularly good . . . for we see in them how utterly unfit for government the senate had become."[31] Just so. In the satiric production Antonio cannot be a mere buffoon: malaise, not amusement, should be the effect sought in these scenes. And we should be forcibly reminded that

---

way's 'Venice Preserv'd'," *Notes and Queries*, 203 (1958), 65–66, and Hauser (note 25, above).

31. Henry Crabb Robinson, *Diary*, ed. Thomas Sadler (Boston: Fields, Osgood, & Co., 1870), I, 121. Cited by Taylor, *Next to Shakespeare*, p. 54n.

the woman who plays these games is Pierre's "love." (2) The conspirators are not to be attractive young idealists but rather scoundrels and scum. There can be no excuse for Jaffeir's alliance with them. (3) The conspirators choose death rather than pardon (p. 259), and they die bravely (p. 283). The pathetic production should let us glory in their moral resolution. The satire should make their choice seem idiotic (via responses of others), their resolution on the scaffold mere gallows bravado. The refusal of pardon is spoken by Pierre *and* Renault; this production will emphasize that linkage. (4) The ghosts in the finale (p. 286) will be imaginary in the satire, where we do not want to distract the audience with theatrical fantasy. In a pathetic production visible ghosts are optional.

Our instructions to the actors might run something like this.

Jaffeir and *Belvidera* operate much more as a tandem than in the pathetic production. They are both about twenty-five—old enough that they should not simply be innocents at large in the world of Venice. This Belvidera is quite conscious of her sex appeal, and dresses to display it (her body attracts Renault, not to mention her nightgown and the bed). She listens attentively (not blankly or passively) when others speak, and she is always trying to figure things out. Because Belvidera looks for motivations and is an expert manipulator of people, she immediately understands more about the conspiracy than Jaffeir does. She plays the defenseless female, and though she is more helpless than she realizes, she is not nearly as helpless as she seems to Jaffeir. The elopement may well have been Belvidera's idea. She wants a successful but biddable husband, and she probably knows that she can get help out of Priuli if it is really needed, as she proves in Act V. Belvidera lets Jaffeir strike poses and speechify because in the process he lays himself wide open to her manipulation. Her impatience with his posturing should be manifest to the audience, though never apparent to him. Jaffeir is not stupid, merely idealistic, inexperienced, and a bit woman-simple. He has long been insulated from reality by family money; only when he is without it does he start to realize what the world is like. He is, however, a dreamer, and quite incapable of doing anything practical. He would wreck Priuli's business if he inherited it. Jaffeir accepts Belvidera's analysis of the conspiracy (pp. 240–41), but without any clear idea what he should do next. The director might even want to imply that Belvidera delivered the anonymous warning to the senate—which has arrived via Priuli.[32] She is quite capable of alerting the senate anonymously and then pushing Jaffeir to do so openly, so he will get the public credit (and cannot blame her). This Jaffeir commits suicide to escape a situation he cannot cope with, not to affirm a code. Belvidera's death is more the result of shock than grief. Her mad scene continues the devastation and becomes an important part of the climax because she was relatively strong. The climax in this production is the cumulative deaths; Priuli is the coda.

Pierre is about thirty-five—distinctly older than Jaffeir and Belvidera. He wants to be a leader (much should be made of his competition with Renault for the position of second-in-command), but he has been done down by the system. Pierre is a power-hungry user of people: he would never let a woman control him as Belvidera does Jaffeir. He has a rather improbable view of himself as a martyr—a self-image that makes a felon's death acutely distasteful to him. He knows exactly what he wants from Jaffeir in Act V, and he skillfully gets his friend to do just what he has in mind.

Aquilina is obviously foreign, young, coarsely attractive, dressed to leave no doubt what she is. She finds Antonio's games a bore, and the soldierly Pierre genuinely attractive, but whoredom is her life. She is not really "corrupted"; she can imagine no other life, and she will never rise above it. For Pierre to be jealous about this woman tells us a great deal about him, none of it flattering.

Priuli is older in this production (sixty or more), a conspicuously wealthy fat cat. Clothes, house, and attendants suggest lots of money, made none too honestly. He protected Belvidera from the outside world but talked to her about it. Without consciously

32. Probably best done by appropriate delivery of Priuli's "from unknown hands / I had this warning" speech (p. 254).

meaning to, he raised her to be somewhat like the son he never had. Losing her to an empty poseur like Jaffeir was a terrible blow to his pride. The quasi-incestuous appeal[33] is a deliberate ploy by Belvidera, chosen because she knows it will work. This Priuli may not in fact die; he would be likelier to recover from the blow and raise his grandson to succeed him. We could even introduce the child in a nurse's arms in the final moment of the play. Stressing this possibility contributes to the irony of the title. Venice is indeed preserved—and the corruption can continue to flourish.

Antonio is another business tycoon, not significantly different from Priuli, except for his sexual preferences. Unlike the pathetic production, this one does not make Antonio a buffoon. He must look like a distinguished senator, not like Alderman Gripe. He is frightened not only by the uprising but by any threat to his status quo. He is a formidable enemy.

The Duke is a Tammany Hall politician—fat, indifferent to everything but his own advantage. He should be made enormously vain, addicted to ceremony and titles.

Bedamar is in his fifties; foreign dress aside, he looks and acts very much like Priuli. He would like to overthrow Venice, but he is a professional diplomat and agent provocateur, not an idealist. He knows exactly how to twist the likes of Jaffeir and Pierre to his own ends. This production will make much of Bedamar's escaping the conspirators' fate. All we need to do is introduce him as a cool, detached onlooker in Acts IV and V (e.g., at pp. 258 and 281–82).

Renault is an older version of what Pierre would be if he lived. He is capable, cold-blooded, and untrustworthy. Not manifestly a villain, and the worse for that.

33. Belvidera reverses Priuli's position with astonishing celerity and completeness in Act V (pp. 269–73). She introduces the subject of her dead mother and stresses their resemblance. She tantalizes Priuli with hints that Jaffeir is mistreating her, and that her father is her only refuge. She misreports the conspiracy in several details, either deliberately to inflame Priuli or because her grip on reality is already loosening. In the satiric production, Belvidera will consciously manipulate Priuli, watch his reactions closely, touch him whenever possible, and play up the phallic dagger.

Sympathy for the protagonists is not an object of the satiric production. Jaffeir should be made petulant, feckless, and easily manipulated. Our focus here is the world of Venice, not the protagonists' feelings, which mostly seem unrealistic and self-deceptive. This production needs lots of guards, servants, people in the streets. Lighting will be bright and bluish, illuminating the whole stage in a pitiless glare. (The pathetic production will be lit in warm tones, and will concentrate light on the principals.) Priuli's house (Belvidera's background) is redolent of big money; Aquilina's "house of fair reception" is pretentious but shoddy. (Compare the Ritz in its heyday and cheap imitation-Hilton modern.) The senate rooms are fancy but decayed.

Otway's original view of the play was indubitably political. As staged in 1682, it presented a corrupt Whig world "threatened" by a foreign-inspired plot attractive only to self-seeking scoundrels and befuddled idealists. How much sympathy was allowed Jaffeir, Belvidera, and Pierre we can only guess, but given the casting, possibly a good deal. The political point evaporated almost immediately: what remains is a peculiarly centerless play. The values of *Venice Preserv'd* are almost entirely negative. A critic can consider this a frightful defect; alternatively one can take this to be Otway's point. Clifford Leech sees the play in strictly pathetic terms, and since he dislikes pathetic drama he condemns it. "Otway was not concerned with a coherent dramatic structure, but aimed at a strenuous emotional exercise. The woes of Jaffeir and Belvidera are not derived from things as they are: they exist to furnish theatrical excitement." This is, assuredly, what the production history would suggest. Thomas B. Stroup offers us the alternative: a "satirical tragedy," one "more akin to Jonson's *Sejanus* or Shakespeare's *Timon of Athens* or *Troilus and Cressida* than to the great tragedies." The devastating pessimism of Otway's later plays is not what we expect of a tragedy, but it does constitute a serious point. Our "happy ending" is the preservation of a Venice rotten to the core. And unless we choose to regard suicide (leading to Belvidera's madness and death) as satisfactory affirmation, that is where Otway leaves us.

We have here a play on which production history and modern criticism are decidedly at odds. The play can be taken in either direction: the question is simply whether one seeks or rejects sympathy for Jaffeir and Belvidera. Few star performers care to work against audience sympathy (a preference which accounts for the production history), so the obvious way to make the play work in the theatre is to furnish the emotional exercise at which Leech sneers. The alternative, though more difficult to sell an audience, is to show us the ineffectuality of muddled idealism in a world corrupt beyond redemption.

APPENDIX: THE SCENE PLAN

At several points Otway is irritatingly vague about setting. A certain amount of deduction produces the following set of locations.

Act

I: Jaffeir provides the *liaison* among the three scenes, which evidently take place in the street where Pierre and Belvidera can meet him by chance.

II: p. 216: evidently Aquilina's house.
     p. 218: "The Ryalto."
     p. 222: "*Aquilina's* house."

III: p. 230: evidently Aquilina's house.
     p. 235: evidently the same.

IV: p. 250: evidently the street. (Jaffeir and Belvidera are going to the senate.)
     p. 254: "The Senate-house."

V: p. 269: evidently another room in the senate building. (Cannot be the senate chamber proper, since Antonio wonders if Priuli has gone there at p. 273; cannot be Priuli's house, since Aquilina wanders in at p. 274.)
     p. 276: evidently the street. (Otway does not indicate the scene change.)
     p. 281: evidently the Rialto. ("Scene opening discovers a Scaffold and a Wheel." "Scene shuts" at p. 286.)
     p. 286: Priuli's house. (Priuli takes Belvidera home.)

199

This translates into a straightforward scene plan.

2.3   Rialto/scaffold
2.2   Other room in senate building
2.1   Senate chamber

1.3   Aquilina's house
1.2   Priuli's house
1.1   Street

7

Amphitryon (1690)

D RYDEN'S LAST and greatest comedy was long dismissed with
faint praise as a workmanlike Englishing of Molière and
Plautus. In the introduction to the California edition (published
in 1976), Earl Miner had the courage to say that "*Amphitryon* is
one of the unrecognized masterpieces of English comedy," and
that "with *All for Love* and *Don Sebastian*, it is at the peak of Dryden's achievement as a playwright."[1] With the exception of an
important article published in 1980 by James D. Garrison, however, no substantial critical work has been done on the play.

On its most obvious level, *Amphitryon* works as a situational
farce, and its popularity on the eighteenth-century stage almost
undoubtedly derived from its comic potentialities. But the critic
or director prepared to consider the more serious elements in the
play will quickly find that it presents ambiguities and problems of
no common order. Does audience sympathy rest with Amphitryon and Alcmena or with Jupiter and Mercury? Why did Dryden write Phaedra and Gripus into the story? Do they debase the
heroic ethos of Amphitryon and Alcmena? How should Dryden's
peculiar ending be staged, and to produce what effect? The special brilliance of the comedy lies in its unusual combination of

1. *The Works of John Dryden*, Volume XV, ed. Earl Miner and George R.
Guffey (Berkeley and Los Angeles: Univ. of California Press, 1976), 472. All
parenthetical page references are to this edition.

201

stock comic elements with a dark moral vision implied by its tone of cynical disillusionment. Racy, witty, and funny it is; a happy play it is not.

We are going to argue that Dryden—unwilling to write a pot-boiler but anxious for financial success—cleverly wrapped a potentially biting satire in inoffensive garb. How much of the satire would come through in performance depends entirely on production choices. A production seeking only detached indifference toward the characters could be done as pure farce. Inviting the audience to identify with Jupiter and Mercury makes the play a kind of sanitized Carolean sex-comedy—sanitized because the fantasy element makes moral judgments largely irrelevant. To invite serious sympathy for Amphitryon and Alcmena makes the work a distinctly bitter satire on the abuse of power. As was his custom, Dryden chose not to force unwelcome conclusions on the audience. As Garrison suggests, however, his handling of Jupiter's prophecy of the birth of Hercules, so differently treated in his sources, opens the possibility of a production that could be "a severe indictment of the contemporary world."[2]

CONTEXT AND SOURCES

Dryden was always a hard-headed commercial playwright, but never more so than in the first years after the Revolution of 1688, when the loss of his government positions made him more dependent on new plays for his income than he had been at any time since the mid-1660s. *Don Sebastian* (December 1689) proved successful, but in general new comedies were doing better than new tragedies, and Dryden evidently felt constrained to return to a form he had not essayed since the ill-fated *Mr. Limberham* in 1678. His enthusiasm for straight comedy had never been great; and in approaching it again after this long hiatus, he had no formula in hand. Audience taste had altered markedly in the course of the 1680s, a fact of which Dryden must have been quite con-

2. James D. Garrison, "Dryden and the Birth of Hercules," *Studies in Philology*, 77 (1980), 180–201; quotation from p. 180.

scious when he set out to write *Amphitryon* during the winter of 1689–90. Cuckolding comedy was less and less acceptable to "the Ladies"; what would replace it was far from obvious.[3] Dryden's own sympathies were more with the satiric comedy of the 1670s than with the "humane" comedy becoming popular at the end of the eighties, and he seems to have had no use for "reform" comedy of the sort being written and championed by Shadwell (e.g., *The Squire of Alsatia*, 1688). Dryden's personal preference was for "raised" tragicomedy like *Marriage A-la-Mode*, but that was out of fashion, and he could ill afford a flop.

Aware of the growing audience reaction against sex comedy, Dryden also knew that cuckoldry still appealed to a significant part of the audience. The choice of the Amphitryon legend as his subject was ideally calculated to let him display sex without ruffling many moral feathers. As a pagan god, Jupiter is beyond ordinary moral bounds, and because he deceives Alcmena her adultery is entirely unwitting. Only a pretty heated moralist could see much point in moral objections to the sexual proclivities of pagan gods. Dryden presents a morally spotless heroine, and he can transfer the love game to secondary characters, Mercury and Phaedra, who need not be taken very seriously.

If Dryden asked himself, as he surely did, what sort of comedy seemed to be doing well of late, the answer was plain to see: magic-and-machinery farce. In all probability he thought these works contemptible. Many years earlier he had sneered at his own farcically-inclined *An Evening's Love* (1668),[4] and all we know of Dryden suggests his disdain for farce, but he was never above using popular formulas to his own ends. The obvious kinship of *Amphitryon* to these works leaves little doubt that Dryden deliberately borrowed from their successful formulas.

The first of these plays, Nahum Tate's *A Duke and no Duke*

3. For discussion of trends in comedy in the 1680s see John Harrington Smith, "Shadwell, the Ladies, and the Change in Comedy," *Modern Philology*, 46 (1948), 22–33; and Robert D. Hume, "'The Change in Comedy': Cynical versus Exemplary Comedy on the London Stage, 1678–1693," *Essays in Theatre*, 1 (1983), 101–18.

4. Pepys reported that Dryden's publisher Herringman "tells me Dryden doth himself call it but a fifth-rate play" (*Diary*, 22 June 1668).

(August 1684), an adaptation of Cokain's *Trappolin Suppos'd a Prince* (pub. 1658), is a good example of the form. Trappolin is magically transformed to look like the temporarily absent duke, imprisons his advisors, and generally misbehaves. Predictable contretemps follow upon the return of the real duke, and are sorted out in due course by the magician. There is little point beyond situational farce, but the duke is nicely discomfited when he is made to look like Trappolin and treated accordingly. Jevon's *The Devil of a Wife, or a Comical Transformation* (March 1686) is a very lightweight romp but one with a genuine point. Sir Richard Lovemore's wife is a horrible shrew who makes life miserable for everyone around her. By enchantment she is made to change places with a cobbler's wife: after she has been thoroughly humbled, the charm is undone, she confesses her faults and promises to reform, and everyone prepares to live happily ever after. Both of these plays were enormously successful, and Dryden was to make good use of the comic possibilities arising from mistaken identity and impersonation. But where Tate uses the impersonation to show us something about acceptance of authority and Jevon to illustrate a homily about good behavior, Dryden's purposes, beyond simple amusement, have not seemed so immediately evident.

Neither Tate nor Jevon did much with machines, but Aphra Behn's tremendously popular *The Emperor of the Moon* (March 1687) makes lavish use of all sorts of fancy staging, employing spectacle almost on the scale of semiopera. The dancers who materialize out of a tapestry (an incident passed off as an enchanted dream), the changing phases of the moon, and the emperor's appearance in a flying chariot (his train held by four cupids) are the stuff of which Betterton had long concocted Dorset Garden spectaculars. Mountfort's bastardized *The Life and Death of Doctor Faustus* ("Made into a Farce," the title page says) likewise employs all sorts of staging tricks—thunder and lightning, books flying out of hands, a giant coming to pieces in full view, a flying table, horns grown on a dupe's head, Faustus getting torn asunder only to have his parts reassemble for a dance. Dryden does not indulge in such stuff, but his use of flyings for the gods and his employment of impersonation and mistaken identity place *Amphitryon* squarely in the farce tradition of the 1680s. With the exception of *Faustus* (ca. March 1688), all of these plays had been highly successful, and Dryden had reason to hope these devices would help sell his show.

The prominence of the "Two Sosias" (touted in Dryden's subtitle) and the sexual persiflage of Mercury and Phaedra provide familiar fare for the unsophisticated part of the audience and should prove amusing in any kind of production. But even a casual reading of *Amphitryon* should show that Dryden was not simply prostituting himself by writing farce. One could argue that *Mr. Limberham* is no more than an expert imitation of Durfey's trashy *A Fond Husband*, done at the king's request; but Dryden's departures from his sources in *Amphitryon* prove that it is more than a concession to popular taste begotten by Jevon upon Mrs. Behn. Had Dryden been content with a fantasy sex farce, he would surely have stuck closer to Plautus and Molière and written a tidy, straightforward ending instead of a flagrantly inconclusive one. Though Dryden follows his sources quite closely at times, he departs quite radically from them at others.[5] What possibilities did Dryden see in this familiar tale?

Jupiter impersonates Amphitryon in order to sleep with Alcmena, whom he impregnates with Hercules. Given the basic outline of the story, we must ask whether at the end Amphitryon is to be happy with these events, resigned to them, or deeply resentful and unreconciled. Plautus chooses the first option, and Molière apparently the second, while Dryden (whose finale is the least explicit) gives us a text that hints strongly at the possibility of a production taking the third option—i.e., of offering no resolution at all.

Plautus' *Amphitryon* presents the most positive view of the story. We are entertained with confusion over identity, but at the end the dazed Amphitryon accedes to Jupiter's prerogative. "I guess I've no complaint if I have to share my possessions with the great god Jupiter," says the cuckold, and hastens off to tell his

5. For a convenient summation, see the California edition.

wife the good news about Hercules.[6] In Plautine ideology what Jupiter does is normal for the king of gods, an honor and not something to be resented. Molière's version entirely desanctifies the gods. Plautus can joke about them, but he grants their special status without question. Molière preserves the story but presents the characters in essentially human terms.

> This Jupiter is not a god but a *grand seigneur*; this Amphitryon is not a Theban warrior but a testy young nobleman of secondary, but not inferior, rank, vain, irascible, youthfully rash, aristocratically impatient; but yet upright, understandably and humanly angered and bewildered; this Alcmène is no passive human instrument for a divine will, but a virtuous young wife, tender but not lacking in mettle; this Sosie is not a slave but a gentleman's valet; this Mercure is neither a vaudeville clown nor a stooge nor a divine flunkey, but a worldly wise and slightly world-weary courtier.[7]

Molière's Amphitryon gets very hot indeed when he believes himself cuckolded, and the text is largely silent about the resolution. Jupiter appears in full glory ("on his eagle, armed with a thunderbolt, amid thunder and lightning," according to the stage directions in the 1682 edition) and lays down the law. Alcmena is absent from the stage, and Amphitryon utters not a word, leaving Sosia to mouth some comfortable platitudes. Thus Molière chooses to throw the emphasis on Amphitryon's confrontation with an authority he cannot flout, and resignation to the inevitable seems his most probable response, though of course actor and director have some latitude here. Molière shows us class conflict couched in safely supernatural terms, and the "lesson" that comes across is a rather unpleasant one: you submit if you cannot resist.

The story as Dryden inherited it has two obvious centers of interest: situational confusion (stressed by Plautus) and arbitrary exercise of power (made prominent and disturbing by Molière). In Dryden's hands the pagan gods emerge visibly akin to the

6. *Amphitryon: Three Plays in New Verse Translations*, trans. Charles E. Passage and James H. Mantinband (Chapel Hill: Univ. of North Carolina Press, 1974), pp. 104–5.
7. Ibid., p. 130.

gentleman-rake of Carolean comedy, and as we have suggested in discussing *The Country-Wife*, a "rake-hero" can be presented in a wide variety of ways, from enthusiastic acceptance to overt condemnation. The real puzzle in Dryden's version is the degree to which he refuses to make his point of view explicit, leaving the director a play that can be given a range of quite contradictory "meanings" in performance.

FOUR CRUXES

Point of view. In any production that claims to go beyond fantasy/farce the director must decide whether the audience is to sympathize with the omnipotent adulterer or with his human victims. The play will support either concept, but Dryden's departures from his sources seem designed to provide opportunities for blackening the gods. Both Plautus and Molière use Mercury for an introductory proem and open Act I with Sosia's return to Amphitryon's palace, where he finds Mercury/Sosia barring his way: Jupiter has already bedded Alcmena. Dryden chooses to open Act I before Jupiter has taken Amphitryon's form and gives us a lengthy, smutty scene with Jupiter, Mercury, and Phoebus. When we first meet Alcmena (p. 239), she is longing for her husband's safe return from the war, and Dryden actually shows us her loving welcome to her "husband." Thus Dryden displays Jupiter's treachery from the outset rather than presenting us with a fait accompli. This change could generate much more hostility toward Jupiter (and concomitant sympathy for Alcmena). As we will see, a great deal depends on the tone and atmosphere of the initial scene between the gods.

Mercury and Phoebus open the play with gossip. "What news in Court?" asks Phoebus. Mercury replies: "There has been a devillish Quarrel, I can tell you, betwixt *Jupiter* and *Juno*: She threaten'd to sue him in the Spiritual Court, for some Matrimonial Omissions: and he stood upon his Prerogative. Then she hit him on the Teeth of all his Bastards; and your Name and mine were us'd with less reverence than became our Godships. They were both in their Cups; and at the last the matter grew so high, that they were ready to have thrown Stars at one anothers Heads" (p. 232). Are we to be amused or disgusted by such gods? When Jupiter appears, confessing that he is "in love," Mercury wonders "into what form your Almighty-ship would be pleas'd to transform your self to night. Whether you wou'd fornicate in the Shape of a Bull, or a Ram, or an Eagle, or a Swan: What Bird or Beast you wou'd please to honour, by transgressing your own Laws, in his likeness; or in short, whether you wou'd recreate your self in Feathers, or in Leather" (p. 233). Phoebus asks why Jupiter will commit a "Crime" and is told first that it is "Fate" and then that the begetting of Hercules is "for the good of Humankind" (p. 235). Mercury observes that if Jupiter "had been a Man, he might have been a Tyrant, if his Subjects durst have call'd him to account," but concludes that objections are pointless: "No more of your Grumbletonian Morals, Brother; there's Preferment coming, be advis'd and Pimp dutifully." Even the stuffy Phoebus concedes that "Since Arbitrary Pow'r will hear no Reason, 'tis Wisdom to be silent"—a statement that might well stand as an epigraph for Molière's play.

Dryden's explicit introduction of crime, tyranny, and arbitrary power, right at the outset, together with Mercury's cynicism, hardly invite the audience to admire the gods. But the gods can be played as likeable pranksters, amused by their own outrageous behavior (with Phoebus overplayed as a pompous prig); or they can be presented as heartless bullies. The director must decide whether Jupiter is genuinely besotted with Alcmena or whether he is snickering to himself over her gullibility throughout the play. Jupiter can be quite unable to help himself, or he can be coldly self-controlled—comic rogue hero or ugly predator. Obviously, the presentation of Amphitryon and Alcmena is equally important, but the handling of the first two scenes goes a long way toward establishing audience attitudes. When Alcmena appears in I.ii. spouting romantic verse ("wou'd I were there . . . and I might die for him!"—p. 240), she can project the passionate sincerity of the heroine or the self-dramatization of a potential sucker. The comedy Dryden weaves into these scenes (Night going backwards at p. 239; Phaedra's mercenary tricks) can work either as comic contrast or as satiric deflation.

We see three basic options. Everyone can be treated as an inhabitant of Cloud Cuckooland, in which case the whole business is a farce to be watched with cheerful indifference. Alternatively, the audience can be asked to identify with the rake (sex comedy), or they can be invited to sympathize with his victims (satire).

The appearance of the gods. Do Jupiter and Mercury really *disguise* themselves as mortals? Or do they just don some token difference in costume? In a play with mistaken identity as a central device, the director has a choice: make the people involved look as much alike as possible, or just ignore the matter and count on costume similarity to make the point. "Resemblance" need not be an issue in casting. The durable convention is that if the text says that they look alike you dress them identically and make a joke of the fact that they look different. The original Mercury and Sosia were quite dissimilar in appearance (Leigh fat, Nokes not, for a start).

Appearance helps tell the audience several things. It can underline or minimize the god/mortal distinction, depending on how the "disguise" is handled. When Jupiter leaves the stage to "drop *Jove*, and take *Amphitryon*'s Dress" (p. 237), exactly what happens? Does Jupiter display a Greek statue's upper torso in I.i. and then cover it with tunic and armor to become "Amphitryon"? Mercury does not normally go about dressed as a slave, so his appearance in the relevant costume is enough to signal both changes. How "human" do the gods look? If they appear ageless, never tired, never dirty, never out of countenance, the god/mortal distinction is continuously emphasized.[8] Alcmena must then overlook differences that are perfectly clear to the audience: Jupiter's

---

8. Giraudoux makes a joke of the difference in *Amphitryon 38* when he has Mercury deride Jupiter's excessively faultless appearance: "You're wearing immortal clothes. I'm sure that they are waterproof, dye-fast, and that if a drop of oil fell on them from a lamp it wouldn't leave a spot." *Collected Plays of Jean Giraudoux*, trans. Phyllis La Farge with Peter H. Judd, 2 vols. (New York: Hill and Wang, 1964), II, 96–97.

reminders about towels for washing up become a joke, since he plainly does not need them.

A Jupiter not just mature but overripe would let the play make fun of the gods, while implying that mortals who are taken in are fools—pitiable fools, if we like. A confrontation between a mature, commanding Jupiter and a noticeably younger Amphitryon favors the authority figure, the more so if the mortals fail to acknowledge the age difference (which then functions only for the audience). For an older man to command and be obeyed is normal. If the gods look just like the mortals all the time, especially if Jupiter and Amphitryon are the same age and the difference is only in names, what we see is explicable basically as comic confusion. A modern director who wants to stress identical appearance could put Jupiter and Amphitryon (and possibly Mercury and Sosia as well) in vacuform life masks that would display identical features on both faces. Jupiter could don such a mask at the end of I.i. or before his appearance in I.ii. Obviously, he would remove it before or during his final appearance.

The director can choose to make Jupiter and Mercury either alike or different in their relationship to their human counterparts. Because one pair is twins does not mean the other needs to be. If both pairs of gods and mortals genuinely look alike, mistakes are much more understandable, and the satire is softened to comedy. To make Jupiter identical to Amphitryon is potentially threatening because it deprives Amphitryon of his identity and Alcmena of any chance to distinguish between them. For Mercury and Sosia to be indistinguishable is much less threatening, except to Sosia, whose distress is entirely comic.

In the original production either Nokes had to be heavily padded or the original Sosias looked much less alike than Betterton and Joseph Williams did as the two Amphitryons. Achieving close visual resemblance for both pairs would hardly be feasible in most repertory companies and would not be easy today even in casting for a movie. The key questions about appearance are (a) whether it contributes to a major differentiation of gods from mortals—or to a lack of difference; and (b) whether the appearance and bearing of the gods constantly reminds the audience of differences to which the mortal characters remain oblivious.

The function of Phaedra and Gripus. Why did Dryden add these characters? They supply the fullness and plot diversity expected of English comedy at the time, but we need to ask why *these* characters. They have been seen as a topical hit at contemporary English society,[9] but if so they seem no more than incidental and awkwardly added to a play whose main action has little to do with England. Garrison seems closer to the mark when he comments on the effect of the juxtaposition of their values with those of Amphitryon and Alcmena. "At first we are likely to wonder what Phaedra and Gripus are doing in a play about the birth of Hercules; by the end, however, we should be wondering what idealists like Amphitryon and Alcmena are doing in a world finally dominated by the relative values of Phaedra and Gripus."[10] We would argue that the juxtaposition is significant, but that its effectiveness depends on the production concept.

Amphitryon can in fact be read as a "three-level hierarchy" play,[11] and if it is, Dryden's additions seem very much to the point. The action involves three triangles: Jupiter-Alcmena-Amphitryon, Mercury-Phaedra-Gripus, and Mercury-Bromia-Sosia. Sosia's fear of being cuckolded by his double echoes his master's (albeit groundlessly). Sosia's fear of being cuckolded is especially comic because his battle-ax of a wife craves more sex than he is able to provide. Phaedra's willingness to sell herself for a good price contrasts pointedly with her mistress' passionate chastity. The "courtship" of Phaedra by Mercury, and their odd proviso scene in Act V, are harder to interpret. Mercury admits his identity, and they bargain.

---

9. For example, by Garrison, pp. 196–98, and by Abdel-Rahman Shaheen, "Satiric Characterization in John Dryden's Later Comedies," *Forum* [Houston], 17, No. 2 (Spring 1979), 2–10.

10. Garrison, p. 198.

11. For this concept see Richard Levin, *The Multiple Plot in English Renaissance Drama* (Chicago: Univ. of Chicago Press, 1971), and discussion in Chapter 5, above.

Mercury. *Memorandum*, that she be always constant to me; and admit no other Lover.

Phaedra. *Memorandum*, unless it be a Lover that offers more: and that the Constancy shall not exceed the Settlement.

Mercury. *Item*, that she shall keep no Male Servants in her house: *Item*, no Rival Lap Dog for a Bedfellow: *Item*, that she shall never pray to any of the Gods.

Phaedra. What, wou'd you have me an Atheist?

Mercury. No Devotion to any He-Deity, good *Phaedra*.

Bromia. Here's no provision made for Children yet.

Phaedra. Well remember'd, *Bromia*: I bargain that my Eldest Son shall be a Hero, and my Eldest Daughter a King's Mistress.

Mercury. That is to say, a Blockhead, and a Harlot, *Phaedra*.

Phaedra. That's true; but who dares call 'em so? (p. 314)

Is this a "reality" beside which the romantic notions of Amphitryon and Alcmena seem silly? Or is this a tawdry normalcy that serves as foil for genuine love? Much depends on whether the actors play the courtship as a genuine attraction disguised by antagonistic games or as strictly a matter of lecherous god and mercenary whore. But whatever production concept is employed, Dryden has chosen to interpose a middle level, and no longer does the Amphitryon-Alcmena-Jupiter line contrast *only* with its comic reflection in Bromia and the two Sosias.

The staging of the finale. After Amphitryon's angry confrontation with his double in Act V, "*Jupiter* re-enters the House: with him *Amphitryon, Alcmena, Polydas, Tranio,* and Guards." Following the Mercury-Phaedra proviso scene, "It Thunders; and the Company within doors . . . all come running out." Amphitryon and Alcmena then deliver their final speeches:

Amphitryon. Sure 'tis some God: he vanish'd from our sight,
And told us we shou'd see him soon return.

Alcmena. I know not what to hope, nor what to fear.
A simple Errour, is a real Crime;
And unconsenting Innocence is lost. (p. 315)

A second peal of thunder follows, "After which, *Jupiter* appears in a Machine." The delivery of Jupiter's speech could be admonitory, overbearing, severely authoritative, or avuncularly comforting. In the midst of the speech Mercury comments, aside, "*Amphitryon* and *Alcmena*, both stand mute, and know not how to take it." Jupiter concludes with the announcement of Hercules' forthcoming birth and "is carry'd back to Heaven." The stage-picture is all important. Are Amphitryon and Alcmena flabbergasted? cowed? resentful? faintly hopeful? Do they look at each other or just stare at Jupiter? Do they turn to each other as Jupiter departs? Does Amphitryon clasp Alcmena to him? Or do they stand apart, hostile and alienated? The first response to Jupiter's speech is "*Omnes*. We all Congratulate *Amphitryon*"—which could be said enthusiastically, doubtingly, or ironically. Mercury rejoins, "Keep your Congratulations to your selves, Gentlemen," and recommends that Amphitryon accept "the favour of *Jupiter* in patience." As in the French play, the summing up is left to Sosia. But where Molière has Sosia deliver advice ("We're best off when the least is said"), Dryden gives these lines to Mercury. Dryden then gives Sosia a flippant speech regretting that he has not been similarly honored and rewarded, which concludes, "In fine, the Man, who weighs the matter fully, / Wou'd rather be the Cuckold, than the Cully." Sosia is at best a suspect spokesman, and nothing we have seen of Dryden's Amphitryon suggests that he will settle cheerfully for counting his blessings.

Amphitryon and Alcmena can be visibly reconciled, left to accept their fate and make the best of it. Or they can be left physically apart, stunned, unhappy, unable to cope with the shambles Jupiter has made of their lives and marriage. If the latter, then the message is that the Sosias and Phaedras of the world can do business with such gods, but more honorable people cannot. What this "means" depends on the context in which the audience has viewed the gods all along. For us, as for Dryden's audience, if they are taken as anything but denizens of Cloud Cuckooland, they stand for power and privilege in society. Produced in that way, Dryden's play is a satiric extension of Molière's, and a very harsh one. Given the distinctly unappetizing picture of the gods and the addition of Phaedra, this is very likely what Dryden had in mind. But so ambiguous is the ending and so thoroughly is the whole play hedged with situational farce and fantasy that it can be successfully staged without attention to its satiric potentialities.

CASTING AND DIRECTORIAL CHOICES

In casting this play the director needs to start with a clear idea of how audience sympathy ought to be conferred. All roles save Sosia and Bromia offer considerable leeway in performance. Production history tells us less about this play than it does about many others, but comparison of a pair of casts from 1708 with the original 1690 cast is instructive (see Table 7.1). The September 1708 production was obviously lightweight, especially on the male side. If the audience is to take Amphitryon seriously, he must stand up credibly in his confrontation with Jupiter, even though he cannot win. John Bickerstaff versus George Powell is a match appropriate only to farce or sex comedy.

Jupiter could be played as a dashing young rake (Wilks), as an older and more threatening rake (Betterton), as a debauched and cynical old libertine (Betterton, if he chose), or as the rake-hero of an old-fashioned sex comedy (Powell). So wide was the range of Betterton's roles that his appearance in the part tells us almost nothing about Dryden's concept of it in the original production. This casting does, however, ensure that Jupiter will appear powerful.

Amphitryon can be presented either as a much perplexed and anguished hero (with Jupiter his sadistic tormenter) or as a hot-tempered dupe, erupting afresh at each provocation (while a libertine-hero Jupiter watches his thrashings-about with cool amusement). Shadings are certainly possible: a comic production might stress Amphitryon's confusion rather than his torment, a choice especially appropriate to farce. The keys to Amphitryon are his relations with Alcmena and Sosia. The quarrel scenes in Acts III and V can be played either as stock routines or as potentially tragic. Beyond Alcmena's romantic adoration of her husband (e.g., pp. 239–40, 243), we get little sense of the normal workings of their marriage. Consequently, Amphitryon's attitude

Table 7.1
Casts for Three Productions of *Amphitryon*

Role	1690	3 Feb. 1708	16 Sept. 1708
Jupiter	Thomas Betterton	Robert Wilks	George Powell
Mercury	Anthony Leigh	Richard Estcourt	Francis Leigh, Sr.
Phoebus	John Boman	?	Henry Fairbank
Amphitryon	Joseph Williams	John Mills	John Bickerstaff
Sosia	James Nokes	George Pack	Richard Cross
Gripus	Samuel Sandford	Henry Norris	Benjamin Johnson
Alcmena	Elizabeth Barry	Mrs. Barry	Frances Knight
Phaedra	Susanna Mountfort	Margaret Bicknell	Mrs. Saunders
Bromia	Katherine Corey	Mary Powell	Mrs. Powell

toward Sosia is critical in determining audience response to him. Whether it is overbearing or exasperated but affectionate will be established during their long scene together when Amphitryon makes his first appearance (III.i.). Amphitryon is, of course, extremely angry, and constantly threatens to beat his harried slave. By comparison with his counterparts in Plautus and Molière, however, Dryden's Amphitryon seems much less humorless and generally better in control of himself. Several times his exchanges with Sosia verge on comic crosstalk, and suggest an affection lacking in Dryden's sources. ("Nothing but the Truth, and the whole Truth, so help thee Cudgel. . . . *Imprimis* for Fustian . . ." —p. 266.) When Sosia says "as he beat me last Night cross-ways, so you wou'd please to beat me long-ways . . . that at least my Skin may look like Checquer-work," Amphitryon replies, "This request is too reasonable to be refus'd" (p. 265). Such exchanges fit well in a farce production; in a more serious one they tend to humanize Amphitryon. If he seems a decent master the audience will tend to assume that he is a good, if domineering, husband. Alcmena is extremely submissive throughout.

Amphitryon's age and presence are important. Joseph Williams, who created the role, was about forty in 1690, a veteran actor who had taken such roles as Bertran in *The Spanish Fryar*, Polydore in *The Orphan*, the Prince in *The Princess of Cleve*, General Bacon in *The Widdow Ranter*, and Don Sebastian. While hardly able to compete with Betterton, he must have brought force and stature to the role, as John Mills would have done in later years. To put a journeyman like John Bickerstaff in the part automatically reduces the potentiality for serious response to the play. To cast for maximum effect one would want a tragic actor of the force of Barton Booth (of whom we have no record in the role) as Amphitryon.

Alcmena is less susceptible to interpretive variation than Amphitryon, serving more as victim than as active agent in the play. Elizabeth Barry, who held the role for two decades, presumably invested it with the maximum of tempestuous emotion. (To imagine Bickerstaff as a credible husband for her takes some doing.) The alternative in a serious production would be a more patient and suffering Alcmena along the lines of Anne Bracegirdle or Lucretia Bradshaw (neither of whom essayed the role). We would guess that Sarah Thurmond (who later took the part at Drury Lane) presented it more this way. Audience response will depend in large part on how well we like Alcmena. Plainly, she is a very desirable woman; but if we are on her side, we cannot be comfortable with Jupiter's deception, and when he returns and talks her round after her Act III quarrel with her husband, our response to this manipulation can be made very negative. Here her relationship with Amphitryon is all-important: is she his beloved or his prize possession? Whether we take Alcmena's woes seriously depends largely on how Jupiter and Amphitryon are presented.

Mercury can be a comfortable cynic or a junior Jupiter. Tony Leigh (like Richard Estcourt, who followed him in the role) was a low comedian of formidable abilities. In their hands the role was evidently a burlesque presentation of a "god," and a decided contrast with the powerful Jupiter of Betterton or the polished gentleman of Wilks. There is nothing in the role, however, to prevent a director from casting Mercury as a smoothie, a gentleman-rake in his own right. In 1690 William Mountfort might have been used this way. To cast a low comedian as Mercury softens the god/mortal distinction by demeaning the secondary god. Mercury can be amused or sadistic with Sosia, infatuated or predatory with Phaedra. We can assume that Mercury is not genuinely going to "marry" Phaedra, and their proviso scene in Act V can be a fantasy spoof or a bargain cynical on both sides. The contrast between Phaedra and Alcmena is stark and conspicuous, and unless we view both as inhabitants of Cloud Cuckooland we are forced to judge that contrast.

Phaedra can be a comically avaricious jillflirt with a sharp tongue, or a mercenary whore. Physically, she must be quite attractive, or Mercury will hardly be panting for her. Susanna Percival Mountfort, who created the role, was a comedienne who could play anything from the virtuous Isabella in *The Squire of Alsatia* to Charlotte Welldon in *Oroonoko*, the rake Sir Anthony Love, and Mrs. Wittwoud in *The Wives Excuse*. In contrast to Mrs. Bicknell (the original Cherry in *The Beaux' Stratagem*), Mrs. Mountfort probably came across as a strong Phaedra, one capable of standing up to Mercury and enforcing a genuine bargain. To play Phaedra as an ordinary servant diminishes the importance of this plot line and moves the whole play more toward farce.

Sosia is a brilliant vehicle for a low comic actor in almost any version of this play. Molière wrote his Sosie for himself; Dryden added quite a bit of comedy, probably tailored to James Nokes. Often more than just a butt, Nokes took such roles as Gomez in *The Spanish Fryar*, Doodle in *The London Cuckolds*, Sir Davy Dunce in *The Souldiers Fortune*, and Peregrine Bubble in *A Fond Husband*. Cibber speaks admiringly of Nokes' "plain and palpable Simplicity of Nature," an ideal characteristic for Sosia.

> The louder the Laugh the graver was his Look upon it; and sure, the ridiculous Solemnity of his Features were enough to have set a whole Bench of Bishops into a Titter. . . . In the ludicrous Distresses which, by the Laws of Comedy, Folly is often involv'd in, he sunk into such a mixture of piteous Pusillanimity and a Con-

sternation so ruefully ridiculous and inconsolable, that when he had shook you to a Fatigue of Laughter it became a moot point whether you ought not to have pity'd him. When he debated any matter by himself, he would shut up his Mouth with a dumb studious Powt, and roll his full Eye into such a vacant Amazement, such a palpable Ignorance of what to think of it, that his silent Perplexity (which would sometimes hold him several Minutes) gave your Imagination as full Content as the most absurd thing he could say upon it.[12]

In Nokes' performance Sosia must have been immensely likeable as well as funny, and such a response must have affected the audience's view of Amphitryon and Mercury. Sosia is a Sancho Panza role, and Thomas Doggett—a great Sancho—could have done wonders with it, had he tried it. But played by a journeyman like Richard Cross or an ordinary low comic like George Pack, Sosia is merely amusing. Performed by an actor who can evoke warmth from the audience, Sosia becomes almost a touchstone for the play: if Mercury or Amphitryon genuinely mistreats him, the audience will turn against the bully. Here the blows Sosia suffers in Acts II and III make an important difference. If he is genuinely hit and hurt, we have one sort of play; if he comically overreacts to near misses or taps, we have quite another.

Bromia is a stock role, the unattractive older wife who henpecks her husband and hounds him for sex. Katherine Corey was a natural for the part. (We have already met her as Octavia in *All for Love* and are about to encounter her as Mrs. Teazall in *The Wives Excuse*.) Bromia's standard but amusing interchanges with her harassed husband (neatly burlesqued in II.ii. when she pursues Mercury, who is in Sosia's guise) help give the play the farce foundation on which it rests.

Surveying these questions of cast, one quickly realizes that a variety of combinations are possible. A choice for Jupiter does not necessarily imply a corollary choice for Amphitryon or Mercury or Phaedra. Beyond the basic issue of whether sympathy is

12. Cibber, *Apology*, I, 141–45.

to go to Jupiter or to his victims, a number of combinations and permutations are possible. For analytic purposes, however, we will do well to consider relatively discrete production concepts— but first the question of satire must be faced.

SATIRE OF WHAT?

If *Amphitryon* can be staged as a satire, what does it satirize? The humorous possibilities in confusion of identity are obvious, and ways of presenting Jupiter as a gentleman-rake are easy to visualize. But while we have talked at length about how audience sympathy might be directed against Jupiter, we have not yet considered the larger implications of doing so. Granting that Jupiter can be made unpleasant, Amphitryon and Alcmena quasi-tragic, what does the play mean if produced this way? Several quite different satiric readings have been proposed and must be considered.

1. "Dryden by his treatment of the amorous activities of Jupiter ridicules the similar activities of Charles II and his courtiers."[13] This idea has only superficial plausibility. We possess no actual evidence that Dryden intended such an identification, or that the original audience made the application. Charles II did not usually seduce wives of his courtiers, and there was nothing either covert or divine about his womanizing. And five years after his death, what would be the point? We agree with Garrison that satire of Charles II would have been "decidedly irrelevant" by 1690.[14] Nor does such an identification seem to lead the audience toward any message or conclusion. Structurally, the play is not set up to do anything with it.

2. As an alternative allegorical reading, Garrison suggests that "we are invited to see in the Jupiter-Alcmena-Amphitryon tri-

13. Frank Harper Moore, *The Nobler Pleasure: Dryden's Comedy in Theory and Practice* (Chapel Hill: Univ. of North Carolina Press, 1963), p. 198. As far as we are aware, the suggestion was first made by Ned Bliss Allen, *The Sources of John Dryden's Comedies* (Ann Arbor: Univ. of Michigan Press, 1935), pp. 234–36.

14. Garrison, p. 192.

angle an allusion to the political struggle between William (false Amphitryon) and James (true Amphitryon), vying to occupy the bed of England (Alcmena)."[15] We find this reading farfetched. Jupiter's resemblance to the dour William is hard to see; and in what way does Alcmena (totally faithful to her husband) resemble the England that had turned from James to William in 1688?

3. Phaedra and Gripus can be taken as satiric depictions of contemporary English society. Garrison points to such speeches as Phaedra's "thou Weather-cock of Government" (p. 303) as evidence that Dryden inserted material having "nothing to do with the situation in Thebes, but a great deal to do with seventeenth-century English politics."[16] This is absolutely true, but such miscellaneous additions hardly make the play a satiric depiction of Williamite England (and indeed Garrison does not make any such claim). Gripus is little more than a bit part, and he cannot reasonably be blamed for failing to distinguish the true Amphitryon, so Dryden cannot be reflecting negatively on the quality of justice in Gripus' court. Phaedra's covetousness is comically exaggerated, but as it goes unpunished we have trouble seeing exactly how she is satirized.

4. The most interesting and persuasive satiric reading of the play to date is Garrison's argument that Mercury's condemnation of "Our Iron Age" at the end of Act IV, together with Dryden's idiosyncratic handling of the prophecy of the birth of Hercules at the end of Act V, constitute "a severe indictment of the contemporary world."[17] Up to a point, Garrison is unquestionably correct. Mercury's speech is stinging ("Such Bargain-loves, as I with *Phaedra* treat, / Are all the Leagues and Friendships of the Great. . . . Our Iron Age is grown an Age of Gold: / 'Tis who bids most; for all Men wou'd be sold"—p. 302). And the glum terms (well-analyzed by Garrison) in which Jupiter describes Hercules' prospective labors in "an Impious Age" that does not welcome such a hero suggest profound disillusionment on Dryden's part (p. 316). We would argue, however, that while *Amphitryon*

15. Ibid., p. 194. This reading is not central to Garrison's interpretation.
16. Ibid., p. 196.
17. Ibid., esp. pp. 180, 199–200.

certainly embodies and expresses a sour and pessimistic view of life, it was not designed primarily as a satire on contemporary England, and nor was it stageable that way. The supernatural element and the remote setting work against topical satiric application. Then too the features on which Garrison concentrates simply do not loom large enough to dominate the play in performance, and most of them come very late, long after the audience's basic response is established. There is no reason an audience member in 1690 could not "apply" the fallen world of the play to his or her England, but the play itself does not thrust such an identification on reader or viewer.

A satire—even just a satiric production—needs a clear target. Incidental sniping at covetousness aside, the target pretty much has to be Jupiter if it is to be playable. To satirize abstractions in performance is extremely difficult: audience hostility is almost always to people. What does Jupiter stand for? Two things: the rake of Carolean sex comedy and abuse of authority. Obviously the two are compatible.

For the original audience to see Jupiter as a gentleman-rake was inevitable. Betterton had played such characters for a generation, and he continued to do so in a number of stock plays (*The Libertine*, *The Man of Mode*, *The Souldiers Fortune*).[18] The terms in which Jupiter is presented in Act I leave no room for doubt of his libertine nature, though whether he is to be presented as an "extravagant rake" or a "debauchee" the text does not specify. Given Dryden's longstanding views on libertinism (which he presents but disapproves of), we can hardly imagine that he envisioned *Amphitryon* as a bedroom farce or that he intended Jupiter as a "hero." The flippant and degrading presentation of the gods in I.i. can be played lightly or sourly, but in comparison with the approaches of Plautus and Molière, Dryden's picture of them is distinctly hostile. This attitude ties in explicitly with the theme of abuse of power.

The first scene of the play says in so many words that Jupiter is

18. As Peter Holland rightly says (*The Ornament of Action*, p. 147), even in the mid-1690s "it is clear that Betterton still embodied the cynical single-minded egocentric rake better than any other actor."

free to use his omnipotence to commit a "Crime." "'Tis our Part to obey our Father," says Mercury (p. 231), and Jupiter asserts that

> Fate is, what I
> By vertue of Omnipotence have made it:
> And pow'r Omnipotent can do no wrong. (p. 234)

Whether Jupiter is a smug tyrant, a sophisticated rake, or a tongue-in-cheek opportunist is entirely a matter of directorial license. Jupiter's final appearance can be at one extreme a deus-ex-machina end to farce complications, or at the other a sneering, triumphant "explanation" that Amphitryon is powerless to answer or resist. A tyrant Jupiter in conjunction with a sympathetic Amphitryon and Alcmena would be easy to stage and would offer a harsh and consistent vision. The fantasy elements and the farce confusion keep the play from becoming too grim, but if we take the suffering of Amphitryon and Alcmena seriously and there is no hint of reconciliation in the final scene, we are left with a dark and disturbing play. John Loftis comments that "the reader or spectator, informed from the beginning of the true relationships among the characters, cannot feel a concernment comparable to that evoked by the [Dryden's] tragicomedies, partly because he is already informed that the troubles are transitory, and partly because the tragic potential of the situation is obscured by the cynical comments on it of the secondary characters."[19] To a considerable degree, however, this is a matter of production choices. The brevity of the suffering is nowhere guaranteed in Dryden's text, and Phaedra can serve either as parody or foil. To stage the play to show a swaggering rake who cavalierly takes his pleasure where he will and thereby wreaks havoc in the lives of good people is entirely feasible. What is satirized in such a production is the behavior and values of the rake.

19. John Loftis, "Dryden's Comedies," *John Dryden*, ed. Earl Miner (London: Bell, 1972), pp. 55–56.

THREE PRODUCTION CONCEPTS

A brief comparison with the Amphitryon plays of Kleist (1807) and Giraudoux (1929) helps put Dryden's version in perspective, if only by making plain what he did not do. Consider the attitude taken toward the gods. Both Plautus and Molière show us decent and honorable mortals forced to accept the dictates of a higher authority. Even for Plautus the gods are basically a donnée. Kleist takes an entirely different tack in his "Comedy after Molière." Instead of concentrating on the cuckolding, Kleist chooses to emphasize Jupiter's motives, taken as read by his predecessors. Kleist's Jupiter is a lonely hero, glumly immortal and omnipotent, vainly seeking to win a true love. His almost sadistic testing of Alcmena gives her a new prominence in the story as Kleist explores her mind and feelings. Instead of being a pawn in a conflict between man and authority, Alcmena becomes the psychic center of the play. The notion of the god seeking love is a romantic concept quite foreign to Dryden. Nor is character psychology per se central to Dryden's play. For Dryden as for Molière, the heart of the play lies in the situation itself.

Consider also the handling of the conclusion. However Dryden's finale is presented in performance, he makes plain the fact that Amphitryon and Alcmena know precisely what has happened and will have to live with that knowledge. Giraudoux's *Amphitryon 38* is startlingly different in this respect. The presentation of Alcmena is quite brilliant (as in Kleist's play she is the central figure), but her moving and convincing acceptance of human destiny is seriously undercut by Giraudoux's having Jupiter confer "forgetfulness" of the whole episode at the end. This tidy resolution totally betrays the seriousness of the story. Whatever we may think of Dryden's coarse gods and addition of "distasteful persons,"[20] we must credit him with unflinching refusal to evade the implications of Jupiter's perfidy.

20. Passage and Mantinband are scathing in their condemnation. "The modern reader . . . comes away saddened at such high talents squandered for the mere diversion of *monde* and *demimonde*. To say that Dryden was ruined as a

Dryden stuck closely to the outlines of the story as he inherited it: his changes seem designed to develop the potentialities for multiple interpretations. Granting that a hybrid production is possible, three sharply different productions are easy to conceive.

Fantasy farce

The venue is Cloud Cuckooland. The pace must be fast, emotions shallow and formulaic. Knockabout and contretemps will be emphasized (recalling the subtitle, "The Two Sosias"). Everybody except Sosia and Bromia is pretty and snazzily costumed. Lavish visual display is in order, with maximum use of flyings and special effects. Jupiter gets an eagle in Act I, a *gloire* in Act V. The concept is musical comedy: logic and emotion are not to be taken seriously. Had Dryden thought of it, Jupiter might have a catchy song called something like "That's the kind of god I am" in I.i.[21] Jupiter does what he does, and we are entertained by the unfolding complications. A gross but fun-loving Mercury is spokesman for this production. The quarrel between Amphitryon and Alcmena can be played as a situation comedy routine, easily forgotten. In the finale they will fall happily in each other's arms as Jupiter winks benevolently and flies off. The production means nothing, but everyone can enjoy the jokes, games, and confusion.

---

dramatic poet by his public is not to say anything very new, but the pity of such a waste is none the less deplorable. If Alcmena comes off tolerably well, and if Amphitryon is not the worst of men, the two of them together cannot offset a stageful of distasteful persons that range from the unprincipled scoundrel of a Jupiter to the unprincipled Harpy of a Phaedra. What the play lacks is humanity. And if the author's purpose was the castigation of vice by merciless depiction of vice, then the Amphitryon scenario was not the proper vehicle for his purpose. The vices of gods in whom neither the author nor the audience believed cannot make for effective satire." (p. 196) This view seems to us to miss the satiric potentialities of the play.

21. For discussion of the actual music provided by Purcell, see Curtis A. Price, *Henry Purcell and the London Stage* (Cambridge: Cambridge Univ. Press, 1984), Chapter 4. Although Purcell's music evidently made some splash, and was printed in Q1 (extremely unusual), it appears to have been an afterthought and the songs are not really integrated with the play. Only "For Iris I sigh" (as Purcell rephrased Dryden's lyric) is thematically apropos (p. 299).

Sanitized sex comedy

The concept is mid-1670s cuckolding comedy, made accept-able to a bourgeois audience (whether of 1690 or the 1980s) by importation of gods to create unreality and eliminate choice on the part of the adulteress. We are invited to identify with the gods (especially Jupiter) and to enjoy the abuse of Alcmena in a sexist way. In this production Amphitryon becomes a pompous, pos-sessive husband whose inability to cope with the situation is comic. The gods look, think, and act like reincarnations of the earl of Rochester—high-spirited, unscrupulous, and devilishly attractive. Here we definitely want Mountfort, not a low come-dian, as Mercury. Since our sympathy is to be entirely with the rakish Jupiter, we might go so far as to cast the young George Powell or John Boman as Amphitryon and Charlotte Butler as Alcmena, thus ensuring that they will be totally overwhelmed by Jupiter/Betterton. The finale need not be very serious. Jupiter breezily lays down the law; Amphitryon and Alcmena are ini-tially confounded, but there is nothing they can do, so they go willingly into the house together as Sosia finishes off the play with his cheerful conclusion that a smart man would rather be the cuckold than the cully.

Satire on libertinism and abuse of power

This production asks us to sympathize with Amphitryon and Alcmena as victims of Jupiter's cynical duplicity. Dryden's epi-graph, manufactured from a pair of lines in Book IV of the *Aeneid*, may be taken as a hint toward this production concept: "Splendid indeed is the praise and rich the spoils ye win . . . if one woman is subdued by the guile of two gods!" The gods can be slick and sophisticated or tawdry and dissipated. Mercury could be Mountfort, someone like Cardell Goodman, or Tony Leigh. Elizabeth Barry would be a splendid choice for Alcmena, though a more passively pathetic conception with Anne Brace-girdle would be fine, too. Joseph Williams is a reasonable choice as Amphitryon, though we might prefer a higher-voltage tragic actor like Barton Booth. Staging and line delivery would emphasize that Jupiter is a sadistic bully, and he would positively revel in the disclosures of the finale. Amphitryon and Alcmena would be left devastated, and no hint of reconciliation should be allowed. During Sosia's concluding speech we could even have Alcmena make a timid, appealing gesture toward her husband, only to have him turn coldly away and depart for the city, leaving her to exit sadly into the house. In this production Sosia's cheery summation functions very much the way the final sextet does in Mozart's *Don Giovanni*—it demonstrates how little "ordinary" people comprehend of the events we have just witnessed.

Dryden certainly does not demand that the play be produced this way. He is much too professional a dramatist to force unwelcome perceptions on his audience, and even the darkest and bleakest imaginable production of *Amphitryon* will be considerably leavened by all the jokes and the farcical confusion. If we had to make a guess about how the 1690 production worked, we would suppose that it made Jupiter moderately unsympathetic without pushing pathos for Amphitryon and Alcmena to the point that the audience really felt uncomfortable. A "compromise" production might have them exit sadly into the house together, hurt but resigned, leaving the audience to make just about anything it pleased of the affair. Dryden gives the director leeway for radically different choices, and the text will work for a variety of compromises as well as for the radically distinct productions we have described.

APPENDIX: SCENE PLAN

Despite the showy use of flyings in Act I (and again for Jupiter in Act V) *Amphitryon* is in fact a very simple show to stage. The song and dance routines in Act IV (pp. 299–302) call for the performers to appear from "underground," summoned in the traditional fashion through the traps by stamping on the stage—but this is hardly vital. Only four settings are required. Act I scene i takes place outdoors at night—in midair, if the director wishes. Scene ii requires an interior setting in Amphitryon's palace, used again in II.ii. The beginning of Act II specifies "Night-Scene of a

226

Pallace." Acts III, IV, and V take place in a courtyard in front of Amphitryon's palace. The scene plan is straightforward.

    2.3   Courtyard in front of Amphitryon's palace
    2.2   "Night-Scene of a Pallace"
    2.1   The heavens at night (for I.i.) [22]

    1.1   A room in Amphitryon's palace

In general, the fancier the original staging, the more like an "opera" it would have seemed; but beyond that, to signal production concept in stock scenery would have been almost impossible. A modern production would naturally adapt scenery and costumes to interpretation. Sets by Sempé would immediately suggest fantasy; Gahan Wilson would signal a very bleak satire indeed, with Jupiter as monster and Amphitryon as paranoid victim.

22. There is actually no need for a special scene for I.i. The "Night-Scene of a Pallace" used for II.i. would be perfectly satisfactory. If a special scene was used for I.i. it might well have been handled with a cloth drop rather than shown on the shutters. All that is needed is a dark background with some stars visible.

8

The Wives Excuse (1691)

*T*he Wives Excuse* is the least familiar of the plays discussed in
this book, and the only one not to succeed in the theatre. A
phrase in Dryden's commendatory poem ("bore but a single
show") is generally taken to mean that it came off after the first
night. This utter failure is the more startling because Southerne's
Sir Anthony Love had been a tremendous success a year earlier,
and *The Wives Excuse* was mounted with a stellar cast, innovative
staging, and brilliant music by Purcell.[1] But neither Dryden's
praise nor Southerne's later successes got the play another hearing. Early twentieth-century critics found no virtues in the piece.
Nicoll dismisses it with contempt; Dodds calls it "dreary" and
"fetid."[2] Its first champion was John Harrington Smith, who argued that *The Wives Excuse* should be rated "one of the five most
considerable comedies written between 1660 and 1700."[3] This

1. For a splendid analysis of the highly functional use of music in this play,
see Curtis A. Price, *The Theatre Music of Henry Purcell* (Cambridge: Cambridge
Univ. Press, 1984), Chapter 4. For a brief account of the extant music, see the
Appendix at the end of this book.
2. Allardyce Nicoll, *A History of English Drama, 1660–1900*, rev. ed., 6 vols.
(Cambridge: Cambridge Univ. Press, 1952–1959), I, 240–41; John Wendell
Dodds, *Thomas Southerne Dramatist* (New Haven: Yale Univ. Press, 1931),
pp. 80, 82.
3. *The Gay Couple in Restoration Comedy* (Cambridge, Mass.: Harvard Univ.
Press, 1948), p. 144. The others, in his opinion, are *The Man of Mode*, *The
Country-Wife*, *The Plain-Dealer*, and *The Way of the World*.

favorable opinion has been endorsed by a number of later scholars,[4] but to date the play has received remarkably little critical
analysis. We include it because we agree with Smith's glowing assessment: Southerne's play is among the most serious, complex,
and original of all late seventeenth-century comedies.

Three questions seem crucial to an understanding of *The Wives
Excuse*. (1) Why did the play flop so dismally in 1691? (2) What
is the play really about? Critics since Genest ("wants incident
sadly")[5] have disparaged the plot, and most critical commentary
has stressed marital discord to the exclusion of almost everything
else.[6] This leaves much unaccounted for, and the play out of balance. What is the audience to be interested in, if not the plot?
(3) What attitude does the play invite us to take toward its characters and events? This is a very slippery problem, the answer to
which must be the premise of any production.

There are two obvious ways to produce *The Wives Excuse*: (1) as
a problem play about marital discord, evoking pity for the betrayed wife; or (2) as a satire on society. As a problem play *The
Wives Excuse* has been compared with Vanbrugh's *The Provok'd
Wife* (1697); as a satire it has been likened to Wycherley's *The
Plain-Dealer* (1676). Both concepts are valid and producible, but
we are going to argue that the most interesting thrust of the play
is toward (3) a wry and cynical realism about society presented
with a critical detachment that is downright Chekovian.

CONVENTIONS USED AND ABORTED

The Wives Excuse is every bit as complicated as *The Way of the
World*, and, if anything, harder to follow. Southerne restricts the

4. A. H. Scouten, "Notes Toward a History of Restoration Comedy," *Philological Quarterly*, 45 (1966), 62–70; James Sutherland, *English Literature of
the Late Seventeenth Century* (Oxford: Clarendon Press, 1969), p. 145; Hume,
Development, pp. 386–87. For a competent descriptive appreciation, see Robert L. Root, Jr., *Thomas Southerne* (Boston: Twayne, 1981), Chapter 4. The
best critical account of the play remains Harold Love's "*The Wives' Excuse* and
Restoration Comedy," *Komos*, 2, No. 4 (n.d.; ca. 1971), 148–56.

5. Genest, II, 22.

6. See Anthony Kaufman, "'This Hard Condition of a Woman's Fate':

action of the play to about twenty-four hours (moving from the end of a concert one evening to a masked ball the next night). Despite the seeming flux of characters, he keeps the two main actions separate from the end of his exposition in Act I until the climactic masquerade.

Mr. Friendall, a coward and philanderer, pursues his wife's friend Mrs. Sightly. He is caught *in flagrante delicto* with Mrs. Wittwoud (whom he has mistaken for Mrs. Sightly) in Act V. Lovemore, an experienced rake, pursues Mrs. Friendall throughout the play, trying to show up her husband as a means of shaking her fidelity. At the end of the play the Friendalls agree to separate.

Lovemore's friend Wellvile has long been attracted to Mrs. Sightly. In a complex subplot they become estranged and then reconciled. He makes a half-hearted proposal of marriage at the end of Act V; she puts him off.

Not much changes in the course of the play. At the end the Friendalls have agreed to separate; Wellvile has proposed to Mrs. Sightly without immediate result; young Fanny has been seduced. But the impact of these events is minimized: the finale is presented so tersely and flatly as to be almost a throwaway. And our concern for Fanny is limited by the extreme brevity of her appearance: she speaks only one line, and that in Act I. Action is not as important in this play as in most other comedies in the period. By contrast even *The Man of Mode* seems action-packed. Other elements outweigh plot, and when we analyze the play we quickly discover that this is only one of many ways in which Southerne frustrates his audience.

Throughout the play, Southerne works so systematically against audience expectations that we must assume he chose this strategy deliberately. There are literally dozens of particular instances, some of which we will review below. But anyone analyzing the

---

Southerne's *The Wives' Excuse*," *Modern Language Quarterly*, 34 (1973), 36–47; Robert D. Hume, "Marital Discord in English Comedy from Dryden to Fielding," *Modern Philology*, 74 (1977), 248–72.

play needs to realize just how disconcerting the principal violations must have been.

The audience must have anticipated an utterly different kind of play. None of Southerne's earlier work is anything like this; *Sir Anthony Love*, its immediate predecessor, is a rollicking adventure farce that features Mrs. Mountfort as the title character, a runaway mistress strutting through the play as a libertine and talking like a rakehell. She pursues the man she loves to France, and in company with Ilford they chase French girls. Sir Anthony eventually cheats her keeper, Sir Gentle Golding, out of £500 a year for life. The whole play is dazzlingly energetic and extravagantly witty. Morality is simply not an issue. To playgoers expecting something along these lines *The Wives Excuse* must have come as a dreadful disappointment. An audience which arrived primed for a new Neil Simon and found itself confronted with one of Pinter's most bleak and cryptic efforts would probably feel much the same way.

The full title is *The Wives Excuse, or Cuckolds Make Themselves*. The implication seems plain: Mr. Friendall will get cuckolded. But he does not, although Southerne sets up the action to make us expect a cuckolding: Mrs. Friendall has to cover up her husband's cowardice. She refuses Lovemore's proposition. Mrs. Sightly tells her that Friendall is pressing for an assignation. Mrs. Friendall, masked, hears her husband say that he married her for her money and in order to womanize more easily. Lovemore renews his addresses; Mrs. Friendall admits that he attracts her, but still refuses him. Friendall is caught copulating with Mrs. Wittwoud by a large group which includes his wife and all their friends.

Every insistence upon virtue is followed by fresh provocation to rebellion, but Mrs. Friendall clings to her virtue. Southerne could easily have written the play to include her fall, perhaps to confront her husband with it and to justify it. Why did he leave the issue dangling? Perhaps in the hope of making the audience think more seriously about what is involved; perhaps because he was conscious of growing objections to adultery in plays, especially from "the ladies."[7] Justifying this frustration of adultery in the epilogue, Southerne says "Ladies, all his aim, is pleasing you." And in the dedication he admits that "Sparks" were "Affronted at Mrs. *Friendall* . . . offended with her Virtue" (p. 41).[8] The audience expected sex it did not get. Lovemore is a Dorimant balked in his schemes.

Convention would dictate that Wellvile and Mrs. Sightly marry, or at least agree to marry—but they do not. Compare the Courtine-Sylvia plot in Otway's *The Souldiers Fortune* (1680), set against "justified" adultery in the main plot. Even in sex comedies like *The Country-Wife* and *The Man of Mode* we get serious romance plots brought to fruition in Harcourt and Alithea, Young Bellair and Emilia. Southerne declines to provide this conventional good cheer in his finale, merely hinting that Wellvile and Mrs. Sightly *may* someday agree to marry. This contributes to a flat and depressing conclusion.

Late seventeenth-century comedies are generally very negative in their treatment of fools and cowards. Friendall is shown up mercilessly from beginning to end, but despite the harsh satire he is left quite unpunctured. He feels no hurt or shame; he is not disgraced by his cowardice; even his public discovery with Mrs. Wittwoud does not faze him—he is sorry only that he was not found with a more glamorous lady. Why leave this repellent creature so untouched? Arguably, Southerne is making a more general satiric point about what society accepts and is really like. But in any case his leaving Friendall unpunished must have surprised and disconcerted the original audience.

Beyond these major frustrations of expectation Southerne indulges in a whole series of smaller ones. For example, the opening scene in which servants gossip outside the music meeting is

7. John Harrington Smith, "Shadwell, the Ladies, and the Change in Comedy," *Modern Philology*, 46 (1948), 22–33. Cf. Robert D. Hume, "The Change in Comedy: Cynical versus Exemplary Comedy on the London Stage, 1678–1693," *Essays in Theatre*, 1 (1983), 101–18.
8. Textual references are to Thomas Southerne, *The Wives Excuse*, ed. Ralph R. Thornton (Wynnewood, Pa.: Livingston, 1973).

unprecedented in late seventeenth-century drama. The idea is brilliant: the servants' talk is neatly paralleled by the society chat of the next scene. In practice, the audience was probably thoroughly befuddled. Exposition is provided by servants whose identity is uncertain. (A reader can laboriously sort them out, but in performance it would be almost impossible.) The parallel between servants and gentry was as unusual as it was probably unwelcome.

Turning to character relationships, as another instance of frustrated expectation, we find that the exchanges between Lovemore and Mrs. Friendall are given only very fragmentarily, a pattern maintained throughout the play. Southerne titillates us, but deprives us of the sex game. The conspicuous tête-à-tête in Act I is mentioned by almost everyone, but we do not hear it (pp. 52–55). Equally unexpected is Springame's shockingly cavalier view of his sister. "She has satisified her Relations enough in marrying this Coxcomb: now let her satisfie her self, if she pleases, with any body she likes better." He adds in so many words that she is welcome to cuckold Friendall with Lovemore (p. 52).

Mrs. Wittwoud is an extraordinary and disconcerting character: an upper-class bawd. Mistress of a married man not in the play, she is quite indifferent to her cousin Fanny's seduction. And she is no more distressed by public exposure than Friendall. But not only does she go unpunished, she turns out to be one of the most accurate judges of events in the play. Southerne replaces the traditional rake's dressing room scene with Wittwoud's she-wit toilette (II.i.), which gives us a different perspective on the rake's game. When Mrs. Teazall asks Mrs. Wittwoud what she will do if she gets pregnant (p. 65), the question sheds a sour light on Wilding's jokes about Fanny's possible pregnancy two scenes later. We hear only one line of the Wilding/Fanny flirtation, and the actual seduction occurs offstage. Unlike the Dorimant/Bellinda episode, this one gives us no chance to enjoy the rake's success, and Southerne proceeds to dwell on what is to become of Fanny. Prostitution or marriage to a gull are the possibilities. Wilding's discussion of his conquest with his servant (II.iii.) imitates the notorious Dorimant-Handy scene ("tying up Linnen") but is disconcertingly explicit about the rake's contempt for his conquest.

Joint cowardice prevents the duel between Friendall and Ruffle in Act III—but nothing is made of that cowardice, though public revelation of it would be a form of social death. Likewise, Friendall's attentions to Mrs. Sightly are clumsy, obvious, and to some of their circle embarrassing—yet she gets little to say to discourage him. Nor does she seem surprised or distressed by him. The implications about what is to be expected in this society are unappetizing. Respectable old ladies do not usually counsel adultery, but this is precisely what Mrs. Teazall suggests to Mrs. Friendall ("use him as you please, no Body will think you wrong him"—p. 85). Wilding pursues Mrs. Sightly after giving Wellvile his word not to, and his breaking his word produces a near duel at the end of Act IV. But nothing comes of it! Southerne makes his point: in this society a gentleman's word is not to be taken seriously. Nor is the word of a woman, as Mrs. Wittwoud's protestations to Mrs. Sightly in Act IV make clear ("as I hope to be sav'd, upon the Faith of a Christian, and may I never rise off my Knees into your good Opinion agen"—p. 107).

The events of the rest of the play continue to run against all general expectation. When Friendall brags to his wife and Mrs. Sightly (who are masked) in V.ii., nothing happens: no unmasking, no confrontation, no reproaches—not even some wifely lamentation in private afterwards. Nor, when Wellvile and Mrs. Sightly make up during the masquerade dance, do we hear their conversation: Southerne deprives us of the explicit emotional expressions we expect. He does much the same thing at the end, which comes very abruptly indeed. In two pages we get the *in flagrante* discovery, Wellvile's half-hearted proposal, and the Friendalls' agreement to separate. The separation is discussed briefly but realistically: the tone is entirely different from the obvious precedents—Shadwell's *Epsom-Wells*, for example. Far from having the separation forced on him, Friendall welcomes it. There is no conventional sense of an ending. Mrs. Friendall is stuck; Wellvile and Mrs. Sightly fail to fall into each other's arms;

Lovemore hopes he may benefit, but is not sure. No dance, no marriage, no punishments, no resolution of problems: a very odd ending indeed.

Southerne's epigraph from Cicero hints that the audience was confused by the play: *Nihil est his, qui placere volunt, tam adversarium, quam expectatio* (Nothing is so adverse to those who wish to please as expectation). We can well believe Dryden's comment that the play was not "damn'd or hiss'd, / But with a kind Civility, dismiss'd." The title page tells us that *The Wives Excuse* is a "COMEDY." True, but a most unusual comedy for 1691. Southerne was asking his audience—albeit unsuccessfully—to reconsider its assumptions about the conventions of Carolean sex comedy.

THE CHARACTERS AND THE ORIGINAL CAST

If the point of *The Wives Excuse* does not reside in events or wit (and the wit is nearly as minimal as the action), then we must look to the characters for some sense of what Southerne was trying to communicate to his audience.

Mr. and Mrs. Friendall

Mrs. Friendall is clearly crucial to the impact of the play, and in particular to the amount of pathos in a production. We learn from the servants in I.i. that Mrs. Friendall has been married less than three months (p. 46) and that she "has discover'd some of my Master's Intrigues of late" (p. 47). She is embarrassed by her husband's songwriting (p. 58), and unhappy that he turns their house into "one of the publick Places of the Town" (p. 84). Nevertheless, she can say in Act I, "I think he loves me, and that excuses him to me" (p. 58). She displays intelligence and energy in her attempts to shield her husband from exposure as a coward when Ruffle insults him. She hauls him away; takes responsibility for his inaction upon herself (pp. 61–62); then writes a challenge in his name and manipulates Springame and Lovemore with skill to bring off her scheme. She realizes that if her husband looks bad, so does she: "I must appear to the world, only in that

235

rank of honour, which you are pleas'd to maintain," she tells him (p. 66). She hopes to prevent Friendall from openly displaying cowardice *to her* (p. 67). She explains her motive in soliloquy: "if he had betray'd that baseness to me, I shou'd despise him; and can I love the Man I most despise?" (p. 68). She wants to love her husband; failing that, she is determined to present the appearance of loving him. The action of the play is contrived to make this impossible.

When Mrs. Friendall repulses Lovemore in Act V, she makes a number of significant admissions (pp. 116–17). Her husband is "her Cross." She does not blame Lovemore for pursuing her and admits that their society might sanction her adultery. ("I don't blame you for designing upon me, custome has fashion'd it into the way of living among the men; and you may be i'th'right to all the Town.") She admits that her "Vertue" has been "try'd" by his attentions, "but all beyond that tryal is my crime, and not to be forgiven." She goes so far as to say, "Nay more, I will confess my heart to you: If I cou'd make you mine—. . . But I am marry'd, only pitty me." She is determined to remain "i'th'right . . . to my Sex and to my self."[9]

Her immediate reward for her virtue is public exposure of her husband's infidelity. At first she says nothing. When Lovemore prods her for a response, she addresses her husband and explains her feelings. She resents being condemned "to a Slavery for life" in marriage. She has considered legal separation (divorce being impossible), but rejects it: "if by separation we get free, then all our Husband's faults are laid on us. This hard Condition of a Woman's fate, I've often weigh'd, therefore resolv'd to bear. And I have born, O! what have I not born? But patience tires." Her response to Friendall's proposal of a separation is bitter: "I must be still your Wife, and still unhappy." Audience reaction would of

9. Harold Love points out to us that this speech of Mrs. Friendall's is actually in blank verse, and will be set that way in the forthcoming Love-Jordan Oxford edition. Both Q1 and Thornton print the speech as prose. Putting the speech in verse (as Southerne clearly intended) is obviously meant to draw special attention to what is said, and to invite the audience to regard the speech with special seriousness. Southerne does this at a number of points in the play.

course be affected by the staging of the final scene. Dryden's poem suggests a hint that Lovemore will succeed in due course: the wife "not accepting, did but just refuse. / There was such a glance at parting; such a look / As bids thee not give o're, for one rebuke"—i.e., Lovemore will get Mrs. Friendall to bed, and Southerne will succeed with his next play. A longing glance would give one forecast, a withdrawal into isolated sorrow, quite another.

Act by act, Southerne knocks the props out from under Mrs. Friendall. Are we to admire her virtue? By the standards of her society it is silly. The epilogue implies that Southerne anticipated contempt from at least part of the audience:

> Damn me, cries one, had I been *Betterton*,   [i.e., Lovemore]
> And struts, and cocks, I know what I had done;
> She should not ha' got clear of me so soon.

We must assume that Mrs. Friendall finds Lovemore genuinely attractive. She says so in V.iii. (p. 117), and we see her politely but firmly refuse Courtall, the only other rake who approaches her (p. 59). She is virtuous, but not innocent or ineffectual. How much pathos is she supposed to evoke? Production choices would make a considerable difference here, but the text does not suggest a fundamentally pathetic conception. We get no tears, and minimal lamentation. Mrs. Friendall is too active and vigorous a character to come across as a Banks heroine translated into comedy. Nor is she a Fidelia in search of a way out of London society. Marital problems aside, she is very much a town lady and at home in this milieu. She takes obvious pleasure in the rituals of her social world—conversation, music, tea-drinking, parties, gambling.

The role of Mrs. Friendall was created by Elizabeth Barry, a piece of casting which raises some questions. Barry was about thirty-three years old in 1691, an actress of tremendous force of character who would contribute to the impression that Mrs. Friendall was not a helpless innocent. She had done some highly pathetic roles (e.g., Monimia in *The Orphan*, 1680), but by this time authors were generally casting Barry in more lurid parts,

Anne Bracegirdle in pathetic ones. A more obvious choice for Mrs. Friendall in the United Company at this time would have been Susanna Mountfort (then twenty-four), who had done so well for Southerne in the title role of *Sir Anthony Love*. Finding Mrs. Mountfort cast as Mrs. Wittwoud—a tough, scheming female rake, rather long in the tooth—is a surprise: Barry would seem to have been a natural for that role. We have no information about Southerne's casting plans when he wrote *The Wives Excuse* in early 1691, but we do have evidence that by the time of the premiere in December Mrs. Mountfort could not plausibly have taken the part of the younger, trimmer Mrs. Friendall: she was five months pregnant.[10] Barry might well have been Southerne's original choice for the part, but one can readily imagine Mrs. Mountfort as a softer, more pathetic Mrs. Friendall.

Mr. Friendall is neither a stock figure nor a particularly complex one. He regards himself as a ladykiller, though his unsubtle tactics do not seem notably successful. Our first impression of him is of an amiable but pretentious fool. Later we may wonder if his cowardice contributes to his blindness to all mockery. He delights in his belief that Lovemore is his confidant and, mistakenly sure of him, needs no other close friends (pp. 106, 111–13, 119).

In case we should be in any doubt about Friendall's despicability, Southerne convicts him out of his own mouth in V.ii. by way of preparation for the unmasking in V.iii. He admits that he is indifferent to his wife: "to tell you the Truth, the chief End of my marrying her, (next to having the Estate settled upon me) was to carry on my Entrigues more swimmingly with the Ladies" (p. 112). He always copies out half a dozen identical love letters every morning, to have them ready for any occasion.

Friendall displays little emotion about anything. He seems to feel nothing but passing irritation at being caught with Mrs. Wittwoud. His response to his wife's lamentation is unembarrassed, unfeeling, and self-serving. "I see we are both disap-

10. See Albert S. Borgman, *The Life and Death of William Mountfort* (Cambridge: Harvard Univ. Press, 1935), p. 171n for the baptismal record.

pointed in this affair of Matrimony; it is not the condition you expected; nor has it the advantages I propos'd. Now, Madam, since 'tis impossible to make it happy between us, let us ev'n resolve to make it as easie as we can. . . . Your own Relations shall provide for you at pleasure, out of my Estate; I only article that I may have a freedom of visiting you, in the round of my acquaintance" (p. 124). As he says in his final speech, he is happy to recover his liberty: marriage has not been as helpful to his philandering as he had hoped it would be.

The impression made by Friendall in performance could hardly be favorable. The role was created by William Mountfort, then about twenty-seven, an actor of exceptional versatility. He played exemplary heroes and romantic leads (Belfond Junior in *The Squire of Alsatia*, Sir William in *The Scowrers*) as well as fops and fools of various sorts (Bayes in *The Rehearsal*, Sir Courtly Nice, Novel in *The Plain-Dealer*). He was often cast in rakish roles (Lopez in *The Libertine*, Willmore in *The Rover*). We can assume that he was capable of carrying out any production concept with skill. The obvious question is whether Friendall should be actively unpleasant or merely contemptible. In a production stressing pathos his treatment of Mrs. Friendall might be made overtly contemptuous rather than just offhand. For example, when he declines to stay with his wife in St. James's Park ("I'll go home with you like a good Husband . . . but no man of fashion, you know, walks with his Wife, besides there's a Noble Lord I must walk with"—p. 84), he could be either jocular or insulting. Likewise her response ("Any thing to be rid of my Company") could be either a cry of despair or an attempt at a playful reproach.

Friendall could be made a dandified fop, but there is nothing in the text to suggest this. He probably dresses expensively, but Southerne does not seem to picture him as a visibly ridiculous character. In a production not dedicated to pathos, Friendall should probably appear presentable in dress and manners. If he does not, his wife's attempts to put the best face on things seem implausible, and his superficial acceptance in society is hard to believe. Friendall is a less obvious fop and fool than Sparkish, but the characters have some similarities. Wycherley spares Alithea such a marriage; Southerne asks us to consider the feelings of a woman trapped in one.

The contrasting women: Mrs. Sightly, Mrs. Wittwoud, Fanny, Mrs. Teazall

Mrs. Sightly is young, good-looking, and well to do. Her life is probably a hint of Mrs. Friendall's before marriage. She expresses few opinions about anything; her main concern is her reputation, though she seems to think herself invulnerable to the hazards of this world. Until warned by Wellvile, she has no inkling of Mrs. Wittwoud's plot against her. When provoked into a confrontation she can show some spirit, as both Wellvile and Mrs. Wittwoud discover. Mrs. Sightly is virtuous but hardly innocent. She knows about Wittwoud's married lover (p. 107); her response to Friendall's dropping a billet for her is "Fye, fye, before your Wife—" (p. 61). She is a genuine friend to Mrs. Friendall, telling her calmly about Friendall's unwanted attentions (p. 101) and going with her to the masked assignation.

On the printed page, however, Mrs. Sightly remains obstinately shadowy. The role was taken by Anne Bracegirdle (then about twenty-eight), celebrated for her portrayals of beautiful virgins. Wellvile tells us that he has "followed" Mrs. Sightly "these seven years" (p. 88), and Mrs. Wittwoud sneers at him as a "Platonick Lover" (p. 86). But how does Mrs. Sightly respond to him? Is she simply an unawakened virgin? Much depends on her apparent age. If she is visibly twenty-five, something is amiss. If, however, she appears more like twenty, we might deduce that Wellvile simply spotted her young and has been waiting for her to grow up.

Why has Mrs. Sightly not married? Perhaps she is still quite young, but she must have had opportunities for marriage or affairs. (Friendall and Wilding are both panting for her.) Mrs. Sightly is naturally dismayed by the example of the Friendalls' marriage. Is her status an indication of serious reservations about marriage? Her response to Wellvile's proposal is ambiguous enough to permit a wide variety of constructions in performance: "This is too sudden to be serious: when you're in earnest,

you won't need an answer" (p. 123). This could be played freez-
ingly or meltingly, as either a put off or a bit of encouragement.
But however Mrs. Sightly was played—and we tend to favor the
dubious-about-marriage interpretation—she is clearly not part
of a romance line that offsets the Friendalls' marital discord plot.

Mrs. Wittwoud serves principally as a foil for Lovemore. Both
can be considered villains; both are cynical manipulators of their
friends. Mrs. Wittwoud is getting a bit old to be marriageable.
We learn in II.i. that she is the mistress of a married man ("I own
he is my curse, doom'd for my plague, and pleasure") and that
she is both an unpleasant tease and genuinely promiscuous. Mrs.
Teazall says in exasperation, "All your Relations know you, and
are afraid to have you in a House with 'em." She brings her "Fel-
lows" home, a practice Mrs. Teazall regrets having been "Fool
enough to allow of," since one of them seduced her elder niece
(p. 65). Whether Wittwoud has money is unclear: she may be
living off Mrs. Teazall (as is hinted on page 66) or she may actually be a paid bawd. Courtall remarks that "She's never the worse
Bawd . . . for being a Gentlewoman" (p. 87); Wellvile calls her
"Bawd" both in soliloquy and to Mrs. Sightly (pp. 89, 105).
Mrs. Wittwoud's long soliloquy about herself tells us that she
wants to be pursued by men (p. 75), but she hates "a Blockhead,
that will never give a Woman a reputable occasion of refusing
him" (p. 86).

Mrs. Wittwoud is clearly unpleasant, destructive, and exceed-
ingly dishonest. As an older woman, a kind of female rake and
Machiavel, she seems ideally designed for the talents of Elizabeth
Barry and rather out of the way for Susanna Mountfort. As the
play was cast in 1691, Wittwoud probably came across more
"mischievous" than villainous, but the role certainly has both potentialities. (Wellvile comments that she is "every thing that's
mischievous; abandon'd and undone; undone her self, she wou'd
undo the Sex"—p. 89.) Wittwoud is not, we should emphasize, a
Lady Cockwood: she is still attractive enough that she can get sex
if she wants it, as Springame's attentions prove. Mrs. Mountfort
was a comedienne. Had Barry taken the role, Wittwoud's plotting would probably have seemed a good deal more threatening

than the younger woman could make it. Several of Wittwoud's scenes offer considerable latitude in performance. When, for example, she goes down on her knees to Mrs. Sightly and begs for mercy (pp. 107–8), is she genuinely in a panic? Or is she simply smart enough to know how to get Sightly to keep her mouth shut?

Of Fanny and Mrs. Teazall little need be said. Fanny is a young fool who proves easy game for Wilding. Her function is to remind us of the fate of foolish girls and to illustrate Mrs. Wittwoud's evil influence. Mrs. Teazall is the most obviously farcical character in the play—a comic old prude. She worries constantly about what the neighbors will think—of Fanny, of Mrs. Wittwoud's roistering, of masquerades—but she also envies younger women. Mrs. Wittwoud tells Wilding that her aunt once deserved the name Teazall, but now can enjoy only card playing (p. 94). The old lady's concern that Fanny not repeat her sister's disgrace seems genuine, though it may spring as much from wanting to be rid of responsibility as from love of the younger niece.[11] She disapproves of Mrs. Wittwoud's liaison with a married man, yet she advises Mrs. Friendall to go ahead and have an affair (p. 85).

Mrs. Teazall was played by Katherine Corey (then about fifty-six), long a specialist in ridiculous old women, though she acted serious roles as well. She could do anything from Octavia in *All for Love* or the sympathetic mother Sysigambis in *The Rival Queens* to the Widow Blackacre in *The Plain-Dealer* or Mistress Barebottle in *Cutter of Coleman Street*. Teazall is clearly a figure of fun in this play, but not an entirely helpless one. She has no illusions about her niece, as we discover in V.iii.: even before Fanny's slip with Wilding, Mrs. Teazall was making all possible haste to marry her off to "Mr. *Buttybun*" (p. 121). Content to have appearances maintained, she accepts the mores of this society.

11. Fanny's unseen sister Biddy has been seduced and impregnated by one of Wittwoud's friends, and has had to be married hastily "below her Rank . . . into the City, where 'twas less scandalous" (p. 65). Wittwoud admits responsibility for "my Cousin *Biddy's* Miscarriage."

The contrasting men: Lovemore, Wilding, Courtall, Springame, and Ruffle

Because Lovemore represents a choice for Mrs. Friendall, he has an important part in determining the impact of the play. He is conspicuous on stage, but Southerne does not tell us much about him. We see him as a casual participant in this social circle and as a rake with designs on Mrs. Friendall—but as precious little else. We learn early in Act I that he has "hopes of the Wife depending upon the senceless behaviour of the Husband," and that he is actively plotting "to expose him" "before her face" (p. 60). He gets Ruffle to insult Friendall, and ever alert for advantage comes away with the forged challenge, even though his first scheme fails. His soliloquy as he puzzles out what has happened is a clear demonstration of his formidable abilities (p. 83). He finds Mrs. Friendall impervious to romantic adoration: she takes over the conversation and makes him look foolish. But when he returns the challenge—out of regard for her, he says— she is mollified. His comment is blunt: "he that won't lye to his Mistress, will hardly lye with her" (pp. 97–100).

In contrast to Friendall, Lovemore looks good. He is smarter and more socially adept; he knows how to be gracious and attentive to a lady; he is not a coward. Eugene Waith has gone so far as to conclude that Lovemore "appears to be sincerely in love with" Mrs. Friendall.[12] This is, however, not what the text says. When Mrs. Friendall "*Goes from him*," saying "But I am marry'd, only pitty me," Lovemore's reaction is contemptuous and self-serving (p. 117)—and it comes too late in the play to be modified. For interpretive purposes, let us examine his speech in three parts. (1) "Pity her! She does not deserve it, that won't better her condition, when she may." But exactly how is Mrs. Friendall to "better her condition" via adultery? She might enjoy the sex for a while,

---

12. See Eugene M. Waith, "Admiration in the Comedies of Thomas Southerne," *Evidence in Literary Scholarship*, ed. René Wellek and Alvaro Ribeiro (Oxford: Clarendon Press, 1979), pp. 89–103, esp. p. 97.

but this is sophistry. (2) "But she's marry'd she says; why, that was the best of my reasons of following her at first; and I like her so well, as she's another Man's wife, I shou'd hardly mend the matter by making her my own." Lovemore would not marry her if he could. (3) "I won't think yet my two months thrown away on her . . . but I begin to believe that every Man loses his labour this way sometimes." In other words Lovemore has deliberately fixed on this young wife as a likely prospect for seduction, and he sees her as merely one of a series. He has nothing invested in her but two months of his time.

Lovemore was played by Betterton, who was indubitably versatile enough to put any imaginable construction on this part. He had played glamorous rakes like Dorimant, repulsive rakes like Nemours, and plain villains like Lee's Caesar Borgia and Shadwell's Don John. He was fifty-six in 1691, and though Lovemore is presumably much younger than that, Betterton's age would have allowed him to play this character as a man in his thirties, well settled into a bachelor pattern. A Lovemore the same age as Friendall could not readily appear so calloused and infinitely experienced. In company, Lovemore is polished and might even seem charming. But his soliloquies afford ample opportunity for displaying the icy manipulator and predator he really is. In a production oriented to pathos he could be made quite unpleasant. Even in a more positive interpretation he cannot legitimately be presented as the husband Mrs. Friendall deserves. How is the audience to react? If Lovemore chased Margery Pinchwifes and Lady Fidgets, we might cheer him on. But he is chasing an Alithea who has had the misfortune to marry a Sparkish. Given the context presented in this play, we cannot feel outraged (even Mrs. Friendall admits it's the way of the world), but nor are we encouraged to identify with Lovemore.

Wilding aspires to be a Lovemore. He would like to attempt Mrs. Friendall, but apparently realizes that Lovemore would not tolerate competition (p. 57). He takes advantage of an easy mark like Fanny, but his ineptitude under Mrs. Wittwoud's tutelage suggests that he is an eager beginner not yet capable of handling an intrigue that calls for subtlety. In significant contrast to

Friendall, he does not flinch from a duel (p. 108). Wilding is an attractive young man: even Mrs. Teazall comments that "He looks like a modest, civil Gentleman" (p. 93). Joseph Williams (then about twenty-nine) played a lot of secondary roles—Cassio, Aeneas in *Troilus and Cressida*—but tended to get cast as a dashing and successful young rake—e.g., as Roebuck in *Love and a Bottle*, Rains in *Epsom-Wells*, Townly in *The London Cuckolds*. Here he does no great harm to anyone the audience cares about, but he is a rather nasty piece of work. He breaks his word to his friend, and his public declaration to Mrs. Teazall in Act V that he has taught Fanny "a very good Trade" (p. 122) does not leave him in a good light. To what extent he should be foppishly dressed and unpleasantly impudent would vary with the production concept.

Courtall's name explains him: he is a pseudo-gallant who loves to provoke scandal and has little interest in actual seduction. The servants tell us in I.i. that "Mr. *Courtall* will do everything, but what he ought to do, with a Woman" (p. 48). As played by John Boman (aged about forty), a professional dandy, he would probably have been affected and overdressed. A modern production might make him recognizably homosexual, but in 1691 he certainly did not sound effeminate, whatever he looked like. Boman had a powerful bass-baritone voice, and had, for example, sung the part of Grimbald in *King Arthur* earlier that year. Affected yes, ineffectual no. He is a perfectly plausible choice to break up the duel between Wellvile and Wilding at the end of Act IV.

Springame, an army officer in winter quarters, is a junior version of Wilding. His inept pursuit of Mrs. Wittwoud reveals his lack of experience. His principal importance lies in his willingness to sanction his sister's adultery. If this is the attitude of an affectionate brother, where can Mrs. Friendall find support for virtue?

Ruffle is merely a plot device imported by Lovemore—"a Spark, that has had the misfortune of being kick'd very lately," encouraged to repair his honor by insulting "a greater Coward than himself" (p. 62). Beyond his cowardice, all we know of him is that he can pass as a gentleman in this group of people. Today

Ruffle's name might suggest a frilly little fellow with a squeaky voice. In the original production, however, the name probably conveyed the now-archaic sense of "to swagger" or "to bully" (*OED*). In 1691 Ruffle's cowardice was a particular joke since George Bright would have been playing against type. He created Ajax in Dryden's *Troilus and Cressida*, and he had played a long succession of toughs and pseudo-toughs—e.g., Bully Bounce in *Greenwich-Park*, Hackum in *The Squire of Alsatia*. This makes Ruffle's terror in III.i. all the more comic, but it also keeps Friendall's cowardice from being quite so obvious in Act I.

The detached observer: Wellvile

Wellvile technically occupies the role of friend and confidant to the "hero." He is the only male in the play (excepting Ruffle) not anxious to be a rake, or at least to seem one. Lovemore calls him "grave" (p. 85), and he comes across that way—a sober observer, though not an ineffectual man. (He is quite ready to fight a duel with Wilding.) He ridicules Friendall and sees through Wittwoud, but he seems to have no objections to Lovemore's designs on Mrs. Friendall. His dignity and reserve would have been well conveyed by Edward Kynaston (then forty-nine). Kynaston had taken such roles as Leonides in *Marriage A-la-Mode*, Harcourt in *The Country-Wife*, and Freeman in *The Plain-Dealer*. Wellvile and Lovemore have an air of assurance which the younger men try with varying success to imitate. They are clearly separate from the other men in the play, and they discuss their situations frankly together (pp. 60, 62–63, 85, 115). In Act III we learn that Wellvile is writing a play called *The Wives Excuse, or Cuckolds Make Themselves* (p. 91). His playwriting associates him with Southerne, and raises the possibility that he may have been intended as a fairly literal self-portrait. If so, his failure to challenge the mores of the group in which he moves seems doubly significant and contributes strongly to a sense of the author's entrapment in a degraded society. He is a bemused and alienated observer who seems unable to imagine any alternatives.

The impact of *The Wives Excuse* depends on the characters—or more precisely, on what they imply. Among the women we find little sign of support for Mrs. Friendall's insistence upon virtue. We are shown no examples of successful marriages, no rewards for chastity maintained, and no solutions for a wife caught in an impossible marriage. Southerne does not, we should note, allow Mrs. Sightly to function as Mrs. Friendall's confidante, which leaves Mrs. Friendall extremely isolated. Compare Mrs. Sullen in *The Beaux' Stratagem*: she can talk openly to Dorinda, and Sir Charles Freeman (her brother) is no Springame. Such confiding as Mrs. Friendall does is to Lovemore.

Southerne's men exhibit a disconcerting lack of differentiation—surely one of the major points in the play. Friendall is despicable—but how fundamentally different is he from the others? He is hardly unique in being a womanizer: even Wellvile accepts that as the normal thing for men. Anthony Kaufman complains of Southerne's "failure" to demonstrate a "stylistic distinction" "between the chief wit, Lovemore, and the chief oaf, Friendall." But Kaufman himself points to an explanation a few pages later when he suggests that "the very fact that one cannot distinguish one of the numerous fine gentlemen from another adds to the sense of their worthlessness and interchangeability."[13] Wellvile is different, but only passively so. He is, after all, Lovemore's friend and confidant. Southerne evidently meant us to see Mrs. Friendall's virtue isolated in a hostile environment. And he does not give us even a pro forma positive norm among the men, as Wycherley does in Harcourt.[14]

Analysis of the characters tells us why a good marriage is nearly impossible in this society. Southerne makes this point without much overt rancor or regret. Men and women are adversaries. Men try to avoid marriage and prey on women for sexual satisfaction; women are deluded in their hope of marrying happily and wind up bitterly disillusioned. Southerne proposes no

13. Kaufman, pp. 38, 41.
14. For an interesting if sometimes overingenious analysis of the original cast in terms of biographical implications and audience expectations, see Peter Holland, *The Ornament of Action*, pp. 141–48.

solutions; he offers avoidance of marriage as a possibility, but without enthusiasm. Directorial choices can emphasize the pathos of the women's position, or alternatively anger (at men? at sex itself? at society?). Since the text gives us a minimum of either, the third choice is detachment and irony. Our twentieth-century society has many of the same problems, though common attitudes toward a Friendall or a Wittwoud differ somewhat. Some people prefer to deny the problems (and hence the relevance of the play). To see divorce as a solution is simple-minded. It would be some help to Mrs. Friendall, but it does nothing to change the predatory nature of human relations in this society. Whether the problem is human nature or this particular society Southerne does not speculate: neither seems subject to improvement. This bleak outlook is too negative to appeal to many people, but Southerne is an unsettlingly dispassionate observer.

DIRECTORIAL CHOICES AND
THE IMPACT OF THE PLAY

Before we discuss directorial choices, we must make clear what Southerne chose not to do in this play. Practically all critics have been unhappy about the plot: less happens than one might expect. But Southerne had several obvious possibilities open to him. (1) The Cibber solution: reform. Southerne might have let the shock of public exposure with Mrs. Wittwoud bring Friendall to his senses. Following a pathetic lamentation by Mrs. Friendall (delivered in Mrs. Barry's most thrilling tones) he could have had Friendall fall on his knees to beg forgiveness. The character reversal is improbable and unprepared for, but then so is that of Loveless in Act V of *Love's Last Shift*. (2) A radical variant on the Cibber pattern is suggested by Southerne's title. Let Mrs. Friendall succumb to Lovemore, and let Friendall's discovery of her adultery shock him into reform and forgiveness. This might have been unacceptable to the audience of 1691. Erring husbands get reclaimed in this drama; seduced maidens sometimes manage to marry their penitent rakes; but female adultery is something else again. Nonetheless, if Friendall were altered a bit, the play would seem to support such an extension. (3) Vanbrugh's solution in *The Provok'd Wife*: a contrast with a satisfying romantic plot line. The marital situation of Sir John Brute and his wife is horrible. But by having Bellinda (Lady Brute's niece) decide to marry Heartfree rather than look for a wealthier suitor, Vanbrugh contrives to suggest that good marriage is possible, however depressing the example of a bad one can be. Southerne had his couple right to hand in Wellvile and Mrs. Sightly. Why not write them a few witty exchanges and let love conquer all in Act V? The answer is obvious: Southerne did not want to let us take such easy comfort. (4) Vanbrugh's alternative solution in *The Relapse*: let Mrs. Friendall's virtue charm Lovemore into at least a temporary reform while convincing Wellvile to go ahead and propose to Mrs. Sightly.

Had Southerne wanted the effect appropriate to any of these possibilities he would presumably have written his play that way. By eschewing both reform and a countervailing romance plot, he forces us to face the bleakness of the world he has depicted. We cannot take refuge in facile solutions or distractions from the main issue. There is, however, some lingering doubt about just what that main issue really is. Depending on the production concept, we can see at least three different ways for a director to conceive the point and impact of this play.

The pathetic problem play

The Wives Excuse departs from the practice of Carolean comedy by focusing on a married couple. In this respect it anticipates what Scouten calls the "marriage group" comedies by Vanbrugh, Cibber, Steele, and Farquhar in which marital discord rather than romance is central to the plot.[15] Southerne does not openly discuss "divorce" (the word is never used), but the implication hardly needed underlining. Without a divorce law in England the position of a woman like Mrs. Friendall was intolerable. Divorce for persons other than Henry VIII had started to become a public issue with the Lord Roos case in 1670, and the feminist move-

15. Scouten, pp. 66–67.

ment of the 1690s made the issue topical. Southerne's resolute refusal to provide a solution via "reform" gives *The Wives Excuse* a thematic point.

Regardless of production concept, *The Wives Excuse* is a cogent argument in favor of adopting a divorce law. If this is conceived as the central thrust of the play, then the most appropriate production concept would seem to be pathetic: we should be made sorry for Mrs. Friendall, and our sympathy will translate into support for a social reform that would give her a way out.

To elicit pathos, Mrs. Friendall should be made as passive as possible—sweet and longsuffering, humiliated by her husband's neglect, and inclined to blame herself for it. Her husband should be made overtly unpleasant, nasty to his wife's face: we should see callous mistreatment, not just indifference.

Lovemore could be handled either of two ways. He could be young and attractive (William Mountfort might be moved to this role), and his unpleasant side could be downplayed. If he is visibly besotted with Mrs. Friendall (instead of coldly predatory), his rakishness could be treated as a kind of game he plays from habit, and his nastiest outbursts the result of momentary frustration. The implication would be that if she were unmarried he might (in the fashion of Dorimant) succumb to marriage. This would give us a romantic-pathetic production. The alternative is to make Lovemore as predatory as possible, stressing Mrs. Friendall's attraction to him as a way of heightening her delusion. We then feel doubly sorry for her, because not only has she got an awful husband but she is about to get into an exploitative affair in which she will be used, hurt, and discarded. This depressing-pathetic production seems to us more plausible and more fully consonant with the text.

The principal objection to the pathetic concept is that it seems to have nothing to do with a great deal of the play. At best, the pathetic concept is incomplete. A second objection is lack of contrast. The pathos would work better if Southerne showed us a good marriage or a pleasing romance, as Vanbrugh does in *The Provok'd Wife*. The paleness of the Wellvile-Sightly line, and its incompleteness, are a strong argument that Southerne was not simply trying to make our hearts ache for Mrs. Friendall. A third objection to the pathetic concept is the lack of direct emotional appeals to the audience. Southerne displayed a considerable talent for wring-it-out pathos in *The Fatal Marriage* (1693) and *Oroonoko* (1695), and his penchant for it appears as early as 1684 in the character of the wronged but patient Erminia in *The Disappointment*. If he had wanted high voltage pathos in *The Wives Excuse*, he would almost certainly have written in some pathetic set-pieces, and Elizabeth Barry was just the actress to make the most of them.

The satire

The obvious virtue of a satiric approach is its ability to encompass the entire play. The assumption behind such a production is that Southerne was trying to show up a corrupt society. This production would seek to rouse contempt and hostility for what it shows. Depending on how negative a view is intended, Mrs. Friendall's belief in virtue could be contradicted, eroded, or ridiculed. In a satire Lovemore is definitely predatory and Mrs. Friendall deluded about him. Friendall is worse than the other rakes only in degree. Wellvile and Mrs. Sightly have little future: no marriage can be satisfactory in this milieu. The audience will realize that there are really no rules. Only Mrs. Friendall and Mrs. Sightly try to believe in rules, and they look foolish for doing so.

Southerne gives a satiric production some excellent material to work with. The servant/master parallels contribute to a sense of "*the world is all alike*" (as Gay puts the point) and are devastatingly effective satire.[16] So, cumulatively, are Southerne's flood of aborted conventions. Originally, the play could definitely have been conceived and staged as a protest against the assumptions of cuckolding comedy. Otway's *Friendship in Fashion* (1678) did this by emphasizing falsity between "friends," something Southerne

16. Brilliant as the opening scene is, it would be almost impossible to make comprehensible in performance. A modern production might go so far as to try a gimmick in order to help sort out the allusions—e.g., send the people referred to into sight at one of the balconies above the proscenium doors, or project pictures of them.

does too, though less shrilly. Lee's *The Princess of Cleve* (1682) takes a hard look at a Dorimant shorn of the protection of comic conventions. Otway's *The Atheist* (1683) shows the unhappy married life of a young couple whose romance the audience had enjoyed in *The Souldiers Fortune* three years earlier. None of these satires had proved successful. Southerne tackles a similar problem not with indignation but through false expectation and changed perspective. Here for the first time the abused wife is central. The point of *The Wives Excuse*, however, is neither pathetic display nor psychological analysis. Conceivably, Southerne gave us relatively little interior psychology because he was afraid of stirring up sympathy for Mrs. Friendall. In a satiric production she is simply not the point.

The most obvious objections to this production concept are the play's failure to uphold positive alternatives to this society, and its extraordinary lack of heat. Late seventeenth-century playwrights were not in the habit of being subtle when they opened up their satiric guns. Manly's raging against society in *The Plain-Dealer* is an extreme example, but Dryden and Congreve are pretty blunt in showing up villains, and Southerne is hardly roundabout in *The Disappointment* or with the Lieutenant Governor in *Oroonoko*. Here Friendall is exposed, but goes unpunished. Indeed, we may note that although Wellvile functions as *raisonneur* throughout the play, he never confronts Friendall directly. (Compare the role of Orgon's brother Cléante in *Tartuffe*, for example.) Thus Southerne chooses not to have Friendall resist good advice, and thereby makes Wellvile's constant mockery seem captious, merely a private game. Wellvile's intimacy with Lovemore and his lack of objection to his friend's design on Mrs. Friendall likewise diminish Wellvile's stature as a satiric spokesman. He is too implicated in this world, and too uncritical of it, to help the play work as a direct satire. And how effective is a satire which is both indirect and dispassionate? We could certainly make the characters ugly and obnoxious in performance, but the central thrust of the text does not really seem to be condemnation of this society.

252

The dispassionate comedy

The essence of this production concept is to treat the characters and their actions as natural—deplorable, perhaps, but so much the way of the world that there is no point to indignation, and precious little even to criticism. Had Southerne thought of it, *The Way of the World* would have made a good title for this play.

The key to this production is *ordinariness*. Southerne packs no great amount of action into twenty-four hours, and he does not ask us to accept major changes in outlook wrought in that time. Like Chekovian characters and like real people, these characters have tantrums over nothing (Ruffle, Mrs. Sightly) but small reactions to major crises: Wellvile does not reply to Mrs. Sightly's refusal to take his proposal seriously; neither of the Friendalls seems much affected by the prospect of separation. Southerne shows us everyday life among city gentlefolk, where hearts are broken while tea is being prepared (to paraphrase Chekov's summary of action in his plays). Southerne does not think the situation very healthy, but he does little more than present it, offering no solutions. He does not entertain us with an atypical situation among special and witty people as Etherege and Noel Coward do. He is no more genuinely critical of his social system than Shakespeare or Neil Simon. He takes neither a satiric position (in the fashion of Wycherley or Otway in his comedies) nor a didactic one (Shadwell or Shaw). He recognizes abuses, follies, and evils, but he does not suggest that they can be solved by good will, or evaded by isolating oneself from them. In this respect Southerne's position seems akin to that of Molière in *Le Misanthrope*. Unlike Congreve, Southerne cannot believe that a couple truly in love can make a satisfactory separate life for themselves within a corrupt and unsatisfactory society.

In a comic production the characters' selfishness, folly, and malice need to be neither emphasized nor minimized. There is no point either to indignation or to great sympathy for Mrs. Friendall: we must live with the world we find ourselves in. Lovemore

253

is selfish and unscrupulous, but not a villain. The tone should be wry, but not bitter. Southerne's identification with Wellvile should be stressed: this production epitomizes Wellvile's view of the world—detached, sardonic, morose, but resigned to its ineluctability. Unlike Chekov, Southerne sees no end to this pattern. Wellvile is trapped in a degraded society, but it cannot be changed and there is no other. Southerne himself remained a bachelor until he was well into his thirties;[17] this production should probably minimize any suggestion that Wellvile will marry Mrs. Sightly, let alone live happily ever after. She can wave him aside, and he can respond with a shrug.

Southerne's tone is uncompromisingly realistic. If he feels affection for these characters, it does not show. He manipulates them with a detachment bordering on indifference. Indeed, one serious question about this play is whether he develops Mrs. Friendall sufficiently to make us care whether she uses "the wives excuse" or not.

The static plot has led to complaints about lack of character development from some critics, especially those who wish to see the play as a problem piece focusing on Mrs. Friendall and the lack of a divorce law. Laura Brown, for instance, is disappointed by Southerne's failure to move in the direction of novelistic realism.[18] This seems both an incomplete view of the play (which contains more than Mrs. Friendall) and an unreasonable demand to place upon a work that cannot have the length in pages and duration in time possible in a novel. Southerne seems, in fact, deliberately to have avoided major and instantaneous character changes. In this respect he is highly realistic, refusing to employ the conventions that make drastic Act V reversals possible if not probable.

A comic production should reflect two of the play's most disturbing features: its very limited characters and the frustrating in-

17. For details see R. J. Jordan, "Thomas Southerne's Marriage," *Notes and Queries*, n.s. 21 (1974), 293–95.
18. Laura Brown, *English Dramatic Form, 1660–1760* (New Haven: Yale Univ. Press, 1981), pp. 111–12.

conclusiveness of both main plot and subplot. Southerne evidently wanted to keep us from getting too interested in any single character as a person, and he does not want us to feel that anything gets settled.

One hint of Southerne's own view of *The Wives Excuse* is the epilogue. How much of it would come across to an audience in performance is open to question. But in the course of the epilogue Southerne makes four important points. (1) Mrs. Friendall's character is "not . . . much in Vogue"—but, says Southerne, he is not trying to "disparage / That ancient *English* Perquisite of Marriage"—i.e., adultery. (2) How so? "Our Author does not set up for reforming." We might read this ironically, but indeed the play does not seem very didactic. Then what was Southerne trying to do? (3) "Our Author has his ends, if he can show, / The Women ne'er want cause for what they do." Thus Southerne says his aim is to show the effect of male libertinism upon the women of their society. (4) The audience is afraid "such Plays may spoil" its "Game." Not so, says Southerne:

> . . . Flesh and Frailty always are the same:
> And we shall still proceed in our old way,
> For all that you can do, or Poets say.

In other words, satire is pointless because human nature cannot be changed. Unless we read this in a very Brechtian way, we are left to conclude that Southerne was bent on showing us society as it is, not on criticizing it or trying to improve it. Conceived this way, the play would seem to be bleakly amusing (not pathetic, not angry)—a comedy on the text "what fools these mortals be."

By way of conclusion, let us return briefly to the questions with which we began. What is the play really about if plot and character development are minimal? Our answer is the nature of the society it presents. Is this a dangerously abstract center? It certainly is, as well as being a most unusual one for this period. What attitude are we invited to take toward the characters? We would say analytic detachment, though a production could cer-

255

tainly tilt audience response toward pathos or revulsion. Is the play producible today? Its quality hardly needs defense: *The Wives Excuse* is thoughtful, provocative, and highly innovative. Its failure in 1691 was most likely the result of audience bafflement at a play that deliberately frustrates almost every expectation the audience could have brought to it or developed from it. Its problem today would be almost the opposite: audiences would probably have trouble with a play so heavily grounded in unfamiliar conventions, especially since it uses the conventions mostly to violate them. A production dedicated to taking a hard look at the society of 1691 would work only insofar as an audience could be made to take such analysis as paradigmatic for any age—no easy task across the historical barriers involved. The likeliest design for a modern production would be emphasis on the marital discord problem and divorce law, which is workable, but presents the play largely as a museum piece. *The Wives Excuse* is probably too complicated, unfamiliar, and dependent on its original social and dramatic context to be more than a curiosity on the twentieth-century stage. It is, however, one of the toughest, most serious, and most original comedies of the seventeenth century. Its Chekovian ellipticality and detachment are unique in its time.

APPENDIX 1: STAGING PROBLEMS AND SCENE PLAN

The staging of *The Wives Excuse* presents a number of points of interest. Ten distinct settings are specified, but four of them (the lodgings of Mrs. Wittwoud, Wilding, Ruffle, and Friendall's house) would probably have been treated as identical and covered with a single interior set. Nothing in any of these scenes makes a setting distinct from the others necessary. We require then (1) the outer room of the music meeting, discussed below; (2) a deep interior room for the music meeting itself; (3) a street scene; (4) a shallow interior for the various lodgings and Friendall's house; (5) St. James's Park, a stock scene for comedy; (6) a garden; and (7) an interior room at Friendall's house, deep on the stage, used for the card game and the finale.

Schematically, the scene plan was probably something like this:

256

2.3   Music meeting
2.2   St. James's Park
2.1   Inner room at Friendall's house

1.3   Lodgings/Friendall's house
1.2   Garden
1.1   The street
0.1   Drop curtain showing outer room at music meeting

The arrangement for Act I.i., the outer room at the music meeting, is extremely unusual and has been the subject of considerable debate and confusion.[19] The scene appears to be a discovery ("*Several Footmen at Hazard, Some rising from Play*"—p. 45), and it is terminated by a discovery ("*The Curtain drawn up, shews the Company at the Musick-Meeting*"—p. 51). If the first scene is indeed a discovery, it cannot be played in front of the main curtain, which was usually raised at the end of the prologue. Drop curtains are not customary in the late seventeenth-century theatre, but they were probably used in Betterton's staging of *The Prophetess* (1690), and we would guess that the company took the trouble to have a specially-painted drop prepared for this play. The rest of the staging is routine, despite the frequent changes. There are at least twelve, probably thirteen visible scene changes.[20] The only awkward transition occurs when we move from the street to a set scene in Mrs. Wittwoud's lodgings the next morning—a change probably covered satisfactorily by the act music at the end of Act I.

APPENDIX 2: STAGING THE SONG IN ACT I

The three production concepts considered here would call for markedly different tones throughout the play. There are a great many exchanges between the characters in groups of two and

19. For a sensible summation, see Thornton's edition, pp. 27–29.
20. We have allowed for an actual street set at the end of Act I because Southerne specifies "SCENE *Changes to the Street*" (p. 61). Street scenes were often simply played against the proscenium arch—a possibility here, since the stage is cleared at the bottom of page 60.

three which could either be made private or overheard. In general, the difference in treatment would be something like this:

Pathetic. The characters should be attentive to all exchanges which do not have to be private, and they should respond with appropriate empathetic emotion, especially where Mrs. Friendall and Mrs. Sightly are concerned—embarrassment, surprise, hurt, sympathetic indignation. Lovemore and Wellvile would be the principal guides to audience response, but to some degree all of the characters can help induce a reaction against Friendall.

Satiric. The characters should watch and listen attentively, but in a spirit of derision rather than sympathy. All save Mrs. Friendall (an unhappy cipher) are prepared to laugh unsympathetically at everyone else.

Comic. The characters should be made either inattentive or unresponsive. Blocking should separate and isolate them; when they definitely see and hear they should be neither visibly supportive nor critical unless personally concerned. They should exhibit neither the warmth of the pathetic concept nor the hostility of the satiric one. In this production the characters remain aloof.

Southerne's text frequently does not specify character reactions, which must be supplied by the production concept with which the actors work. As a specific illustration, let us consider the events around the English song performed at Lovemore's instigation at the end of the music meeting (pp. 57–59). Lovemore, wishing to get his proposition across to Mrs. Friendall, is arranging to have a particular song performed by the musicians. Friendall takes the opportunity to show off as poet and songwriter. Wellvile sneers at Friendall's Italian taste. (Does Friendall hear him? Does he respond? Does anyone else?) The music master says Friendall's words are unsettable. (Who hears and reacts?) Mrs. Sightly asks if it is his "own." (Is she merely curious? Trying to conciliate him? Deliberately needling him?) He tries to say that she inspired it. (Who overhears this?) Friendall admits that he has "told a Dozen" women the same thing already. (To whom is this said? With what reaction?) Mrs. Sightly asks Mrs. Friendall about her husband's songwriting; she replies that she thinks he loves her, and this excuses his follies, though she does not like

258

them. Mrs. Wittwoud makes a snide remark about Mrs. Friend-all. (To whom?) Mrs. Friendall reproaches her husband for making them both ridiculous. (Who hears this? With what visible reaction?) The song Lovemore wanted is duly sung. (How many of the people present know that Lovemore is after Mrs. Friendall? How many of them show that they get the message? If Mrs. Friendall understands, how does she respond?) Friendall complacently thanks Lovemore for the song. (Is anyone visibly amused?)

The entire company is on stage for this episode. The people uninvolved (Springame, Courtall, Wilding, Ruffle, and Fanny) can scatter and chat in dumb show, oblivious to the conversation and uninterested in the song. Or they can pay attention—responding with sympathy, derision, or impassivity, as directed. Their response need not be visible to the Friendalls. This is a public concert, and hence the scene could be staged with a flock of extra people to dilute the visible reactions of the insiders. What those reactions are is pretty much up to the director.[21]

21. We are grateful to Harold Love, Robert Jordan, Curtis A. Price, and Julia Rich for helpful critiques of this chapter.

9

Love for Love (1695)

C ONGREVE'S most popular comedy has attracted far less critical attention than *The Way of the World*. As a stage vehicle,
Love for Love is clearly the more effective play, though it lacks the
marvelous verbal polish and psychological subtlety of the later
comedy. As a literary text, *Love for Love* seems quite straightforward, which makes lack of critical consensus rather surprising.
Criticism has proved more chaotic than directly contradictory—
so much so that the lines of argument are far from clear. Some of
the most interesting criticism (for example, that by Norman Holland and Aubrey Williams) has been written without concern for
the practicalities of performance, with the result that in our opinion several standard interpretations turn out to be virtually unproducible. The play works in the theatre, but why it works, and
what can be done with it in performance, remain problems well
worth investigation.

Unlike such plays as *The Country-Wife* and *The Beaux' Stratagem*, *Love for Love*'s production possibilities do not reduce tidily
to a romp/satire spectrum. Congreve's fundamental sympathy for
Valentine and Angelica is written ineluctably into his play, and
only by doing violence to it could one present a production hostile to the protagonists. The basic question for a director boils
down to whether one chooses to present the play as a humours
comedy or as a romance.

260

CRITICAL PERSPECTIVES

When Congreve set out to write *Love for Love* in early 1694 he had behind him a smash hit (*The Old Batchelour*, March 1693) and a disappointingly modest *succès d'estime* (*The Double-Dealer*, November 1693). The former is a lighthearted pastiche of Carolean sex-comedy elements; the latter, a deliberate move toward the manner of Wycherley's *The Plain-Dealer*. Congreve evidently believed that a serious comic writer needed to produce satire. Current literary theory certainly said so, but audience taste tended to favor something rather fizzier. As an ambitious young writer seeking success and fortune, Congreve must have been given serious pause by the cool reception of his second play. His return to theatrical clichés in *Love for Love*, and its altogether lighter tone, are evidence of his determination to recapture his audience. One can view the play as a bouillabaisse of proven devices: tricked marriage, extravagant humours characters, inheritance achieved by trick, foolish beau, satire on an astrological pretender and a heavy father, country ingenue, rustic (here nautical) bumpkin, witty heroine, love game, and outwitting plot. Congreve's prologue expresses the hope that "tho' of Homely Fare we make the Feast," the "variety" of humour, plot, and satire will include "something that may please each Taste." John Harrington Smith points out that though many of the elements of the play derive from the cynical comedy of the 1670s, there are major differences in the handling. Valentine is not involved in the cuckolding of Foresight; Prue does not actually get deflowered; her near-seducer is Tattle, not Valentine or Scandal. Angelica is witty, but she tests Valentine, and is thus "revealed as a lively-serious heroine, intent on making sure of his sincerity." The concern for testing and sincerity is a cliché of the new humane comedy that had sprung up in the nineties as an alternative to the more satiric sex comedy of the seventies tradition. Smith is entirely correct in saying that "the love action of the play is a mixture."[1] Congreve well

1. John Harrington Smith, *The Gay Couple in Restoration Comedy* (Cambridge, Mass.: Harvard Univ. Press, 1948), pp. 156–58.

261

understood "the change in comedy," and he adapted his materials accordingly.

The obvious importance of the 1690s' context notwithstanding, a great many critics (including some with good things to say) have explicitly or implicitly started from a question: what is the play about? The diversity of their conclusions has not been as discouraging as it should have been to like-minded critics.

For Fujimura, *Love for Love* is simply a "witty and naturalistic" expression of Congreve's outlook on life, and not in need of further point. We admire the Truewits (Valentine, Angelica, and Scandal) and laugh at the follies and deficiencies of the others.[2] As Fujimura reads the play, emphasis is on the "outwitting" plot, and Valentine undergoes no significant change—a position startlingly different from Norman Holland's "education of Valentine" discussed below. For Fujimura, there is no subject: "it is the fine wit of Valentine and Angelica that gives real substance to the comedy."

For a critic bent on finding a "subject," family relationships are an obvious possibility. The idea has been explored most fully by Susan J. Rosowski, who believes that "the relation of the individual to society" is "the central theme" in all of Congreve's comedies.[3] The line of argument is obvious: *Love for Love* displays a variety of good and bad marriages and parent-child relationships. Whether this is particularly significant, however, is another matter. Most comedies display good and bad family relationships, just as they tend to exhibit "appearance and reality," but that does not make either family relationships or appearance and reality the point of a play. To extract commentary on family relationships from *As You Like It* and *King Lear* is perfectly easy, but in the theatre neither play comes across as a dissertation on the subject. Arthur W. Hoffman is perfectly correct in seeing Valentine's failed relationship with his father as a crucial fact in this

2. Thomas H. Fujimura, *The Restoration Comedy of Wit* (Princeton: Princeton Univ. Press, 1952), pp. 176–83.

3. Susan J. Rosowski, "Thematic Development in the Comedies of William Congreve: The Individual in Society," *Studies in English Literature*, 16 (1976), 387–406.

play, but to us it seems more donnée than subject.[4] Charles R. Lyons is likewise right in seeing Angelica as Valentine's salvation, and their marriage based on "a conception of the marriage relationship which is not within the convention of the convenience marriage of earlier Restoration comedy."[5] But how much does Congreve show us or tell us about their relationship? Astonishingly little. Indeed, we never see a conversation between them in which both are speaking openly and honestly.

If the play is not about family relationships or marriage, does it ask a question? Virginia Ogden Birdsall asserts that "the central question which the play asks . . . is whether either naturalness or any kind of honesty is often possible in human relationships given a world where people almost invariably behave inhumanly, unnaturally, dishonestly, and where interest is the dominant motive."[6] But wherein lies the question? One might better say that the play shows us the possibility of genuine love and honesty in a corrupt world. Lyons and Birdsall are quite right in pointing out the nonlibertine nature of this play: Congreve presents something closer to romantic love than to the taming of a rake. But as a production concept this seems dangerously limited, especially when the love relationship is so sketchily presented.

Is *Love for Love* a statement about epistemology? F. P. Jarvis works from the premise that "John Locke's *Essay Concerning Human Understanding* (1690) . . . [is] the informing source of *Love for Love*."[7] Jarvis argues that the point of the play is its attempt to "deal in social terms with the fundamental problem that Locke poses in the *Essay*, that is, the certainty and extent of human

4. Arthur W. Hoffman, "Allusions and the Definition of Themes in Congreve's *Love for Love*," in *The Author in His Work: Essays on a Problem in Criticism*, ed. Louis L. Martz and Aubrey Williams (New Haven: Yale Univ. Press, 1978), pp. 283–96.

5. Charles R. Lyons, "Congreve's Miracle of Love," *Criticism*, 6 (1964), 331–48.

6. Birdsall, *Wild Civility*, p. 215.

7. F. P. Jarvis, "The Philosophical Assumptions of Congreve's *Love for Love*," *Texas Studies in Literature and Language*, 14 (1972), 423–34. Jarvis acknowledges Norman Holland as the source for this discovery, but Holland does not get so carried away with the idea.

knowledge." Jarvis reads the play as a skeptical attack on Locke. This is an excellent example of unproducible interpretation. The play does not mention Locke, or even allude to him in any clear way. The chance that anyone (let alone everyone) in the audience of 1695 went home thinking "so much for Locke," or even pondering "the limitations of human reason" seems remote. Analytically, one can certainly see Congreve's characters as exhibiting different degrees of "comprehension," but then one can do the same with almost any play.

Lack of specific reference to Locke does not, of course, mean that the play does not address epistemological questions. Harriett Hawkins offers a much more sophisticated epistemological reading, and unlike Jarvis she talks about what the play itself shows us. Congreve does repeatedly have his characters comment on the difficulty of interpretation, generally in connection with Foresight's astrology and the incomprehensibility of women.[8] As Valentine says despairingly of Angelica, "Understood! She is harder to be understood than a Piece of *Ægyptian* Antiquity, or an *Irish* Manuscript" (p. 297).[9] As Hawkins reads the play it "shows us the dilemmas which arise from the fact that it is almost impossible to know, with certainty, how others will act, why they are acting, or indeed when they are acting. And the play asks whether there is, in truth, any 'effectual Difference between continued Affectation and Reality.'"[10] Hawkins prudently refrains from suggesting that the play exists to convey any message about epistemology or apprehension of reality, and confusion and uncertainty can indubitably be projected by actors. But if the "idea" of the play were epistemological skepticism, the happy ending

8. For a sensible interpretation of such references, see Maximillian Novak, "Foresight in the Stars and Scandal in London: Reading the Hieroglyphics in Congreve's *Love for Love*," *From Renaissance to Restoration*, ed. Robert Markley, in press. We are grateful to Professor Novak for sending us an advance copy of his essay.

9. All page references are to *The Complete Plays of William Congreve*, ed. Herbert Davis (Chicago: Univ. of Chicago Press, 1967).

10. Harriett Hawkins, *Likenesses of Truth in Elizabethan and Restoration Drama* (Oxford: Clarendon Press, 1972), p. 111. She is quoting Valentine's statement that he knows no such effectual difference (p. 254).

would be all wrong, since certainty about Angelica's feelings runs exactly counter to the incomprehensibility Jarvis and Hawkins want to see as the point. And in performance, if you want the audience to think about "the limitations of human reason," you must have the characters talk about it much more directly than Congreve chose to have them do. Epistemology quickly proves a dead end for the would-be interpreter of this play.[11]

Is *Love for Love* a satire? Congreve's prologue says it is.

> Since the *Plain-Dealers* Scenes of Manly Rage,
> Not one has dar'd to lash this Crying Age.
> This time, the Poet owns the bold Essay.

Few critics have taken this claim seriously. Valentine, Jeremy, and Scandal take turns railing at the state of society:[12] as Novak observes, Congreve "clearly conceives of satire in terms of direct invective, such as that delivered by a constantly satiric spokesman—a misanthrope like Manly or personified figures like Folly or Truth."[13] But is this display of spleen supposed to be taken as Congreve lashing the age or as his way of characterizing his witty and disaffected gentlemen and pert servant? Only Bonamy Dobrée has taken *Love for Love* as a serious attempt at satire, and he condemns it as "ponderous" and "overweighty."[14] Prologue notwithstanding, this seems to us to confuse Congreve's purposes

11. A methodologically similar approach to the play is offered by James Thompson in "Reading and Acting in *Love for Love*," *Essays in Literature*, 7 (1980), 21–30, who starts from Valentine's reading Epictetus in I.i. His discussion is better fitted to the text of the play than Jarvis', but save for the occasional playgoer deeply steeped in Epictetus, the explicit terms of the reading are unproducible.

12. Scandal serves as a kind of licensed, plain-dealing railer, and so on occasion does Jeremy. But all of the hardest hits are delivered by Valentine under the guise of madness. "I am Truth. 'Tis hard I cannot get a Livelyhood amongst you. I have been sworn out of *Westminster-Hall* the first Day of every Term" (p. 280). "Prayers will be said in empty Churches, at the usual Hours. Yet you will see such Zealous Faces behind Counters, as if Religion were to be sold in every Shop." (p. 289)

13. Maximillian E. Novak, *William Congreve* (New York: Twayne, 1971), pp. 108–9.

14. Bonamy Dobrée, *Restoration Comedy* (Oxford: Clarendon Press, 1924), pp. 132–38.

with the internal workings of his play. Clifford Leech aptly observes that however wittily critical Congreve allows his characters to be about their society, his work usually seems to lack the "animus" of the serious satirist.[15] Try as he may to be a satirist, Congreve's equable good humor keeps creeping in. *Love for Love* is far too cheerful to be played as a satire: one need only look at Otway's *Friendship in Fashion* or Southerne's *The Maid's Last Prayer* to see the difference.

Love for Love gives us a sardonic view of most of its characters and their world, but whether Congreve tried to embody an "idea" or a "question" in his play seems much to be doubted. On the whole, we agree with Novak's comment that the play presents "debate and points of view" but that it "would be doing violence to Congreve's art to suggest that it was a play of ideas," though "it is one of contrasts and paradoxes." Provocative the play can certainly be, but we have to suppose that if it encapsulated a tidy point, that point would long ago have been perceived and expounded. Usable production concepts are rarely subtle. Let us turn, therefore, to some critical approaches which whatever their other virtues or vices can claim to deal with the play in a broader way.

THREE INCOMMENSURABLE READINGS

How does Congreve want us to view Valentine's renunciation? What does it mean, and what does it tell us about the play as a whole? Three quite different approaches have been tried by critics prepared to tackle the structural problem posed by the ending. Summarily put, one can see the play as the education of Valentine (Norman Holland), as a demonstration of Providence (Aubrey Williams), or as a kind of fairy tale (Novak). Each approach has virtues and limitations, but for production purposes only the third seems fruitful.

The education of Valentine. The best known interpretation of

15. Clifford Leech, "Congreve and the Century's End," *Philological Quarterly*, 41 (1962), 275–93.

Love for Love is undoubtedly Norman Holland's. Holland sees the play almost as a philosophical disquisition: "Congreve . . . wrote his third play about three different kinds of knowledge, three different ways of life—we might call them presocial, social, and suprasocial."[16] We doubt that Congreve conceived his play as an illustration of an abstract proposition, though one can certainly agree that Ben and Prue are unfitted to cope with this society, and that Valentine and Angelica will try to live on a higher plane of honesty and love. Holland explicitly sees the action of the play as "based on the idea of an education or therapy" in which Valentine progresses "through three confinements" relating "to knowledge as well as madness." For Holland, "the end of Valentine's education is to bring him to a higher kind of reality, a Providence or God's justice, that transcends the chance and show of ordinary social reality."

Holland's analysis is genuinely brilliant, and it presents us a play with a satisfyingly tidy point. The deceptions and affectations of ordinary society must be rejected. To survive in "a dog-eat-dog world" people need "knowledge"—not Foresight's astrology, nor Sir Sampson's authoritarian concept of nature, not the "skeptical naturalism" of Scandal and Jeremy, but rather "the religion of love" to which Valentine and Scandal are "converted" in the finale. Holland's predilection for right way/wrong way readings is again evident here.

Analytically tidy though this account is, it presents considerable problems for a director. For a start, Holland ignores both Angelica's motivation and the impression she makes on the audience before the finale.[17] We see her as a pert chit in Act II, slanging her uncle, teasing the nurse, and evidently enjoying her gadding about town (pp. 236–39). We see her as a witty love-game

16. Holland, *The First Modern Comedies*, Chapter 14; quotation from p. 161. Following quotations from pp. 162, 164.

17. William Myers finds Angelica's "behaviour . . . dramatically unaccounted for." See "Plot and Meaning in Congreve's Comedies," *William Congreve*, ed. Brian Morris, Mermaid Critical Commentaries (London: Benn, 1972), pp. 75–92; quotation from p. 83. The original audience would probably have recognized both the "Scornful Lady" archetype and the "testing" pattern discussed below, but as far as the text goes, Myers is quite correct.

heroine when she outsmarts Jeremy and Scandal and decides to "play Trick for Trick" on Valentine (pp. 276–77). We see her as a slick social operator when she ensnares Sir Sampson. But until the last three pages Congreve has done singularly little to establish her as the representative of higher truth and "emotional sincerity." The simplest explanation of Angelica's behavior is probably the best, and the most playable: she wants to be sure Valentine really loves her. Angelica has a fortune of £30,000, and as she is no fool, she has qualms about the sincerity of her suitors. Novak points out that Congreve's subject and title are reminiscent of Durfey's successful *Love for Money* (1691). Durfey's *The Richmond Heiress* (1693) is likewise apropos, and ends with the disgusted heiress deciding not to marry at all. Angelica's world is nothing if not materialistic, and we should not forget Penelope Gilliatt's sarcastic comment that Congreve ought to have called his play *Love for Loot*.

Is Angelica waiting for Valentine to "learn" something, or does she just want to make certain of his sincerity? If the former, then what exactly is to be learned? And how? Holland's explanation seems to us unconvincingly high-flown. "Valentine's problem in winning Angelica is that he is still too close to social pretense; he is trying to win her by putting on a show of poverty or madness. He must learn to transcend his social habits through an action completely asocial, resigning both his fortune and his love; he must learn that intrigue is not effective on the suprasocial level. It is to the education of Valentine that the title *Love for Love* refers: Valentine learns to substitute real love for showy love."[18] This is fine social philosophy, but it does not grow out of the play. How are we shown Valentine's transcendance of "social habits"? He gives up his struggle against his father when he believes Angelica lost, and his declaration of his love (made when he apparently has nothing to gain) convinces her of his sincerity (p. 312). This is certainly not a reform comedy. Valentine has no sudden change of heart; he does not repent his former ways.

Critics have been astonishingly obtuse about looking at the ac-

18. Holland, *The First Modern Comedies*, p. 172.

tion of *Love for Love* in its most obvious terms. Valentine, though well born, has outspent his allowance and is about to be disinherited, but he continues to woo a very wealthy woman. How can she be sure that he truly loves her, and not just her money? What she says in the finale concerns not education but proof: "I was resolv'd to try him to the utmost; I have try'd you [Sir Sampson] too, and know you both" (p. 312). When she knows Valentine, she is prepared to marry him. The speech with which Angelica closes the play stresses "Constancy," not reform or achievement of a higher understanding à la Norman Holland.

> Men are generally Hypocrites and Infidels, they pretend to Worship, but have neither Zeal nor Faith: How few, like *Valentine*, would persevere even unto Martyrdom, and sacrifice their Interest to their Constancy! In admiring me, you misplace the Novelty.
> The Miracle to Day is, that we find
> A Lover true: Not that a Woman's Kind.   (p. 314)

Angelica has not educated Valentine; she has tested him and found him "A Lover true."

An effective "education" play needs to show us a process of transformation and a fairly explicit recognition of right way and wrong way on the part of the protagonist.[19] *Love for Love* does nothing of the sort. Holland's reading is plausible psychology, but Valentine's education is not specified in the text in ways that would allow us to play it comprehensibly for an audience.[20]

19. As for example in Behn's (?) *The Debauchee* (1677), Shadwell's *The Squire of Alsatia* (1688), Centlivre's *The Gamester* (1705), or Fielding's *The Modern Husband* (1732). Or ranging more widely we might point to Calderón's *Life is a Dream*, Lessing's *Miss Sara Sampson*, O'Neill's *Ah, Wilderness!*, and Brecht's *Good Person of Setzuan*.

20. A better view of education in the play is offered by Harold Love, who comments on "three sets of lessons each involving a teacher and a pupil." Tattle instructs Prue; Mrs. Frail gives lessons to Ben; "at an altogether higher level" Angelica must teach Valentine that he cannot "trick or bribe her into loving him." We are uncomfortable with the view of Angelica and Valentine. How does he try to "bribe" her? He tries to trick her into *admitting* that she loves him. Dr. Love feels that the finale shows that "Valentine has learned to trust and to give, absolutely and without reservation," but what has taught him to "trust" and how is this shown? See Harold Love, *Congreve* (Totowa, New Jersey: Rowman and Littlefield, 1975), Chapter 4.

Providential pattern. Aubrey Williams' reading starts from "Congreve's unusual deployment of religious diction and imagery."[21] No one can deny the explicitness of the religious terminology of the finale. Valentine exclaims "On my Knees I take the Blessing," and says to Tattle, "you would have interposed between me and Heav'n; but Providence laid Purgatory in your way." Scandal says to Angelica, "you have converted me." Angelica speaks of "Worship," and "Faith," and "Martyrdom." Williams argues that *Love for Love* presents a "testing pattern," and that Angelica's "role as a vigilant, yet also solicitous, guardian angel" and the religious language employed in the play (for which it was violently denounced by Jeremy Collier) would have made the original audience see it as an illustration of the operation of God's providence in our world.

We entirely agree with Williams that the play is structured and developed as a test, not as an education. Beyond that, we have some problems with his assumptions. We need to consider two separate issues. Is the action an illustration of providence? Would the religious language have made the original audience judge the play in religious or potentially religious terms? On the first question we would answer unequivocally no. What brings off the happy ending is Angelica's skillful dissimulation. She deliberately pays court to Sir Sampson, invites and accepts a proposal of marriage, and so gains control of the crucial paper. What is so marvelously providential about this? Angelica engineers the happy ending by means of blatant lies and outright dishonesty. We approve, to be sure, but Angelica hardly seems as "suprasocial" as Norman Holland would have her, let alone "an intimation of another personage, a shadowy reminder of those who 'execute the divine plan for human salvation.'"[22] What we see of Angelica makes her seem attractive, human, and comfortable in the world of the play. That Congreve was capable of employing a genuinely providential design in a play should be obvious to any reader of

21. Aubrey L. Williams, *An Approach to Congreve* (New Haven: Yale Univ. Press, 1979), Chapter 8; quotation from p. 157.
22. Williams, p. 175.

The Mourning Bride (1697), a play to which Williams' predispositions are ideally suited. Comparison with a genuinely providential play should suggest to any but a hardened Christianizer that *Love for Love* is a very different kind of work.[23]

The effect of religious language in late seventeenth-century comedy has been hotly debated.[24] Properly speaking, the issue comprises two quite separate questions: Did Congreve intend religious signification? Would the original audience (or some part of it) have responded to the language on a religious plane? Unless we are to believe that Congreve was simply a liar, we have to accept his denial of religious signification in his language. "Because Mr. *Collier* in his Chapter of the Profaneness of the Stage, has founded great part of his Accusation upon the Liberty which Poets take of using some Words in their Plays, which have been sometimes employed by the Translators of the Holy Scriptures: I desire that the following Distinction may be admitted, *viz*. That when Words are apply'd to sacred things, and with a purpose to treat of sacred things; they ought to be understood accordingly: But when they are otherwise apply'd, the Diversity of the Subject

23. For a sober, balanced, and historically sophisticated assessment of Williams' approach, see Harold Love, "Was Congreve a Christian?" *Themes in Drama*, 5 (1983), 293–309. Considering Williams' insistence that "providentialist patterns in the designs of these plays" make "what might otherwise have seemed casual or even parodic patterns of religious allusion and theological language . . . carry a real charge of doctrinal meaning," Love makes the important point that "Congreve's use of providential patterns of plot construction" need not imply "a Christian world view." As Love says, "The *Oedipus Tyrannus* of Sophocles and the *Aeneid* of Virgil are at least as good examples of providentialist plot structure as *Incognita* and *The Double Dealer*, while many of the comedies of Plautus and Terence make use of plot formulae based on rebounding deceptions of a kind that Williams identifies when they recur in Congreve as indications of providentialist influence. To me it seems difficult to claim that Christian doctrine is the sole or even the main reason for Congreve's use of these formulae when they were available as an established convention in pagan writers whom he revered as models of literary excellence and often imitated directly. . . . Williams has failed to acknowledge a purely literary influence that would have produced the same effect as a devotional one."

24. For the two sides of an ongoing argument, see Harriett Hawkins, *Likenesses of Truth*, Chapter 5 (a vigorous reply to Williams' early work), and J. Douglas Canfield, "Religious Language and Religious Meaning in Restoration Comedy," *Studies in English Literature*, 20 (1980), 385–406.

gives a Diversity of Signification."[25] We must allow for the fact that Congreve is replying to a harsh attack, but surely the terms in which he chose to respond are significant. Congreve denies religious signification. If, as Professor Williams believes, practically everyone in the audience would automatically have drawn the religious implications, such a denial would have been both disingenuous and unconvincing. If Williams' assumptions are correct, why would Congreve not simply have replied that any good Christian should take the religious allusion in a positive way, to produce a "*moralisé*" reading?

Turning to our second question, we should ask what evidence we have of seventeenth-century readers or audiences reacting to comedies in explicitly Christian terms. Our principal evidence is the Reverend Jeremy Collier, who denounced *Love for Love* for blasphemy. "Here you have the Language of the *Scriptures*, and the most solemn Instances of Religion, prostituted to Courtship and Romance! Here you have a Mistress made God Almighty, Ador'd with Zeal and Faith, and Worship'd up to Martyrdom!"[26] Collier's reaction proves that a contemporary reader could find lots of religious signification in *Love for Love*; of course, he objected violently to it. We think it significant that his contemporaries never state their positive response to plays in religious terms, and that none of the many replies to Collier dared tackle him directly on the issue of "correct" religious reading, which would surely be the case if this were the natural bent of the audience. That most of Congreve's audience believed in "Providence" in Christian terms we do not doubt; whether they would have taken a reference to providence in a bouncy comedy as possessing serious religious signification is a different matter. Vanbrugh's comment seems to the point: "Every body knows the word Providence in Common Discourse goes for Fortune. If it be answer'd,

25. *Amendments of Mr. Collier's False and Imperfect Citations &c.* (1698), *The Complete Works of William Congreve*, ed. Montague Summers, 4 vols. (Soho: Nonesuch, 1923), III, 174. Williams does not discuss this passage, though he devotes a long (and generally helpful) chapter to the Collier controversy.

26. Jeremy Collier, *A Short View of the Immorality, and Profaneness of the English Stage* (London: S. Keble, 1698), esp. pp. 74–77, 142–43.

Let it go for what it will, it is in strictness God Almighty; I answer again, That if you go to strictness, Fortune is God Almighty as much as Providence, and yet no one ever thought it Blasphemy to say, Fortune's blind, or Fortune favours Fools: And the reason why it is not thought so, is because 'tis known it is not meant so."[27]

That some part of the contemporary public responded to religious language in comedy is clearly true—though the response was hysterically negative. That other readers or viewers could have drawn positive implications in a *moralisé* reading is entirely possible. Such a response would depend almost entirely on the predisposition of the individual. We have no evidence that a substantial portion of the audience did respond this way, and if it did, Congreve's denial of religious signification would have been more than a little odd. The providential reading would not work for a twentieth-century audience; we see no evidence that it worked for a significant part of the seventeenth-century audience.

The fairy tale. A major problem with both the education and providential readings of *Love for Love* is their failure to account for more than a small portion of the play. Congreve shows us a social world. Are we to take it as an ugly picture of society in 1690s' London, or are we to enjoy it as a largely separate comedy world? Scholars familiar with comedy of the time have all recognized Congreve's heavy dependence on formula, and have been disinclined to take the implied world very seriously. Within the play, no one comments on the illegality of the tricked marriage. Novak sensibly comments that "it belongs to the absurd dramatic world of *Love for Love*, and that world has only the most tangential relation to reality."[28] Harold Love likewise observes that "it is a world without many points of contact with the real one."[29]

If we ask what *Love for Love* is, taken in toto, our answer is that it is a mélange of devices from 1690s' comedy, mingling elements

27. *A Short Vindication of the Relapse and the Provok'd Wife* (1698), *The Complete Works of Sir John Vanbrugh*, ed. Bonamy Dobrée and Geoffrey Webb, 4 vols. (London: Nonesuch, 1927–28), II, 201.
28. Novak, *William Congreve*, p. 120.
29. Love, *Congreve*, p. 60.

from Carolean comedy and from the more romantic tradition of Fletcher that was being reasserted in the humane comedy of the 1690s.[30] Novak's reading is an excellent one. "Congreve has found his mode—lyricism, romanticism, and optimism superimposed upon that world of cynical libertines and imbecile cuckolds which was the tableaux of Restoration comedy." Valentine "was a libertine, remains a wit, and is capable of true love"; Angelica is a version of the Scornful Lady archetype; "the satire . . . is not concerned with the problem of love for money, but with the entire context of social action." For Novak, the ending exists to make the audience happy: "that Valentine should act unwisely and still find his reward is the beautiful, satisfying fairy tale which Congreve serves as a delightful feast."[31] Novak seems to us to overstress the importance of "irrationality" of love in the play, and to miss the importance of "testing" in the design of the play (thereby diminishing its potential seriousness), but his fairy tale concept is clearly producible, and it neatly avoids the pitfalls that have plagued most scholarly interpreters.

CHARACTERS AND CASTING

How "real" is the world of *Love for Love* to seem? This is not the same question as asking about the relationship of the world of the play to ordinary reality as known to the audience. Even in 1695 the connection was remote. But if we play the text as though it were serious, we get one sort of production (romance); if we play it as comic formula, we get quite another (humours comedy). The choice has important implications for our concept of both the characters and the casting.

The original cast presents some problems and puzzles. The play must have been complete by November 1694. Cibber informs us that "this valuable Play had a narrow Escape from fall-

30. For discussion of these types, see Shirley Strum Kenny, "Humane Comedy," *Modern Philology*, 75 (1977), 29–43; and Hume, *Development*, Chapter 9, and *The Rakish Stage* (Carbondale: Southern Illinois Univ. Press, 1983), Chapters 5–7.
31. Novak, *William Congreve*, pp. 108, 110, 117, and 121.

ing into the Hands of the Patentees; for before the Division of the Company [in December 1694] it had been read and accepted of at the Theatre-Royal: But while the Articles of Agreement for it were preparing, the Rupture in the Theatrical State was so far advanced that the Author took time to pause before he sign'd them; when finding that all Hopes of Accommodation were impracticable, he thought it advisable to let it take its Fortune with those Actors for whom he had first intended the Parts" (*Apology*, I, 197). Despite this assertion there are grounds for doubt that the cast of 1695 was exactly what Congreve originally had in mind. As Peter Holland points out in a helpful discussion, three important performers stayed with Drury Lane: Joseph Williams, John Verbruggen, and Susanna Mountfort Verbruggen.[32] The oft-repeated notion that Valentine was originally intended for Joseph Williams rather than the sixty-year old Betterton is entirely speculative, but it is plausible. Holland observes that "casting Betterton as Valentine reverses the approach to Betterton that Congreve had taken and would take in casting his comedies." Betterton's other roles in Congreve's comedies are Heartwell, Maskwell, and Fainall, *not* Bellmour, Mellefont, and Mirabell. The obvious role for him in *Love for Love* is Sir Sampson. A production with a dashing young man as Valentine (Joseph Williams) and a heavyweight villain as Sir Sampson (Betterton) could be startlingly different from one with a famous if elderly rake as Valentine (Betterton) and a "natural comedian" displaying "the Stiff, the Heavy, and the Stupid"[33] as Sir Sampson (Cave Underhill). Tony Aston says that Underhill "did great Injustice to Sir *Sampson Legend* in *Love for Love*, unless it had been true, that the Knight had been bred a Hog-driver,"[34] whereas Cibber praises his Sir Sampson highly. The difference, we suspect, was one of production concept. Underhill would fit into a humours comedy quite nicely, but he would not be the more credible father and blocking character needed for a romance production.

Unlike such plays as *The Country-Wife* and *Amphitryon*, where

32. Holland, *The Ornament of Action*, pp. 224–33.
33. Cibber, *Apology*, I, 154.
34. Supplement to Cibber, *Apology*, II, 308.

the way we conceive and cast Horner and Jupiter is crucial, *Love for Love* does not turn on the presentation of a major character. In large part this is because the audience will identify with Valentine and Angelica regardless of production concept. Nonetheless, a brief survey of the characters (in the order of the dramatis personae list) suggests a considerable range of possibilities.

Sir Sampson Legend plays heavy father, though without any explanation of his motives. Why is he so determined to disinherit Valentine in favor of Ben?[35] If Sir Sampson is angry about Valentine's prodigality, why would he not favor marriage with a wealthy heiress like Angelica? In a humours production he is simply a monomaniac, and the more he rants, the less we worry about what makes him tick. In a romance the actor will need a better motivation. As Harold Love points out, Valentine keeps expecting to find some humanity in his father.[36] Here a plausible subtext might be that Sir Sampson has only recently discovered that he can no longer assert his authority over his son, and each attempt to get around him just adds to his determination to have his way (rather like Orgon in *Tartuffe*). He is forced to face facts in the final scene and to see how much he has deluded himself not only about Valentine but also about Angelica, and he leaves ashamed. Congreve does not write in the customary reconciliation, which would scarcely be plausible after the boasts of his impending marriage to Angelica. In a humours production Sir Sampson simply storms off and disappears; in a romance he will be distressed and humbled ("You're an illiterate Fool, and I'm another," p. 313), and we can imagine an ultimate reconciliation. Angelica will placate him by treating him as the great patriarch. In the romance Valentine and Angelica can mime "don't go" as he leaves, and the audience can assume eventual peace.

Valentine is basically a conventional 1690s' hero. He has been a spendthrift and a libertine, and has fathered bastards; he is a wit who makes a suitable bosom friend for Scandal; he is passion-

35. Congreve does not explain the legal technicalities, but presumably the estate is under some form of entail requiring Valentine's agreement to his disinheritance.
36. Love, *Congreve*, p. 70.

ately "in love with Angelica" (as in the dramatis personae description). We have no reason to believe that he has ever pursued her with anything but marriage in mind. He has been denounced in moral terms for his suggestion that the mother of one of his bastards "knows my Condition well enough, and might have overlaid the Child a Fortnight ago" (p. 221).[37] But even Aubrey Williams is willing to consider this evidence of the "mixed" character Congreve considered appropriate to comedy,[38] and Valentine—in contrast to his own father—does give money for support of his child. His crack is at best graceless, but it can be delivered jokingly. Valentine is £1,500 in debt; Sir Sampson has offered him £4,000 to sign away his inheritance. He certainly could not live as a gentleman of leisure on the balance. He would have to join the army or marry a rich old widow, as his father suggests (p. 260). Congreve's point is that what worries Valentine is the prospect of losing Angelica: compare the outlook of Farquhar's Archer and Aimwell. Valentine wants the estate because of Angelica, and his lack of concern with money per se marks him as a true lover. Valentine's manner in the final scene is as important as anything he actually says. If he is self-pitying, manic, or full of bravado, Angelica cannot reasonably respond, "Generous *Valentine!*" (p. 312). He must have come to terms with his ruin; if he has lost Angelica, he can embrace it happily. For the first time in the play we see him behaving openly and sincerely, not trying tricks or playing the wit. His "renunciation" proves the disinterestedness of his passion.

Scandal ("His Friend, a Free Speaker") serves as confidant and wit, and functions as a gentleman-rake at a time when heroes could no longer both make cuckolds and marry the heiress in the course of a single play. Like Archer and Aimwell, Scandal and Valentine are the two halves of the "double gallant," gay blade and sincere lover respectively. In a romance they probably need to be about the same age; in a humours production Scandal

37. See especially George Parfitt, "The Case Against Congreve," in *William Congreve*, ed. Morris, pp. 23–38, especially pp. 23–25.
38. Congreve, *Amendments*, in *Works*, III, 200.

might be significantly older, a rakish misogynist comically converted by Angelica's virtue. The original Scandal was William Smith, Betterton's longtime co-manager who came out of retirement to join the Lincoln's Inn Fields company. His age would have helped minimize Betterton's incongruity as a young lover. Because so much of the pro forma "satire" is put in Scandal's mouth, he needs to have enough stature to be a credible moral spokesman. Smith would have filled the bill very nicely in a way that John Freeman or Joseph Trefusis would not. Triumvirate productions generally cast Barton Booth in the part, an indication of the "weight" appropriate for it.

Tattle ("A half-witted Beau") has an exceptional range of production possibilities. John Boman, who created the role, specialized in fops (he was to be Bellair a decade later in *The Beaux' Stratagem*); George Pack, who took the part in early triumvirate productions, probably played a lower-comic version of the role. In a romance production Tattle might be young and shy, his chattering a nervous reflex. We need not believe in his conquests, in which case he can "pursue" Prue with no intention of actually seducing her, and can be visibly relieved at the Nurse's interruption (p. 253). A thirty-ish Tattle who is no fool, married to a domineering Mrs. Frail (a tease, not a slut), may have a future ahead of him as gentleman and M.P. An ineffectual fop in his forties tricked into marrying a young slut will have a wretched life ahead of him. Laurence Olivier's 1965 National Theatre Tattle makes a useful contrast to the usual Beau Didapper concept. In a humours production Tattle's amours would probably be genuine, and he should be insensitive as well as obsessed with himself.

Ben is a delightful irrelevance, a vehicle written for Thomas Doggett, whose vast popularity in the role made it important out of all proportion to its function in the play. He is so far removed from the plot that he and his brother Valentine never speak to each other. Ben is not stupid, merely innocent of town ways and stratagems. He speaks with blunt good sense, but is totally vulnerable to deception. He could be made eighteen and wide-eyed or twenty-eight and quite uninterested in changing his ways.

278

What is done with Ben has almost nothing to do with production concept.

Foresight is a harmless fool, an "illiterate . . . pretending to understand Astrology . . . Omens, Dreams, &c." He is old enough that Sir Sampson (who admits to fifty-three) calls him "Brother" (pp. 241, 243), and he has apparently been impotent throughout his second marriage (p. 270). To contrast with Sir Sampson he should be soft-spoken. His house should be liberally supplied with books, astrolabes, and related paraphernalia, and at home he might well wear a stage wizard's robe and hat. His costume helps explain Angelica's teasing in Act II, and is important in establishing his character. In a romance production he might be shy and ineffectual. As Novak suggests, the Nurse might treat him as another of her children.[39] In his foggy way, he could be compassionate toward the madman in Act IV, and unlike Sir Sampson he remains to witness the finale. The humours Foresight is grotesquely near-sighted, peering dimly through thick spectacles or carrying a small telescope with him and constantly aiming it in the wrong direction. A humours Foresight could be dirty, unkempt, and dangerous when roused. Samuel Sandford created the role (part of his comic old man line, not his villain line): the more repulsive Foresight is, the more understandable Mrs. Foresight's adultery becomes. He is a comic butt in any case, but he can range from half-likeable to genuinely contemptible.

Angelica is an astonishingly underdeveloped role. Because she has no confidante, she says almost nothing that shows us her real thoughts and feelings. She is a beautiful, wealthy, witty lady quite smart enough to play Valentine "Trick for Trick" and keep him in the dark (p. 227). She can enjoy teasing Foresight in a pretty rough way: a humours production could allow her some real bite

---

39. Novak, *William Congreve*, p. 114. Even in a romance production, some of what Angelica says about Foresight's midnight revels with the Nurse may be true (pp. 237–38). Angelica need not even have peeped at the keyhole: she can be as astonished as we are when she finds that her teasing has hit the mark, and she can then go on to embroider the tale out of mischief more than malice. Angelica would be much less innocent in the humours production.

and malice in this scene. She is careful about appearances. Mrs. Frail visits Valentine alone of a morning (p. 230), but Angelica arrives with maid in tow (p. 276). We see almost nothing of her relationship with Valentine. Their first real conversation occurs in Act IV, and Angelica is firmly pretending to believe that Valentine is mad (pp. 294–95). One of the barriers to a serious romance production is insubstantiality in the love relationship. The audience readily accepted Angelica as heroine when played with dash and spirit by Anne Bracegirdle (or later by Anne Oldfield), but the character is mostly a donnée. In some ways, Angelica is a throwback to gay couple heroines (e.g., her refusal to be tricked by Valentine and her expert manipulation of Sir Sampson), but in her determination to test her suitor's sincerity she is very much a creature of 1690s' comedy. One cannot imagine her looking favorably on a Dorimant, offers of matrimony notwithstanding.

Mrs. Foresight and *Mrs. Frail* can be handled in a wide variety of ways. In a romance production Mrs. Frail flirts in Act I, but is careful of her actions (trips to World's End notwithstanding— p. 247), though she is hardly a virgin. Marriage to a comparatively innocent Tattle may not be what she was looking for, but as Angelica says, they will soon get used to one another (p. 310). If Tattle is educable, he can learn a lot from an alert schemer like Mrs. Frail. In a humours production Mrs. Frail will be openly promiscuous (like Mrs. Wittwoud in *The Wives Excuse*), but on the lookout for the security afforded by a wealthy husband. In a romance production Valentine's invitation to "step into the next Room—and I'll give you something" (to which Scandal adds, "Ay, we'll all give you something," p. 231) is a frivolous joke; in a humours production Mrs. Frail might well be visibly interested in some group action with Valentine, Scandal, and Tattle. In the latter case she would have visibly to restrain herself to play innocent when she tries to appeal to Ben-the-heir. Such dissimulation could be extremely funny, especially if she had been tempted at the idea of a foursome earlier. This Mrs. Frail will browbeat and cuckold her husband.

According to the text (p. 247) Mrs. Foresight is twelve years older than her sister. This may have been played as a joke in the original production: Barry-Frail was acting by the time Boman-Foresight was born, if not before. If Angelica and Mrs. Frail are twenty, Mrs. Foresight thirty-two, her marriage, though an uninspiring example, is not relevant the way it is if the disaster of May joined to December is impossible to miss. If we make Mrs. Foresight fortyish and Scandal fairly young, his momentary reluctance (p. 269) to pursue an affair and her later denial of the whole episode make excellent sense. In neither production would Mrs. Foresight broadcast her availability the way her sister does. But the two of them can be anything from highspirited teases who slip once in a while to promiscuous hypocrites always on the lookout for a quick tumble. Their getting the goods on each other in Act II (pp. 246–48) should be extremely funny in either production, but doubly so if both are superficially prim.

Prue, like Ben, is an irrelevant but delightful cameo. Most critics assume she is sex-crazy, but this need not be so. She can be played as very young and staggeringly innocent in the love scene with Tattle (pp. 251–53). Her subsequent determination to "have a Man some way or other" (Robin the butler if need be—p. 305) can be Hoydenish, but it could also be the bright idea of a child who has no real grasp of what she is saying.[40] The dramatis personae calls her "a silly, awkard, Country Girl," not exactly the terms one would apply to Vanbrugh's Hoyden in such a description. Mrs. Ayliff, who created the role, was primarily a singer and had no established line as an actress. She seems likely to have played Prue as a silly innocent, which offers more contrast with the Frail sisters than would Prue-as-nymphet. A decade later the role was taken by Margaret Bicknell (Cherry in *The Beaux' Stratagem*), who could have taken the role in either direction.

With some sense of the spread of interpretive potentialities available in the major roles we are ready to inquire how they might best be combined into coherent productions.

---

40. Hoffman suggests that Prue "is left isolated, rejecting a dildo and howling for a man" (p. 287). We find his interpretation of the "Rod" Foresight refers to (p. 305) strained, though it is playable. But even if her reply ("A Fiddle of a Rod") is played for a laugh, Prue need not understand what she is saying.

HUMOURS COMEDY OR ROMANCE?

The fundamental production choice for *Love for Love* is whether the audience is to be asked to laugh at the characters or to be invited to sympathize more seriously with the protagonists. The performance difference between the two productions we have been imagining is perhaps most clearly conceived if (flying in the face of history) we cast the show for each production out of early 1690s' actors who were members of the United Company. Since we are making up "ideal casts," we have not worried about whether particular performers were available in exactly the same season between 1690 and 1694 (see Table 9.1).

Only brief explanations of these choices should be necessary. If we want an amusing, essentially unthreatening Sir Sampson, then Tony Leigh (Dominic in *The Spanish Fryar*) would be ideal; if we want to make the parental threat serious and play up father-son conflict for romance concernment, then Betterton's weight and authority are appropriate. In a romance Valentine is probably best made fairly young, and the charismatic William Mountfort would be a good choice; otherwise Joseph Williams would make a satisfactory protagonist. In the romance Tattle can be made less obviously silly and contemptible, so we have chosen the relatively colorless Freeman, whose presence in the role does not automatically signal "fool" to the audience. Ben takes no part in the persecution of Valentine, and has no real function in either production, beyond incidental amusement. Actors who later took the role include Cibber and John Bickerstaff, but with Doggett available one definitely wants him. Foresight can be made flagrantly ridiculous by Nokes or Underhill; alternatively, he could be made vague but kindly, a muddled man of good will played by a more dignified actor like Phillip Griffin.[41] Even a role like Jeremy can help tilt the production one way or the other. A gentlemanly Jeremy (William Bowen) is needed for a romance production;

41. Griffin had performed such roles as Serapion in *All for Love*, Manly in *The Plain-Dealer*, Sir Edward Belfond in *The Squire of Alsatia*, Porpuss in *Sir Barnaby Whigg*, and Surly in *Sir Courtly Nice*.

Table 9.1
Ideal Casts for Two Productions of
Love for Love

Role	Humours Comedy	Romance
Sir Sampson	Anthony Leigh	Thomas Betterton
Valentine	Joseph Williams	William Mountfort
Scandal	John Verbruggen	Williams
Tattle	John Boman	John Freeman
Ben	Thomas Doggett	Doggett
Foresight	James Nokes or Samuel Sandford	Phillip Griffin
Jeremy	Jo Haynes	William Bowen
Angelica	Anne Bracegirdle	Mrs. Bracegirdle
Mrs. Foresight	Frances Knight	Elizabeth Barry
Mrs. Frail	Mrs. Barry	Susanna Mountfort
Prue	Charlotte Butler	Jane Rogers
Nurse	Katherine Corey	Elinor Leigh

the grosser absurdities of Jo Haynes would fit nicely in the humours comedy.

Anne Bracegirdle seems ideal for Angelica regardless of production concept, and so does Anne Oldfield, who succeeded her in the role. A less mesmeric actress (like Lucretia Bradshaw, who took the part at Drury Lane in 1709) would have to look for other ways to make Angelica appealing in a romance production. Mrs. Frail should be relatively young and attractive in a romance: her marriage to Tattle should not seem an utter disaster for both of them. Freeman's marrying Sue Mountfort is a far cry from Boman's marrying Elizabeth Barry. Likewise using Frances Maria Knight as Mrs. Foresight[42] gives us a more squalid picture of her marriage and Scandal's seduction than would Elizabeth

42. Frances Maria Knight took such parts as Mrs. Squeamish in *The Richmond Heiress* and Widow Lackit in *Oroonoko*.

Barry. Prue can be made relatively innocent (by the young Jane Rogers) or far from it, however ignorant she is of town ways (Charlotte Butler). For the decorum of a romance production Elinor Leigh[43] would be a more suitable Nurse than the boisterous Katherine Corey.[44]

The humours production exists principally to amuse us with a gallery of fools and a pro forma outwitting plot, topped off with an outrageously romantic finale, its high-flown language verging on burlesque. Visual contrasts are especially important in this production because the major humours characters are not at center stage for long periods of time, and they must make vivid impressions. Sir Sampson and Foresight need to be given maximum business and time to develop visual reactions. This production displays extreme contrasts of age in couples, and insists on physical infirmities and grotesquerie. Foresight is nearly blind; Sir Sampson has high blood pressure and turns purple when questioned or thwarted; Mrs. Frail is constantly in heat; the Nurse could be unhealthily fat, not just plump; Ben keeps his seaman's gait on land; Tattle minces and postures, and is obsessed with smell; Prue is physically clumsy and has not learned how to manage a lady's clothes; Mrs. Foresight's attempts to hide her age are transparent; the lawyer snivels; Trapland is greasy and grasping; Snap is sadistic; Sir Sampson's Steward has been bullied into a hangdog stance. At the end Valentine has won Angelica, but nothing else has changed for the better. Sir Sampson stomps out (and we desire no reconciliation); Tattle and Mrs. Frail have a dismal married life ahead of them. We enjoy the wit and ridicule: the focus of this production, beyond humour for humour's sake, is the outwitting plot.

The romance production shows us more believable people. Sir Sampson, however threatening, is at bottom the decent person Valentine thinks him, and he will ultimately be reconciled with his son. Foresight is kindly and muddled, not unkempt and dis-

43. Lady Woodvil in *The Man of Mode*, Lady Wishfort in *The Way of the World*.
44. Mrs. Teazall in *The Wives Excuse*, Bromia in *Amphitryon*.

gusting. Ben and Prue are quite young and very ignorant, but not necessarily unable to grow up to lead satisfactory lives. Mrs. Frail will turn her energies to making the best of Tattle, and he will be able to give up his chattering affectations. Scandal is a good fellow, overjoyed by his friend's narrow escape and perhaps ready to think of settling down himself. Mrs. Foresight has had her fling and will learn to make the best of her old but decent husband. We enjoy the wit and humour, but the focus of this production is Angelica's test.

Love for Love is basically a ragoût of popular devices from 1690s' comedies of all sorts. The probability seems to be that the original production was something of a hodgepodge, with a strong tendency toward the humours concept. Eighteenth-century production history suggests that the play was taken in either direction, depending on the principal performers available.[45] If you have Wilks and Oldfield, you probably move toward romance.

To try to produce the play as a satire on its society pulls against its natural bent. Peter Wood's 1965 National Theatre production conceived the play as a satire on "the fortune-hunting materialism of the new upper classes."[46] Valentine's lodgings were made "like a pig-sty," and financial distinctions emphasized throughout. But such a production ignores Congreve's fast pace and the spirit of fun that pervades the play. Even in a humours production emphasizing the grotesque, Congreve displays little that we should hate or fear. Harold Love acutely notes that "whatever we may feel as outsiders about the world of *Love for Love*, we can hardly deny that its inhabitants are thoroughly satisfied at being part of it."[47] And unless we are to despise the protagonists—a tack more easily taken with a play like *The Country-Wife*—this acceptance gives the play an air of ease and good humor hard to play against.

45. On stage history, see Emmett L. Avery, *Congreve's Plays on the Eighteenth-Century Stage* (New York: Modern Language Association, 1951).

46. For commentary on this and some other twentieth-century productions of Congreve, see Kenneth Muir, "Congreve on the Modern Stage," *William Congreve*, ed. Morris, pp. 133–54.

47. Love, *Congreve*, p. 71.

Both Love and Novak comment on the festive air of *Love for Love*. Reading Norman Holland, one might suppose that it was all a very solemn business, and that at the end "the hero retreats from the social world of deception and illusion to a personal haven of psychological truth and emotional sincerity." This seems contrary to the world of the play and to Congreve's own life. Where are Angelica and Valentine to go? Valentine is hardly an Alceste who finds his antisocial soulmate. We trust they will lead a happier life than most of those around them, but surely they will continue to live in London society. Angelica is a lively young lady who enjoys gadding about town in a coach; we are given no evidence that she proposes to retire to Northumberland to read Locke—or even Epictetus.

Critical unhappiness with the ending (Leech finds it "unconvincing"; Zimbardo denounces its "sentimentality")[48] seems to stem largely from false expectations. *Love for Love* can be staged as a romance, but it is not a romantic comedy of the Shakespearean variety: Congreve shows us almost nothing of the relationship between hero and heroine. Likewise, to see the play as Valentine's education demands that it do something Congreve seems never to have intended. He presents us a test of sincerity, not an education in "the religion of love."[49] Part of the problem lies in critics' failure to understand that what starts as Valentine's play ends as Angelica's. Considering how the play is "loaded"[50] (how each part is distributed throughout the play), the director must realize that after Angelica's visit to the "mad" Valentine in IV.i. initiative is entirely in her hands, and her prominence in the action reflects this fact. Valentine continues to struggle and scheme, but the audience should recognize both that Angelica loves him and that she, not Valentine, will have to engineer a happy ending. Conceived as "Valentine's awakening," the play fails for the

48. Leech, "Congreve and the Century's End"; Rose A. Zimbardo, *Wycherley's Drama* (New Haven: Yale Univ. Press, 1965), pp. 7–15.

49. Holland, *The First Modern Comedies*, p. 170.

50. For this concept, see Kenneth Tynan's interview with Laurence Olivier, *Great Acting*, ed. Hal Burton (London: British Broadcasting Corporation, 1967), p. 22.

simple reason that Valentine does not reform, repent, or visibly achieve a heightened state of consciousness. All of Norman Holland's ingenuity and special pleading notwithstanding, Valentine does not change. We see no reason to apologize for the finale: Congreve knew exactly what he was doing. In a humours production we enjoy the fairy-tale ending; in a romance we rejoice when Valentine's love is proved by the utmost trial Angelica can impose.

APPENDIX: SCENE PLAN

The staging of *Love for Love* is extremely simple. Action alternates between Valentine's lodgings (Acts I and IV) and Foresight's house (Acts II-III and V). For the mad scene in Act IV we have a discovery. The act opens in "Valentine's Lodgings" and at the crucial moment Jeremy "Goes to the Scene, which opens and discovers *Valentine* upon a Couch disorderly dress'd" (p. 279).[51] If necessary Valentine's lodgings and Foresight's house could be represented by the same interior set, but a sharp visual difference is desirable. In both cases one set of proscenium doors leads toward the street, the other toward more private space (e.g., Prue's bedroom). To get at Tattle and Prue the "back way," the Nurse probably exits upstage between the flats, not through a proscenium door (p. 253). Aside from the discovery in Act IV there are no scene changes except between acts, and so we can put both lodgings on the second set of shutters, which gives us plenty of maneuvering room for Congreve's numerous private conversations.

2.2   Foresight's House

2.1   Valentine's Chamber

1.1   Valentine's Lodgings—Antechamber

51. In discussing this play Peter Holland says that "the discovery of a tableau, particularly someone lying on a couch . . . [is] a direct invocation of the world of Restoration tragedy" (*The Ornament of Action*, p. 231). He cites only a scene in Tate's *Lear* as evidence for this assertion. But discoveries are commonplace in comedy, as for example in Act V of *The Wives Excuse*.

Foresight's house might be made solid but old-fashioned, Valentine's lodgings more showy, as befits a gentleman-spendthrift.

We should note that Congreve seems quite conscious of the *liaison des scènes*. He breaks it three times in this play, and on each occasion there is a good reason. In Act II Valentine and Jeremy deliberately avoid speaking to Mrs. Foresight and Mrs. Frail, emphasizing the secrecy of the ladies' confession scene and subsequent plot (p. 246). In Act III the stage is cleared when Mrs. Foresight takes Prue away and Mrs. Frail leads Ben to her chamber, so that when the fathers arrive there is no courting couple to be found (p. 265). In Act V Sir Sampson and Angelica hurry off to plot in secret (p. 301). Congreve's concept of scenes has been the subject of considerable argument and misunderstanding, much of it connected with his adoption of French-style scene division in the *Works* of 1710. The quarto texts are clearly closer to the performance practice of the 1690s, but Congreve already thought of scenes in terms of a change of actors on stage, as is indicated in his comment in his 1695 dedication that "one whole Scene in the Third Act" was "omitted on the Stage." In the quarto there is only one scene in Act III, but in the 1710 edition there are fifteen separate scenes.[52] D. F. McKenzie has argued persuasively that though the quartos use the English system, with a scene changing when location does, Congreve always thought in terms of a scene being defined by a group of people in conversation, and that consequently his adoption of the French system in 1710 "is no middle-aged editorial affectation of French fashion but only the proper and belated expression of the author's early, indeed constant, intentions."[53]

52. Anthony Gosse argues that the eleventh was the one dropped in the first production—i.e., lines 513–74 in the Davis edition. See "The Omitted Scene in Congreve's *Love for Love*," *Modern Philology*, 61 (1963), 40–42.

53. D. F. McKenzie, "When Congreve Made a Scene," *Transactions of the Cambridge Bibliographical Society*, 7 (1979), 338–42.

10

The Beaux' Stratagem (1707)

*T*he Beaux' Stratagem remains one of the most accessible comedies of the period and is produced with some regularity by academic theatres; it is even attempted occasionally in the commercial theatre.[1] Directors find it an effective stage vehicle. Literary critics, however, have been able to come to little agreement about the play. Is it sentimental slush? A serious comment on bad marriage and England's divorce laws? Is it about attitudes toward money? marriage? something else? Literary critics have emphasized some aspects of the play not usually apparent in production and other aspects difficult or impossible to communicate in the theatre.

Critics disagree about what the play means, but a directorial eye can at least tell us what is—or was—feasible in performance. We will start with a look at two major interpretive problems, go on to consider the circumstances of the original production, and then ask if any of the "subjects" critics have found in the play are communicable in performance. We are going to argue, finally, that between two quite disparate extremes there is a range of valid production possibilities in the script.

1. A production by T. Edward Hambleton and Norris Houghton at the Phoenix in New York in 1959 was praised by Atkinson in the *Times*. The National Theatre production by William Gaskill in 1970 was successful enough to tour.

MAJOR INTERPRETIVE PROBLEMS

Archer and Aimwell. These younger sons have left London to go fortune hunting, alternating as servant and master. They have agreed that if one can marry an heiress he will split the take with the other. If all else fails, they will go "to Brussels"—i.e., enlist in Marlborough's army (p. 15).[2] This possibility is passed over lightly, but the audience of 1707 would have been well aware of the potentially fatal results. Is the stratagem just the lark of a pair of young scamps? Or could a production play off Farquhar's working title, *The Broken Beaux*,[3] and emphasize the parallels with the highwaymen they are mistaken for? In the eighteenth century the play was generally advertised as *The Stratagem*, a title with some interestingly ambiguous implications.

Aimwell and Archer follow a long tradition of paired rakes, but they are not twins. The distinction between them is aptly summed up by William Appleton, who contrasts "the self-seeking Archer . . . in the tradition of Hobbes" with "the tender-hearted Aimwell . . . a follower of Shaftesbury."[4] Philosophical labels are difficult to translate into production, but we may agree that Archer is earthy, pragmatic, even cynical, while Aimwell is more emotional, less detached. The beaux seem to think of themselves as playing a game, and they certainly win. No one in the play serves as an alternative "right way" to their behavior, nor does anyone criticize them directly. Audiences usually respond favorably to Archer and Aimwell, though a production could be slanted to make them ugly and predatory.

Are the beaux twenty-two or thirty-two? The original Dorinda, Lucretia Bradshaw, was young and beautiful, which makes Aimwell's love-at-first-sight raptures technically plausible. But

2. All references are to *The Beaux' Stratagem*, ed. Charles N. Fifer (Lincoln: Univ. of Nebraska Press, 1977).

3. See Verlyn Flieger, "Notes on the Titling of George Farquhar's 'The Beaux' Stratagem,'" *Notes and Queries*, 224 (1979), 21–23.

4. "The Double Gallant in Eighteenth-Century Comedy," *English Writers of the Eighteenth Century*, ed. John H. Middendorf (New York: Columbia Univ. Press, 1971), pp. 145–57, quotation from p. 149.

Farquhar does not, we should note, give that relationship more than minimal development. Indeed, he does not even bother to write the customary series of love exchanges. This makes the relationship of the courting couple exceptionally superficial, particularly as a basis for Aimwell's sudden recantation and confession in Act V. Farquhar makes a joke of the whole convention of heroes loving heiresses at first sight. The joke would become ironic if Dorinda were portrayed as decidedly plain. There is not a great deal in their lines to support an overtly negative view of the beaux, but some hints could be developed. In III.ii., having just seen Dorinda for the first time, Aimwell goes into raptures. But not two pages later, as Archer goes off to pump Scrub, Aimwell asks him, "Can't you give me a bill upon Cherry in the meantime?" (p. 48). This can be played as a pleasantry, but it could also be a blunt reminder that Aimwell is a rake after Dorinda's money. Likewise when Archer rejoices at the availability of the false priest Foigard ("He shall marry you and pimp for me"—p. 95), we see a potentially ugly side to the pair. With the beaux made older and predatory, Dorinda plain and gullible, marital discord emphasized (with Mrs. Sullen as a warning), and highwaymen parallels stressed, we could be given a fairly sour view of wastrel rakes.

This is not what the surface of the text says, and production history suggests that the beaux are normally attractive and the audience in favor of their success. But what can success consist of? Do we want to see Dorinda cheated of her £10,000? Mrs. Sullen seduced and abandoned? Short of magically eliminating Aimwell's brother and making him the Viscount he has pretended to be (which Farquhar proceeds to do), no morally tidy resolution is possible, and Mrs. Sullen's problems remain unresolved in any case. By adopting the expedients he does, Farquhar lets us enjoy the beaux' success, but only via flagrant improbability. Whether this is to be taken in the spirit of *H.M.S. Pinafore* or whether a significant ironic comment is to be understood is a matter of choice. The play can be produced either way.

What happens in V.iv. A great deal of the critical disagreement about the play stems from the "divorce" of the Sullens in Act V.

Mrs. Elizabeth Inchbald denounced *The Beaux' Stratagem* because of "the free manner in which . . . [Farquhar] bestowed the hand of Mrs. Sullen upon Archer, without first procuring a divorce from her husband."[5] Leigh Hunt made the same assumption, but took the "want" of a proper divorce as a piece of social criticism. As recently as 1966 A. J. Farmer said blithely that Archer "will presumably marry" Mrs. Sullen and her ten thousand pounds.[6] Such readings ignore the reality of 1707: the "divorce" was illegal and impossible, and hence was strictly a piece of fantasy. A formal separation was legally possible, but of course it would not have permitted either partner to remarry.[7] And even if we take Farquhar's use of the term "divorce" to mean "separation," nowhere does he explicitly give Mrs. Sullen to Archer.

The version originally written by Farquhar and preserved in the quarto of 1707 (the source of all modern editions) quite clearly does not pair them off. Sullen agrees to release his wife but not her fortune (pp. 129–30), whereupon Archer announces to Sullen that Gibbet has stolen "all the writings of your estate, all the articles of marriage with this lady, bills, bonds, leases, receipts to an infinite value." Archer concludes: "I took 'em from him, and I deliver them to Sir Charles." In short, Sullen is forced to accept the loss of his wife's estate in order to get back his own bills, bonds, etc., and Mrs. Sullen is returned to the guardianship of her brother, not given her dowry outright.[8] On the last page Archer invites Mrs. Sullen to lead a dance with him and then speaks the finale, in which he says, "'Twould be hard to guess which of these parties is the better pleased, the couple joined or the couple parted" (p. 131). The reference is singular in both

5. Comments by Inchbald, Hunt, and others are reprinted in *Farquhar: A Casebook*, ed. Raymond A. Anselment (London: Macmillan, 1977), esp. pp. 35, 41.

6. *George Farquhar* (London: Longmans, Green & Co., 1966), p. 26.

7. For discussion, see Gellert Spencer Alleman, *Matrimonial Law and the Materials of Restoration Comedy* (Wallingford, Pa.: privately printed, 1942), pp. 43, 106–7, 111–12.

8. See Eric Rothstein, *George Farquhar* (New York: Twayne, 1967), p. 159. Rothstein's reading of the motivations behind the ending seems correct except for this detail.

cases: Aimwell and Dorinda have been joined, the Sullens parted. Nothing is said of joining Archer and Mrs. Sullen, whether in matrimony (impossible) or "justifiable adultery" (as Alleman assumes will happen). Rothstein observes that Sir Charles does not "seem to be a man who would forward a sister's adultery." Nor, we might add, does Archer seem likely to defy the rules of his male society and seduce the sister of a friend.[9] The printed page does not, however, specify the visual details of the end of the play. If Archer speaks the finale with an arm around Mrs. Sullen and goes off with her, we get one idea about their future; if he moves away without looking back, while her brother leads her off, we get quite another.

At this point we must take note of a textual problem. In the edition of 1728 Count Bellair's part is printed in italics (a sign of omission in performance) with a note saying that it was "cut out by the Author, after the first Night's Representation." The count's lines in the last scene are given to Foigard, and Archer's speech about Sullen's papers concludes, "and, if the lady pleases, she shall go home with me." This is not decisive (the staging of the finale remains important), but Archer's invitation certainly moves the play away from the implications of the original ending. We cannot be certain that this line was written or approved by the dying Farquhar, or even that he made the decision to cut Bellair. Moreover, many critics' assumptions about the ending stem from an anecdote recorded forty years later by William Rufus Chetwood, who says that Wilks visited Farquhar in his final illness and told him that "Mrs. *Oldfield* thought he had dealt too freely with the Character of Mrs. *Sullen* in giving her to *Archer*, without a proper Divorce, which was not security for her Honour."[10] But whatever the eighteenth-century performance tradition may have been, nowhere in the text does Farquhar ex-

9. Archer: "Sir Charles Freeman, brother to the lady that I had almost—but no matter for that" (p. 121). Archer is, as it were, mopping his brow after a narrow escape from a serious social contretemps.

10. William Rufus Chetwood, *The British Theatre* (Dublin: Peter Wilson, 1750), p. 131. The anecdote seems inauthentic both in relation to Oldfield's private life and to some of the roles she was already playing.

plicitly join Mrs. Sullen and Archer. Even the 1728 text leaves the matter up to the reader's or director's choice, rather like the second ending of *Great Expectations*.[11]

Archer's character supports a romantic ending with Mrs. Sullen only with difficulty: his philosophy has been and remains to avoid entanglement. Archer accepts Dorinda's £10,000 from Aimwell (p. 124), and with Mrs. Sullen's like fortune (supposing her "available") he would be distinctly well off. But though Archer willingly participates in the "divorce" hearing, he hands Mrs. Sullen's marriage settlement directly to her brother. Nor does he seem interested in using his new-found security to pursue Cherry. He cries "Rot the money! [the beaux' £200] My wench is gone," when he hears of Cherry's disappearance. Yet he persuades Aimwell to have Dorinda take Cherry into her service (p. 125)— providing for her, but not as his responsibility.[12]

If the ending simply dissolves into happy fantasy, then we can rejoice at the good fortune that allows the new Lord Aimwell to claim Dorinda, and we can use the celebratory ending of the comedy to award Mrs. Sullen to Archer. In reality, Mrs. Sullen is not much better off than the unhappy title characters in *The Wives Excuse* and Vanbrugh's *The Provok'd Wife* (1697); and if the director separates her from Archer at the end, we have a distinctly gloomy comment about her future. How serious the play is depends on the attitude a production takes toward the marital discord. The evidence provided by eighteenth-century casting and textual history (a steady diminution in the marital discord speeches) suggests that the play was staged as a romp. In such a production Archer might well escort Mrs. Sullen offstage, an exit

11. At least one eighteenth-century production presented a more drastically altered text. An ad for a performance at the Little Haymarket, 26 August 1735, states that the play has been extensively revised: "tho' . . . the Chief Characters in this Play, are drawn with a great deal of Life and Spirit; Yet . . . there are several obvious Faults. That as the Character of the French Count, and that of the Irish Priest, are in no sort conducive to the Plot of the Play; they may therefore be looked on as superfluous: That the Parting of Sullen and his Wife, is extremely unnatural; and that the Ending of the Play (with respect to Archer) is abrupt to a Degree, &c. &c." See *The London Stage*, Part 3, I, 505.

12. Fifer considers that "Archer's real interest" is in Cherry, but he assumes that, Archer not being a marrying man, he only wants "access to her" (p. xxxv).

which would maintain the fantasy world set up by the deus ex machina and the "divorce."

Farquhar is careful not to introduce discordant points of view in the finale. Lady Bountiful is not on stage while her daughter is given in marriage and her son is "divorced." Nor is Scrub present: he would be seriously disconcerted to discover that he could no longer aspire to emulate "Martin," which Farquhar avoids by leaving him in the cellar guarding prisoners. The fantasy evidently remained unpunctured for those members of the original audience who wished to enjoy it. But a production which, against the expectations of comedy, separated Archer and Mrs. Sullen might—then or now—replace the fantasy with an interestingly discordant ending.

THE IMPLICATIONS OF SETTING, ORIGINAL CAST, AND CHARACTER CONFIGURATIONS

Setting. The Beaux' Stratagem is physically simple to stage. Only five locations are specified: the public room of an inn; a gallery in Lady Bountiful's house; Mrs. Sullen's bedroom; another bedroom; and another room in the house not described more precisely—a scene which could be played in the gallery.[13] Indeed, the only apparent reason for the second bedroom in Act V is to permit the removal of a practicable bed at the end of V.ii. (p. 114). We may hypothesize an arrangement such as is shown in the scene plan below. Action alternates between inn and house (i.e., gallery) until V.ii., when we move from the inn to Mrs. Sullen's bedchamber. At the end of the scene we move to "*another apartment*," which closes off the stage at the first group of shutters for ninety lines while Mrs. Sullen's bed is removed. At the end of this brief scene we return to the gallery for the finale. This staging could be simplified. The stage directions for V.ii. lead us to hypothesize a practicable bed, but if we opt for a bed painted on a wing we could move the scene to the gallery and cut our loca-

---

13. Act III.i. specifies merely "*Lady Bountiful's house*" (p. 42). The most conservative reading is to assume that this refers to the same set as II.i.

tions to three—inn, gallery, and Mrs. Sullen's bedroom. The issue of the bed is far from trivial: the presence or absence of an actual bed could make a major difference to the seriousness with which the audience takes Mrs. Sullen's confrontation with Archer. A painted bed not only defuses audience anxiety about "rape," but makes their struggle comic because clearly nothing is going to happen. A real bed alerts the audience to the possible consequences of what Mrs. Sullen has regarded as a game.

All four settings were probably pulled from stock—nothing was advertised as new. A modern production might try to make points visually about the inn or the house, but Farquhar's descriptions of settings imply no authorial commentary. We should, however, note that the whole play takes place indoors. Critics, especially Rothstein, have emphasized the "country" setting (Lichfield) and talked about Lady Bountiful's association with "Nature." But the interior settings, the London longings of the four principals (not to mention at least two of the supporting characters), and the London-based deus ex machina all work against a visual connection of the country setting with "Nature." A director eager to stress nature could provide the gallery with windows looking out on the grounds of the estate,[14] or could move some of the action outside the house, but there is nothing in Farquhar's text to suggest thematic significance for the country setting. In this context "Lichfield" is no more specific a location than "upstate New York" is to a Manhattanite. The action takes place away from London because the logic of the plot demands it. The whole point of the stratagem is to let the gallants return to high life in the city.[15]

The original cast. Farquhar presumably wrote each part with its original actor in mind. In any case, the 1707 Haymarket cast tells

14. The illustration showing Aimwell's fit in the 1711 edition of Farquhar's *Works* has windows opening onto a garden but is clearly an interior setting. We have no way of knowing whether it reflects the current staging practice.

15. Archer and Aimwell both rhapsodize about life in London (pp. 15–16, 94); Mrs. Sullen sneers at the country (p. 26); Dorinda gloats over the prospect of life in London (p. 92); Gibbet expects to buy a place in the Royal household (p. 100); Cherry tries to put on the airs of a London lady (pp. 31–32); Scrub aspires to "Martin's" higher condition as a London servant.

2.3   Vacant
2.2   Gallery
2.1   Mrs. Sullen's Bedroom

1.3   Vacant
1.2   Inn
1.1   The Other Apartment

Figure 10.1. Scene plan for *The Beaux' Stratagem*.

us a good deal about the probable balance and impact of the production. Archer is the last of the succession of leads Farquhar wrote for his friend Wilks.[16] Of the three women in the play whom Wilks might pursue (Bicknell as Cherry, Bradshaw as Dorinda, and Oldfield as Mrs. Sullen), Anne Oldfield is the only one with whom he was regularly paired in 1706–07. She had already chased or been chased by him in at least seven plays this season, six times in *The Recruiting Officer* alone.[17] By comparison, the audience had seen Wilks matched with Margaret Bicknell and Lucretia Bradshaw just once each.[18] The Wilks-Oldfield combination clearly tips the balance of interest against John Mills and Mrs. Bradshaw as Aimwell and Dorinda, a weighting reflected in their proportion of lines. We may also note that not all Wilks-Oldfield couples remained together at the end of the play.[19]

John Mills' roles suggest that he was overprepared for what

16. For a helpful account of Wilks' effect on Farquhar's characterization of his male leads, see Shirley Strum Kenny, "Farquhar, Wilks, and Wildair; or, the Metamorphosis of the 'Fine Gentleman'," *Philological Quarterly*, 57 (1978), 46–65.

17. Wilks and Oldfield were paired in *The Spanish Fryar*, *The Recruiting Officer*, *The Platonick Lady*, *The Tender Husband*, *The Comical Revenge*, *Wit Without Money*, and *The Orphan*.

18. Bicknell was paired with Wilks in *The Northern Lass* and as part of a triangle in *The Careless Husband*. Bradshaw played Ophelia to Wilks' Hamlet later in this season. She was paired with Mills in *The Royal Merchant*, *The Tender Husband*, and *Sir Courtly Nice*.

19. They remained apart in *The Spanish Fryar*, having discovered that they were siblings. In previous seasons their attraction had remained unfulfilled in *The Humour of the Age*, *The Basset Table*, and *Hampstead Heath*.

little Aimwell has to do.[20] He provided solidity and plausible sentimentality as a contrast to Wilks' famous airiness. Mrs. Sullen's French suitor, Bellair, offered nothing special to John Boman, a professional dapper dandy.[21] But the choice of Boman over lighter-weight and less-experienced actors like William Bowen, George Pack, Henry Fairbank, and Benjamin Husband is informative, indicating an attempt to make Bellair a believable rival to Sullen and Archer.

The most interesting choice of actor was John Verbruggen to play Sullen. Verbruggen's age (ca. forty) and versatility allowed him to play Alexander in *The Rival Queens*, Iago opposite Betterton's Othello, and Hotspur to Wilks' Hal. He had the dignity to play Colonel Bruce in *The Comical Revenge*, but he could unbend to become Surly in *Sir Courtly Nice* and Ramble in *The London Cuckolds* ("a great designer on Ladies, but unsuccessful"). Sullen is generally played as a dimwitted rustic. The National Theatre production of 1970 presented him as an alienated intellectual— an interesting but improbable twist. William Gaskill is simply wrong in saying that "there is no indication that he is a rustic."[22] The dramatis personae calls him "a country blockhead, brutal to his wife" (p. 6), and Boniface says "he's a—he wants it here, sir [*Pointing to his forehead*]. . . . Icod, he's no better than—" (p. 11). The real question about Sullen is whether he is a potentially violent dolt or a blustering buffoon. Verbruggen could have taken the character in either direction. But since he, with Boman, was set up against Wilks and routed by Keen (as Sir Charles Free-

20. For example, Worthy in *The Recruiting Officer*, Edmund in *Lear*, Morelove in *The Careless Husband*, Cortez in *The Indian Emperour*, the King in *The Maid's Tragedy*, and Volpone.

21. Boman (or Bowman) played more serious characters than Bowen and other fop actors—e.g., Frederick in *The Rover* and Don Carlos in *The Adventures of Five Hours*.

22. "Finding a Style for Farquhar," in Anselment, p. 215. Gaskill does, however, have helpful technical suggestions about working with twentieth-century actors on "Restoration" plays. For directors who use script-based improvisations *The Beaux' Stratagem* offers some obvious possibilities—e.g., "Martin" teaching Cherry "Love's Catechism," the church scene where Aimwell sees Dorinda, the beaux planning the "fit" scene, Aimwell and Dorinda's love scene, the confrontation between Cherry and her father about the robbery.

man), we believe his Sullen posed a real threat. Keen took over as Sullen when Verbruggen left the company at the end of the season, whereas Benjamin Johnson, Francis Leigh, or even Richard Estcourt would have been more likely choices for a comic Sullen.[23]

Farquhar's knowledge of the company inspired him and at times overstimulated him. Gibbet and Boniface have more stage time than they really need, perhaps because they were written as vehicles for Cibber and William Bullock. Not surprisingly, they just disappear at the end of the play. Gibbet's old and dirty regimentals (pp. 36, 50) contrast amusingly with the usual run of fops Cibber played. Boniface represents a plum for Bullock, an actor in the low-comedy tradition of James Nokes, Tony Leigh, and William Pinkethman. He took country bumpkins, fops, coarse fathers, old ladies (*travestie* parts), comic Irish and Scots roles. To use a low comedian as the local kingpin of a gang was both a challenge to the actor and a joke the audience could be comfortable with: Bullock posed no threat to sympathetic characters. The best-integrated of the smaller roles is Scrub, a gift for Henry Norris, Jr., whose "Jubilee Dicky" had contributed so much to the success of Farquhar's *The Constant Couple*. Scrub's naïveté and servant status are casting to type: Norris specialized in such roles as Gripus in *Amphitryon* and Littlewit in *Bartholomew Fair*. Foigard was taken by Bowen, a notable joker and public personality in the tradition of Jo Haynes. Bowen was an Irishman specializing in such roles as Teague in *The Committee* and Raggou in *The Old Troop*.[24] Lady Bountiful continues Mrs. Powell's line of comic old women. Gipsy's character is mostly reported rather than demonstrated, and the use of Mrs. Mills in the role only confirms her lack of importance.

Cherry is the most problematical of the minor characters. The role was created by Mrs. Bicknell, then perhaps twenty-two, who specialized in pert servants and sprightly young women. She

23. Keen had appeared as Acasto in *The Orphan*, Ballance in *The Recruiting Officer*, Voltore in *Volpone*, and the King in *Henry IV* and *Hamlet*.

24. The original casting was ideal for the wonderful brogue scene between Archer and Foigard (pp. 96–98): Wilks had come from Ireland, and he must have been able to do a most convincing "countryman" to Bowen's Foigard.

took such roles as Margery Pinchwife, Hoyden in *The Relapse*, Edging in *The Careless Husband*, Prue in *Love for Love*, and Melantha in *Marriage A-la-Mode*. To attract Archer, Cherry is presumably clean and energetic rather than sluttish and lazy. How old is she? How experienced? Archer calls her "child" and she objects (p. 21), but this need not mean that he is cradle-snatching. The word was a common term of endearment, and Mrs. Sullen calls Dorinda "child" (p. 26). If we present Cherry as circa eighteen and far from genuinely naïve, then the relationship with Archer is potentially serious, at least in terms of sex. If she is fifteen or sixteen and he is just playing games with her, then she is much less a genuine alternative to Mrs. Sullen. Why does Farquhar entangle Archer with both women? "Love's Catechism" (pp. 37–39) is a neat variation on the sort of thing Congreve does with Prue in *Love for Love*, but Cherry is not just a gullible adolescent. Indeed, she has a very hard head: "Depend upon this, sir, nothing in this garb [footman's clothes] shall ever tempt me, for though I was born to servitude, I hate it" (p. 40). One possible explanation for Farquhar's emphasis on Cherry is that he intended parallels with Dorinda and Mrs. Sullen—who are also looking for ways out of country servitude. Lady Bountiful is Cherry's godmother (p. 105), and Cherry has evidently learned something of the manners and affectations of the gentry. Are we to rejoice at her replacing Gipsy as lady's maid? Since Farquhar has given Cherry the love scenes which might normally have gone to Dorinda, this hardly seems likely. Here again the happy ending will not bear much reflection.

Character configurations. Casting tells us how the original audience might have expected couples in the play to match up. If we look at the order in which potential couples are presented, paying attention to the class distinctions in the play, we see how Farquhar both piqued and controlled these expectations. The rhythm of the play is more like a series of interruptions than development of a harmonious theme.[25] Farquhar tries out eight different male/fe-

25. Farquhar is unusually specific about times for particular scenes. The action begins Saturday night and concludes in the small hours Monday morning. The two scenes in Act II are overlapping if not simultaneous: both occur before

male combinations, six of them shown, two only reported. Of these couples, only one (Aimwell and Dorinda) has any likelihood of enduring: the rest are mismatches of some sort, most of them explicitly abandoned by the end of the play.

We hear first of the Sullens, whom Boniface considers mismatched (p. 11), and who play a series of variations on that theme in their several encounters. The first pair we actually see together is "Martin" and Cherry, but the exposition is hardly complete before both of them have told us that there is no future in the relationship. The obstacles are ambition on her part and pride on his.[26] Between their two flirtations, Mrs. Sullen explains to Dorinda that she intends to use Count Bellair as a sham rival, hoping to "rouse" her "lethargic sottish husband" (p. 30). The original audience would assume that no heroine would have a real interest in a captured French officer, count or not.

In the first two scenes in Act III, Aimwell and Dorinda separately report their love at first sight—a placeholder for their relationship. Since there is no real blocking figure, Farquhar uses other scenes to keep the lovers apart as long as possible. By way of contrast Scrub then tells "Martin" about his infatuation for Gipsy—a negative parallel for the "Martin"-Cherry relationship.

The rest of Act III as originally written works rather poorly. Bellair represents a piece of ponderous point making about chastity by Farquhar, and is probably best dispensed with in performance. First we see Mrs. Sullen attracted to "Martin" ("The devil take him for wearing that livery . . . I should like this fellow better [than Bellair] in a design upon myself," pp. 64–65). We then see her with her husband (pp. 65–66), with Bellair (pp. 67–68), and with the two of them (pp. 68–70). Mrs. Sullen makes

---

church. The first two scenes in Act III are definitely simultaneous, occurring after church but before Sunday afternoon dinner. And Act V.i. and ii. both occur at 2:00 A.M., while scene iii. follows so quickly that it must have begun simultaneously, though we are shown only the end of the action.

26. Archer: "Let me see—two thousand pound! If the wench would promise to die when the money were spent, Igad, one would marry her, but the fortune may go off in a year or two, and the wife may live—Lord knows how long? Then an innkeeper's daughter—ay, that's the devil. There my pride brings me off" (p. 41).

plain that she has no intention of taking Bellair as her lover, and at the end of the act she laments the inadequacy of divorce law (pp. 71–73). The sequence has two functions: it emphasizes Sullen's intractability, and it is "ocular proof" that Mrs. Sullen means to keep her marriage vows. Cutting the Bellair scenes removes the evidence that Mrs. Sullen will be faithful, while keeping them lessens the probability that she will go off with Archer at the end of the play. But even if Bellair is left in, a French fop does not make a convincing rival for Archer. This flaw in the structure admits of no easy solution.

Farquhar's presentation of Aimwell and Dorinda is most unusual. Not until the finale do we hear the couple talk. When Aimwell recovers from his "swoon," he addresses some flagrantly contrived verse to Dorinda ("Delirious, poor gentleman," says Lady Bountiful), and we see him *making love in dumb show*" (pp. 85–87). In place of the lovers' dialogue, Dorinda later repeats some of his compliments to win a bet with Mrs. Sullen (pp. 91–92), but what is emphasized is her rapturous vision of what marriage with "Viscount Aimwell" will mean:

> [*Dorinda*] Why, my ten thousand pounds may lie brooding here this seven years and hatch nothing at last but some ill-natured clown like yours. Whereas, if I marry my Lord Aimwell there will be title, place, and precedence, the park, the play, and the drawing-room, splendor, equipage, noise, and flambeaux.—"Hey, my Lady Aimwell's servants there—Lights, lights to the stairs—My Lady Aimwell's coach put forward—Stand by; make room for her Ladyship."—Are not these things moving? (p. 92)

The love-at-first-sight convention notwithstanding, this speech reveals Dorinda as a thoroughly selfish social climber. Mrs. Sullen endorses this vision by congratulating Dorinda; she then weeps and makes the unhappy comparison: "And must the fair apartment of my breast be made a stable for a brute to lie in?" The effect is not that of the conventional love scene.

The moment of Aimwell's transformation is worth close scrutiny. He has confessed to Dorinda, and Archer has reproached him ("too late for pardon. You may remember, Mr. Aimwell . . ."—p. 120). Dorinda rushes in to say "You are the true Lord Viscount Aimwell" (p. 122). Sir Charles confirms this and explains: "Your brother died the day before I left London," whereupon Aimwell (amiable creature that he is) exclaims, "Thanks to the pregnant stars that formed this accident." Archer then speaks up: "My lord, I wish you joy. . . . My lord, how d'ye? A word, my lord, how d'ye? A word, my lord" (p. 123). Not "Mr. Aimwell" but "My lord"—four times in five lines. Is Archer thunderstruck? fawning? ironic? A page further on Aimwell says to Archer, "Our money's gone, Frank"; a moment later Archer says, "By this light, my lord, our money again." From artificial distinction between Aimwell and Archer we have moved to a very real one, and Archer shows no signs of liking it. The more stress is laid on the chorus of "My lords" the more artificial and even obnoxious does the happy ending become. Most productions play right over the point, but it is there if wanted. Aimwell and Dorinda have merely to assume a condescending air and the whole impact of the ending can be tilted.

From this survey of cast and characters we learn that Farquhar threw his emphasis heavily toward Archer and Mrs. Sullen; that small parts were cast to type; and that Sullen was given to an actor who could make him more than an obvious comic butt. With Wilks and Oldfield cast as they were, the audience would expect Archer and Mrs. Sullen to get together. If Archer's interest in Cherry is genuine, it becomes a rather disturbing diversion. And if Archer and Mrs. Sullen are visibly separated at the end, then expectation has been strikingly frustrated.

IS THE PLAY ABOUT SOMETHING?

When asked why he chose to stage *The Recruiting Officer*, William Gaskill replied, "I wanted to do a Restoration comedy that was *about* something." He had in mind the "social-critical documentation" of the recruiting scenes. *The Beaux' Stratagem* lacks that kind of explicit "realism," but a number of critics have found the play to be what Ronald Berman calls "drama of ideas,"[27] and we need therefore to consider whether it makes some sort of formal statement. The possible subjects proposed to date are money, marital discord/divorce law, country values, and social criticism of robber-beaux.

Money. Berman refers to "the final cause of the play, the sum of ten thousand pounds," and Michael Cordner rightly points out the "formidable influence of money upon the characters' lives and world."[28] Farquhar emphasizes money rather than true love by constant, specific references throughout the play: we count more than thirty examples. This reverses the usual pattern in late seventeenth-century comedy, where money is assumed to be necessary but is not discussed at length. Impecunious rakes simply do not consider falling in love with women who are not "fortunes." Aimwell's "reform" technically reasserts the priority of love, but given the meager development of the romantic plot, the reform does not fundamentally alter the play's values. The rakes require money.

Berman says that "whatever order is being asserted is very plainly determined by cash and contract." He finds the play "dishonest" in its failure to "account" for the change in Aimwell, but denies that the end is "merely sentimental" or that the "analytical structure" invalidates the love. He says that Farquhar is trying to "move from the world of Hobbes to that of Shaftesbury." In other words, Farquhar is trying to transcend a money ethic. We find this too generalized to be convincing. Archer gets money, though he does not reform. If Farquhar had wanted true love to outweigh money, he could have developed his romantic couple more fully.

The emphasis on money yields unflattering implications (at least to us) about the society of the play. To marry money was of course a commonplace of both comedy and real life, one which

27. Ronald Berman, "The Comedy of Reason," *Texas Studies in Literature and Language*, 7 (1965), 161–68.
28. *The Beaux' Stratagem*, ed. Michael Cordner (London: Benn, 1976), p. xxii.

provides happy endings for a host of plays in this period.[29] Dorinda is not, however, simply treated as a pot of gold at the end of a rainbow. The sums of money specified in the play seem realistic. John Loftis has compiled a list of fortunes and incomes mentioned in some contemporary plays. Congreve gives Millamant £12,000 (or £6,000 if she marries without her aunt's consent). Vanbrugh provides Hoyden £1,500 a year, and Lord Foppington £5,000. Lady Lurewell in Farquhar's *The Constant Couple* is worth £3,000 per annum; Sir Harry Wildair, £8,000. Gregory King estimated that ordinary gentlemen had about £280 per annum; esquires, £450; knights, £650; and temporal lords, £2,800.[30]

We are told that Dorinda's entire fortune is £10,000 (which coincidentally is the sum wasted by Archer and Aimwell in an unspecified length of time). Sullen's annual income is £3,000; Lady Bountiful's, £1,000. Cherry can get hold of £2,000 (by stealing from her father?): Archer estimates "a year or two" to spend it. From a marriage portion of £10,000 Archer might make as much as £500 a year; from the £5,000 he is entitled to by the bargain, half that. If Aimwell got Dorinda without inheriting his brother's money, would he be wishing her dead in five years so he could pursue another heiress? How different is Dorinda with £5,000 from Cherry with £2,000?

In short, a £10,000 fortune is a good haul but not wealth by itself. If we look at the real-life marriage settlements recorded by Narcissus Luttrell between 1701 and 1707 we find some twenty of them, only two as low as £10,000, and only six under £30,000. Dorinda is worth a lot of money, but not nearly enough for the scale on which the beaux dream of living. Without the lucky death of Aimwell's brother she is no more than a temporary expedient.

---

29. Farquhar himself reputedly tried to marry money and found himself tricked. Critics willing to use biographical material differ about whether this experience affected *The Beaux' Stratagem*, and if so, how.

30. John Loftis, *Comedy and Society from Congreve to Fielding* (Stanford: Stanford University Press, 1959), pp. 45–49. Loftis points out that Bellinda is

Marital discord and divorce law. The prominence of these elements in the 1707 text is obvious. Eighteenth-century performance tradition seems to have minimized them, and plainly a production does not have to emphasize them. How serious a comment did Farquhar hope to make in performance? Marital discord had been a popular theme in comedy since about 1690. There were two distinct traditions. Problem plays (*The Wives Excuse*, *The Provok'd Wife*) left the unhappy couple together in misery or arranged an explicitly unsatisfactory separation, actual divorce being impossible. Solution plays—"reform comedy," if we want a less unflattering title—moved to reconciliation, often implausibly (*Love's Last Shift*, *The Careless Husband*).[31] Farquhar hits on a novel expedient: happy ending (but how happy?) by means of fantasy divorce. Rothstein feels that the play presents a marriage problem and argues for divorce as a solution, though without presenting a genuine resolution for this play. Hopper and Lahey see no better than a clumsy achievement of an unrealistic happy ending. Where Rothstein sees Farquhar's use of Milton's divorce tracts as part of a serious justification of an otherwise "dubious proceeding," Hopper and Lahey find it superficial (mere "plumage") and say that Farquhar "wanted a few colorful feathers for the nest of a happy ending."[32] Kenneth Muir finds the divorce neither fantastic nor farcical but deliberately "Utopian."[33]

Much depends on whether Sullen is a comic rustic or a "brutal" one (as the dramatis personae specifies). Mrs. Sullen's initial description of her "sad brute" ("beware of a sullen, silent sot"— p. 27) is certainly funny, but its effect will depend on whether she is ironically amused, exasperated, or genuinely bitter. The fact that Farquhar gives Mrs. Sullen no other name indicates how completely he conceived of her as a wife. The question is how she

---

able to marry Heartfree in *The Provok'd Wife* because "she herself possesses £10,000, enough to enable them to live modestly" (p. 46).

31. See Hume, "Marital Discord" (Chapter 8, note 6, above.)

32. Vincent F. Hopper and Gerald B. Lahey, ed., *The Beaux' Stratagem* (Great Neck, N.Y.: Barron's, 1963), p. 36.

33. Kenneth Muir, *The Comedy of Manners* (London: Hutchinson, 1970), p. 150.

reacts to her circumstances. We see her seriously tempted by "Martin" in the picture gallery scene, but Farquhar keeps her from following her inclinations. In V.ii. Archer comes to her bedroom under the mistaken impression that she expects to receive the count. But despite his having become the gentleman of her fantasies, she resists him. This is the ultimate test of Mrs. Sullen's resolve. Farquhar then proceeds to graft a solution onto what had been a problem plot. One cannot really say that *The Beaux' Stratagem* is about marital discord: it makes no complex statement. A production in the early eighteenth century that stressed the "marriage problem" would have implied the need for a divorce law, but that is hardly raison d'être for the whole play or for producing it today.

Country values: inn versus house. For four acts the scene oscillates between Boniface's inn and Lady Bountiful's house. Eric Rothstein has read the play as essentially a contrast of the values attached to these settings.[34] Lady Bountiful, in this reading, "stands for a limited but benevolent nature," since she lives in the country and practices "natural healing." Her thematic opposite, Boniface, violates "natural, social, familial, and personal relationships." Boniface's inn "is appropriate for the beaux," since like them Boniface "is a hypocritical user of beauty and bounty for his own ends." According to Rothstein, the "healing manorhouse" is beset by "interlopers," but its values are upheld. The "central metaphor" is "nature," most clearly associated with Lady Bountiful, who "gives freely and unaffectedly whatever she has." But is Lady Bountiful the "normative character" Rothstein finds her? Even he admits that "naivete . . . confines her to superficial judgments of people," and hence "she must be excluded from the dialectic of the play."

We find this reading ingenious as literary criticism, but not easy to stage convincingly. Though Lady Bountiful is spoken of earlier, she does not appear until IV.i. and has only sixty-nine lines in the whole play. She dotes on the obnoxious Sullen; is easily deceived by Aimwell's simulated fit; has helped infect

34. Rothstein, *Farquhar*, pp. 151–57.

Cherry with ambitions difficult for her to fulfill. She is a kind but clearly ineffectual character. In most productions she is an incidental figure of fun: how to make her much else is hard to imagine. She could be made middle-aged rather than old, and handsomer than usual, but she has so little stage time that she cannot loom large—the more so since she is absent from the finale. Alan Roper goes so far as to say that "the beaux are intent upon carrying the values of the inn to the house," and that "in the last act the inn and its values make a bodily assault upon the house and its values." [35] But what makes the audience see the house in such terms?

Stress on "nature" seems to us misguided. Rothstein is correct when he says that Sir Charles justifies his sister's "divorce" in terms of "the procedure of natural law." But Sir Charles is a London gentleman, an inhabitant of the town world Archer and Aimwell are struggling to remain part of. We might ask, in Northrop Frye's terms, whether a new society emerges at the end of the play. Will Aimwell and Dorinda live in the country? (That is not her vision, and nor has he suggested it would suit him.) Will Archer? Will Sir Charles immure his luckless sister in a country seat? Who upholds Lady Bountiful's values, much less gets converted to them? House and inn notwithstanding, the action of this play really has its origin and destination in London—and its values are London values.

Social criticism: rakes = robbers. Rothstein sees a significant analogy between rakes and the Boniface-Gibbet gang, a reading accepted by both Roper and Cordner. In some terms it clearly makes sense: the beaux have come to cheat an heiress out of her money and will divide the spoils. Farquhar definitely puts the beaux in an unflattering light in this respect. But to expect Farquhar to raise basic questions about the mores of the society he lived in may be asking too much.

The metaphoric parallels are certainly available to the reader,

35. Alan Roper, "*The Beaux' Stratagem*: Image and Action," *Seventeenth-Century Imagery*, ed. Earl Miner (Berkeley: Univ. of California Press, 1971), pp. 169–86, esp. 184–85.

and perhaps to the spectator, but three factors work against such identification in the theatre. First, whether Farquhar's audience saw anything wrong in wanting to marry money is much to be doubted. Second, at a time when specific costume descriptions are rare, Farquhar goes out of his way to indicate differences between rakes and robbers. Scrub reports "Martin's" fancy dress (p. 45): if "Martin" wears lace, high-tongued shoes, and a periwig, carries a silver-headed cane, and struts after the French fashion, then surely Aimwell is even more resplendent.[36] By contrast both beaux sneer at Gibbet's shabbiness (pp. 37, 50). True, Gibbet has on his working clothes, not what he swells around London in, but they are the only outfit we see him wear. One might argue that the contrast is ironic, but the direct visual impression works against the rakes/robbers parallel. Third, although Boniface and Gibbet leap to the conclusion that the beaux are their competitors, Scrub and the ladies do not. As early as page 44 Scrub reports various rumors about their presence (spies, mountebanks, Jesuits), but these do not imperil their reception at the house. Archer does enter by subterfuge in Act V and is taken for a robber by Scrub, who has seen and heard the real robbers. But Scrub is too terrified at that point ("O, pray, sir, spare all I have and take my life"—p. 109) to be a serious critical/authorial voice. And Archer recognizes no parallel after rescuing the ladies from Gibbet's gang when he moralizes on "the rogue's destiny" (p. 115).

The finale offers no criticism of the beaux: no one in the play except Sir Charles has the distance from which to assess them, and he shares their values. In Brecht's hands this might be ironic:

36. Evidence of the contrast between Scrub and "Martin" is easy to find. In the 1730s and 1740s Hippisley wore "Scrubs jacket." See Philip H. Highfill, Jr., "Rich's 1744 Inventory of Covent Garden Properties," *Restoration and Eighteenth Century Theatre Research*, 5 (1966), 17, under "Modern cloaths in wear." For a 1775 description of "business" used by Weston as Scrub in III.iii., all admiration for Garrick's "Martin," see George Lichtenberg, *Lichtenberg's Visits to England*, trans. Margaret L. Mare and W. H. Quarrell (Oxford: Clarendon Press, 1938), pp. 25–27. Their pattern was followed by the earl of Barrymore and Captain Wathen at the earl's Wargrave Theatre in 1791–92. See Sybil Rosenfeld, *Temples of Thespis* (London: Society for Theatre Research, 1978), Plate 1.

low-life rogues get punished, high-life rogues rewarded. But most early eighteenth-century playwrights are quite explicit about morals, and Farquhar does not even specify the punishment of the captured gang. To make the rakes/robbers analogy potent, he would have had to let the beaux' stratagem work. If the play ended with Dorinda gloating over her future as Lady Aimwell while Archer and Aimwell sniggered over her delusion and split the loot, we would leave with a different impression. The reader (more than the spectator) may say "what if . . . ?" but the fact remains that Farquhar does not bring matters to that pass. He is always conscious of the economic disadvantage of the younger brother,[37] but given the nature of this finale we have to regard any reading that stresses Farquhar's criticism of his own society as exaggerated. How we evaluate that society in comparison with our own is another matter.

ROMP OR SATIRE?

The answer to this question is plainly "either." The text of *The Beaux' Stratagem* presents us with a range of possibilities, and a particular production could be made to come out almost anywhere between the extremes. For the sake of clear contrast let us sketch the essentials of two very different productions.

The Romp

Motto: Love makes the world go round.
Philosophy: Benevolism.
Act I. Play the beaux as highspirited youngsters—comfortable anywhere, good humored about everything, uncritical. Their stratagem is a lark, not a serious enterprise. They play hard, but have never worked at anything. They do not necessarily expect to succeed, and are not worried about failing. Brussels is a dream, not a threat. The war is just another game, one they do not believe will really endanger them. Parallels to highwaymen can be

---

37. A point well made by Eric Rothstein in "Farquhar's *Twin-Rivals* and the Reform in Comedy," *PMLA*, 79 (1964), 33–41.

minimized by dress and by emphasis on differences in manners and polish. Such villainy as exists in this comedy world is embodied in the highwaymen, of whom Boniface is an unwilling dupe. Gibbet can be treated as a comic-book villain, and the gang made hyperanxious and bumbling. Cherry does not present a genuine alternative to Dorinda (as fortune) or to Mrs. Sullen (as love interest). She should be markedly younger than the ladies and attractive to Archer only as a flirtation—in which she should take the initiative.

Act II. The Sullens should be sharply differentiated in appearance and behavior from Aimwell and Dorinda. The marital discord scenes can be played boisterously as Darby-and-Joan comic routines: perhaps they are the Sullens' form of fun. Mrs. Sullen is not desperate, but she is bored by her situation. Yet she remains hopeful of catching her husband's interest. Sullen might be a bewildered blockhead (a twenty-three-year-old mama's boy) or alternatively a comic villain (perhaps a thirty-five-year-old who never wanted to get married and sees no reason to change his bachelor ways). In neither case should Sullen seem threatening enough to worry the audience.

Act III. The adolescent love-sickness that Aimwell and Dorinda suffer is still a familiar convention: they revel in their agony and inarticulateness. The attraction between Archer and Mrs. Sullen should be played from their first meeting, without regard to disguise, class, or any other rational consideration. The Bellair scenes get cut, the rationale-for-divorce speeches shortened.

Act IV. Mrs. Sullen's medical advice to the countrywoman is nasty enough that it is hard to read as a joke in good taste. But if she is miffed at being mistaken for her mother-in-law and hence made mischievous, the sting is lessened. The countrywoman might also be deaf. Aimwell's feigned fit is a masquerade which the beaux constantly expect will be uncovered. As their implausible game succeeds, we share their astonishment as well as their pleasure. Foigard is a comically inept plotter, and his ineptitude rather than his adopted religion should be emphasized. The edge can be taken off Dorinda's vision of life as Lady Aimwell if she is visibly moved by Mrs. Sullen's response and plight (pp. 92–93).

Act V. Sir Charles Freeman becomes a benevolent authority figure, older than the beaux, to whom Sullen can also listen with respect. The misunderstanding in Mrs. Sullen's bedroom should be played with enough obvious encouragement from her and enough restraint from Archer to avoid any threat. (Berinthia's "rape" in *The Relapse* is the obvious predecessor of this interpretation.) The robbery is then an unwelcome interruption, not a relief. Of course, the thieves put up no effective resistance. Aimwell's reform is played through quickly and at face value, and gets him his heiress. Instant "divorce" follows upon lucky inheritance and is topped off with a bit of convenient blackmail. However improbable, these events are a series of exhilarating surprises, and the audience goes away pleased with the fairy tale.[38] Under these circumstances Mrs. Sullen may just as well be given to Archer. In a modern production the validity of the divorce hardly matters, and hence the issue of "justifiable adultery" need not arise. Everyone who is important comes out fine, and everyone else is kept out of sight.

The satire

Motto: Money makes the world go round.
Philosophy: Hobbesian self-interest.

Act I. The beaux should be cast and played as adults—twenty-eight-year-old wastrels who have never worked and would rather chance getting killed in Marlborough's wars than start working now. They are inclined to sneer at their country surroundings. Their goal is abstract: any fortune will do. The usual procedure in plays of the late seventeenth and early eighteenth centuries is to introduce the rakes, then take up discussion of a current intrigue. Instead, we hear first of their dislocation from London, then of their disguise, and then of an unfeeling design to trick an heiress out of her fortune. The plan is born of desperation, and it brings out the worst, usually undramatized features of the court-

---

38. The same sort of inheritance of title and money occurs at the end of Caryll's *Sir Salomon* (1670), which remained popular in the London theatre around 1707.

ship pattern in this society. The better "understanding" the beaux seem to have with Boniface and his cohorts, the more easily we can see parallels between their values. Cherry should be made older (ca. eighteen), experienced at teasing and perhaps more, and determined to marry a prosperous Londoner. In this production she represents a genuine alternative to Mrs. Sullen, albeit a short-term one from Archer's point of view.

Act II. The Sullens show us the results of marriage for money, even when the match is not deceitfully arranged. The pace and tone of their discord should convey rancor, not comedy. Sullen must appear genuinely "brutal" and contemptuous of his young wife; he should be neither stupid nor ineffectual. If their encounters seem funny because of accidentals like his hangover, the audience can hope for Sullen's reform and a happy ending. A serious production must not allow this to happen.

Act III. Dorinda's raptures over love at first sight should be exaggerated into fatuousness. Any tendency to take the "love" seriously can be counteracted by emphasis on Aimwell's explanation a few pages earlier of just how he will behave in church if he spots a prospect (pp. 32–33). Heavy stress should be laid in that scene on Aimwell's waving off Archer's advice to concentrate upon fortune rather than beauty: "Pshaw, no woman can be a beauty without a fortune. Let me alone, for I am a marksman." This phrase is picked up at the start of III.ii. as the beaux discuss Aimwell's success and Archer comments: "Well, Tom, I find you're a marksman." Aimwell insists upon his "passion" (p. 47), but this can be treated as deliberate hyperbole—irritating to Archer, but helpful to Aimwell in playing the lover's role. Class should be stressed in the scene between "Martin" and Mrs. Sullen: she is desperate enough to take up with a footman or a French fop, and Dorinda helps her find an excuse for pretending that the footman is a gentleman in disguise (pp. 64–65).

Act IV. Lady Bountiful is an atypical parental figure, introduced very late. The norm in comedy is for the lover to assume a disguise to get round the blocking figure. Here the parent fosters the trick and does her best to push it along (pp. 81–82). She is no less foolish, but she is more forceful than in the romp production. Stress should be laid on the beaux' deception: Dorinda and Lady Bountiful are rapturous at the prospect of her snaring a lord. Dorinda's vision of life as Lady Aimwell should be given full measure of selfish gloating—and of course it is illusionary, since Aimwell is merely pretending to be a lord. Dorinda is a fool blinded by her own ambition—a point to be underlined.[39]

Act V. Farquhar presents us with a series of blatantly improbable "rescues." (1) Mrs. Sullen is saved from assault when Scrub enters crying, "Thieves, thieves, murther, popery!" (p. 109).[40] (2) The beaux save the house from the robbers. (3) Aimwell gets Dorinda even after confessing. She knows what her marriage portion makes her worth, and he is a passport to London, if not one quite so grand as she had first thought. (4) Sir Charles Freeman enters to announce that Aimwell has inherited his brother's title and money. (5) Archer is rescued from poverty by getting the whole of Dorinda's £10,000. On top of this improbable series of events we get (6) the Sullens' "divorce." Vivid contrast here between the serious treatment of Mrs. Sullen and the over-romanticization of Aimwell and Dorinda should lead to a completely insubstantial happy ending. Mrs. Sullen escapes from her marriage, but only into limbo: this production will separate her from Archer. Dorinda will indeed become Lady Aimwell, but only a deus ex machina has prevented her from being hoodwinked and robbed, and nothing we have seen of the relationship should suggest a basis for a happy marriage, especially with the example of the Sullens before us.

The Beaux' Stratagem can certainly be played as a happy-ending romp, and for a twentieth-century audience playing it any other way would be difficult.[41] The audience of 1707, steeped in

39. For a useful discussion, see William L. Sharp, "Restoration Comedy: An approach to modern production," *Drama Survey*, 7 (1968–69), 69–86.

40. Why this night of all nights for the robbery? Boniface and his cohorts have apparently been operating for years without this target's having occurred to them. But the suspense over the robbery, juxtaposed with Archer's invasion, helps prepare for the rapid-fire series of events at the end of the play.

41. Getting twentieth-century actors to treat these characters as real people rather than as assumed artificial identities is of course a major problem. The

the generic norms of the day and well aware of divorce law problems, would have been much more sensitive to the serious issues. Farquhar's text offers at least the potentiality of a tongue-in-cheek satire on comic norms, and it might be pushed further to raise questions about social and economic reality.

Overtidy endings are the norm in comedy. Why should this one be unsatisfactory, even if akin to fairy tales? Farquhar's seven previous plays show that he was not in the habit of writing sloppy and improbable endings, or of leaving romance relationships completely undeveloped. Here the happy ending comes as a surprise to almost all the characters, who comment on how implausible it is. We are left to conclude that Farquhar wanted it that way.[42]

For anyone not prepared to accept the events of Act V at face value, the play is well-calculated to undermine romantic conventions. Until late in Act V Farquhar reverses the usual presumption that love outweighs money, and if the marital discord is played seriously it should cast a pall over so underdeveloped a love relationship as Aimwell and Dorinda's. The magical unraveling of all complications in Act V is deliberately overdone: Farquhar is either mocking the conventions of comedy or taking refuge in farce and Cloud Cuckooland. A literary critic might berate Farquhar for allowing his audience to enjoy the ending and hide from the "point." But production history suggests that from very early on—perhaps from the first production—the potentialities

---

beaux' assumptions about living on inherited money (or marrying into inherited money), the lack of a divorce law, and the dependent position of the woman in marriage are all major barriers to comprehension by actors as well as by audience.

42. Farquhar drops some rather flagrant hints in the course of the play. Regarding problem marriages: (a) Mrs. Sullen: "If I go a step beyond the bounds of honor, leave me" (p. 31); (b) Gibbet: "a poor lady just eloped from her husband . . . told me of her husband's barbarous usage, and so I left her half a crown" (p. 34); (c) Dorinda: "Your divisions don't come within the reach of the law for a divorce" (p. 72); in preparation for the deus ex machina and Aimwell's transformation, (d) Mrs. Sullen: "I expect my brother here tonight or tomorrow. He was abroad when my father married me" (p. 93); and (e) Mrs. Sullen: "I have heard my brother talk of my Lord Aimwell, but they say that his brother is the finer gentleman" (p. 58).

315

for an effective romp have swamped the play's more serious implications. Calling the play a treatise on divorce law or an exemplar of country values makes it something it could never have been in performance. An interpretation should definitely acknowledge these topical and thematic elements, but they are more important to the reader than to the viewer, and their impact would vary greatly with the nature of the production. Indeed, even a determinedly serious and satiric production would probably never have carried all members of the audience to the "correct" conclusion: anyone who wanted to buy the magical solutions of Act V could do so.

The romp has always been the obvious and surefire way to stage the show. Such a reading trivializes and plays over much in the script, but it is certainly valid. The alternative is an extension, not a negation of the romp. Farquhar was, after all, a commercial playwright anxious to please his audience and provide for his soon-to-be-fatherless family. What he gives us in *The Beaux' Stratagem* is a satire subtle enough not to offend those members of the audience determined to take the happy ending straight.

Appendix
Index

APPENDIX
MUSIC FOR THE PLAYS

F OR DISCUSSION of music and musical practices in the late seventeenth-century theatre, the reader should consult Curtis A. Price's *Music in the Restoration Theatre* (Ann Arbor: UMI Research Press, 1979). Price's book includes a "Catalogue of Instrumental Music in the Plays 1665–1713." For the next century the standard reference work is Roger Fiske's massive *English Theatre Music in the Eighteenth Century* (London: Oxford Univ. Pr., 1973). Songs from plays of the late seventeenth-century period that were collected in song books are conveniently indexed in Cyrus Lawrence Day and Eleanore Boswell Murrie, *English Song-Books 1651–1702: A Bibliography* (London: Bibliographical Society, 1940)—hereafter cited as D&M. The best source of information on theatre music extant only in "single sheet" form (often gathered into nonce collections) is *The British Union-Catalogue of Early Music* [printed before 1801], ed. Edith B. Schnapper, 2 vols. (London: Butterworths, 1957)—hereafter cited as *BUCEM*. Happily, within the next few years most of the extant music for English plays 1660–1714 will be published in Series A of *Music for London Entertainment, 1660–1800* (Richard Macnutt Ltd.).

Essentially all plays staged in the public theatre in London in the late seventeenth century were performed with preliminary music and with "act tunes" following each act except the last. The preliminary music generally consisted of the "first music" and "second music" (each comprising a pair of contrasting pieces), plus an overture or "curtain tune." Special music was written for each new play or revival. Such incidental music usually consisted of nine pieces—the first and second music, plus overture and four act tunes. A surprising amount of this music was published, and as Curtis Price has shown, quite a lot of it is extant in both printed and manuscript form.

The constitution of the playhouse orchestra varied considerably from theatre to theatre and time to time. The "normal" orchestra seems to have consisted of ten or twelve musicians, though this group could swell in excess of thirty for fancy operatic productions. The music is in four parts—two trebles, tenor (viola), and bass. Although songs would have been accompanied by harpsichord or theorbo realizing the continuo, there is little evidence that these instruments would have played with the orchestra; as in the French theatre, symphonies and act tunes were probably performed by the strings alone.

A substantial amount of the original (or near-original) music is extant for six of the eight plays analyzed in this book. Given the wealth of available music, we see no excuse for not using the real article in any performance with pretensions to authenticity. The capacities of the available singers must be considered. Price documents the seventeenth-century practice of using surrogate performers in place of non-singing actors where required (*Music in the Restoration Theatre*, pp. 42–47). In some instances substitution of other seventeenth-century music might be in order, either to supply a piece feasible for the available performer or to introduce better music. For *The Beaux' Stratagem*, for example, a modern director might select some of Purcell's act tunes in preference to the act music composed by J. C. Gillier. But there is no excuse for the Greensleevesitis of which Flanders and Swann so justly complain. The musical requirements (and the known music) for the plays we have analyzed are listed below. When only unique sources are known, we have given fuller bibliographical information than when several sources are available.

The Country-Wife. No music is extant. A song is sung by Lady Fidget (played by Elizabeth Knepp) in V.iv.: "Why should our damn'd tyrants oblige us to live," and "A Dance of Cuckolds" is required at the end. Sir Jaspar and Pinchwife have just been assured that they are not cuckolds: the music presumably sends a different message. Gerald Weales suggests that the tune "Cuckolds All a Row" from John Playford's *The Dancing Master* (1651 and often reprinted) might have been used for the dance (*Complete Plays of William Wycherley*, [Garden City: Doubleday Anchor, 1966], pp. 370–71), but the suggestion is entirely speculative. (On this tune, see Claude M. Simpson, *The British Broadside Ballad and Its Music* [New Brunswick: Rutgers Univ. Press, 1966], pp. 145–47.) In a modern production the dancers might be supplied with cuckolds' horns to convey the message. Since Lady Fidget's song is thematically apropos, a modern production cannot substitute for it without loss, and a new setting in an appropriate style should be obtained if possible.

All for Love. No music is extant. Beyond the ordinary act music the only music required is "(Soft music)" during Antony's fit of melancholy in Act I—an important scene (line 230). For act music Curtis Price suggests using one of the unascribed sets in British Library Add. MSS 29,283–85, soon to be published in facsimile in Series A of *Music for London Entertainment*.

The Spanish Fryar. Act music by Robert King (probably written for a revival ca. 1690) is preserved in British Library Add. MS 35,043, fols. 41v-42 (first treble), and five of the pieces are in part books in Magdalene College Library, Cambridge, fols. 118 and 136 (all four parts). One of the pieces was published in *Apollo's Banquet* (1691), no. 42 (first treble), and another in *40 Airs Anglois, II* [ca. 1701], p. 1 (first treble). John Eccles' chorus "Look down, ye bless'd above" for I.i. ("A Procession of Priests . . . follow'd by the Queen . . . the Choristers singing") is preserved in British Library Add. MS 29,378, fols. 138–138v. The song in Act V ("Farewell ungratefull Traytor") is D&M 974, music by Pack, published in the 1706 *Pills to Purge Melancholy* (and reprinted in later editions). Henry Purcell set a song not in the text, "Whilst I with grief did on you look," for a revival; see the Purcell Society edition, Vol. XXI (1917). Price suggests that this song was probably inserted into Act V. Another song not in the text, "Silvia, how could you e'er mistrust," was published in John Eccles' *A Collection of Songs* (1704), sung by Mrs. Hodgson. Where it was sung in the play we do not know.

Venice Preserv'd. Act music by Solomon Eccles is preserved in British Library Add. MSS 29,283–85, fols. 15v-19v (two trebles and bass); all nine pieces are also in New York Public Library Drexel MS 3849, pp. 55–59; eight of them are in Yale Univ. Music Library Filmer MS 6, pp. 23–29. Act music by John Lenton for a revival ca. 1696 can be found in the Royal College of Music (London) MS 1144, fols. 4–4v (treble and bass). Eight of these pieces are in British Library Add. MS 24,889 (four parts); seven, in Bodleian MS Mus. Sch. c.72 (3 parts); seven, in part books in Magdalene College Library, Cambridge (four parts). Single pieces were published in the *Compleat Flute-Master* (1695), [fol. 26], and *Apollo's Banquet* (1701), no. 125 (first treble). Music for the mad scene in V.ii. ("Soft Music. Enter Belvidera distracted . . .") is not known.

Amphitryon. Henry Purcell's act music was published in *A Collection of Ayres for the Theatre* (1697), pp. 28–30, and republished by the Purcell Society, Vol. XVI, in 1906. For commentary and corrections by W. Barclay Squire, see Summers' edition, *Dryden: The Dramatic Works*, VI, 539. Purcell's settings of the three songs were published in Q1690 and are reprinted by Summers, though not in the California edition. For a listing of the songs and dances, see Franklin B. Zimmerman, *Henry Purcell 1659–1695: An analytical catalogue of his music* (New York: St. Martins, 1963), No. 572. For analysis of the music, see Curtis A. Price, *Henry Purcell and the London Stage* (Cambridge: Cambridge Univ. Press, 1984), Chapter 4.

The Wives Excuse. The act music is apparently not extant. Four of the songs, all by Purcell, were published in contemporary collections. "Ingrateful Love!" in I.ii. (D&M 1817) was published in *The Banquet of Musick* (1692), p. 2, singer unspecified, though from the music we can deduce a soprano (Charlotte Butler?)

rather than the music master in the scene (Joseph Harris), to whom the song is assigned by Thornton in his edition of the play. "Say Cruel Amoret," sung by Mr. Friendall (William Mountfort) in IV.i. (D&M 2852), was published in *Joyful Cuckoldom* (1693?), no. 8. This song is allegedly set by Mr. Friendall himself. As Curtis Price comments, it contains no "Hoffnung blunders," but is "a theatrical representation of an incompetent song, not the work of the fool himself." "Corinna, I excuse thy face," a soprano song to a Scots air (D&M 732), was published in *The Banquet of Musick*, p. 4, singer unspecified. A fourth song, "Hang this whining way of wooing," also published in *The Banquet of Musick* (1691/2), p. 3 (D&M 1233), is said in the play quarto (which gives the words following "Corinna" in Act V) to belong "In the First Scene of the Fourth Act" (p. 116). Unfortunately, it does not fit there. Zimmerman assigns it to IV.iii., but there is no such scene. Price sensibly suggests that it was sung between the acts or, more probably, performed during the Act V masquerade. When the song was reprinted in *Joyful Cuckoldom*, no. 9, the singer was specified as Mrs. Butler. All four songs were often reprinted, and are available in the Purcell Society edition of his *Works*, Vol. XXI. What "Italian song" was performed in the Act I music meeting we do not know. Price suggests that something like "Amor prepara mi," an anonymous aria published in *The Gentleman's Journal* (January 1692), pp. 28–31, would be appropriate. The dance music for the masquerade is unknown. All four of the preserved songs fit the themes and action of the play brilliantly.

Love for Love. Godfrey Finger's act music is in Bodleian MS Mus. Sch. c.72, pp. 8–10 (three parts). All nine pieces are in the Finney part books at UCLA (four parts), and also in King's College Library, Cambridge, MS 122 (treble and bass), Royal College of Music MS 1144, fols. 24–25 (two trebles), Yale University Filmer MS 9. Several of the pieces were published in contemporary collections: for a full listing, see Price, *Music in the Restoration Theatre*, pp. 191–93. The song in III.iii. ("A Nymph and a swain to Apollo once prayed") is D&M 2443, and was published in *Thesaurus Musicus*, The Fourth Book (1695), pp.

25–27, the music by John Eccles, the singer Pate. Ben's song in III.iv. ("A Soldier and a sailor," also by Eccles) sung by Thomas Doggett, D&M 3019, was published in the same collection (p. 27) and was often reprinted. A song in IV.iii. ("I tell thee, Charmion") is D&M 1603 and was published in [*Two Songs*] (1695), music by Godfrey Finger, the singers specified as Pate and Reading. Price hypothesizes that the music for Ben's dance with the sailors in III.iv. is the tune "Danc'd in the Play Love for Love" published in *The Dancing Master*, II (1696), p. 20. James Thompson has suggested that this tune was used for the dance at the end of Act V and says that "as a formal social dance, it contrasts visually, aurally, and thematically with the Sailors' Jig in Act III." See *Notes and Queries*, n.s. 25 (1978), 34. However, Congreve does not specify that the dance in Act III is a jig; indeed, Ben says, "you shall see that we Sailors can Dance sometimes as well as other Folks." The point in the play at which this music was used remains conjectural.

The Beaux' Stratagem. Jean-Claude Gillier's act music is preserved in a British Library collection, g.15 (four parts). No music is known for the "Country Dance to the Trifle that I sing to Day." A dance called "The Beaus Stratagem," for which the first treble part was published in the *Dancing Master* (1718), p. 169, may be associated with this play. Farquhar's published playtext states that Archer's "Trifling Song" in III.iii. is sung "to the tune of *Sir Simon the King*" (p. 62), a popular ballad. On the ballad see Simpson, *The British Broadside Ballad and Its Music*, pp. 545–51. Publication of music by Daniel Purcell for "The Trifle" in single-sheet form ca. 1707 suggests that the theatre may have decided to employ a more formal setting. According to the *BUCEM*, II, 855, this version of "The Trifle" is to be found in the British Library and elsewhere.

Until very recently, neither literary critics nor music historians understood just how wonderfully effective analysis of the music can be as an aid to "literary" interpretation. There are plenty of plays with mediocre music, and many with wholly inorganic music—but the music is often enough integral and significant to warrant careful consideration of the possibilities in every case.

For a brilliant demonstration of the possibilities of this approach, see Curtis A. Price's *Henry Purcell and the London Stage*. Anyone who wishes to hear spirited and historically authentic performances of Purcell's theatre music should listen to the recordings made by The Academy of Ancient Music under the direction of Christopher Hogwood. As we write, six discs are now available in the L'Oiseau-Lyre Florilegium series: DSLO 504 (*Abdelazer*, *Distressed Innocence*, *The Married Beau*, *The Gordian Knot Untied*); 527 (*Bonduca, Sir Anthony Love, Circe*); 534 (*Don Quixote*); 550 (*The Virtuous Wife, The Old Batchelour, Amphitryon*); 561 (*The Double-Dealer, The Richmond Heiress, The Rival Sisters, Henry the Second, Tyrannick Love*); 590 (*Theodosius, The Libertine, The Massacre of Paris, Oedipus*).

Index

Some single and peripheral references are omitted. Full bibliographical information on some works will be found in the list of "Works Frequently Cited" in the front matter.

Index

329

Index

Index

Polwhele, Elizabeth
—*The Faithful Virgins*, 45n
—*The Frolicks*, 41, 41n
Porter Mary, 133, 134, 179
Powell, George, 60n, 61, 62, 95, 215, 225
Powell, Mary, 215, 299
Price, Curtis A., 224n, 228n, 319–25
Prior, Moody E., 107, 107n, 192, 192n
Pritchard, Hannah, 179
Producibility: as a criterion for judgment of interpretation, 11–12
Producible interpretation: defined, 3; related to date of production, 21–22; versus valid interpretation, 17–19
Production process: casting, 47–53; important questions concerning, 35–36; in seventeenth-century, 36–40; rehearsals and acting, 59–66; scenery and staging, 52–59; seventeenth-century production concepts, 66–69; sources of scripts, 41–47
Proffitt, Bessie, 188n
Purcell, Daniel, 324
Purcell, Henry, 228, 321, 322, 324

Quin, James, 64, 179

Rabkin, Gerald, 31, 31n
Rabkin, Norman, 32n
Racine, Jean, 107, 109, 149–50
Rapin, René, 113, 165
Ravenscroft, Edward
—*The Careless Lovers*, 43
—*The London Cuckolds*, 9
Rehearsal practices, 59–64
Reinert, Otto, 122–23, 123n, 138
Reiss, Timothy J., 137, 137n
Rich, Christopher, 37, 38, 42, 42n, 43, 44
Righter, Anne [now Barton]: on *The Country-Wife*, 74, 77, 78n, 80, 82, 90, 92n, 96, 96n; on *Venice Preserv'd*, 193, 193n
Rochester, John Wilmot, earl of, 20, 79, 82, 225
Rogers, Jane, 48–49, 49n, 283, 284

Rogers, Katharine M., 24, 25, 25n, 77–78, 78n
Root, Robert L., 229n
Roper, Alan, 308, 308n
Rosenfeld, Sybil, 53n, 309n
Rosowski, Susan J., 262, 262n
Ross, Robert H., 50n
Rothstein, Eric: on *The Beaux' Stratagem*, 292n, 296, 307–8, 307n; on *The Plain-Dealer*, 26n; on theories of tragedy, 113n, 165n; on *Venice Preserv'd*, 186, 186n, 192
Rowe, Nicholas, 107, 192
Ryan, Lacy, 179
Rymer, Thomas, 110, 112, 165

Sadler, Thomas, 194n
Sandford, Samuel, 50, 50n, 160, 215, 279, 283
Saunders, Mrs., 215
Schilling, Bernard N., 115n
Scenery and staging, 52–59
Schnapper, Edith B., 319
Scouten, Arthur H., 6, 40n, 185, 185n, 229, 249, 249n
Sedley, Sir Charles, 169
—*Antony and Cleopatra*, 111, 114
Segre, Cesare, 14n
Seltzer, Daniel, 32–33, 33n
Settle, Elkanah, 42, 42n
—*The Female Prelate*, 148
Seymour, Mrs., 179
Shadwell, Thomas: compared with Southerne, 253
—*Epsom-Wells*, 234
—*The Lancashire Witches*, 148
—*The Miser*, 43
—*Psyche*, 43
—*The Squire of Alsatia*, 18–19, 46n, 203, 269n
—*The Virtuoso*, 41n, 100
Shaftesbury, Anthony Ashley, first earl of, 147, 173–74, 177
Shaheen, Abdel-Rahman, 211n
Shakespeare, William, 107, 109–11, 113
—*Antony and Cleopatra*, 107n, 109, 118
—*As You Like It*, 32, 65

334